Publishing with
InDesign

THE ENCLOSED CD-ROM CONTAINS TRIAL VERSIONS OF:
DIMENSIONS 3, ILLUSTRATOR 8, INDESIGN 1.5,
GOLIVE 4, LIVEMOTION, AND PHOTOSHOP 5.5
PLUS SEVERAL OTHERS FOR BOTH WINDOWS AND MAC

IN ADDITION THERE ARE OVER $300 WORTH OF FREE FONTS!

Publishing with InDesign

By David Bergsland

OnWord Press
Thomson Learning™

AFRICA • AUSTRALIA • CANADA • DENMARK • JAPAN • MEXICO • NEW ZEALAND
PHILIPPINES • PUERTO RICO • SINGAPORE • UNITED KINGDOM • UNITED STATES

NOTICE TO THE READER

OnWord Staff:

Business Unit Director: Alar Elken
Acquisitions Editor: James Gish
Editorial Assistant: Fionnuala McAvey
Developmental Editor: Fionnuala McAvey
Executive Marketing Manager: Maura Theriault
Channel Manager: Mona Caron
Executive Production Manager: Mary Ellen Black
Production Coordinator: Larry Main
Art/Design Coordinator: Rachel Baker
Cover Design: David Bergsland

Printed in Canada
1 2 3 4 5 6 7 8 9 10 05 04 03 02 01 00

For more information, contact Delmar, 3 Columbia Circle, PO Box 15015, Albany, NY 12212-0515; or find us on the World Wide Web at http://www.delmar.com

International Division List

Asia
Thomson Learning
60 Albert Street, #15-01
Albert Complex
Singapore 189969
Tel: 65 336 6411
Fax: 65 336 7411

Japan:
Thomson Learning
Palaceside Building 5F
1-1-1 Hitotsubashi, Chiyoda-ku
Tokyo 100 0003 Japan
Tel: 813 5218 6544
Fax: 813 5218 6551

Australia/New Zealand:
Nelson/Thomson Learning
102 Dodds Street
South Melbourne, Victoria 3205
Australia
Tel: 61 39 685 4111
Fax: 61 39 685 4199

UK/Europe/Middle East
Thomson Learning
Berkshire House
168-173 High Holborn
London
WC1V 7AA United Kingdom
Tel: 44 171 497 1422
Fax: 44 171 497 1426

Thomas Nelson & Sons LTD
Nelson House
Mayfield Road
Walton-on-Thames
KT 12 5PL United Kingdom
Tel: 44 1932 2522111
Fax: 44 1932 246574

Latin America:
Thomson Learning
Seneca, 53
Colonia Polanco
11560 Mexico D.F. Mexico
Tel: 525-281-2906
Fax: 525-281-2656

South Africa:
Thomson Learning
Zonnebloem Building
Constantia Square
526 Sixteenth Road
P.O. Box 2459
Halfway House, 1685
South Africa
Tel: 27 11 805 4819
Fax: 27 11 805 3648

Canada:
Nelson/Thomson Learning
1120 Birchmount Road
Scarborough, Ontario
Canada M1K 5G4
Tel: 416-752-9100
Fax: 416-752-8102

Spain:
Thomson Learning
Calle Magallanes, 25
28015-MADRID
ESPANA
Tel: 34 91 446 33 50
Fax: 34 91 445 62 18

International Headquarters:
Thomson Learning
International Division
290 Harbor Drive, 2nd Floor
Stamford, CT 06902-7477
Tel: 203-969-8700
Fax: 203-969-8751

Library of Congress Cataloging-in-Publication Data

Bergsland, David.
Publishing with InDesign / by David Bergsland.
p. cm.
Includes index.
ISBN 0-7668-2001-7
1. Adobe InDesign. 2. Desktop publishing. I. Title.
Z253.532.A34 B47 2000
686.2'25445369--dc21

00-031637

I dedicate this book
to my lovely and patient wife,
The Rev. Patricia H. Bergsland.
She is the reason
I keep pushing for excellence.
Her love is the best thing in my life.

On the CD-ROM you will find many things

There is a complete Web site with all of the exams and assignments for coursework associated with this book. There are many trial versions from Adobe and Macromedia. There are eleven of the author's fonts (worth over $300) that are free for purchasers of this book.

Acrobat Reader, Dimensions, GoLive, Illustrator, InDesign, LiveMotion, and Photoshop are all Registered Trademarks of Adobe Systems Incorporated. Flash and FreeHand are Registered Trademarks of Macromedia, Inc. Quicktime is a Registered Trademark of Apple Computer, Inc. The Macintosh and PC installers of these trial versions are presented "as is" with no guarantee or warranty implied. These are limited versions of the software -- some are save-disabled and some are time limited. There is no promise that they work -- you are expected to be thankful for whatever works. If there is a problem with a font, write the author and he will send you a new copy.

ACKNOWLEDGMENTS

Over the years, many people have helped me along the way. Personally, I have to thank my friends Nob Hill Foursquare for their immense help in bringing me greater maturity. Their love and support have been essential to my growth as a person, as a teacher, and as a writer. This wouldn't have happened without their prayers and support.

At school, I have to thank my Dean, Lois Carlson; my friend and Associate Dean, Susan Cutler; and my Program Directors, Dan Valles and Marcella Green. They have given me leeway to pursue this new pedagogy and a great deal of support and kindness. We creative types can be very hard to live with, but they have hung in there with me even though I am severely bureaucratically challenged. I am grateful.

Many thanks have to go to my students in my Business Graphics and Communication degree program and in my commercial mentoring venture, Pneumatika Online School. It is horribly unfair to name names, so I won't. We've had a great deal of fun. They didn't volunteer as guinea pigs. In fact, most of them think I know what I am doing.

There are two students who have gone far above the call of duty. They have been a major encouragement to me. Darrylin O'Dea on the North Island of New Zealand has been a wonderful help. Locally, Marcia Best has helped, encouraged, proofed, and supplied PC graphics as needed. Both of these women have worked their mousing finger to the bone trying to figure out what the heck I am doing.

At Delmar, all of the original people I knew from *Printing in a Digital World* have moved on except for Larry Main, their production manager. His experience, stability, and encouragement have been a huge help in the practical matter of allowing an author to do all of the production work as well. Pamela Lamb supplied the copyediting and index professionally and very fast. Jim Gish, my editor, I just met today, but I like him. His assistant, Fionnuala McAvey, has been a rock and extremely able. Sandy Clark, executive editor, has answered every question and been great help.

My major gratitude is reserved for my incredible wife, the Rev. Patricia H. Bergsland. Her ability to put up with my foibles is staggering. Without her love and support, I would have quit a long time ago. In addition to being my wife, she is also my pastor which, as you can imagine, is a fantastic help. Serving as one of her elders has given me a glimpse into true leadership and a teaching ability that has been the core of my inspiration as a teacher and mentor. Her friendship has been my stability. Our love is my reason for going on ...

June 1, 2000 • Quail Wood, New Mexico

Table of Contents

Table of Contents

FRONT MATTER

Table of Contents

Table of Contents

Table of Contents

Forward

It's been a wonderful ride. About six years ago, a sales rep from Delmar called me on the phone in my lab where I taught Commercial Printing at Albuquerque TVI. She wanted to know if I was using any of her books. I explained that I couldn't because they were all application-specific and I taught all the major software at the same time in the same lab. As a result, I was forced to write all of my own materials. I had to create everything from scratch because nothing existed that taught the basic principles of the paradigm shift our industry was undergoing. She said, "You interested in writing a book?" Like an idiot, I said, "Sure!"

About a month later I received a call from an editor from Delmar, in Albany, N.Y.. He asked me if I was serious about that book. Again, in blissful ignorance, I said, "Sure!" I explained that I was a nobody who just liked to write. I told him that I needed a conversational book, in the style of my lectures, or the students would refuse to read it. Actually, we talked for about forty-five minutes. The result was that he told me they were receiving proposals on a book like this and he'd like to see one from me.

That time around

That first book was a revelation. What I discovered was a paradigm shift. All of the rules that worked when I was in industry were changing faster than anyone could write them — except for in the magazines. One of the advantages of a paradigm shift is that the new persons start on the same footing as the old hands. Everyone has new rules. Often, in fact, the new people are not hindered by the habitual reactions from the old paradigm.

My sources were *MacWorld, MacUser, Publish, Step by Step* (both), NADTP, GATF, NAPL, *Graphic Arts Monthly, American Printer, Southwest Graphics, Aldus* (now *Adobe*), and several others. The best was and is *Before & After* by John McWade. Here I found a man after my own heart ... and look at what he is doing!

There were no textbooks on this new trail. I used Roger Black's *Desktop Design Power* and Robin Williams's books. These two authors are probably my biggest influences. They had a conversational tone that I liked — clear, concise, and entertaining *PLUS* my students would actually read it. The old printing textbooks were never used at all. I needed a retail book, but none of the well-written computer books covered printing problems adequately or even accurately.

The advantage of being forced to start from scratch became obvious. Not being hampered by traditional ways of doing things, I developed an entirely new method of instruction. Based on my twenty-plus years in the industry, I knew what employers needed. I discovered that students also thrive when they are taught real-world solutions to real-world problems.

This time around

This textbook is written as an entertaining read. It is meant to be conversational and a little controversial. My primary concern is the higher learning skills — we need graduates who can think and solve problems. This means asking difficult questions.

Table of Contents

This book is quite different from the first book in that it actually teaches software. It is different from my second book in that is assumes much more advanced knowledge. This third book contains a lot of review materials for those who do not have comprehensive training. But it is primarily directed to advanced students and people with prior publishing knowledge obtained through informal training or simple work experience.

Going online

In 1996, it became obvious that most industry communications were going to be over the Net. As a result of that, I converted all of my coursework to online instruction. At present, all of my students have the option to do all or part of their work online. This is a real boon for students who are convinced that they can survive professionally on a PC (my lab is all Mac). More than that, it has enabled employed personnel to upgrade their skills while working. What I saw in 1996 has become fact. For this book, all communication with the publisher has been via email, the final digital documents will be PDFs FTPed to the printer in Canada, and everything is moved around attached to emails.

My goal is extremely practical. What do you need to succeed in this industry? I am relentless about that. I call it reality orientation. That's what this book is all about.

June 1, 2000

PS: For those of you compulsive about these things, except for illustrations taken from *Printing in a Digital World*, I created everything. I wrote all the copy, shot or own all the photos, and drew all the drawings on my iMac, 96 MB RAM, 6 GB hard drive, plus a ZIP, JAZ, APS 4x4x20 CD-RW, and an Epson 636 scanner. My word processor is Mariner Write. My illustrations were done in FreeHand 9. The bitmaps were done in Photoshop 5.5. Everything was assembled in InDesign 1.5, from which I directly exported the PDFs for printing. Finally, I designed all my own fonts for this book.

MY EMAIL ADDRESS IS:
graphics@swcp.com

MY HOME PAGE IS:
http://kumo.swcp.com/graphics

Welcome!

As you begin this book, I want to give you both a word of welcome and a word of encouragement. This book is the result of eight years of study, research, trial, and experience. It has been field-tested with hundreds of students. I welcome you to their number. I think I can promise you a fun ride.

However, this will be training like you have never had before – unless you have used my materials in another class. Please do not expect the normal, "All right now, kiddies, let's open our books to page ..." There are no lockstep tutorials contained herein.

Adult education (even for teenagers)

For most of you, this will be your first experience with truly *adult* education. I realize that some of you are still in high school, but it's high time you were treated like an adult anyway. So what do I mean by "adult education"?

Adult education assumes that you are in this class because you choose to be here. It assumes that you are genuinely interested in learning digital publishing, and that you have a well-considered interest in becoming a professional designer. It assumes that if you get confused or feel like you are in over your head, you will ask questions and seek help.

Adult education is not a baby-sitting service. When you get hired or start producing jobs for real clients, they will not hold your hand. They will hand you a job ticket, ask if there are any questions, and tell you it's due tomorrow morning.

Your instructor and staff will be glad to help you get to the point where you can work freely and unsupervised. There are no stupid questions, only stupid students who do not ask questions. This is your chance to learn how to work.

The nature of graphic design

The first thing you will notice, as we go through the theory, miniskills, and skill exams found in this book, is that there are usually no right or wrong answers. The best we can do as designers is to find competent, professional solutions to the problems presented by the design projects we are given to create. For the essence of graphic design is problem solving.

We will talk a lot about this throughout this book. You will discover that there are essential problems like, "Who is the desired reader for this piece and what are they looking for?" Plus there are hundreds of little problems like, "Does this yellow triangle help the readers make the connection to this important point they need to understand?"

In fact, graphic design is one of the most difficult jobs in existence. This is problem solving as a way of life: dealing with subconscious motivations of the readers; meeting the needs of demanding clients; reading everyone's mind trying to figure out what they are really saying; analyzing your content and message to see where they touch the reader with a genuine need; and doing it all incredibly fast under ridiculously tight deadlines.

You will discover shortly that graphic design is very much a service industry where you have to serve and satisfy many different people with different, and often conflicting, needs. The readers need to be shown why they genuinely need this product or service. The client needs to survive. Your boss needs you to stay well within budget so the profit keeps you employed. And the production staff needs a design that prints or downloads quickly, easily, with no snags or difficulties.

These are the normal tasks of the graphic designer. As you can clearly see, there is little room for the person who *"just likes to draw."* You have to really like this line of work. If you do not, the pressures will be too great and you will quit.

Table of Contents

How to tell if you belong

It is not hard to determine if you are cut out for graphic design. There are common characteristics in most, if not all, commercial artists. There is usually a real joy in the experience of visual beauty. Most find that visual stimuli are extremely enjoyable. Many of us use elegance of design, richness of packaging, and a high level of craftsmanship to help determine which products to purchase personally.

There is commonly a compulsiveness to our art. We draw or at least doodle all the time. Often we cannot really look at something without trying to figure out how to make it better, prettier, or more useful. Often we are highly critical. When we go to an art exhibit, we are either blown away by the beauty or almost disgusted by what we consider mistakes – often in the same piece of art. Usually we really think we can do it better, and often that is true. Somehow for us art, designs, and graphics really matter – more than they do for most.

These things are not grounds for arrogance. They are simply indicators that we have been given a creative personality. Often there will be an insatiable curiosity, an intellectual quickness, an emotional sensitivity that makes us different from most of our peers. Again, this is nothing wrong, it is merely who we are.

This book and this career give you an opportunity to make a living using these attributes of your character. Some of you will discover that you really cannot work within these restrictions. Just go on into fine art, where your personal vision is all that matters.

You are part of what my wife and I were once called – exotic people – those strange creatives: artists, writers, musicians, and the like. The world at large may never understand, but we are a neat group of people. One thing for certain, life will never be boring or dull!

For those of you who might be seriously saddened if it were missing, here's the landmark that has faithfully guided you through all of my books — just for nostalgia's sake.

So relax and enjoy the ride.

1

Publishing Software

CONCEPTS

1. **PostScript Illustration**

2. **PostScript**

3. **Page layout**

4. **Publishing**

5. **Bitmap image**

6. **Vector image**

7. **Image manipulation**

Definitions are found in the glossary.

A software overview of the publishing industry: what is used, when it is used, and how it is used

CHAPTER OBJECTIVES:

By presenting the options and capabilities of the publishing industry's software, this chapter will enable you to:

1. Describe the capabilities and usage of PostScript illustration software including FreeHand and Illustrator
2. Describe the capabilities and usage of paint and image manipulation software
3. Describe the capabilities and usage of page layout software
4. Describe the capabilities and usage of WYSIWYG Web creation software for pages and graphics

LAB WORK FOR CHAPTER

- Become familiar with the computer you will be using for the course: system software, publishing software
- Adjust the defaults and preferences of the software you will be using, saving the resulting files so you can make any computer yours, and restore your defaults as needed

We begin a new great adventure, learning how to use yet another of the powerful publishing applications. I wish I could tell you that we have finally found the Holy Grail, the software application that does it all. However, that program does not, and will not, exist. Digital publishing now requires, and will always require, at least three software applications to do it well. As we go through this chapter you will soon see that, in reality, you will be using about seven applications all at the same time. Any software large enough to do it all would consume your computer.

InDesign is a remarkable 1.0 version. The Version 1.5 update is remarkable. Adobe has created page layout software that is extremely powerful. It truly has great promise. It is an obvious competitor for Quark with all of their strengths and weaknesses. In fact, it works much like a more intuitive version of Quark. Right out of the box, it solved all my personal problems with that program – poor link management, a clumsy interface, and a poor type engine.

It is obviously designed with the Quark user in mind, doing everything possible to make the transition from Quark to InDesign as painless as possible. I am actually naive enough to believe that Adobe has a real good chance with this program. At the very least, Quark finally has some obvious competition, even though the latest versions of PageMaker already provided that level of competency (for those of us who used it).

Nothing is enough

The basic fact of publishing remains. We need a suite of programs to do what we do. Formerly, this was called the Big Five. Now, we have to add two more to the mix. The programs necessary for us to work in this industry are: InDesign, PageMaker, QuarkXPress, FreeHand, Illustrator, Photoshop, and Acrobat. We cannot do without any of these. Even if we do not use them all, we will receive pieces of our documents on all of these programs.

Though it is true that InDesign can open and convert PageMaker 6.5 and Quark 3 & 4 files, we still have to deal with them. One of my old digital presses, for example, has an old PostScript Level One clone for a RIP that will not print Quark, Illustrator, or InDesign files. I am certain there are other older RIPs that can only print Quark files. It could be argued that several non-PostScript printers do best with Publisher. But that is another story.

THIS IS ADVANCED INSTRUCTION

THIS BOOK ASSUMES PRIOR KNOWLEDGE

Unlike my first four books, this one assumes that you have been either working in or studying publishing production for a little while. InDesign, like Quark, is for advanced users only. For those of you who are coming from PageMaker, you will discover that InDesign strongly inhibits spontaneity. However, on a 1 to 10 scale of spontaneity to rigidity, InDesign is about a 5 (if PageMaker is a 2 and Quark a 7). Neither Quark nor InDesign are for the faint of heart, the publishing ignorant, or those not familiar with the PostScript workflow.

Although we will cover basic reviews of all topics you need to know, I have to assume introductory knowledge, at least, of PageMaker and/or QuarkXPress; FreeHand, CorelDraw and/or Illustrator; and Photoshop and/or PhotoPaint. I must assume that you have exported graphics from creation programs and imported them to page layout programs. I also have to expect that you know basic file management techniques, mouse usage, text editing, the Clipboard, and so forth. We won't mention basic computer literacy.

In other words, I expect you to have a basic working knowledge of your computer and how to use it. My experience suggests that many (if not most) of you were poorly taught in these areas. In fact, unless you have used some of my earlier books and curricula, it is quite possible that my euphemistically named *reviews* will be brand new knowledge for many of you. But we will cover those things as we go.

Please notice clearly that I am not using *desktop publishing*. That phrase has become meaningless for most of us – having only nostalgic meaning for those who remember Paul Brainard and the early days. In most cases, desktop publishing currently refers to what I would call secretarial use. Those front office people, who spend most of their time with business correspondence and materials, who are called upon to do the monthly newsletter for the personnel or customers. These people have no publishing knowledge, and certainly little printing experience.

Digital publishing is the new paradigm of several old industries: marketing, advertising, publishing, and printing. We are the service industry for marketing and advertising agencies. Or, we are doing all of the marketing, advertising, and public relations for a company. Or, we are working for a printing or design firm who services these people. As part of this industry, we are responsible for producing the artwork and digital documents for printing projects from business cards to billboards, from brochures to books, from envelopes to point-of-purchase displays.

In addition, we are commonly responsible for the graphics and page production of Web sites. Often, we are also responsible for simple multimedia in the form of simple interactive CDs and PDFs. Finally, because we are often the only artist in the place, we also produce all the graphics and set up the PDFs or HTML for presentations.

No wonder that there is no one program that will do it all. In fact, in some shops there is no one person who is allowed to do it all. So, before we can go on, we must discuss the software that we must use to do the things we do. I will try to mention all the options.

 Please keep in mind: I offer many of these rather strongly stated opinions for several reasons. One is obviously to entertain. Another is to provoke discussion. A third is to give a hint of the wide variety of publishing solutions used in the industry. If you think I am wrong, good for you.

Publishing Software

State of the Industry

In an article in an issue of *Electronic Publishing* during the summer of 1999, a statistic was found that claimed digital publishers spent 40% of their time in Web work. My curiosity wonders about the time spent in simple multimedia using the interactive capabilities of Acrobat, for example.

What is important is that you think. Focus some time on software available, holes in your capabilities, and purchases you need to make.

Publishing software

For some of you, this is review. Even for you power users, the conceptualization of how our software is used will be helpful. Many of you do not know why we use the programs we use. It is not because they are popular. Keep in mind that if popularity were the issue, Quark would be out of business. PageMaker has sold ten times as many copies. It still has over half the market, even considering InDesign.

There are several important distinctions to be made concerning publishing software. First and foremost is the quality level. Software suitable for professional-quality publishing is top-end stuff. It has to support PostScript fluently and resolutions of 1,200 dpi or higher if it produces bitmapped lineart; or have the ability to produce a screen frequency of at least 100 lines per inch for tints, halftones, and separations. Most professional work is at 133 line screens or finer and 2,400 dpi or more. Also, this software must be able to read and use the common formats for graphics and text. At the minimum, this means support for EPS, TIFF, and the various word processing formats in common use, especially Rich Text Format. In addition, it has to support HTML, GIF, JPEG, and (increasingly) SWF and PNG.

It must be remembered in digital publishing we are not competing against in-house secretarial productions, but slick "Madison Avenue" photographically imaged pieces. This takes a fast computer with a lot of memory (both RAM and storage) plus top-level software. (We'll cover the hardware needs in the next chapter.) Printed pages are amazingly complex images that use both conscious and subconscious techniques to communicate. We live in a culture that has received printed perfection for years, with clients who often refuse to pay for anything less. Courier and a spell checker will not cut it. We need kerning, tracking, various fonts, virtually infinite size, leading, and width controls, and we need them at the touch of a key or mouse button.

The problem with word processors

Normally, the first step in digital production is word processing. This is only the first step because word processors simply do not have the typographic capabilities required to produce professional-looking documents. Interestingly enough, InDesign has left this capability out of its environment. Like QuarkXPress, it basically cannot do word processing. That is, it always works in WYSIWYG page layout view. Multiline composing and screen redraws make writing in either Quark or InDesign a virtual impossibility.

By always working in layout view, InDesign sacrifices the speed and editing ease of the best word processors. **Watch out!** Here comes the first of many opinions. You will do well to get rid of the normally accepted word processors like Word and WordPerfect. What publishing professionals need in a word processor is speed in the writing and editing of copy. All the fancy bells and whistles of the modern word processing behemoths are useless in a professional publishing environment

A little heresy for fun

On one of the lists I'm on, a few weeks ago, one of the contributors from England made the following observation, "If you eliminate all evidence of MicroSoft software from your computer, you will experience a 20% to 40% speed increase." He was right! My increase was about 25%.

anyway. In addition, that copy of Office you have on your machine is using huge quantities of disk space and your precious digital fluids (RAM). Is it really necessary?

I strongly recommend that you purchase (if you haven't already) a dedicated word processor that has drag'n'drop editing and style palette capabilities that can be assigned with a keyboard shortcut. My preference is Mariner Write. It takes barely 3 MB of hard disk space, less than 2 MB of RAM, is lightning fast (opens in less than 3 seconds) and has all of the powerful text editing tools needed (plus the list price was less than $80). I have also heard very good things about Nissus Writer. On the PC side, I do not know names, but it wouldn't surprise me if there is a freeware word processor that will do the job.

One of the problems you will run into is the unusable state of word processing files as received. We will cover cleanup techniques in Chapter 7. If you do not do your own copyediting and cleanup, you will truly need a person who is trained typographically who can apply styles that you can import and automatically format. This person may take some real effort to find (or train). I highly recommend that you compensate him well to avoid losing him. The typographic errors in copy produced by people trained to type are a major hindrance to production speed. The fact that they were trained to type as they do doesn't help the morass of double spaces, double returns, tabs for indents, and all of the other anomalies you will run into.

The need for PostScript

One of the most important things you must understand to work in this industry is PostScript. It is a page description language brought out by Adobe in 1985 that was part of the enabling technology (along with the LaserWriter and PageMaker) that created desktop publishing and saved the Mac. There were other competitors, but PostScript won out and became the absolute standard. Some others claim that their software can do as well — don't believe them. The problem is not in the creating software — there are many competing programs that can produce results that superficially appear professional (*even Word!*). The difficulty is in the final output. For the foreseeable future, all professional-quality output devices will continue to use PostScript.

For example, CorelDraw is not used much in our industry. That says nothing about the power and quality of the software. Right or wrong, there are basically three reasons: one, it was not available on the Mac until recently; two, it does not use the standard industry terminology; three, it does not produce files that can be relied upon with imagesetters and platesetters (it writes PostScript code that causes printing problems). Supposedly versions 8 and beyond have solved the PostScript problem, but many of us are justifiably leery. That alone is enough to make it unusable for our purposes.

Publishing Software

The important thing to remember is that PostScript works by describing pages in terms of shapes. These shapes are described mathematically in a page description language. Even bitmapped images must be put in a box that is described mathematically, with screens and separations described in PostScript code. As we continue, this will become more clear. At this point, we'll emphasize that you need a firm grasp of the concept of pages as assemblages of shapes written as mathematical equations.

The software we use

Publishing software has at least three major categories: illustration – PostScript and paint; image editing or image manipulation; and page layout. To produce professional results, you will need at least one program in each of the categories. Like mentioned, you probably need all of the Big Seven.

ILLUSTRATION SOFTWARE

PostScript illustration

On the left is a scan of a watercolor painting. On the right is a PostScript illustration version of the same painting. Neither version is better or worse. They are simply different.

This book uses the term PostScript instead of other terms, such as vector drawings or object-oriented software, for a simple reason. PostScript is the standard in our industry. Future developments will likely be improvements on PostScript. Even if there is a radical change, it will probably be called PostScript. The much discussed PDF workflow is a use of a cleaned up and streamlined PostScript. The concept we are discussing involves creating shapes by describing them with a mathematical equation of the outline and various fills.

This sounds much more clunky than it actually is. The equations used work elegantly, and transparently. They are exquisitely precise and can be modified easily. If there is a problem with this type of illustration, it is this precision. PostScript illustration can easily be too perfect. This is why much computer art is easily recognized. There is a perfection that cannot be found in the natural world. There is a matte smoothness that cannot be produced with a buffer or even hand polishing. There is no dirt, no breaks, no randomness, unless the artist works at it (and draws it in). For clean work with little or no visual distraction, PostScript software is the ideal solution. Adding the human touch is more difficult. All the dirt and abuse of reality must be drawn.

Another major advantage is that EPS graphics are generally much smaller than Tiffs unless they are used to save bitmapped art. Because a large shape can be described with an equation instead of a huge, laborious list of each pixel or dot, vector drawings take up much less space in RAM, in storage, or in modem time. They can become so complicated that output is impossible, but this can easily be avoided with simple compassion for the imagesetter operators. EPSs are more portable by far.

In general, PostScript illustration is used because of the ease of manipulation. Any part of a vector drawing is treated as a separate object. As a result, any piece of a drawing can be cloned, duplicated, flipped, skewed, rotated, scaled, or filled with an almost infinite number of patterns, gradients, or tints. The professional programs allow layers to be built that can be moved above or below any other layer and turned on or off at will. Layers can be locked, grayed out, and made nonprintable (so they can be used for tracing). The creative freedom is totally exhilarating. The only problem is that illustrations can become so complicated that no imagesetter can handle them.

> **TIP: If you have a PostScript Illustration that approaches or exceeds 1 MB, it is far too large. In fact, it may not print. You need to be very careful about excessive complexity in PostScript illustrations. All it requires is a little planning and forethought.**

Since the early 1990s there have only been two real competitors, FreeHand and Illustrator. The also-rans, primarily CorelDraw and Canvas, never quite matched up. Draw completely changes the technical language the rest of us use, plus it has always had problems with graphics that

would not print. Even though it is possible to export as an Illustrator file, resave, and reexport as an EPS, this is obviously a bit clumsy. Canvas has always advertised itself as the one-stop-shop, with many neat tricks. However, all reports indicated, that until very recently, Canvas lacked some of the basics and had trouble with PostScript. There are currently rumors that both Draw and Canvas are now professionally usable. I think the problem now is that we are all deeply invested in FreeHand and/or Illustrator. There is no reason to change, and we don't want to take the chance. If they work for you, go for it.

As far as the two majors are concerned, Illustrator has always had the reputation. FreeHand has had the ease of use and most of the innovations. In my experience, Illustrator has been a lot like QuarkXPress. It takes a great deal of memory and constant use to remember the keyboard shortcuts necessary to function in both these programs. They are not very intuitive until you have learned to think like they think. Without the shortcuts, the amount of mousing required greatly slows production. However, once the shortcuts are learned, Illustrator is universally acclaimed as "the most elegant" PostScript illustration program. Illustrator is undeniably the choice of full-time professional illustrators. Its use will probably increase a little now that it is so strongly fit into the standard Adobe interface of PageMaker, InDesign, Illustrator, and Photoshop.

FreeHand, on the other hand, is very easy to use. Its functions are both easier to understand and easier to access. Its capabilities like drag'n'drop color, multiple pages, graphic styles palette, 25,600% enlargements, 222-inch square pasteboard, are not matched by any one else. No other program can handle type so fluidly. There are also direct interface ties to Dreamweaver, Flash, and Director that appeal to many Web designers. Beyond that, until InDesign, FreeHand was the only program that allowed the almost complete customization of the interface to fit your needs. FreeHand can almost do the Adobe interface better than Adobe.

FreeHand is the clear winner for people who are responsible for the entire process of digital publishing – working with several programs open, every day, on a constant basis. Illustrator will probably remain the favorite of people who specialize in drawing and illustration, exclusively. FreeHand is probably the best choice in production environments. There is a real reason why the wire services settled on FreeHand for their graphic delivery to newspapers.

The final software in this group would be MultiAd Creator. I know very little about it. All reports make this an incredibly powerful, extremely functional tool in the intensely production-driven newspaper and magazine environment. I have no idea why it isn't used more. But then I have never figured out why VHS beat out Beta, or why Iomega put SyQuest out of business. Often, the best simply does not win out.

Though the possibilities are amazing, many illustrations can still be done only by the other type of graphic illustration software, a painting program that works with bitmapped images.

PAINT ILLUSTRATION

This discussion will separate paint from image editing because of the complexity of the tools. In this case, we are talking almost exclusively about Painter (or the 3D paint programs). Painter tries to emulate traditional fine art tools and techniques with remarkable success. It uses "real" brushes, like a Sumi brush or a round sable, doing a remarkable job of mimicking the look of the tool. In fact, fine art is the key to understanding this program. It uses fine art language and a fine art attitude for an interface that is nearly incomprehensible in its complexity. The learning curve is very steep in the beginning. This is a program for full-time illustrators. No one else really has the time to learn the interface.

Publishing Software

Once you are in and working, Painter has amazing power. You start by specifying the surface to be worked on—watercolor paper in smooth, rough, hot press, cold press, and several variants; canvas of many kinds and textures; and so forth. Then you pick the color of the surface and the direction of the prevailing light source.

The tools have fine art names — brushes, markers, pencils, pastels, crayons, and so on. Unlike Photoshop's limited, single brush of varying size and color, Painter offers watercolor sables, worn bristle brushes, Sumi brushes, and so on. These brushes actually give the same results as their namesakes. Painter 6 has brushes where each bristle or hair produces an individual single-pixel-wide line. You can drop water on a wash and produce the same bleeding and hard edge found in watercolors. All of these have many variations, and the penetration and saturation of the colors can also be controlled. The erasers come in ink, fine point, gum, dry, kneaded rubber, plus a full set of bleach tools. The erasers take you back to the surface color. The bleaches take you to white.

The tools can get rather exotic — spinners, rubber stamps, airbrush, smudgers, and so on. In addition, there are cloning tools, selection tools of many kinds, and blending tools. It becomes relatively easy to produce multiple strokes or multiple image parts. There is complete control of transparency and blending. Many fine artists are now producing watercolors in Painter and printing them out on large Iris inkjets on watercolor paper. It is virtually impossible to tell whether they were done by hand or by computer.

The only limits are your imagination and coordination. The main thing, as in all fine art, is practice, practice, practice. It is obvious

that virtually any type of picture can be produced **IF** (this is really a large if!):

- If you have a lot of time
- If you have a lot of RAM – 128 MB or more (512 MB RAM is commonplace in this rarefied arena)
- If you have a lot of storage – raid arrays and huge multigigabyte disks are normal
- If you have a fast CPU – G3 or Pentium III or faster (a multiprocessor G4 would be nice)
- If you have a lot of skill and much experience.

This is the major problem with painting. These bitmapped documents commonly run into hundreds of megabytes. Gigabyte paintings are not unheard of. Most of the applications require that there be 3 to 5 times the size of the file in RAM and the same amount available on the hard drive for manipulation purposes. Some of the three-dimensional paint programs still take days to render the image on the screen, even in the Pentium III/G4 era. It is certainly possible to cover the surface of a shape with textures ranging from shiny metal through any fabric, stone, tile, whatever. It takes time. Often it takes a lot of time. With digital production time measured in minutes, painting is often a luxury that must be forgone. Often, there is only time for much simpler solutions.

Portability difficulties

Another problem that is often forgotten is, "What do you do with that admittedly gorgeous image when you are done?" If the document reaches several gigabytes, how can it be transported to a service bureau, unless you simply unplug your hard drive and carry it there? In fact, the current crop of pocket-sized, hot-swappable FireWire drives is the only real solution, so far. Even these technological wonders only hold a dozen or so gigabytes. Huge, multipage, process-color pieces like programs, magazines, or annual reports can easily total several gigabytes. It is too late to prepare for this when the document is finished at 2 GB and your largest removable is an old 1 GB JAZ drive. Even T1 lines into 100BaseT Ethernet will be tied up for a ridiculously long time.

A final concern with painted images is the need to create them to size. Unless you calculate accurately, the resized image can develop a severe case of the "jaggies." At the very least it will be softened. Transformation tools do the same. Unlike PostScript graphics, which rasterize the image at the printer, painted images have designated pixels. The image is mod-

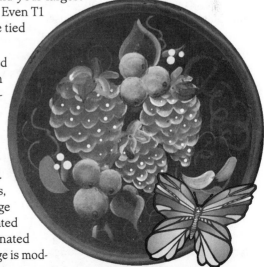

ified in page layout at the risk of the designer. As a result, you should plan carefully in advance and produce an image that is transformed and sized for the final output directly in the creating software. Then it will print with no problems.

SCAN MANIPULATION

IMAGE EDITING SOFTWARE

Technically, image editing software could be called painting programs, but their purpose is different and the tools are more limited in quantity, though not in scope. In reality, image editing software can be called Photoshop (even though CorelPaint is a distant also-ran). The major purpose of image manipulation software is to work with scans of photographs, artifacts, and continuous tone artwork. They do this extremely well. Beyond that, image manipulation software does an amazing job of compositing multiple images.

Professional manipulation software can work in color up to 48-bit. They can produce RGB or CMYK, grayscale, and bitmap images. They can export the finished images in a very wide variety of formats including the required EPS, TIFF, GIF, JPEG, and PDF. In fact, one of Photoshop's common uses is converting strange formats into something more acceptable to the software being used for page layout. Unprintable TIFFs, from nonprofessional software, can simply be opened and resaved in Photoshop to fix them, for example.

Halftone through separation production

Photoshop can produce halftones, duotones, tritones, quadritones, and separations in process color. It can produce virtually any screen frequency or angle in a wide variety of dot patterns, including round dot, square dot, elliptical dot, line, mezzotint, and custom dots. It provides complete control over color, tint range, highlights, midtones, or shadow dots, and so on. *(If this paragraph seems to be in a foreign language, read Chapter 11.)*

One of the major abilities of this type of software is another result of the paradigm shift. It has become relatively easy to blend many photos or scans into one. We are not talking about simple collages where images are pasted together into a single image. This is a brand new ability: New York balanced on the edge of Crater Lake with the Matterhorn looming in the background. This is the technology used for all the reality distortions in movies and commercials.

Every image can be placed in its own layer. That layer can be infinitely doctored up with color modifications, feathering, and transparency control. When all the layers are flattened into a single image, it is impossible to tell that the image has been messed with — except for the obvious fact that it no longer has any attachment to reality known to mankind.

In addition, image manipulation programs offer a huge variety of filters to blur, sharpen, twist, pointillize, distort, lighten, darken, or otherwise play with the image. Because it is easy to edit at the pixel level, it is relatively simple to put one person's head on a different person's body, and so on. Retouching photos has taken on an entirely new meaning. In fact, it has become an ethical problem. Are we required to tell when we've removed a deformity? Photographs can no longer be considered legal evidence, as they used to be; no one can tell whether the photo has been modified.

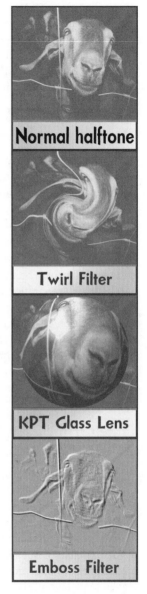

Normal halftone

Twirl Filter

KPT Glass Lens

Emboss Filter

The major source of "professionally ugly" design

The filters and multiple layers of various images have become a real visual problem. In recent years, many illustrations have become mere filter and compositing demos with little artistic merit. They are bad design covered with fashion. At its worst, modern image manipulation illustration becomes what could be called professionally ugly — distorted collages of images whose sole purpose is to convince the viewer of the creator's sophistication. John McWade calls it *grunge collage*. What most fail to remember is that this style of image is often appealing only to their fellow Photoshop video warriors. In fact, many schools and books teach Photoshop like fun and games — a true video game.

"Wow! Look, ma, what I can do!"

The size and transportation problems are the same as for painting programs. The hardware requirements are very stiff. Photoshop professionals are always complaining about memory even at the norm of 256 MB of RAM. Every new version of Photoshop requires more RAM. The minimum requirement is now 32 MB. Even then you can only work on small, simple images. In reality, the minimum is more like 128 MB.

DOCUMENT ASSEMBLY

PAGE LAYOUT

We have finally arrived at the focus of this book. Though it can be argued that image editing takes the most skill (*PostScript illustrators can squeal now*) and digital image assembly takes the most computing power (*let's hear the whines of the animation crowd*), page layout software is the cream of the crop, the top of the heap, the end of the chain. This is where the document comes together.

Though image assembly comes after page layout, creativity truly ends with layout. The master designers work in page layout. Illustrators can be hired, separations can be subcontracted out, and image assembly can be handled by the printer as a separate contractor. Page layout creates the publication in a very real way. Though writers and illustrators are often more creative (classically), page layout is what ties the document together and creates the overall image. Writing is not read unless the publication convinces readers that they want to read it. Illustrations usually make little sense unless they are tied to the writing that goes with them in a way that communicates accurately.

... *creativity ends with page layout.*

In a lot of ways, page layout software is like a Jack or Jill of all trades, but a master of one: document assembly. You can write in them, but writers prefer a good word processor. You can draw in them, but many of the good abilities are missing. It is even possible to do some image manipulation, but only at the expense of quality. What page layout does better than anything else is final production of the artwork. Once a document leaves page layout, the rest of the production is concerned with duplication rather than creation.

Creative freedom with ultimate typography

A document in the hands of a master designer has the fluidity of paint. Type can ebb and flow like water into the channels prepared for it by the creator. Graphics become points of inspiration and clarification. The concepts of the writer communicate clearly, and the reader is powerfully motivated to respond as intended. Professional page layout software uses type, graphics, and color as malleable media. The freedom of photographic pasteup is nothing compared to digital expression.

Publishing Software

The use of page layout is not optional.

Even though FreeHand, CorelDraw, and Canvas claim to be the full solution to all of your digital publishing problems, do not believe it. Where they come up very short is in their page layout capabilities. If you do not use InDesign, Page-Maker, FrameMaker, or QuarkXPress, you will be extremely sorry — sooner or later.

These applications allow a control of type size, leading, tracking, kerning, scaling, and positioning that is astonishing to traditional professionals. You can vary these from a few points to hundreds at the touch of a couple of keys or the click of a mouse. Paragraph styles can be preformatted to allow text to be imported and automatically flowed into place with an exciting amount of control. Character palettes allow for consistent typographic accents.

Graphics can be linked to the text so that reflowing the words brings the pictures along with them. Colors can be assigned freely and applied precisely. Everything can be "snapped" to a predefined grid to provide creative freedom with an underlying structure that prevents chaos. Type sizes and leading can be changed by minute amounts to eliminate extra lines or paragraphs.

Beyond all of these are such things like text wrap, which allows the designer to drop a graphic into the middle of copy and watch the words fit themselves around it automatically. Linking is so complete that you can open the original graphic directly from the page layout software. When changes or repairs are made and saved, the image is simply updated in the final document. If the wrong graphic is imported or you simply change your mind, relinking allows you to bring in the one you really intended to use.

When the body of the document is complete, tables of contents and indexes can also be created automatically. The chapters or sections can be tied together with automatic page numbering and "continued to" or "continued from" tags. Multiple master pages can be set up that automatically place repeating elements on every page as needed while remaining completely editable. Columns, guide lines, margins, alignment, and virtually any other element of a publication can be controlled with exquisite precision, often with the nudge of an arrow key. Power users can control all of these techniques on the fly with a complete set of keyboard shortcuts that can be adjusted to fit the designer's working style.

When everything is complete, the document, all linked graphics and text, fonts, and whatever else is necessary can be automatically assembled into a final folder for easy transportation to the imagesetter, printer, image assembly facility, or platesetter. For even more streamlining, everything can be condensed into a universally usable PDF. The creation is complete and packaged – all that remains is production. The rest of the production team is charged with duplicating the artwork produced in the page layout software.

The varieties available

Within the constraints of PostScript, there are four page layout programs that can work professionally: FrameMaker for the scientific, technical, and long document market; PageMaker for spontaneous creation where the designer is also writing or editing all of the copy; QuarkXPress for process production with automatic assembly into precise templates; and the newcomer on the block, InDesign – the focus of this book.

Adobe's claims for InDesign are really quite astonishing. They claim all the functionality of both PageMaker and Quark adding transparent interaction with all of the creating graphic software. InDesign has added a new typographic engine that is far superior to anything currently available in the desktop publishing market. It has added graphic abilities like gradient strokes that are unheard of. It works natively in PDF, writing prepress level PDFs directly without the need for Distiller. For a 1.5 application, InDesign is truly amazing.

However, InDesign 1.5 is still a brand new program. Several of the capabilities need a little fleshing out. Some abilities require third party plug-in manufacturers (think Xtensions). But there is little doubt that 1.5 and beyond offer real competition to Quark, and in many areas raise the bar to astonishing heights. Even 1.5 is a remarkably powerful and fluid document assembler.

Even as it is, I find it feels like a well-developed, fully functional piece of software. I, for one, am willing to give Adobe the benefit of the doubt. I am convinced that this will be at least a worthy competitor to Quark — with high hopes that it will far surpass it.

ASTONISHING COMPLEXITY: THE REALITIES OF SKILL

Professional publishing software is complex enough to make it virtually impossible for anyone to be expert at all of it. Attempting to do everything usually compromises the quality of the finished product. If at all possible, the norm should be to let writers write, illustrators illustrate, and designers design. Try not to expect creativity out of prepress wizards — it will reduce their accuracy (and you are paying them for their accuracy and technical skill). Technicians in the image assembly department are chastised if they change the image without signed prior approval from the artist, at least, and usually the client.

Training requirements are huge

Finally, no matter how much talent one demonstrates, it takes a fair amount of time for anyone to become proficient at any one program. Expect that close to 200 hours of practice *(not work!)* will be required for power use of each program (much more than that for publishing novices). This is specifically 200 hours of practice and experimentation, as opposed to routine production, with each program. Also remember that the yearly upgrades often take considerable time to assimilate. This time should be planned for. Compromising training time will mean shorting your company on production speed and accuracy. If your superiors do not understand this, it might be appropriate to look for a new position elsewhere.

Beyond that there is the problem of wetware storage. It is the rare brain that can be truly expert in all areas of digital design. You are a fool to try. The adage is true. The jack-of-all-trades is truly master of none. Look at your personal strengths and head in that direction, spending your training time where it will do the most good. You really do not have to do everything. It is the wise person who subcontracts his weaknesses. The good news is that InDesign fits very well with your existing workflow.

Publishing Software

InDesign has a slightly steeper learning curve, but not as severe as QuarkXPress. In fact, if you know Quark well, you are very well prepared to pick up InDesign relatively quickly. The almost completely customizable interface will enable you to make InDesign fit smoothly into your workflow.

PDF workflow

Recently there has been a huge amount of excitement about the last program in the Big Seven. There really is good reason to believe that it is about to become the center of your workflow procedures. Most of you have at least heard of PDFs by now. So, what's the big deal? From our point of view here, we will not get into the entire procedure for using a PDF workflow. However, InDesign not only creates beautiful PDFs, it can also edit PDFs (if they are not encrypted).

For now, let's just describe what they are. PDF stands for Portable Document Format. It was one of a group of formats developed in the late 1980s and early 1990s to solve the cross-platform dilemma. The basic idea is a universal format that can be read by anyone on any platform. PDF does this well. Acrobat Reader is free. You have a copy of the installer on your CD and it can be downloaded free from http://www.adobe.com for any platform you need: Mac, PC, UNIX, Sun, Silicon Graphics, Next, and others. This reader can read any PDF regardless of what platform it was created on (provided it is recent enough). One of the real problems I had when I first installed InDesign was that none of my students could read the PDFs I produced until they installed Reader 4.0.

HYPERMEDIA PARADIGM

CHAPTER 22:
PRINTING WELL
IN BLACK & WHITE

Doing black & white well.

Contents

Check out a Rembrandt etching.
Most jobs are limited
B&W brings clarity
The single color majority...
Linescreens
Continuous tone
Tips on halftone production
Dot gain
Commercial printers use presses
Quick printers use duplicators
Generational shifts
Miscellaneous problems
Target dot ranges
A 7 step process
#1—Photo Location
#2—Set the size & resolution
#3—Adjust the scan
#4—Crop the scan to size
#5—Clean up the image
#6—Adjust the levels
#7—Sharpen with unsharp mask
Final comments
Terminology
Suggested Reading

RADIQZ PRESS

© 1998 David Bergsland, Radiqz Press

Publishing Software

However, PDFs go far beyond universal readability. Because they embed the graphics, PDFs produce an extremely accurate view of the original document. They can even be color calibrated to be used for contract proofs. More than that, the image will be crisp, clear, and will not suffer badly when you enlarge it to see things better (as long as the bitmap graphics have high enough resolution). This is because the PDF format is a streamlined, cleaned-up version of PostScript. All the fonts can be embedded, so you do not have to convert them to paths — and once the fonts are embedded, they show up perfectly on PC or MAC. This solves the major cross-platform issue: the fact that Macs cannot read PC fonts and vice versa.

InDesign reads PDFs directly, importing them like EPSs. Because PDF is so much a part of it, InDesign can create PDFs by simply exporting without any need for Acrobat Distiller. Much of the excitement surrounding the release of InDesign was about the new ability to truly implement a PDF workflow.

My last book, *Digital Drawing*, was created entirely in PageMaker (InDesign had not been released). When I was done writing, assembling, and formatting the book, I printed the document for each chapter to disk as a PostScript file. Then I distilled the .ps files into PDFs using the parameters set by my printer in Canada for Distiller 3. I then uploaded the PDFs to my printer's server (over 2,000 miles away). They printed beautifully with none of the printing problems I experienced with my first book in the summer of 1996. This time I fully expect to merely export each chapter as a PDF and upload them.

Annotation

During the process of creation, I regularly use PDFs for proofing. I send PDF proofs to each of my proofers and they add the corrections in the form of annotations. These are little notes that can be added to PDFs with Acrobat Exchange 3 or Acrobat 4. These notes have my proofer's name on their title bar. When I get the proofs back I can assemble the notes from each of my proofers into a single PDF file. This makes adding the corrections extremely easy. The annotation procedure is not detailed enough for my copyeditor — after the book is completed. However, it makes a wonderful visual proofing medium for catching layout errors and so forth.

Beyond that, PDFs have proven to be the enabling technology for teaching these materials on the Web. Without the ability of students to easily send in projects in a complete package, online critiques would be impossible. More than that, without a way to annotate those projects as they work their way to professionalism, it would be impossible to offer suggestions or help that could be understood.

Compression

I have mentioned that PDF is a streamlined PostScript, but that would not be enough in itself. For Web delivery, we have to go much further than that. So Acrobat offers very powerful downsampling and compression capabilities. It offers both lossy and lossless compression to what

printers would consider ridiculous extremes. But then the Web is ridiculously crude from a printer's point of view.

TIP: You really need to remember that PDF was developed for Web delivery, among other things. The default when you install the Distiller package is for Web graphics. This means heavy downsampling (to 72 dpi) and extreme lossy compression (using JPEG at the maximum). Acrobat 4 offers three job settings: Screen Optimized for the Web and CDs; Print Optimized for your laser printer or inkjet; and Prepress Optimized for your service bureau, imagesetter, or platesetter. You will need to carefully set up your job options when you start using this software regularly. My printer for this book, for example, wants me to be sure that I only use lossless compression and no downsampling.

Do not be dismayed, the Web *is* ridiculously crude from a historical designer's perspective. Extreme JPEG compression cannot even be seen online. While it is true that JPEGs can hardly be used in printing, because of the compression artifacts, at 72 dpi those artifacts are not even rendered on the screen. However, ImageReady in Photoshop 5.5 now makes lossy GIFs that are often far superior to JPEGs.

Interactivity

Beyond all of this, PDFs can be made interactive very easily. Internal linkages are made as fast as you can type. Links can be added to external URLs. Clicking on the Web link opens your browser and goes to the link. You can embed Quicktime movies that will play with a click on a link – or music. There is really nothing better for the generation of electronic books at the present time.

The front cover of one of my chapters for an early version of my PDF book now called Image Manipulation can be seen on page 17. That Table of Contents is linked to the locations in the book. If I click on a TOC entry, it takes me to that page at an appropriate enlargement. There are also many interactive links inside each chapter. The glossary on the last page of each chapter is linked directly to the definitions in the chapter, for example. References to illustrations are linked to those illustrations. Most importantly, all of the linkages were added in about 15 minutes. It really makes a marvelous method to publish exploratory or limited edition books.

We haven't even talked about Apple's proposed change from QuickDraw to PDF for monitor graphics in System X. How far they go with that remains to be seen. There is a reasonable chance that PDF will become the standard for all monitor graphics in addition to becoming the output standard for digital publishing. It is easy to foresee all of publishing becoming dependent upon PDF as we are now dependent upon PostScript for printing.

1. Why are virtually all logos drawn with PostScript illustration software and moved around as EPSs?

2. Why do we need to be able to use all of the Big Seven?

3. What is the graphic purpose of Painter?

4. What is InDesign's place in publishing?

5. What are the advantages of a PDF workflow?

WHERE SHOULD YOU BE BY THIS TIME?

This is the introduction to your studies around InDesign. If you are in a class, your instructor will be showing you what is expected with file management, which software is available, what hardware is available and so forth. It is time to get yourself settled in. This would also be a good time to quickly go through the tutorials that came with InDesign. They should be located in your InDesign folder on one of your hard drives, in a folder called Learning Adobe InDesign. Inside is a PDF called Tutorial Contents.pdf – open it.

DISCUSSION

You should be meeting your classmates and finding out their history and goals. You will become increasingly convinced during your career in publishing that lone wolves make lousy graphic designers. Publishing is a team sport, and you might as well get started now.

Talk among yourselves...

A Digital Workflow

CONCEPTS

There is a great deal of printing and publishing terminology in this chapter that assumes you have been involved in printing and publishing before. There is no help for this other than study and experience. My assumption is that you have had a basic digital publishing course using a textbook like, *Printing in a Digital World,* Delmar 1997, that has taught you this terminology. If not, you need to buy a copy. It can be found many places. I recommend the Desktop Bookstore:

http://kumo.swcp.com/ graphics/bookstores

A generalized overview of the printing industry: giving a feel for what you will be working with in your career

CHAPTER OBJECTIVES

By presenting the options and capabilities of the publishing industry's software, this chapter will enable you to:

1. Describe the digital variant of the traditional commercial printing firm
2. Describe digital quickprint
3. Describe top end digital printing
4. Explain the hardware and software needs of a professional digital designer in various settings

LAB WORK FOR CHAPTER

• Do the InDesign tutorials that come with the software
• Look over and read as much of the User Manual as you can stand

There have been a few changes...

Remember, several lists have selected Gutenberg as the most important person of the last millennium — with good reason.

A digital workflow

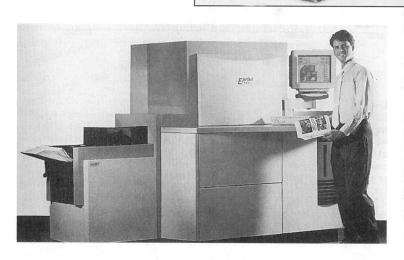

"So, what's new?

"The entire conceptual basis of the publishing industry, that's what. Now that we have talked a little about our software tools, we need to discuss where we are in the industry (as if anyone really knows). For not only have the rules changed, we are in a brand-new ball game. Certainly there are remnants of former careers floating around in this new world. However, they are all strangely realigned, combined, and synergized.

"Here is the major difference. One person can now do it all. It is true that most of us have sense enough to only get involved with that which we can do well. However, there is no longer any limit, conceptually, to these tasks. Moreover, these skill sets are very fluid in scope. Because the same hardware is used for it all, and the same software can do most of it, each individual project has the capability to vary wildly from the one done previously."

This copy originated in the PDF book, *Image Manipulation*, Radiqz Press, 1998. It was radically different from my first textbook, *Printing in a Digital World*, Delmar, 1997. The third book, *Digital Drawing*, Delmar, 2000, went even further. It evolved from a static traditionally printed volume to a Web site, an interactive CD-ROM, as well as a traditional printed book. It was all being done with the normal software tools of a publisher covered last chapter.

So part of the new paradigm is the wideness of options. However, it goes far beyond that. It all started at the beginning of the twentieth century with the concept of a universal tool. The idea was a tool that could do anything – a calculating machine, but much more. Let's go back to those words written in early 1997.

THE DIGITAL AGE

"The big change came with what we now call the digital age ... we entered a new era. Don't misunderstand – it isn't the intelligence of computers that has changed our world. It is the ability to do stupid repetitive things very quickly, without mistakes (the mistakes that harass you are almost entirely operator or programmer error). The now ubiquitous pocket calculator is a clear example of this. We no longer have to waste our mental storage capacities to remember things like multiplication and division tables (we won't even mention such horrible nasties as sines, cosines, tangents, square roots, etc.). Even if we remember how to do those things, the pocket calculator is so much faster, and more accurate to boot.

"This is the revolution – the ability to do stupid repetitive things very quickly

"No more repetitive work to hassle us – we know that this is not literally true. We seem to have an infinite capacity for boredom (and for stupid repetitive tasks). However, this is the basis of the new paradigm. In the publishing industry, this has led to radical, fundamental change. Entire careers have been eliminated by software (which is simply a set of mathematical instructions that execute very difficult, yet precisely definable tasks). The difficulty is simple. Those boring drudge jobs that have disappeared were highly prized by those who find thinking painful. However, there are many who find the creative freedom exhilarating.

"Regardless, it has been a genuine shift in the basic rules of operation. By the late 1990s, the entire industry was radically different. Entire careers are gone – typesetters, hand letterers, pasteup artists, cameramen, strippers, and more. An entire industry of tool manufacturers and graphic suppliers has been wiped out – presstype, Magic Markers™, Format™ screens and rules, parallel rules, waxers, tech pens, stat cameras, and hundreds more. All of these things can now be done by a single person, sitting in front of a Mac or PC, next to their laser printer and their color proofer.

"Now it is possible for a single person, sitting in their converted garage, to produce publishing that is indistinguishable from the big boys on the coasts. (Often it is of higher quality, probably the result of working in a functional environment.) My first textbook rocked my publisher. They had never (before – or since, as far as I know) had an author who wrote all the copy, created all the illustrations, shot all the photos, and produced the finished artwork.

"The Web

"At the same time, traditional publishing was being attacked from a completely different direction. In the 1960s, the Defense establishment had set up… a computer network that would survive a nuclear attack. The result was the Internet. If possible, it was a worse joke than early DOS word processing. You thought DOS was bad – you just hadn't seen UNIX yet…. The Internet was stuck in a similar paradigm as the publishing industry – the code-driven interface. Here the paradigm buster was Netscape, which provided the first publicly popular tool to browse that new graphical portion of the Internet – the World Wide Web.

"Navigator did to communication what PageMaker did to publishing – it brought these capabilities into the SOHO (Small Office Home Office) world that was emerging as a result of the new technology. What many of us wanted to do (after our downsized layoff), we were now capable of doing. With a Website, a computer, and some nerve, we could compete with the big boys on virtually even footing…. Again the early efforts were crude and often annoying – the communication equivalent of 9-pin printers … this was a change of like stature as what desktop publishing became.

"The advantages of the Web rapidly emerged. 'An 800 number on steroids.' 'A friendly face available to your clients 24–7–365.' 'Your entire inventory available at the touch of a keyboard.' 'Communication that avoids the irritation of phone tag.' 'A worldwide presence from

the comfort of your SOHO' ... the synergistic addition of the Web to the Desktop makes SOHO much more viable. Again, the new paradigm has to do with decentralization, creative freedom, and the ability to break out of the corporate coffins. The result is fundamental change to the business world and the publishing industry.

"Remember, this is the basic paradigm. All of the publishing tools, all of the communication tools ... are available on my desktop to help me communicate with you. The larger shops will still have specialization; but even here, we find single persons taking on entire projects. The old paradigm where I needed others to do the things I was incapable of doing for myself has become merely an expensive option.

"Worldwide Fulfillment

"The final difference between the new and the old is the area of influence. Over the past few days, I have had student and client inquiries from New Zealand, Alaska, Italy, England, Virginia, St. Louis, plus several others who haven't bothered to mention their location. It no longer makes any difference. I use the same software and the same delivery method for my next door neighbor as I do for my student on the North Island."

Now, three years later, I cannot tell the difference between my local students and my global students. The online students come from as close as the computer in the lab next to me, to the far side of the world and it makes no difference at all. Let's continue the quote a bit.

"In this industry, where we are selling ideas and designs in a digital format, it is becoming common for the designer to be in one country, the client in another, and the actual production to be spread all over the globe.... The only problem for us is final delivery of the art and proofs, but FedEx and its competitors have solved that. My real problem today is that I have to do an ad and hand-deliver it to the local newspaper. What a hassle! I don't have time for that kind of thing anymore. Why can't I just attach it to an e-mail?"

With thanks to my editor at Radiqz Press, here's a few observations. First of all, this radically new industry was foreseen. Second, our equipment has finally matured to a place where there is little new. InDesign marks the first necessary change in several years. There is no functional difference working in Photoshop 3, 4, or 5. The same is true of the rest of the Big Seven.

Finally we can describe the new industry

It is now possible to describe the shape of the industry in the twenty-first century. Publishing will be increasingly digitized. What cannot be digitized will be automated. There will still be drudge jobs for those who refuse to get educated. Printing will become a highly educated industry, though. Instead of relying on apprenticeship, it will require computer-literate personnel trained on the job in the specific software used by the specific company.

By 1995, it was almost impossible to even get interviewed without Mac experience with PageMaker, Quark, FreeHand, Illustrator, and Photoshop. The maturing of PDF and the release of InDesign are the first real changes we have seen since then. In those years we have seen thousands of traditional shops go out of business or be transformed into all digital or partially digital operations. For designers, it's been all digital for quite a while.

We will look at workflows in three areas:, commercial printing, quick print, and digital printing. There is no way we can cover all the variables. However, we can give you a good feel for what is out there.

The changes to traditional shops

The first thing to note is the disappearance of cameras. Some firms that have them still use them, a little. However, there is often an extra charge for camera-ready art because of the expense of firing up the processor again. What this means on a practical level is that several careers have disappeared also. Camera operators and strippers (film assemblers) are gone. In many shops, even platemakers are gone — replaced by computer-to-plate options or digital presses.

In addition, cameras are no longer needed in the art room because PMTs are no longer needed for enlargement and reduction. Pasteup has vanished as a career now that everything comes out composited. Typesetters are also gone with everything becoming part of digital publishing. Traditional shops have been decimated.

THE CLOSEST TO TRADITIONAL

DIGITAL COMMERCIAL PRINTING

First of all, there are shops that are still tied to some of the old technology. Basically, we are discussing establishments that are still using their old presses. They may be still using their platemaker. That would depend on whether they have an imagesetter or a platesetter. Even if they have an imagesetter, there have been radical changes.

Front office

One of the things that has broken down is the white-collar versus blue-collar segregation that existed before 1990. It is possible that only the pressroom staff still qualifies as blue collar, and maybe not even them. This is due, in large part, to the fact that most jobs are coming on disk. There is a department of CSRs (customer service representatives) charged with handling all the incoming data and taking care of the overall file management for the entire operation. This data room covers those responsibilities, plus basic preflight and electronic job writing.

The rest of this office has not changed a lot. The estimator now sends her data to the CSRs after the quote is accepted. The CSRs and all sales personnel have to be digitally literate and at least functional on an entry level with the publishing software. Everyone communicates by e-mail and cell phone. Many jobs come in as electronic job tickets with the digital files attached. The entire shop is networked. There are still

**The original
desktop publishing**

And they say every-
thing is new — we're
really just a lot faster
(and usually quite a bit
more tense about it).

separate nets for office and production, but even they are connected in the data room. All the computer areas run both Mac and Windows, even though Macs still vastly outnumber Wintel machines.

Digital design and production

The art department does not even look the same. It is air-conditioned, quiet, and decorated. The walls are lined with workstations. They are still using Macs primarily, but they have Windows machines to handle customers working in Wintel (at least to translate them into usable Mac format). All jobs are sent first to a workstation run as a translating station. Here all data is translated to formats that are usable by the software used in the shop. Both the word processing files and the graphics have to be checked, preflighted, and converted, if necessary. When everything is ready, it is placed into an appropriately named folder.

The art director's career has changed a lot. It has become much more administrative. She is a traffic manager and handles all customer relations. Customer conferences are easier that way, and nonadministrative, production employees waste too much time if they are overly involved with customer relations. Her responsibilities are creative supervision, job assignment, and layout approval.

After receiving a job and getting the client to answer any necessary questions, the art director gives the projects to the graphic designer whose skills best fit the client's needs. The graphic designer is charged with producing a layout, a graphic needs list (with sizes, and general typographic decisions).

The designer gives the graphics, outside her expertise, to the creative director. His responsibilities include all illustration, scanning, and tracing plus halftone production. Even those done directly by the graphic designer need to be approved by the creative director. His personnel include at least two illustrators (one in PostScript and one in Paint) and a scanner operator who runs the tracing program and produces halftones. The halftone producer may be an additional person, a Photoshop specialist, who is also charged with the production of duotones and the commodity separations.

Once the graphics are assigned, all copy is sent to the copyeditor. He cleans up the converted files and keys in any additional copy. He is responsible for fixing spelling, grammar, typos, extra returns, extra spaces, superfluous tabs, and the like. He is also a reasonably good copywriter for those projects needing those services. Finally, he adds headlines and subheads when required.

Once the graphics and copy are finished (or brought as far as possible), they are returned to the designer. After an approval conference with the art director, production begins. There may or may not be a rough. Sometimes the client provides a layout. Sometimes the project is a redo with changes. Regardless, the art director has to approve all layouts.

The designer sets all the defaults, flows the copy, and drops the graphics into place. If any additional pieces are needed graphically, she sends them to the creative director for assignment. Simple pieces she does herself (although her machine does not have enough RAM to work effectively in bitmap). Increasingly, production designers are PostScript masters using Illustrator or FreeHand for their production graphics. When complete, the job goes back to the art director with a laser proof.

After art director approval, the rough is sent on to the software specialist. This person is typically a computer nerd, who can fix any software problem in a heartbeat. He is also charged with keeping production flowing, installing software, and maintaining the creative network. His job is to open the folder containing all the pieces to make sure that all the pieces are there. After ensuring that all pieces are present, in the proper format, linked correctly, and in the right folder with a proper name, he generates a prepress PDF. Then he prints a contract art proof, marks it up, and sends it up front. Then the properly named folder is stored in the correct place on the correct drive until approval arrives, with the PDF ready to go if there are no changes.

Image assembly

After the client signs off on the proof, we enter the world of the production manager. Her task is to produce what has been created. She gets all approved jobs as a PDF from the design department plus all the projects that come in already designed, on disk. The first step is serious preflight. The CSRs simply look for missing pieces. Her preflightist just graduated from a local vo-tech and she's checking him out. The word is that he is not creative, but he's a hard worker and a Photoshop wiz. She's hoping that he'll have an eye for color correction – those are really rare.

After checking to see that everything is in working order, the preflightist sends the folder back to the production manager. She sends it on to the separator. By now the job is on a definite schedule. Everyone has a digital schedule that shows where every job is. Before image assembly, a delivery day was only an approximate guess; now everything is scheduled to the half hour.

On the critical color projects, the separator scans color images and separates them – sending low-res placeholders back to the designer or the art department. She also performs the OPI substitutions for the low-res images after they return. This is where the appropriate GCR adjustments are made, where the neutral gray levels are balanced, and the image is sharpened. In some shops this is the same color specialist who works up in the design department under the creative director. When complete, a contract color proof is made and sent back to the production manager.

After the color proofs are approved (sometimes by the client, sometimes not), the production manager sends the folder to the plating department. All projects arrive here as PostScript files or PDFs. Here the trapper and/or the impositor assemble the pages into sigs, and the traps are applied (if required). After determining that everything is in order, blueline or low-res proofs are made. Once the proofs have been signed off by the production manager, either negs or plates are output. They are thoroughly checked by the system manager and then the digital components are stored away. Some shops keep an old prepress master who lays down the prepunched composite negs on standard master sheets and burns the plates. He also makes all the laminated proofs. The old printing expertise is still

A Digital Workflow

A word about traditional software arenas

Commercial printing has traditionally been the stronghold of Quark and Mac. The quickprinter used mainly PageMaker with a lot of Windows clients. This has changed a lot recently. InDesign is obviously designed for top-end commercial printing. At this point, all three can be used anywhere. Because InDesign can open and convert the others, it is a strong position in all areas of printing.

By early 2000, the figures were about 50% PageMaker, 32% Quark, and 18% InDesign. And these figures were for InDesign 1.0.

extremely helpful for quality control, and for producing patches in areas of the negs having fit problems or needing last minute changes.

Pressroom and bindery

The pressroom has not changed much. They do have a new waterless press, but they are still using the same old plates that have worked so well for so many years on the rest of the presses. Rumor has it that the plates are not going to be made any longer. At that point, the plan is to get a new stochastic platesetter and convert the rest of the presses to waterless.

The bindery is also the same. Here the same people are still working as they have since the mid-1980s. There are no plans to change and no need to do so. They don't go up front much. They don't feel like they belong. It's really alien up there these days.

This shop has changed a great deal, but it still looks a lot like it did. The techniques are still the same conceptually. It's just that everything before the composite negs is digitized. The huge horizontal camera has been outside in the rain because they tore out the darkroom. The huge racks of negatives, flats, and plates have largely been digitized, although there are still several old clients who reprint enough to keep the old plates around.

THE NEW QUICKPRINT

Here's an industry segment that has changed a bit more radically. When you walk in the front door, nothing looks very different. After all, quick print led the way into desktop publishing. Because they could work with 85-line screens, laser printers were able to output camera-ready copy years ago. Even here, though, things have changed. First of all, there is now a preflight station next to the front counter. It is presided over by our trusty software guru, who examines all incoming projects that arrive on disk and confers with the customers.

This guru is a bit spiffier and friendlier, in keeping with the retail nature of the shop. It's almost a guru-as-CSR position. She is also kept busy helping the people at the rental computers in the corner. There's a couple of G4s and a Wintel workstation with a couple hundred megs of RAM and a good flatbed scanner available for those who can't afford to buy one. Some customers prepare their files and then come in to rent the computer to add their halftones and separations under the watchful eye of the guru.

The digital publisher is in a little room by himself. He does a lot more keyboarding than the copyeditor in the last shop. He had to pass a typing test to get interviewed, but his 45 words-per-minute rate was sufficient. He had explained that even though he wasn't a very fast typist, he was a very fast editor and an experienced user of OCR. In most cases, fast editing and formatting is worth far more than typing speed. He is responsible for all artwork production: word processing, illustration, halftone production, and page layout.

Formerly, he helped a lot at the front counter, but he got so busy that they hired the guru to manage the CSRs at the front desk. Once he has completed a project, he proofs it, and gets it approved by the customer (quickprint business usually doesn't rate the term client – go figure). Increasingly, he sends soft PDF proofs to the customer for approval and annotation. When the project is approved, he does any imposition or trapping needed (rarely), exports it as PDFs or PostScript files, and sends it to the sign cutter (it still works from EPSs) or the print area (they prefer the PDFs).

The sign cutter is new. The boss decided to get what she saw at a demonstration at a big print show. From the day they got it, business has grown phenomenally. It has become a major profit center. The new employee in the sign shop has done some wonderful pieces, including a huge eight-color graphic covering both sides of a new delivery van. The main source of business seems to be two-foot by eight-foot coated canvas banners announcing sales, openings, and so on.

On the other side of the shop are the largest changes. In the print room, all the smelly old duplicators are gone. They've been replaced by a digital mimeograph, a large production black and white copier with limited spot color capability, plus the trusty old Canon color copier with a powerful new RIP workstation controlling all three. The room is quiet, decorated, odorless, and clean. Everything is controlled by the system manager with her workstation. She runs the files through preflight software, queues them up on the RIP, prints them, and stores them for future use, if necessary. As customer files build up in size, she burns 500 MB at a time for long-term storage on CD-Rs, deleting the hard copied files to free up the server. She is also responsible for maintaining the hard-copy storage of samples for each job. Several times this has saved all of their necks by enabling rescanning and OCR of the sample.

The only other addition are the paper handlers, who work under the system manager. They load and unload paper from the presses, do the preventive maintenance, and move everything back to the bindery after it's printed. Maybe a better name would be print gophers. The bindery has not changed.

THE SERVICE BUREAU PRINTER

THE DIGITAL PRINTSHOP

Now we have finally arrived at a type of company that could not have existed before 1995. Our sample is built out of a service bureau. Service bureaus rose from the ashes of old typesetters, separators, and prepress houses. Some simply saw an opportunity and grabbed it. The best were often started by a desktop computer wiz and an experienced separator. Maybe one hired the other, but these are the ingredients.

The shop we are going to look at was started by the city's digital pioneer. This is the guy who saw it coming back in the early 1980s. He had a copy of PageMaker and a LaserWriter in 1985. Being absolutely fascinated by the process, he kept soaking it up until people started asking him how to get things working. After several years of consulting, he tired of the rat race and looked for a comfortable office and people he could train

A Digital Workflow

Please remember:

These are all speculative samples of possible digital solutions. There may or may not be anything in reality that corresponds to the companies described in this chapter. They are meant to give you a feel for what is happening in the industry.

to do the running around. About that time, one of the local separators was going broke from payments on outdated equipment.

Our pioneer ended up buying most of the equipment at far less than cost and hiring the separator as his production manager. It sounded screwy to everyone else, but they had a chemistry that worked. The front office is a beautiful reception area with a receptionist, a CSR and or job ticket writer, and a huge office for our man.

The production manager runs the back shop. Her preflightist is more experienced than any of the others we have mentioned so far because he is also in charge of file repair. Many of the files come in with broken links, missing fonts, spot color mixed with process, bleeds that stop at the edge, and so on (the average is still nearly two-thirds nationally). When he is preflighting, he fixes what he can immediately.

There are three scanning stations. Two are huge. In this shop that means G4s with a gigabyte of RAM and 75 GB hot swappable RAID arrays. All three have dual monitors, all color calibrated. Each station does its color critical work on huge Barco monitors (one of them cost over $10,000). Even the small station has 512 MB RAM and a RAID array. The shop has two top-end drum scanners (one will scan up to 17 inches by 22 inches) and a top-of-the-line flatbed that has an automatic document feeder they use for production OCR. The production manager runs the color correction station with her years of experience.

The entire shop is hard wired with 100BaseT EtherNet which is starting to really cramp their style. So far they are covering their need by using the hot swappable RAID modules as a massive sneakernet.

The entry-level positions are where this shop's staff assembles the scans for client use. They do a lot of high-res scans for clients, plus artwork and difficult image repairs. They have had to add a station where the newest person is broken in, doing nothing but assembling files for copying to removables and for proper storage.

One of their niches has become composite negatives of imposed and trapped sigs for the 40-inch presses in town. Several of them have refused to go digital, so our group prepares the composite negs for them. They all prefer to burn their own plates, but the town can only support one eight-up imagesetter, so far. This shop is thinking of getting out of it because of the chemistry problems in their downtown high-rise. One of their most experienced women has expressed an interest in moving the photochemical portion of the business to an industrial area just outside of downtown. It looks like this might work, and the phone company will help them install a hardwired fiber optic connection between the two locations.

The fastest growing portion of their business is on-demand printing. They have a 22-inch Agfa Chromapress, an Indigo six-color label printer, a large Iris inkjet for proofing and fine art prints, and two large format inkjets (one is a hi-fi color Roland). They are seriously considering adding two Docutechs to complete their full-service capabilities. Because they are in the middle of downtown, near the phone switching building, it has been easy to network to clients with high-speed ISDN phone lines. They also offer T1 Web access for their clients, in keeping with their plan to provide everything their customers need.

They have had to lease most of the floor below for file storage, hardware, and file management. They have four huge RAID arrays down there; one is just under a terabyte. They have every type of removable drive that exists. The room is radiation-proofed and has its own protected power supply to back up the power company. Their Web server is in there also. Recently they moved the Chromapress and the Indigo down there, leaving room for the proposed Docutechs. This will be a massive change because of the sheer quantity of printing they will putting out. Even with virtually automatic inline binding, an amazing amount of complexity is added to the operation.

Probably the biggest change recently is the addition of a design department. It is pretty stripped down. They have an incredibly creative art director and her husband, who is the town's leading PostScript illustrator, plus a woman who is amazingly fast with document assembly. If the art director can get this person an accurate rough plus all the pieces, the document is basically done.

This has enabled them to offer full-service, on-demand printing. With their new design services, they are thinking of adding a sales department. At this point, however, they can barely handle the business they already have. They keep adding equipment to supply almost anything their clients request.

For example, their large-format inkjet business started years ago with one of the early large-format inkjets. They saw it as a way to offer simple posters. They quickly grew into the largest trade show display producer in the city. They haven't gotten into video or multimedia yet, because of their alliance with one of the best design and production shops in town. But their video displays, surrounded with huge photos, are awesome. Now they are starting to design them. Is seems obvious that there will be much more interaction with the video and multimedia studio in the near future.

The wide variations in reality

We could go on and on, but you have the idea. I haven't mentioned the worldwide access offered by AlphaGraphics™, Sir Speedy, and Kinko's. The online Web printing services that are growing like mad — able to ship anywhere in the world. The digital job ticket that enables accurate service ordered from the SOHO and delivered directly to the client — anywhere.

The main thing I want to impress on you is speed. The deadline pressures in our industry are enormous. There is immense satisfaction in producing beautiful work under these pressures, but you need to be fast enough to cut it. Otherwise you'll be dropped from the team.

Let's give you some sample production times. Obviously, these have to be modified by circumstances and complexity. If you are working in full color for a company making a national push for new markets, you can quadruple these times. If you are working for a small printer these are pretty accurate. Process color, will probably take twice as long. The main thing to remember is that this is always a deadline-driven

industry. If you want time to be creative, you will have to produce at this speed or faster to free up enough time. Most small customers do not want to pay for thinking so you have to make your own. In general, however, this is what you will be expected to produce:

- .... 12-page newsletter   12 hours
- .... Halftone production . . 5 to 7 minutes
- .... Separation production . . a half hour or less
- .... Scan and trace logo . 15 to 30 minutes
- .... Name changes on four-up business cards. . 15 minutes
- .... Small flyer   30 minutes
- .... Produce clipping path on product shot . . 30 minutes
- Headline typographic manipulations included, no charge

In general, you can figure that you have an hour to produce a letter-sized document, 40 minutes for a half letter, 1.5 hours for a tabloid. Creative charges are in addition to this, obviously. If you are marketing your design skills and marketing solutions, clients will be willing to pay for your creative time. In many cases, however, clients need and expect creativity on a deadline or creative production.

You do not get involved in digital publishing because "you like to draw." You have to love print, typography, and beautiful graphics. You have to enjoy pleasing a client. You must take it seriously and learn your craft. This is a highly competitive field. Only professionals survive.

THE NEW PARADIGM IN ACTION

Notice that we haven't touched on the core of the new paradigm. In late summer 1999, *Publish* or *Electronic Publishing* magazine (I really can't remember which) offered a survey on designer compensation which claimed that nearly 60% of graphic designers are self-employed (if I remember correctly). Where I live and work, the figure is closer to 85%. Freelancing is the norm in digital publishing. It isn't mentioned commonly in trade media. All the training and verbiage is directed at the old paradigm of huge printing firms and design agencies employing dozens or hundreds of designers doing highly specialized work under the dictatorship of the account executives and art directors.

The fact of the matter is that most of you (more than half) will probably be working in your own office, often at home – in equal competition for the design projects in your area (or worldwide on the Web). Even if you have employment, the pay for artists is so low that you will normally be freelancing to supplement your income. The survey mentioned above quoted something like $24K to $36K as the normal spread of employed income. Freelancing is necessary.

So, what I think we need to do next is talk about what is needed to set up for business — hardware and software needs, mainly. This will give you a quick handle on where your equipment stands now, what your needs are, and where you must purchase next. The question, in our fast-growing marketing economy, is never "Do I need to purchase more?", but rather, "What comes next?" Your employer will be providing this or more. If not, you'll have to buy your own.

Hardware needs

Most of you are probably familiar with the hardware requirements for InDesign. Adobe requires you to work in MacOS 8.5, Windows 98/NT4, or better. The RAM requirements are 48 MB minimum assigned to InDesign, but Adobe strongly hints that anything less than 128 MB is substandard and talks very positively about 256 MB assigned just to InDesign. Typically, 512 MB is not out of line, and a gigabyte of RAM is no longer uncommon.

The CPU minimum is a Pentium II or a PowerMac 604. They are basically joking. Even a G3 is a little slow and the same is true of any Pentium slower than 450 MHz – this, of course, depends quite a bit upon the RAM you have available. This is a G4 application or it needs a very fast Wintel solution. Hard drive requirements are not too large, but then publishing needs multiple gigabytes, in general.

Peripherals

Obviously, you will need some major removable storage options, unless you are employed and on a very fast network. It will be very helpful to have at least a CD-R burner. ZIPs are the smallest floppies that are functional at all (as simple backup and quick sneakernet). A CD drive is required. You will need a reliable, safe, backup system.

You really need fast Web access. You will do well to have ISDN, at minimum. Simple phone line modem access is frustrating, at best. It is virtually impossible to work in publishing anymore without fast Web communication and the ability to attach or ftp proofs and files for printing. WhamNet! was basically designed for our industry. DSL, cable delivery, or satellite each make good SOHO access. One of InDesign's major moves is in the ability to work in PDF (no longer requiring Distiller), import PDF graphics, and edit PDFs. These greatly simplify the Web transfer of documents. Increasingly you will work online.

You will also need a flatbed scanner. Even if the majority of your work is with drum scans and top quality process color, you will need a good, fast, 600 dpi (or better), 36-bit (or better), legal size (or better) flatbed. You will be scanning constantly, plus tracing logos and graphics. You will also be scanning all of your Web photos. In addition, many of us start our graphics with a quick scan of a sketched rough for proportion. You will probably find this helpful, sooner or later.

The usefulness of your scanner is dependent upon the quality of its Photoshop plug-in.

You will also need a PostScript Level 2 printer, black and white or color – minimum. In reality, InDesign is designed for a PostScript Level 3 printer. My advice is also to make sure you buy a printer

with genuine Adobe PostScript. The cheaper PostScript clones all cause problems sooner or later, in my experience. I do not hear this about the top of the line PostScript RIPS, but then most of you will not have one of those in your office. You do not want to be using a software RIP, either. They are all far too slow.

However, the is now a major qualifier to the last paragraph. Adobe's PressReady and a supported Inkjet offer a viable, professional quality proofer for around $500. The cost per print is still very high, when compared to a laser printer, but professional laser proofs still require several thousand dollars for the printer. The laser printer is still the best solution, but there is now an option.

Having said all of this, I am doing well on this book with an old 333 MHz iMac with 96 MB RAM and an Epson 636, plus a ZIP, a JAZ, and a CD-R. I'm proofing on an old LaserWriter Select 360. But then I do little large process work, and I am primarily a PostScript illustrator, using Photoshop only for halftone and/or separation production and for rasterizing my EPSs for various uses, including all of my Web graphics. This does not put nearly the load on hardware as my former job would. As the art director of a medium-sized process color printer, I would need much more hardware. You simply have to get enough to meet your real needs and the capacity that allows you to express yourself freely.

Software needs

Obviously, for this book, you need InDesign. However, like all page layout programs, it is insufficient by itself. You will definitely need PostScript illustration software: FreeHand, Illustrator, or CorelDraw. We mentioned last chapter the trepidation we old-timers have with Corel, but if it works for you on a practical level, the tools are there professionally. I am personally partial to FreeHand, but Illustrator is very close in capabilities and favored by many.

Most of us use both FreeHand and Illustrator. There are things that are better done in each program. I don't want to get into an argument about the relative merits of each. The fact is that you will have to deal with both. Your clients and the ads you receive will give you both FreeHand and Illustrator files to use. You have to be able to work with them, fix them, and modify them.

Photoshop goes without saying. Everyone needs Photoshop. There is nothing else with the critical color adjustment controls. Many use it as their primary illustration tool. I can easily prove that this is not always advisable, but it is a fact. Regardless, the usefulness of your scanner is dependent upon the quality of the Photoshop plug-in that came with it. You will scan everything into Photoshop to work with — even if your goal is just a cleaned up scan to autotrace in FreeHand.

Font management

You will definitely need font management software. Sadly, this is one of the areas where Windows is still far behind. They are beginning to show up on that platform also, as the need becomes more apparent. On the Mac, there are several choices. Suitcase was formerly the standard, but it has fallen behind. MasterJuggler and Adobe Type Manager Deluxe work very well. There is a newer one with great reviews called Font Reserve. I like it and use it but it's not that much better.

With fonts, there are two things going on. First of all, almost all designers end up as virtual font collectors. The longer you work in the industry, the more you are seduced by the beauty of excellent type. Both MacOS and Windows have limits to the number of fonts that can be installed (active) at any one time. The font managers allow you to keep the actual fonts used to manageable levels, giving you the capability of making font sets for your various clients and projects. You only turn on what you need for the project you are designing. If you find a specific need for your project, you can then add to your active set.

The second reason has more to do with production. When you start a project like an event program, a small magazine, or anything where you will be placing a lot of advertising, fonts can quickly get out of hand. PDFs are helping with their embedded fonts. However, many designers are not as enlightened as we are. Many have not even heard of PDFs.

You will receive ads as Quark pages with embedded Illustrator EPSs and Photoshop TIFFs. You will receive raw FreeHand pages. You will get PageMaker pages. You will get everything imaginable. Every ad will bring two to ten fonts to the mix. I remember doing a little sixteen page, process color, fine arts magazine (a year ago or so) where each issue had over 200 different fonts, just from the advertisements. Every agency sent a different set. They sent over 700 fonts; I only used 200.

At this point, font management is not an option. That many fonts can quickly overload the resources of your machine. The scenario just mentioned was complicated by a printer, in Juarez, who had never heard of PDFs. I'm not sure I would like to try to make a PDF out of a sixteen page document with over 200 fonts and over 600 MB of imported graphics, anyway. (And for those of you asking, the deadlines precluded most repairs and the option of converting most of those fonts to paths.) Without a good font manager, that project would have quickly gone down the tubes.

Miscellaneous software

We all need a copy of Acrobat 4 or better. In addition, all of you will have software that you are certain you cannot do without. It might be something as simple as a macro maker like QuickKeys. It may be a less common program like Canvas or MultiAd Creator. (I even saw someone on the InDesign list the other day talking about using ReadySetGo side by side with InDesign.) It might be as complex as 3D bitmap illustration software. There are chart creation software, table makers, database converters, tag generators, and so forth. The real criteria is that you are enabled to save your graphics in a usable format (EPS, TIFF, PDF – GIF, JPEG, PNG, SWF).

Almost all of you will have a WYSIWYG Web page creator. Some of you will insist that Dreamweaver or GoLive is essential. Some will argue just as fervently that FrontPage or PageMill are more than sufficient. Many of you will have a dedicated Web graphic creator like FireWorks or ImageReady embedded into Photoshop. Most of you will at least be tempted by Flash or LiveMotion. Many more will realize that when you only design a

few Web sites a year (less than 500 pages or so), FreeHand, Illustrator, and Photoshop work just fine for the creation of your Web graphics.

Quite a few of you will quickly discover that you simply cannot survive without barcode creation software. Quite a few will be using Fontographer to solve font problems and to create custom fonts for yourself and your clients. The list goes on almost forever. We haven't even mentioned your copy of Director, Authorware, Premier, and After Effects — or maybe you prefer Final Cut Pro, Alias, or Lightwave or whatever.

The point I am trying to make is simple. Every one of you will have your own personal hardware and software configuration that works well for you. You need to add the pieces that help you do the things you do best. If you don't like to work in Photoshop, don't be ashamed. On the other hand, if you haven't tried PostScript illustration you are missing out on a great tool. Almost all of us use both — to varying degrees. The key is not allowing yourself to be seduced by the video game nature of much of the software out there. There is a time for gaming, but it will certainly mess up production. Find software that improves production efficiency.

Beyond the Big Seven, there is no right or wrong.

1. Why do commercial printers keep as much of their old equipment as they do? (Give at least two reasons)

2. Why were quickprinters the first to go digital?

3. Why does the author insist that our industry has gone through a paradigm shift (a move to a whole new set of rules)?

4. What is the importance of font management software?

5. Why are the new digital printing companies the technocrats of our industry (why do they have the newest equipment and software)?

WHERE SHOULD YOU BE BY THIS TIME?

By now you need to have at least started through the tutorials that came with InDesign. They should be located in your InDesign folder on one of your hard drives, in a folder called Learning Adobe InDesign. Inside is a PDF called Tutorial Contents.pdf – open it. Take a look through the customizing shortcuts dialog boxes (File >>> Edit Shortcuts). I wouldn't advise changing much until you become accustomed to the interface. But take a look and see which shortcuts match up with your normal use, and the other pieces of software you use daily. If you are coming from Quark, look at the Quark 4 setup. The factory setup is basically a PageMaker/Illustrator mix. However, it goes far beyond that.

DISCUSSION

Discuss your computer setups with your classmates. If you are in a lab, find out what is available: scanners, removables, servers, printers, proofers, presses, and so forth. Share with each other things that have worked well for you. Remember, there is no right or wrong – you need to simply find the things that work for your style of creation.

Talk among yourselves...

A Digital Workflow

InDesign's Interface

CONCEPTS

A generalized overview of InDesign's interface with suggestions for preferences, shortcuts, defaults, and templates

CHAPTER OBJECTIVES

By presenting the options and capabilities of the publishing industry's software, this chapter will enable you to:

1. Describe the differences in interface between InDesign, PageMaker, Quark, Illustrator, and FreeHand
2. Set up your preferences
3. Begin to conceptualize the true use of keyboard shortcuts
4. Describe the need for and use of defaults

LAB WORK FOR CHAPTER

- Set up your preferences (FILE >>> PREFERENCES)
- Examine the default keyboard shortcuts (FILE >>> EDIT SHORTCUTS...)
- Look at all of the palettes mentioned in the chapter

InDesign's Interface

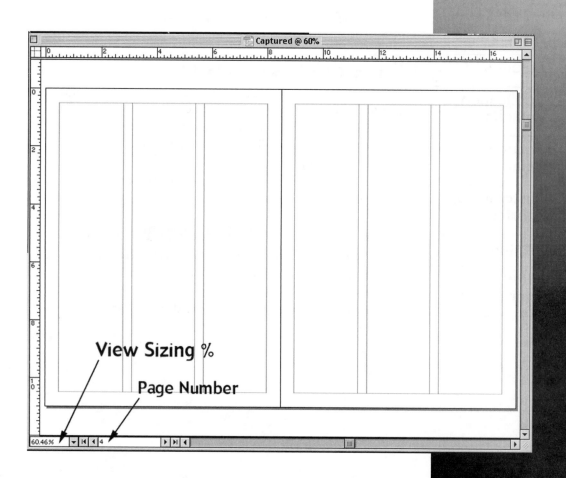

Captured @ 60%

View Sizing %

Page Number

60.46%   4

Let's get started!

You may ask why we didn't start with this chapter. The answer is simple. The first week of class is usually a confusing mess, at best. While everyone is getting settled down, the only thing to do is give some theory to carry you through the confusion. However, that theory was also necessary to get us all on the same page. Now that we are there, let's get started.

First of all, InDesign really is a brand new program. It is not a step up from PageMaker. It is not Adobe's version of QuarkXPress. It is not a multipage Illustrator. It uses pieces and concepts from all of them, but the synergy of the application is very different. It has a very different feel. My basic reaction has been, "This is what Quark should have been."

Now I don't want you to be confused. This is certainly a version 1.5, as far as a few of the more advanced features are concerned. It cannot create tables of contents, indices, tables, and so forth. They are available in plug-ins. However, it is amazingly complete for a 1.5 offering. The largest thing I miss is a built-in word processor, but that simply shows that I come from PageMaker. Quark users have never had that capability. It certainly has changed the way I write books, however. My earlier books were written and formatted as a continuous flow, creating graphics as needed, and writing in explanation of the graphics created. Now I have to work copy and graphics separately.

However, this is the normal procedure for everyone using anything else but PageMaker. The nice thing is that the text import features are as good or better than PageMaker or Quark. You have complete control over where the text will go: manual, semi-automatic, and full autoflow. But we are getting far ahead of ourselves.

THE BASIC DOCUMENT WINDOW

As you can see on the opposite page, InDesign's window looks like almost any other, at first glance. The first major difference you notice when you click on the View% popup menu in the lower left corner. The percentage range is 5% to 4,000%, which is the best of all the normal page layout programs other than FreeHand (which goes up to 25,600%).

As you can see, the only other control built into the window is the page turner. This is quite slow and clumsy, but it works. As you can see from the graphic to the left, the pages are laid out in the typical Quark fashion. The only real difference is that each spread has its own pasteboard, which is relatively generous. However, there is no using the pasteboard as a common library as you could with PageMaker. It is certainly safer this way.

The scrolling list of pages from PageMaker is gone, and there is no dialog box that appears when you double click the page number. You can type in whatever page you want to go to and hit Return or Enter. Of course, this assumes that you know what page you are headed for. One of the most efficient ways to navigate pages is to go to the 5% view and use a Zoom tool marquee to enlarge whatever area on whatever page you desire into the center of the window.

In every other way, the window is standard for your OS with your normal scroll bars, title bars, minimize/maximize/zoom boxes, and so forth. There are no additional surprises here. As you can see, the View choices are very limited. Even in the File >>> Edit Shortcuts dialog, there are only view commands for 50%, 100%, 200%, and 400% to add to the View menu. In addition, the menu commands, either in the window or up above in the View menu, do not center your selection in the enlarged view.

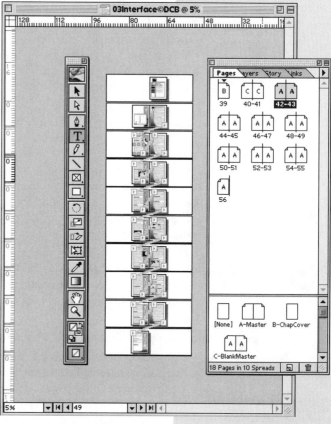

As we will mention when going through the palettes in the next chapter, there is a Navigator palette similar to Photoshop's, but it is clumsy for moving through multitudinous pages. The 5% view with the Zoom tool marquee probably remains the most efficient navigation method.

The plethora of palettes

Those of you who have read my *Digital Drawing* book on FreeHand will remember my apologies for the need to spend a good deal of time organizing the interface because of the multitude of panels. The Adobe interface calls them palettes, and there are quite a few more of them. I hadn't really thought that possible. You will need to spend even more time, in InDesign, organizing them. In 1.5 you are even more restricted, by the *normal* Adobe interface. Here is a quick list, which we will explain in detail next chapter:

1. **Character palette:** This looks almost like the measurement palette from Quark or the Control palette from PageMaker. It replaces the Character Specifications dialog box. The only mildly disconcerting aspect is the lack of a dialog box. In 1.5 this has become a boxy rectangle à la Photoshop — no wide horizontal bar any more.

2. **Paragraph palette:** This replaces the Paragraph Specifications dialog box from PageMaker and the Paragraph Formats dialog from Quark. Again this replaces the dialog box — boxy again.

3. **Transform palette:** This includes all of the functionality of Quark's Measurement palette, plus the handles proxy that makes PageMaker's Control palette version so useful. Everything can be measured from the handle of your choice, plus you have Illustrator's option of dragging the transformation center to whatever location you need — boxy again.

4. **Layers palette:** This one has the full functionality of Illustrator's Layers palette. It's missing several of FreeHand's abilities, but then this is a page layout program.

5. **Story palette:** This is really a preference or command masquerading as a palette. It controls the Optical Margin alignment ability, which takes hanging punctuation to new levels.

6. **Pages palette:** This adds PageMaker's Master Pages palette to Quark's Document Layout palette with very impressive capabilities and a far more useful layout. Nested masters just gives you a hint of the additional possibilities. It is very customizable.

7. **Align palette:** This one contains all of the capabilities of Quark's Space/Align dialog box.

8. **Text Wrap palette:** This one has PageMaker's look. However, it does add the choice to wrap around the frame or around the object's clipping or outline path making it more useful than Quark's.

9. **Links palette:** This palette provides all of the functionality of PageMaker's links dialog and Quark's Picture Usage dialog box. This is very important, because Quark has always lacked the simple abilities to Edit Original and to Relink to a different graphic. It is not as good as Aldus' HotLinks, but it works. Plus, you can multiple-select to update a lot at the same time.

10. **Attributes palette:** This one simply allows you to set the overprint characteristics, both stroke and fill, of selected objects. It is one of the best examples of palette overkill. The overprint option could (and should) be a simple checkbox option when applying a swatch to an object, in the Stroke palette, in the Fill palette, and in the Gradient palette (like it is in FreeHand).

11. **Paragraph Styles palette:** This is the best styles palette I have ever seen. The limited keyboard shortcuts are a little different, but there are far more than enough. In general, this palette gives the best global document control I have used including PageMaker, Quark, and FreeHand.

12. **Character Styles palette:** This long awaited capability basically completes the tool set that has been always needed for document formatting. Quark 4 implemented it first, but it's here and extremely elegant.

13. **Library palette:** This is the first one I have seen that I think I'll actually use. Both PageMaker's and Quark's were obtuse enough to put me off. I realize that this is my problem, and that you have all been using this capability for years. But InDesign's not only makes sense, it seems obviously functional.

14. **Swatches palette:** This color palette works well enough, I suppose. It is very much like Illustrator's version. Adobe's color handling has always been its weak point. It would be superb with FreeHand's drag'n'drop color. However, disregarding FreeHand, Pagemaker's and Quark's are both better. InDesign's palette really needs stroke, fill, and both boxes at the top.

15. **Stroke palette:** This gives control to stroke options. It is very much like Illustrator's version, but better laid out.

16. **Color palette:** This allows you to create colors in RGB, CMYK, or LAB. The colorized sliders are a great help when working in normally foreign color spaces, like RGB and LAB. But then, I may be the strange one – who can think in CMYK.

17. **Gradient palette:** This one again uses Illustrator's model. It works well enough, but it is crippled by the lack of FreeHand's drag'n'drop color. The method of applying color is very clumsy. You are basically forced to add gradient swatches to the swatches palette – the interactivity level is very frustrating.

18. **Color Swatch Library palettes:** These tabbed palettes give you access to a large set of Illustrator's color libraries. I was really down on them until I found the keyboard shortcut to use the search capabilities, but that's always been Adobe's approach. I wish I could remember what it was (it's frustrating to have to go to the help software all the time). I must confess that I miss the Crayon library, but then I'm just an old softy, I guess.

Whew! What a list! And this is the minimum. You could easily have several library palettes open, and several color swatch library palettes. As you can see, palette proliferation is a problem. As we go through this chapter and the next, I will give you a couple of options to help you get a handle on palette control. If you are familiar with Photoshop and/or Illustrator, this should be no big problem because they are very similar in feel.

The palette/dialog box interface option

It should be obvious by now that InDesign has opted to eliminate most dialog boxes in favor of palettes. This will seem frustrating, at first. However, my simple solution is to make the palette opening keyboard shortcut the same as I am accustomed to with the old dialog boxes in other programs. InDesign has already done this in several cases. The Character palette, for example, is opened with the same keyboard shortcut as the Character Specifications dialog box was in PageMaker or Quark (depending on the shortcut set you select). I've done the same thing with Text Wrap, Links, and others.

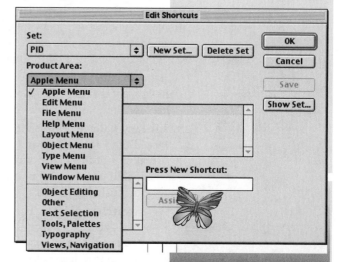

I can see where this is a good thing, but it will be disconcerting at the beginning. Once you get used to the concept, however, you will begin wondering why this hasn't been the standard for years.

Keyboard shortcuts

Throughout this book, I am going to do my best to scrupulously avoid shortcuts. This is not because they are not crucial to efficient production. They certainly are. In fact, as one of my students accused

me, two days ago, "After rejecting DOS because of its code and turning to a GUI, you are now advocating code again." As a retired programmer, in the industry since the 1950s, he found this to be nearly hysterical.

Keyboard shortcuts are... a production necessity.

Let me state emphatically, keyboard shortcuts are not an option. They are a production necessity. With the production speed required by our industry, there is no way you can keep up without fluid use of keyboard shortcuts. However, shortcuts are a very personal thing. I could offer my set of shortcuts , but they would probably help only a few of you. (Please see the sidebar on the next page.)

This is because I have analyzed my particular production style and methods — noting which tasks I use repetitively. I then learn the shortcuts that save me the most time. Now you need to note, I have a photographic memory and I can retain about 500 shortcuts in my active memory. In addition, I teach these materials five days per week to refresh that memory. Most of you will have a great deal of trouble remembering more than a couple of hundred shortcuts, and it takes over 200 to run Quark, Illustrator, or Photoshop alone.

You have certainly noticed that, of the Big Seven, only two are anomalous: Quark and FreeHand. The rest are Adobe products. Adobe is (and has been) making a major push to unify its interfaces. Because we all use Photoshop, those shortcuts are part of all our production procedures. For page layout, we have had the Adobe method and Quark's. As Adobe has told you, InDesign gives you that choice: Adobe's or Quark's. However, this is just the beginning of your need to set up your shortcuts to fit your particular production methodology.

For example, I only use Quark under duress. I can use it well and know all of its abilities. However, it is so far outside of my normal daily procedures that I run Quark with the mouse and menus. Personally, I use FreeHand more than anything else. This is neither right nor wrong, it simply is — my personal choice.

In addition, I am left-handed (supposedly the majority of designers are — because we are right brained?). In addition, I am using Apple's new compromised keyboard (though that will probably change shortly). The result is that my shortcuts are probably very different than most of yours.

The FreeHand commands fit very well because PageMaker and FreeHand came from a common background. (Aldus, remember?) Much of Adobe's shortcut structure is shared by FreeHand. However, the major factor in setting up shortcuts, at this point, is that InDesign and FreeHand are almost completely editable. InDesign lets me set up my shortcuts to fit my personal style.

Left-handed shortcuts

I will mention this heresy (to the *normal* world) because it is nearly normal in the design community (probably over half). All shortcut setups are right-handed. By this I mean that for those of us who use the mouse with one hand and execute the shortcuts with the other, lefties have a problem. (The new compromised Mac keyboard is even more strongly right-handed with the elimination of the modifier keys on the right side.)

All I need to do is remind you of all of the shortcuts built around A, S, D, C, Z, X, C, V. All of those keys are found at the lower left of the keyboard. Seemingly these would work well for lefties. However, in most cases, they mean we have to drop the mouse. As a result, I have experienced large production speed increases by simply basing many of my shortcuts on the ,./l;'iop keys in the right side instead. For example, in InDesign I access the selection tool with the semicolon, the direct selection tool with footmark, and so on. This works for me, but it makes my shortcut set much different than the norm. In fact, I can leave both right and left sides in place to be used interchangeably — depending on which hand is using the mouse at the time. Yes, most of us lefties are at least partially ambidextrous (by necessity in a right-handed world).

Your personal shortcut set

Now that it is possible, you really need to analyze the set of shortcuts you use. Some of you use the ⌘L and ⌘U for lock and unlock. For some ⌘L has always been Spell Check. ⌘U was Ungroup for years. Personally, I almost never lock items except in FreeHand, and there I do it with the Layers palette. So I can freely use ⌘L for spell checking. I did the same with Ungroup. I just is easier for me — neither right nor wrong.

I could go on with examples like this for pages, but I would still not mention some of your favorites. The point is simple, however. **Now you are free to set them up the way that works best for you**. More importantly, you can set them up in the way that you can remember.

My guess is that Photoshop 6, Illustrator 9, and Quark 5 will all allow shortcut customization. It seems to be a natural progression. Maybe it will come to Office 2001. Regardless, by making your core production shortcuts more similar, it is much easier to accommodate those extra programs we all use (like FileMaker Pro, Final Cut, Fontographer, Director, and so forth). We all have limited memory, we need to streamline our shortcuts so we can produce as much as possible with keyboard shortcuts.

Timing concerns

InDesign is missing a toolbar. I imagine that this option will come eventually (at least as a plug-in). However, we need to review basic production speed issues. The figures I am giving here are only approximate, but they are proportionally accurate.

- Mousing menu commands: 2 seconds
- Mousing toolbar clicks: 1 second
- Keyboard shortcut: $^2/_{10}$ of a second

To give a practical example, used many times a day: grabbing the mouse, dragging down the type menu to open the Paragraph palette, double-clicking the Space Before Paragraph field, typing the new spacing, and executing the change can take nearly 4 seconds. The

InDesign's Interface

Shortcut appendix

Originally, I was going to add an appendix showing PC shortcuts, Mac shortcuts, and my left-handed shortcuts. I cancelled that plan when I realized how many we are dealing with. It would have made a ten-page appendix for each of the five options PC, Mac, PC Quark, Mac Quark, and the left-handed option. There were not fifty pages available for this book. However, if you open your EDIT SHORTCUTS... dialog box, there is a SHOW SET button. Clicking that produces a text file that you can save, place into a new document and format as you like. Sorry, but that's the best I could do for this book.

⌘M>>Tab>>Tab>>Tab, *type number, bit Enter* sequence takes far less than 2 seconds (maybe less than 1). If you spend a lot of your time massaging copy to fit better on a page, you might use this command sequence a couple of hundred times a day. If that were the case, these shortcuts would save you over 3 minutes a day.

That time seems insignificant, but there is a real reason why we ol' f**** can beat you young whippersnappers by hours. The going rate for formatting a book like this one is about 5 minutes per page. This includes importing the copy, formatting it, dropping in the graphics, eliminating widows and orphans, spell checking, and printing a proof. I can do an average of nearly twenty pages per hour. Without the shortcuts, I would be lucky to do a half dozen.

The practical shortcut approach

You need to watch yourself work. This is why this diatribe is in an early chapter of this book. Notice which commands you use constantly. Learn the shortcuts for those commands. If you find yourself regularly using (or starting to use) a command from another application by mistake, change InDesign's to match your normal usage. Do whatever you are enabled to do to make your shortcuts common to as many programs as possible.

Obviously, this will take some time and effort. Of course, you will not be able to do this until you are in a daily creation and/or production environment. However, to survive in this industry, this is not an option. All of your competitors are doing it (especially those who can outproduce you by a factor of two or three times).

The faster you can produce the more time there is to create.

Yesterday, one of my students was entering a major state of panic. He has been working on this twenty-four-page event program (that has to proof tomorrow) for about three weeks. He has created (or subcontracted to other students) all of the ads (about thirty-five of them). He found someone to type all of the copy, set up a style palette, and format everything. But the project was just going so slow. His major concern was simply keeping track of all the pieces. (He has never done this before.)

He left class yesterday afternoon a quivering mass of jelly laced with electrical charges (yes, he was nearly spastic). After he left, I took mercy on him, made two brand new documents (cover and insides), tossed everything into them, made master pages, dropped in all the ads, and roughly formatted everything in about 50 minutes. (He had told me exactly what he wanted to do.)

Now, I assume that most of you have more experience than this man. He is a first-termer, working his first major project. However, I would guess that anyone at my experience level could do the same to you. (If you are at my experience level, why are you reading this book?) The time difference might not be quite as dramatic, but it would be substantial. This is the difference a computer set up to your specs, using your customized shortcuts, with applications of your choice, can make.

Remember, we are not talking right or wrong. The focus is on what works and what hinders production speed. Eliminate what hinders and focus on what works best for you. If you want to see my customized shortcuts for InDesign, send me an email. Other than that, I will merely try to make occasional suggestions throughout the book.

STARTING TO SET UP

SETTING THE PREFERENCES

InDesign really doesn't have many Preferences and this is a good thing. One of the major things that always irked me with Quark 3 was the relative inability to set Application Defaults. PageMaker's method was always far superior. In this paradigm, defaults are a major method of setting up your program for your personal use. Preferences are simply long term choices made concerning the applications interface. You Quark specialists will come to really prefer this approach. *Trust me!*

The reason I think this approach is better is that preferences are changed so rarely that it's hard to remember what the options are. In InDesign those that you use regularly (like the Typographer's Quotes option) can be set up with a keyboard shortcut (I use ⌘⌥\). Defaults are something you change regularly (often several times a day), so they need to be readily accessible in familiar locations. We do need to go through the preference options quickly, however, because some of them are reasonably important. However, setting preferences is not a long drawn out affair. More importantly, you don't have to make crucial decisions (like whether or not you are going to use a real em space or not). Let's start with the first one:

General Preferences

Preferences	
General ▾	OK
Images	Cancel
Display: Full Resolution ▾	Prev
Page Numbering	Next
View: Section Numbering ▾	
General Options	
Tool Tips: Fast ▾	
Tools Palette: Single Row ▾	
☑ Overprint Black	

Gradient Tool (G, L)

For this one we'll include the entire dialog box so you can see the Okay, Cancel, Previous, and Next buttons. These are on all pages of the dialog box. Obvious, eh? So are the choices on this page. You

can choose whether you want high resolution images, screen previews, or grayed out boxes for your documents. A new wrinkle to help screen redraws is the Optimized Resolution option. This does not affect printing; it is for viewing and working with those graphics. Your choice is based on the speed of your computer and monitor.

The numbering option should be obvious. If you are using section numbering (like was done with the front matter of this book), it is really helpful to show that on the page turner at the bottom of the window and in the pages dialog box. You have the option of absolute numbering which simply counts all pages from the first to the last even though the section numbers show up with the automatic numbering markers.

As you can see from the image in the sidebar on the other page, tool tips are a little box that pops up to show you what the name of the tool is and its keyboard shortcut. This is usually the easiest method of learning the keyboard shortcuts for the tools you use all the time. While you are doing that, 1.5 lets you set them up to appear fast (normally there is a 2- to 3-second delay).

New to 1.5 is the ability to customize the appearance of your toolbox. As you can see to the left, you can keep it normal or you can make it a single row or a single column. Because all of the palettes are now chunky little boxes, I use the single row, but it is your choice. The single row gives me more width for two-page spreads.

The checkbox at the bottom is also obvious. This is the place where you decide about overprinting black. The default is to always overprint black, as you know. However, for those times when this causes a problem, this is where you turn that default off.

Text preferences

One of the minor frustrations of the past ten years concerns the contents of this page of the preferences. I've spent almost ten years now teaching my students why they need to change the default settings of superscript, subscript, and small cap size. InDesign's defaults are typical, and based on the idea of using superscript and subscript for exponents, footnotes, and chemical formulas: a^2b^3 or $H_2O + NaNO_3$.

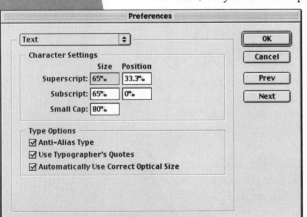

However, very few of us spend much time thinking about, writing about, or typesetting these scientific constructions. I have no figures for the percentage of publishing focused on these needs, but I am certain it is very small. *"So, smart guy, what do we use them for?"* In this industry, superscript and subscript are used almost entirely for constructing fractions.

Yesterday, there was a flurry of recommendations in the InDesign list about setting fractions. Many recommended getting special math fonts, but they are not available in the fonts you will be using. Several others just suggested using the fractions that come with some fonts. Again there is the font limitation, and the fractions that come with fonts are very limited.

Here is one place that PC fonts do a little better. However, even if you have a font that includes fractions for a half, one- and three-quarters, one and two thirds, plus one-, three-, five-, and seven-eighths (and none do), it is still almost useless. You discover that almost as soon as you let fractions onto your page, sooner or later you need $^4/_5$ or $^{127}/_{256}$. These are covered by no font. More than that, you will quickly find that you cannot match your fractions to the ones in the font.

As a result, you will have to construct all of your fractions manually. Some of you will immediately think, "Ah, ha! I can write a little script!" This was the next most common suggestion. But it doesn't work, as you'll see. The final suggestion was to set up paragraph styles. You can certainly do these things, but you will still have to manually construct your fractions.

$\$147^{\underline{37}}$

$37\frac{15}{16}$

$14^{47}/_{64}$

$29^{154}/_{256}$

So, which version of fractions is correct? The modern digital standard is simply that which looks best for a particular project — in your humble opinion.

Setting fractions

Before we go on, let's list the normal procedure I suggest: type the fraction; select the numerator and make it a superscript; select the denominator and make it a subscript; then kern everything precisely. (I wonder if optical kerning covers even that?) Nope, I just checked. It does a reasonable job, but hand kerning will still be required.

That last phrase is the key. Hand kerning is always required. For some of the styles seen to the left, even kerning won't do you any good. Scripts are useless unless they work perfectly every time... and I haven't even mentioned the use of the fraction slash instead of the normal keyboard slash. It's a little more vertical and has very tight spacing built in if your font has one. So you are always stuck with the normal procedure, or you have to construct the fractions in FreeHand or Illustrator and import them. Stylistically, the choice is yours. There were strict standards. Now these vary by situation. *Situational design rules!*

It is certainly true that you can set up a script or a set of character styles. However, this is a lot of work for something that is used so seldom, and for something that changes with every font. It is far better to simply set the super/subscript options to work when you need fractions. The same changes also work for setting prices in newspaper ads, and so forth.

So what are these changes? You can see the normal set up I use in the capture for this preference on the previous page. I usually raise the percent of point size to around 65%. Then I make the superscript position enough to make around 100% when the two are added together – in this case about 34%; 60/40 and 70/30 also work. I just start at 65/33.3. For this book with this font I ended up using 60/28 before I liked the look: $27^{27}/_{32.}$ I wonder if you agree?

If you are starting a long project (like this one), you will need to make sure that the percentages you set work with the font you will be using. The 65/33.3 doesn't work with lowercase numbers. In that case you will have to make special adjustments. The final place you use your new

preference is with ad pricing – $147²³. As you can see in the sample, the cents are often underlined. However, using the underline style is almost always too heavy. You really have to draw the line to get the weight right.

The small caps default is almost always 70% of the point size (75% in Quark). With both of those options, the small caps look noticeably thinner than the caps. (Remember, true small caps are specifically drawn so the strokes of the small caps are the same weight as the strokes of the caps and lowercase.) I have always recommended going to 80% to minimize that weight difference. Of course, this made the cap/small cap distinction harder to see. It is a compromise at best (and one of the reasons, when I was making the fonts for this book, that I made a true small caps font for the heads).

As for the three checkboxes at the bottom, I can't think of a reason why you would want to turn anti-aliasing off. All it does is make the type smoother on the screen. It doesn't affect printing. Maybe if you have a very slow, compromised machine (but, then you aren't using InDesign anyway, right?)

The TYPOGRAPHER'S QUOTES option is the normal one. Turn it on to automatically add curly quotes in the appropriate places. Of course, you'll have to turn it off, if you are working with copy that actually has inches and feet marks in it. One of the really nice features of InDesign is that you can use a keyboard shortcut to toggle the curly quotes on and off. It's the last choice of the Typography area in the Edit Shortcuts dialog box.

The USE CORRECT OPTICAL SIZE option only affects you if you are using a Multiple Master font that has an optical size axis. If you are into MM fonts far enough to use them regularly this will be necessary and obvious. If not, it makes no difference, so you might as well leave it checked. (Why is it here anyway? Adobe no longer even produces Multiple Master fonts.)

Composition preferences

These options are usually left at the factory defaults. But at least I get to make first mention of one of the best features of InDesign – its multiple line composer. This ability (to make justification decisions based on several lines of copy) gives InDesign the best-looking type I have ever seen in an off-the-shelf page layout software application (especially on screen).

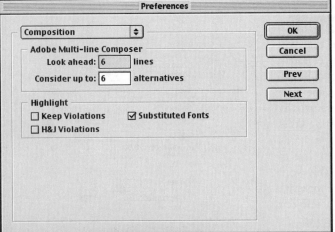

I remember reading in one of Olav Kvern's articles on the InDesign beta in one of the magazines, that you should leave this one at the defaults (5 ahead and 5 alternatives) because of the performance hit of doing more. This may or may not be true (I haven't checked it out). However, because the modern writing style is to use short paragraphs that rarely get longer than 5 lines anyway, the 5/5 setup is sufficient regardless. However, 1.0 used 6/6. So it is a problem.

InDesign's Interface

Nevertheless Ole is right. InDesign is a large program. It taxes my system more than any other program on it. (I don't use 3D.) However, the smoothness of the type color is definitely worth it. If I were writing longer paragraphs, I would go with more lines here — who cares about the performance hit for type that looks this good?

The highlighting options are another story. While these can be helpful, they are certainly visually irritating. As you can see in the capture, the only one I leave on is for SUBSTITUTED FONTS. This flags all fonts that are missing and therefore substituted. The real problem is that InDesign creates a lot of these missing fonts because of the way its Character palette works.

When you are speccing fonts, and adding them to your styles palette, InDesign often adds font possibilities that do not exist. We'll get to this more specifically next chapter. For now, let's leave it at this: if you are working in Akme Black, for example, and change the font to Caslon, InDesign will leave the Black — even though there is no such font as Caslon Black on your machine. You really need the visual flag to eliminate these problems.

KEEP VIOLATIONS will flag places where InDesign was unable to say within your decisions for widows, orphans, column breaks, and page breaks. Because InDesign has still not figured out what a widow is (see Chapter 6) and the rest are all automatic things that are very obvious visually, this option is merely irritating and useless from a practical view point.

H&J VIOLATIONS will flag lines in varying colors that are outside the desired specs for hyphenation and justification. For software like Quark, and even PageMaker, this is necessary. Their type engines are so poor that a lot of manual help is needed. InDesign's engine is so smooth that fixing the minor problems flagged by this enters the arena of butt puckering.

If you get a project for an old account exec accustomed to premium typography, this may become necessary (and you are allowed to charge for the privilege of wasting your time). For 99.8 percent of your clients, this is yet another visual irritant in an interface already littered with guides, frames, and paths. If you set your defaults well, InDesign's type passes muster. More than that, it is beautiful with a good-looking, well-spaced font.

Units and increments preferences

These options are so fundamental that you will usually set them once (now), and never touch them again. If you work globally (in different cultures) this is a little more important. I have to come here regularly because my overseas students are usually metric, many of my students who are upgrading skills work in points, and all of my students in the States work in inches. Because it is hard for you to live in more than one place at a time, you will probably work in one measurement system or another. Then there are those of us who have to remember to ask where our customers live because we work entirely online.

This is also where newspaper work is set up with picas horizontally and inches vertically. Then there are those who use inches horizontally and the leading in points vertically. Regardless, here is where you set those options. InDesign has more options than most, adding centimeters, picas, and custom in addition to inches, decimal inches, points, millimeters, and Ciceros to both horizontal and vertical rulers.

The one new addition in 1.5 is the Origin choice. As you can see I use the spine, but it is just your choice. You get the choice of setting the zero point of your rulers to the Spread, Page, or Spine.

The increment options affect what happens when you change sizes and locations with keyboard shortcuts. The Cursor Key option changes how far a selected object or objects will move when you hit an arrow key. Because I work in FreeHand a lot, I set it at my normal quarter point (0p.25) which is translated to .0035 in. I use the arrow keys to gently nudge things into place, and I don't use snap tos. Your method may be different. This is where you set that.

The next two control how much change occurs when you use the keyboard shortcuts to increase of decrease leading, point size, and baseline shift. The factory defaults are two points a hit. That seems silly to me. Again I use these shortcuts to nudge pieces into position. I have reset my increment to 1 point, and I am thinking about going to a half point. Use what works for you.

The same is true for the kerning/tracking increment. Usually .02 em works fine for me (and this is the factory default). However, you need to set it at what works for you. This again is used for nudging into place. It is not a place for huge movements. Those should be done with tabs and the fixed spaces.

Grids preferences

Use whatever makes you happy. The defaults are a good starting place. This one is not a biggy for most of us. Just remember, that using too many guides and grids brings in a rigidity that is boring, at best. Of course, this is merely my personal opinion, but then I've been doing this for over thirty years now. Version 1.5 has added separate controls for Horizontal and Vertical lines.

Guides preferences

We already covered this in grids – whatever makes you happy. If you are color blind to one of the defaults, change it. If the colors are upsetting your design judgment, use grays. The guides matter if you are using snap to guides a lot. And you may want to move your guides to the front or back. Why InDesign doesn't have a Guides layer that works like FreeHand's Layers palette, I do not know.

InDesign's Interface

Dictionary preferences

In most cases, there are not too many choices here. In areas where you are dealing with multiple languages, this will be used often. It's a pretty obvious choice though. Using a Norwegian dictionary makes little sense unless I speak Norwegian. Even though I might want to do this in remembrance of my ancestry, it seems foolish for ads done in the Southwest of modern American (Spanish helps).

As you can see, for some reason InDesign has added Hyphenation Exceptions for both the User Dictionary and the Document. Why, I am not sure. I would think they should be the same, but it must be an old typographers' thing.

So, now you have your preferences set. If you haven't a clue yet, just do what your instructor recommends. Once you are working full time, fix the ones that irritate you. There really is no right or wrong here. All of these choices really are simply your personal preferences – hence the name.

PREPARING TO SET DEFAULTS

I mentioned earlier that InDesign follows the PageMaker paradigm of using both Application and Document Defaults. It is the best way to handle things. A copy of these defaults is saved automatically into two files in the InDesign folder (InDesign Defaults and InDesign SavedData) every time you quit InDesign (close the application). Application defaults change what happens every time you open a new document. Document defaults change what happens when you reopen an old document.

Application defaults are made by changing anything allowed while no document is open. This would include palette positions, palette contents, page size, margins, text frame options, style palettes for character and paragraph, swatches, stroke, gradient, almost anything in the application.

Document defaults allow you to do the same thing in a document you are currently working with. For example, I have set up fairly elaborate defaults for this book. Defaults like sections, master pages and so forth can only be done to a document.

This is all personal

As we go through the next chapter covering all tools, palettes, and menus, I will continuously be suggesting application or document defaults you might find useful. However, all I can do is share my opinions. There is no right or wrong here either. This is why digital publishing and graphic design are so difficult. You have to understand all of the options and then set them up so they work for you.

Again, this is not a little thing. Your survival in the field is dependent upon functional defaults. Without them, your work speed will be so compromised (when compared to your competition) that adequate

income will prove to be much more difficult (unless you work 16 hours a day — and you will probably have to do that anyway).

As much as possible, you need to have your application set up so upon opening a new document you can simply start working. Most of us have a standard document type that we use most commonly. For myself, it is a handout of some sort with .75-inch margins, one column, and a consistent style and character palette. I have a "normal" color palette that I use. My text wrap is always set to WRAP AROUND OBJECT SHAPE and so forth.

When I have another handout to create, I can simply hit ⌘N >>> Enter, click in the automatic text box, hit ⌘5 for my headline, and start typing. The styles are all set up to flow into one another. Once I start writing, creation becomes almost automated. All my tools are in the same place every day, so when I reach for them they are there.

However, standard defaults are not enough, even though they are essential. All of us have many "normal" documents. We meet that need by setting up templates. **Templates** are documents saved with customized document defaults to enable them to be used as easily as your normal defaults for your most common documents.

To give a personal example, I teach at a community college, have a commercial design studio with a private school, and serve as the church administrator and an elder for the church pastored by my wife. Some of the templates I use regularly are: stationery for my degree and its courses; stationery for my design studio; stationery for my private school; graduation certificate for my school; a newsletter for the private school; an automatically numbered invoice for the studio; a press release form for the church; a fax sheet for studio, school and church; and so on. All of these templates are carefully set up to maintain a consistent look for each of these organizations. They all have customized style and character palettes; customized swatch palettes; custom page sizes and margins, and so on with guides and text boxes set up and ready to fill.

The key thing to remember about these things is not how well organized I am — for I am certainly not. Think absent-minded professor and you have a closer idea. Think about how easy it must be to do these things if even David can get this together. Most importantly, having these templates allows me to keep track of the different organizational images. Plus, and this is key, the use of these templates probably saves me 150 to 200 hours per year.

You should have a set of templates for all of your ongoing clients. Much of this does not need to be formal. When a client comes in with a need for a new brochure, the first thing to do is open their old one. Work from that modifying it to the new need. Start by deleting the graphics you will no longer use. Then use the preflighting packaging command (File >>> Preflight…) to generate a new folder to hold all your new work. That way you will already have copies of the continuing graphics and logos in the folder you are working in.

WHY SPEND ALL THIS TIME?

You don't have to, and as my competitor I hope you don't. As a friend I want to assure you that this will greatly enhance your ability to have fun as a designer. By setting up preferences and defaults, you can free up more time for design, and that is why we got into this career in the first place, right?

The important thing to remember is that setting up preferences and defaults is an occasional thing. If you don't, you have to do the same things for every document regardless. You may get very fast at set up, but it won't compete with someone like me who simply opens a template and starts work. Basically, I will start with a 15-minute to 1-hour lead in my production for every project. You really cannot afford this kind of competitive disadvantage.

Knowledge retention

1. Why do Defaults really matter?

2. Why do you control the superscript/subscript size and locations?

3. Why does this book refuse to specify keyboard shortcuts?

4. What are two advantages of using a palettized interface like InDesign's (and Adobe's in general)?

5. What are some advantages of having almost complete control over your keyboard shortcuts?

WHERE SHOULD YOU BE BY THIS TIME?

By now you should have completed enough tutorials and self-imposed exercises to have a basic, entry level, grasp of the look and feel of InDesign. You need to have your preferences set, and a conceptual grasp of the difference between application defaults, document defaults, and templates.

DISCUSSION

Discuss with your classmates what keyboard shortcuts are most important to you, and which of the changes in factory default shortcuts irritate you the most. Talk about strategies for dealing with the plethora of palettes with different *normal* documents.

Talk among yourselves...

InDesign's Tools and Palettes

CONCEPTS

A specific option-by-option explanation of tools and palettes with suggestions for defaults

CHAPTER OBJECTIVES

By presenting the options and capabilities of InDesign's tools and palettes, this chapter will enable you to:

1. Describe the different tool capabilities
2. Set the defaults for the palettes
3. Begin to learn the keyboard shortcuts for the tools
4. Learn to group palettes rationally
5. Begin to set up your shortcuts and palette arrangements

LAB WORK FOR CHAPTER

- Set up your palette defaults
- Begin changing and memorizing keyboard shortcuts
- Begin setting up the interface for efficient use

InDesign's Tools and Palettes

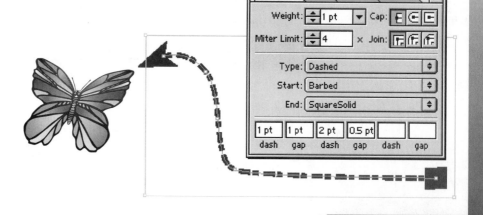

After

the lengthy discussion of why we are here, in InDesign, we can now begin talking about the tools and capabilities of the software. The obvious place to start is with the tools available. For those of you coming from Illustrator, PageMaker, or Photoshop, the Toolbox will look very familiar. In fact, if you consider this toolbox as a finally functional version of a PageMaker/Illustrator hybrid, you are not too far wrong.

It does have all of the relevant Illustrator tools, but they are laid out in a way that is instantly recognizable as page layout. Strange tools like the graphing tool, gradient mesh, blending tool, and so forth are missing, as they should be. This is a page layout program. It does not have Illustrator's incredible brush tool, but Version 1.5 does have FreeHand's indispensable drag'n'drop color. This is not a graphics creation program — vector or bitmap.

If you have been working in an exclusively Quark/FreeHand environment, the look and feel will be a little disconcerting. However, there aren't any of those people that I know of. Most of us have been using either PageMaker, Illustrator, or Photoshop as one of our primary programs for years. As a result, the toolbox looks comfortingly familiar.

There is no doubt, however, that InDesign takes an Illustrator approach to tools. This isn't all bad, but it is reality. However, this is not Illustrator (or a multipage Illustrator). I, for one, am grateful for that. This is closer to the Quark 3/4 upgrade, but Adobe was able to dispose of all the legacy code that Quark is still stuck with.

InDesign is very much what Adobe wishes PageMaker was. At a 1.5 version, it has a way to go, but it is an amazing first step. However, in a very real way, InDesign is what Illustrator can become. There are options and palettes that look like Illustrator, but they have added functionality. The colored sliders in the swatch creation dialog box are evidence of these very helpful additions. These are (and always have been) essential to people who cannot think in RGB, CMYK, or LAB — they just haven't been available before. It's an obvious idea and a great help when working in multiple color spaces.

THE TOOLS

THE SELECTION TOOLS

The SELECTION and DIRECT SELECTION tools are very similar to Illustrator's in appearance. They are also much like Quark's in function. The hollow pointed arrow to the right basically functions as the content tool in Quark, plus it does path editing like the direct selection tool in Illustrator. For those who have not had to deal with the clutter of frames before, this can be disconcerting. However, the powers that be have decided that Quark's style is required. Once you get used to it, the clutter isn't too cumbersome.

For those coming from Quark, the simplicity of InDesign's approach should be a breath of fresh air. The frame changes according to which tool is selected. Any frame can be made into a text frame

InDesign's Tools and Palettes

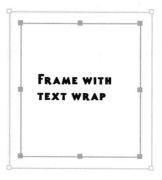

FRAME WITH TEXT WRAP

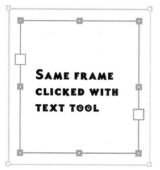

DIRECT SELECT FRAME WITH TEXT WRAP

SAME FRAME CLICKED WITH TEXT TOOL

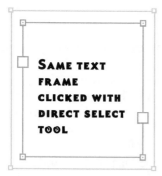

SAME TEXT FRAME CLICKED WITH DIRECT SELECT TOOL

by simply clicking in the frame with the TEXT tool. There is an easy toggle back and forth between the two tools (Option/Alt Tab by default). If you need to move a frame or resize it, you need the selection tool. If you want to modify the shape in any way, you need the direct selection capabilities. As you can see to the left, you can tell which tool you are using by the look of the paths and points of the frame.

 One of the most important changes – and advantages – of InDesign's approach is the simplicity of the various forms of frames. Any frame can be converted to a text frame by simply clicking inside with the Text tool.

Some of more unique features of the frames can be seen at left. Notice that the TEXT WRAP boundary is there for all four frames. You do have to go to one of the selection tools to modify the wrap on the text frames.

 TIP: One of the disconcerting aspects of this new page layout setup is the simple fact that you can have two separate text wraps on the same object. One for the SELECTION tool, and another for the DIRECT SELECT tool.

T THE TYPE TOOL

Only because we have already mentioned it, we will go to the TYPE tool now. All we are going to do is mention it because it is very obvious in use. Basically it works like any other type tool you have ever used in page layout.

Do not ever confuse this tool with word processing capabilities. I am writing this chapter as I go (like I did all of my other books), and it is a real pain in the butt. There is no drag'n'drop editing. In addition, the type rendering function of the software can barely keep up with my typing.

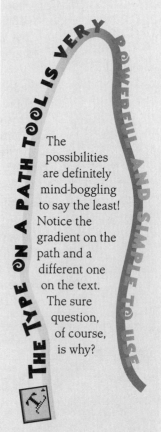

THE TYPE ON A PATH TOOL IS VERY POWERFUL AND SIMPLE TO USE

The possibilities are definitely mind-boggling to say the least! Notice the gradient on the path and a different one on the text. The sure question, of course, is why?

In fact, I find myself watching my fingers because the lag in rendering makes typing almost impossible. It's like Quark 3 was in 1992.

The selection capabilities of the type tool are the same as PageMaker: double-click to select a word; triple-click to select a paragraph; shift arrow to select characters; and so forth. They can all be modified to fit your needs and working style (everything can be modified, almost).

THE PEN TOOL

InDesign's PEN tool is very definitely Illustrator's four part PEN tool, with all of its advantages and disadvantages. In 1.5 InDesign tucks the Scissors tool here as well. Most people seem to believe that Adobe's pen tool is the standard by which others are defined. This is only true if you have used Illustrator's Pen tool for any substantial period of time. For those coming from Freehand's single tool, it will be a shock. I have definitely found that InDesign's version works the way that I wish Illustrator's or Photoshop's did.

Again, for those of you who are not familiar with Adobe's version, you have to closely watch the tool when working with a path to find out what is happening. If you see a little plus next to the tool, you will add a point. If you see a little minus, you will subtract one. If you see the little open pointer, you will change point type from smooth to corner or vice versa. There are shortcuts to access any of the tools individually, which are the same as Illustrator's shortcuts. You can cycle through the tools with the Shift+P.

The basic advice is to remember that holding down the Command (Control) key changes you back to the last selection tool you used. Holding down the Option (Alt) key switches you to the Convert Point tool. The most disconcerting aspect is that there is no way to drag out handles on a corner point. All you can do is drag out the handles with the CHANGE POINT tool and then move the tool over the handles that result. This changes the pointer to a CHANGE POINT icon that allows you to drag the handles individually.

This is disconcerting to FreeHand users only. After a while InDesign's implementation seems very elegant and obvious. However, I am still firmly convinced that, for almost all graphic creation work, Illustrator users will go back to Illustrator and FreeHand users will go back to FreeHand. Even for Illustrator users, there are just too many things missing in InDesign (like the Pathfinder filters). As far as FreeHand users are concerned, there are even more things missing, such as live envelopes, a perspective tool, and so on.

Frame generators

The next three tools are a little confusing, because Adobe has made them two separate menus: the graphic frame tools and the text frame tools. But, it doesn't make any difference which one you are using. If you have a graphic frame and click in it with the TYPE tool, it becomes a text frame. If you have a text frame with no type in it and place a graphic, it becomes a graphic frame. You can almost place anything into any frame with complete freedom. Graphics placed into a text frame become INLINE GRAPHICS (Quark calls them ANCHORED).

 **TIP:** One of the things you quickly learn in InDesign, as you are learning the program, it to carefully watch the graphic signals on the screen. Amazingly, inline graphics still retain their text wrap if you have an automatic text wrap set up as your default. You can only access that text wrap to adjust it by clicking on the graphic with the DIRECT SELECTION tool. Then the wrapping path will appear for editing purposes.

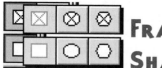 # FRAME TOOLS (F)
SHAPE TOOLS (M)

Shift+F and Shift+M cycles you through the three varieties of each.

THE ELLIPSE TOOL

This tool is a normal ellipse tool. If you hold down the SHIFT key; the shape is constrained to a circle. If you hold down the Option (Alt) key, it draws from the center out. It's just another reason to create graphics in a graphic program. It also draws from handle to handle like all of the older ellipse tools.

THE RECTANGLE TOOL

This tool works normally like the ELLIPSE tool.

THE POLYGON TOOL

This tool is a severely limited version of the POLYGON tool. As you can see from the dialog capture to the above right, the shape of the points of the star must be guessed. There is no preview. With an infinite variety of stars possible with every number of points, this makes this tool useless except for drawing frames for regular polygons (hence the name, I guess).

 ## THE PENCIL TOOL

This is a typical Illustrator triple tool: Pencil, Smoother, and Eraser. Shift+N cycles you through the three of them. It work the way you would expect. The Pencil draws freehand. The Smoother progressively smooths out the line (without any real control, although it often does a nice job). The Eraser does what you would like it to, most of the time.

A really nice capability is that the Smoother and Eraser work on any path you draw, with any tool. The Smoother, for example, will convert a star into a polygon with concave sides (it changes the entire

shape). They even work on type converted to paths, but the effects are rather unpredictable. In general, however, these are a very elegant selection of freehand drawing tools. But then, most of us will be drawing elsewhere.

THE LINE TOOL

What can we say? The tool draws lines. Hold down the Shift key and it draws horizontal, vertical, and 45° lines. The only difference in InDesign is that it is possible to assign a gradient to a line.

THE ROTATE TOOL

InDesign's rotation tool works like Illustrator's. This means that the rotational center of the selected shape or shapes is indicated by the little target you see in the capture to the right. When you move the cursor over the target, it changes to a black pointer that allows you to drag the center to wherever you desire. This very handy, but it is disconcerting to FreeHand users who are accustomed to the click-drag rotation of FreeHand (where the center is determined by where you click. For precise rotation, use the TRANSFORM palette, where the center shows up on the X/Y field.

THE SCALE TOOL THE SHEAR TOOL

These tools work as expected once you take the transform center target into account. This is a capability where those coming from FreeHand will appreciate the Adobe paradigm. The previews while transforming are exceptional, and both of these tools seem much easier to control than their Macromedia counterparts.

In fact, these tools are much easier to handle than Illustrator's versions also. As far as I can tell, this is because InDesign has a frame around everything. That rectangle gives a much more intuitive feel for how the transformation is moving through 2D and 3D space. It makes it relatively easy to use these tools for 2D perspective. Regardless, InDesign's tools for scaling and shearing are very usable.

THE FREE TRANSFORM TOOL

This is Illustrator's and Photoshop's tool. Using the appropriate shortcuts you can interactively apply any transformation to any object. If the tool is over a handle, you can scale. If it is outside the selected shape you can rotate. If you drag a side handle on the side of the bounding box (not a corner) and then hold down Control+Alt (Windows) or ⌘⌥ (Mac OS) as you drag until the object is at the desired perspective. To reflect, simply drag a handle across to the other side. Shift-drag to constrain the tool. It's a wonderful tool!

 THE EYEDROPPER TOOL

This tool copies typographic setting or graphic setting from one object to another. It works with imported graphics. It copies from one document to another. Double-click to set the Options determining what is copied. It can copy almost any attribute.

 THE GRADIENT TOOL

This tool works exactly like its counterparts in Photoshop and Illustrator. It allows you to apply gradient across multiple selected shapes, controlling the angle of the gradient by the direction of the click-drag. The length of the gradient is controlled by the distance between the click and the release. This is a gradient tool that FreeHand should have; but, the interactivity of drag'n'drop gradients is completely missing. In fact, the creating of gradients, as opposed to applying, is far from smooth.

This tool is very good. For InDesign (like with all Adobe products) it is the production of the gradient into swatches that is so clumsy. The only functional method is to add a NEW GRADIENT SWATCH using the popup options menu on the SWATCHES palette. Once you have the gradient on the SWATCHES palette, this tool applies that gradient very elegantly.

 THE HAND TOOL

The GRABBER HAND tool works as expected. However, this is one of the areas of greatest complaint about InDesign. The mere fact that this is a "major" complaint shows clearly how well InDesign works, in general. However, there are many people who do not like the fact that the HAND tool is accessed with the spacebar unless you are working with the TYPE tool. If you have an insertion point in a text frame, this tool is accessed with the Option (Alt) key.

This makes perfect sense to me. The Option (Alt) key is used to modify the actions of many of the drawing and graphic editing tools. This is why all graphics programs use the spacebar to access this tool. However, when the TYPE tool is active, pressing the spacebar adds a space to the copy. Pressing the Option key while working in text has always been PageMaker's option, for this reason. The only frustrating aspect of all of this is that modifier keys are not available, in general, from the EDIT SHORTCUTS command. However, to say that this is major problem is a bit silly.

THE ZOOM TOOL

Here is a tool that is used constantly, that will rarely be accessed through the TOOLBOX. I will mention this again when we get to the NAVIGATOR palette, but this is a keyboard shortcut you must learn ASAP. Pressing the ⌘ Spacebar selects this tool for magnifying.

Adding the Option key makes it a zoom out tool. For PCs, the command is Control+Spacebar adding the Alt key.

This is the only truly efficient method of controlling the % view of your document. First you press the ⌘⌥0 (PC Control+Alt+0) to zoom out to the FIT SPREAD IN WINDOW option. Then you hold down the ZOOM shortcut and draw a marquee around the area you want enlarged and centered on your monitor. The area marqueed will then be enlarged as much as possible and centered on the monitor.

If you can already see the object you need enlarged, you can simply hold down the shortcut and click. However, in this instance you will not be able to control how far it is enlarged. The enlargement will just be to the next step seen in the popup menu in the lower left corner of your document window.

THE FILL AND STROKE TOOLS

These options work exactly like those found in Illustrator (except for the strange fact that the keyboard shortcuts are reversed). You can change them in EDIT SHORTCUTS or you can use the defaults if you don't come from Illustrator. These controls are very obvious and extremely handy if you have any Adobe experience. Pressing the D key gives you the default stroke and fill that you set up with the rest of your defaults. Pressing the X key switches the colors. Pressing the Shift X combination switches which tool is active. It is a little clumsy keeping track of which is active.

TIP: Like any of the other tools, the single letter shortcuts do not work while the Type tool is active. This is obvious, when you think about it, but it can be very irritating until you get used to it. For everyone, except PageMaker specialists, this is a very easy adjustment. For all of us now, we have to make sure that we keep close track of which tool we are using. Blindly using keyboard shortcuts without thought can slow down production to a crawl. There is a major change in shortcuts when the TYPE tool is activated.

As you see above, a wide graduated stroke does make for almost instant buttons

THE APPLY COLOR TOOL

Clicking this button changes the color of the object(s) selected to the color of the swatch currently selected in the SWATCHES palette. The only confusing (and often frustrating) aspect of this procedure is that where the color is applied is determined by whether the fill or the stroke is active. It is relatively common to apply a color and then discover that the stroke is active when you meant to change the fill. Obviously, this problem also applies to the APPLY GRADIENT and the APPLY NONE buttons also.

THE APPLY GRADIENT TOOL

Clicking on this button changes the fill or stroke color of the object(s) selected to the last used gradient swatch in the SWATCHES palette.

A MAJOR NEW ABILITY: InDesign is the first software application that I am aware of that can apply a gradient to a stroke. It actually may not be a major ability, for I cannot remember the last I wished, "Gee, I wish I could apply a gradient to that stroke." However, it is certainly a unique capability of InDesign. I suspect that it will become a major tool of the nouveaux riche designers who are compelled to use every tool as often as possible without regard for grace, elegance, or effectiveness. Remember, please, the importance of style!

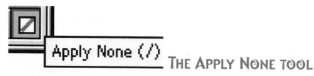

THE APPLY NONE TOOL

Clicking on this button changes the fill or stroke color of the object(s) selected to None, depending upon which tool is selected in the TOOLBOX.

These last three tools are extremely useful methods of applying color without slowing the creative process. If you draw a lot in InDesign, you must learn these shortcuts. Even if you create all of your graphics elsewhere, these buttons will be used often by almost all of us. You will quickly find that, without Stroke and Fill boxes at the top of the Swatches palette, these buttons are essential.

This completes our overview of the tools in the toolbox. As we have seen, InDesign has a reasonably full set of PostScript drawing tools in a powerful page layout package. Naturally, these tools are slanted toward an Adobe Illustrator view of graphic construction. In some areas this helps. In some areas this hinders. What really matters is that what is needed is available.

InDesign's palettes

As I mentioned last chapter, there are at least eighteen tabbed palettes in InDesign. I'm not sure, but I think I found a couple of more last week at school. It doesn't really matter. There are only about fifteen that you will use consistently. We're going to go through them in groups: document organization, typographic controls, color application, and graphic construction. As we go through, I'll give my reasoning for tabbing certain palettes together. You may feel that a different arrangement is better for you.

That does not matter. What matters is that you come up with a layout that works most efficiently for your production methods.

The palettized interface

As you can see, organizing your palettes in not an option. After I made this little screen capture, I realized that I had forgotten to show the Navigator palette or any of the Library palettes for graphics or colors. However, I think you get the idea. This concept of palettes has gotten way out of hand. In fact, without palette organization, it is impossible to work effectively.

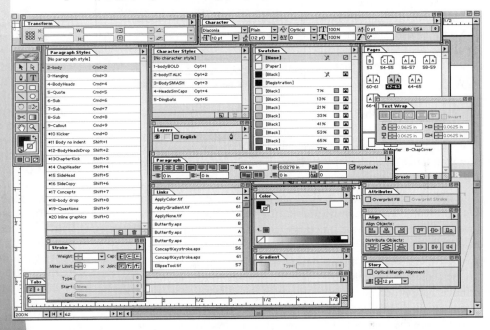

Some of you will certainly point to your second monitor as a solution. Mac has always offered this approach and now Windows does also (98 or better and NT). However, you will quickly find that, as handy as a second monitor is, it does not solve the plethora of palettes problem. While is it possible to organize things "over there" (the side you add that second monitor is controlled by whether you are right- or left-handed), that second monitor greatly adds to your mousing time. It is farther away than the menu bar at the top of your window. Also, for most of us, that second monitor is not calibrated so all of the color palettes have to go on the calibrated screen regardless.

Tabbed palettes

We have three major tools in InDesign for controlling the palettized interface: keyboard shortcuts, tabbing, and what FreeHand calls zipping. We have already covered the basic concepts of customizing your shortcuts. When you find yourself habitually trying to use a certain shortcut to access a particular dialog box, change that shortcut to the one you have already memorized. For me, the LINKS dialog box will always be accessed with ⌘⇧D, so that is what I use. It doesn't matter if you mess up some of the more esoteric commands. You don't use them anyway. Everything has a shortcut. You can't remember them all.

The second method of control is tabbing. Every palette (or dialog box) that has a tab can be grouped onto a common palette with other tabbed palettes. The organization is up to you. Here you can see one of the default groups. One of the major irritants of 1.5 is that these palettes (which have always been long horizontals) are now boxy rectangles that are always getting in the way.

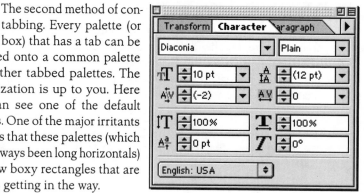

 TIP: Remember that the only thing that matters when customizing your interface, is that it works well for you, and that you can remember the shortcuts easily. Don't let anyone say they have a better way, unless it works for you. They think differently than you do, and they have different memory associations.

The third method of control, zipping, has limited availability in InDesign. However, we can do something very similar. We have a third button in the title bar of the palettes that works like Windows' Minimize button. When you zip a palette you can tuck the collapsed title bar in a convenient, and easy to open, location. When you unzip, the palette pops onto the screen in a predictable place that is easy to use. In InDesign, the minimize button does not tuck minimized palette away. The tabs remain where they were. However, you can place those tabs above your document window where they are out of the way, yet still allow for easy access. The only problem is that this option is still a little buggy. The palettes seem to flop open at random intervals.

With InDesign, the best general practice seems to be to put the palettes away with the CLOSE button and use a keyboard shortcut to reopen the palette. So, what is the advantage to this approach? Simply put, the predictable location allows you to move the mouse there habitually, without looking. This saves a great deal of mousing time. Also by having the palette pop up closer to the center of the screen, you always have the fastest possible access because you move the mouse the shortest possible distance. When you're done with the palette, close it and you have the entire screen to work with again. As I mentioned before, it would be better to have a toolbar to open buttons with a click. Plus there should be a shortcut available to close the active palette. But we always must do the best we can do with what we have.

As we go through these palettes, I will be using the arrangement that works the best for me. Thinking that through, you will probably understand that some of this involves placing palettes where I have

InDesign's Tools and Palettes

Master page items: As mentioned below left, master page items are always placed on the page at the absolute back of the layer to which they are assigned. By clicking on a master page item with the standard shortcut (⌘ Shift – PC: Control Shift), the item is broken from the master page and becomes available on that layer. The only problem with that is that this moves that item on top of the other master page items. **TIP:** You may have to remove all items from the master page to maintain the layering you need.

them popup when I use FreeHand (I already told you that FreeHand is my tool of choice for graphics). If my organization does not work for you, **CHANGE IT!** If you have no real preference, just use the default arrangement until you figure out a faster way to work.

DOCUMENT ORGANIZATION PALETTES

The Pages palette

The most obvious of these is the PAGES palette. As mentioned, this one is the best I have seen. Here you have access to any page in the document or master page. You can easily add multiple page spreads, which Adobe calls ISLAND SPREADS. You can also create MASTER PAGES based on your other MASTER PAGES, just like you can do with paragraph styles. When you change the parent master, those changes appear in the child also. As you can see with the little black inverted triangle on top of page 57, you can start new sections anywhere that is needed. Each section can have its own numbering in its own numbering style. Most of these things have been available in Quark for a while. However, InDesign's implementation is extremely smooth and elegant. Everything I have ever wanted to do in this palette has been available.

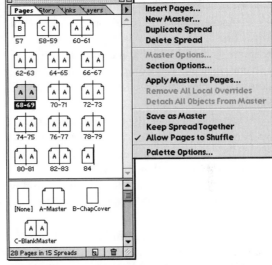

As you can see from the OPTIONS menu, there are many powerful options available. You can shuffle the page order, optionally keep spreads together as you do so. You can directly save a page as a master. To keep Quarkists happy, you can even set up the palette so it looks and works like the one in Quark.

The PALETTE OPTIONS dialog box calls Quark's arrangement Vertical. I have always thought that Quark's setup wasted a great deal of space, but you have the choice. You also have a lot of control over the size of the icons, You can even set your master pages icons to be proportional to the actual page size you will be using.

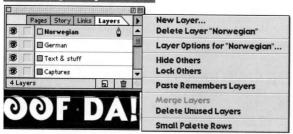

The layers palette

As mentioned, this one works almost exactly like Illustrator's. Personally, I find little use for this type of layers organization in a page layout program. In fact, I find that most designers grossly overuse this capability and end up needlessly complicating their design and slowing their production speed. Nevertheless, when you need layers, there is often no other solution that will work.

As you can see, the capture illustrates the use most often touted by Adobe – the ability to work a document in multiple languages. This is certainly a good use. The tutorial use of placing your photos in one layer, your graphics in another, and your text in another is absurd. In the vast majority of cases, you can do what is needed with the simple shortcuts found under OBJECT >>> ARRANGE used to move selections up or down through the creation order.

Having said that, I am using two layers in this document. It has become a real hassle to access the screen captures when they are brought in. They have to be placed in back of everything because of the fact that I am trying to avoid printing complications by not bothering with clipping paths on the captures. This gives me large white areas that block out type and such. Using the Command/Control key to click down through the layers was a good solution in PageMaker. It doesn't work nearly as smoothly in InDesign. This is mainly due to the fact that you must be in the Selection tool to accomplish the task. Temporary access to the Selection tool with the Command/Control means that the clicking down through layers option is not available until you truly switch tools.

By placing the captures in a new layer under everything else, I have given myself easy access to them any time I need to modify them. Of course this caused another problem (doesn't everything digital?) All of my master page items were in the original layer. The new Captures layer placed the captures behind the master items. So, I needed to go back to the master pages and move all of the graphic elements to the Captures layer.

Master Page items are always at the absolute back of the layer where they are assigned. By moving the master graphics to the back of the Captures layer my problem is solved very elegantly for the rest of this book. Sweet! My frustration is ended. This represents what I would consider a legitimate use of a layer. The new layer solved a specific problem and made production more efficient.

InDesign's Tools and Palettes

This is that mentioned last chapter

One of the problems of the CHARACTER palette is that STYLE field. As mentioned under the font field subhead on the next page, InDesign only shows actual style installed and available. The problem is that when you change fonts the style may no longer be an option. To take an example on the next page, if I change from Akme to Frutiger, Black changes to 85. However, the CHARACTER palette will still show Frutiger [Black], which will not print because there is no such thing. You need to carefully check the style used and have it flagged by the SUBSTITUTED FONTS preference.

The links palette

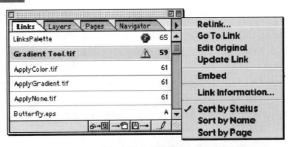

Here we come to a page layout capability that is crucial to understand. The basic concept seems simple enough: if you place a graphic or story, you make a link to that graphic or story. The actual graphic is not embedded into the document unless you specifically tell it to be. One of the most basic problems is where you copy and paste your graphic into your document. This often damages your graphic by converting it to a different format, plus there is no link established. You need to understand that an up-to-date link is the desired goal of graphic management. All graphics in your document need to show up in the LINKS palette with neither bright yellow, triangular warning signs nor bright red, octagonal question marks.

If either of these dreaded icons appear, you need to click the appropriate button at the bottom of the links palette. If the red question mark appears, it mean that InDesign does not know where that graphic went. By clicking on the RELINK button, you can then click on the BROWSE button and tell InDesign where it is. Of course, if you wish to avoid problems, it really needs to be in the same folder as your document. Even if there is no red question you can relink and change to a different graphic of your choice.

 TIP: There is an irritating thing about this palette and how it updates links. If you update a link (or change it to a different graphic), it comes into the existing frame – even though it may be cropped or obviously distorted in proportion. Often it is simpler to delete the graphic and re-PLACE it.

The GO TO LINK button takes you to an enlarged view of the graphic in place in your document. The UPDATE LINK button does what its name suggests – it gets rid of the yellow triangle. The EDIT ORIGINAL button does what you hope it will do: it opens the creating application and opens the graphic for editing. For those of you accustomed to HOTLINKS, this is not that. Normally this does not actually find the originating object. It assumes that EPS graphics are editable, for instance, and opens the EPS (a bad practice because you have no original).

Because all of these button icons are visually vague, you may well need to use the Options menu popup for quite a while until you get the buttons you actually use memorized. TOOL TIPS do give you the name. Just set Tool Tips for Fast under EDIT >>> PREFERENCES >>> GENERAL.

 One final tip: When you import your copy from a word processor, you need to make a decision. Are you going to do any editing in InDesign? If you do, you need to embed the text file using the OPTIONS submenu.

THE TYPOGRAPHIC CONTROL GROUP

Here we get to the core of page layout. Contrary to the imaginations of most designers, "content is king." Graphics are the dressing to display the content to the best advantage. The content is the copy. You didn't buy this book because of its graphic interface. You bought it because you (or your instructor) thought this book was the best available to explain to you how to use InDesign for page layout. Although the book would be very dry without the graphics, without the copy it would be an assortment of mediocre drawings that meant nothing.

TYPOGRAPHY IS WHAT WE DO. This may be hard to tell with some of the offerings of recent designers. The acknowledged standard "splash" page for your Web site is not even questioned, though it irritates many who came to the site looking for content. When was the last time that the title page of a book was a reason, pro or con, to purchase a book? Even with that most typical of splash pages, the magazine or novel cover, when was the last time you bought a magazine because of the image on the cover? My guess is you bought it because of the content – those headlines enticing you to read the articles inside.

Page layout gives you the power to control your document's image typographically.

The Character palette

Most of us will access this palette using the same keyboard shortcut we used in PageMaker or Quark, depending upon where we came from. Hopefully all used the dialog box there. The worst scenario for selecting type changes is to use the menu at the top of the window. What is needed is to memorize the tabbing order of the fields in this palette, the way you memorized those fields in your former software. My problem, coming from PageMaker, is that Adobe has added seven new fields to this palette that were in other places before. The same thing is true for those of you coming from Quark.

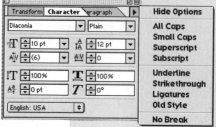

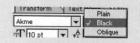

Local formatting

Of course, this palette should really not be used much at all. The choices in this palette are for local formatting, primarily. As we will discuss thoroughly in Chapters 8 and 9, you should do no local formatting, except after all the general formatting with the STYLES when you local format to clean up widows, orphans, and the like.

The font fields

Here you will be a little irritated if, like me, you have been dependent upon a font menu that was WYSIWYG with side menus for the actual fonts. Part of this is the OS upgrade required to run InDesign. Part of it is that InDesign selects fonts differently. There is a popup for the

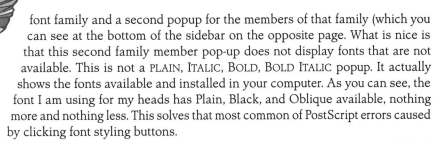

font family and a second popup for the members of that family (which you can see at the bottom of the sidebar on the opposite page. What is nice is that this second family member pop-up does not display fonts that are not available. This is not a PLAIN, ITALIC, BOLD, BOLD ITALIC popup. It actually shows the fonts available and installed in your computer. As you can see, the font I am using for my heads has Plain, Black, and Oblique available, nothing more and nothing less. This solves that most common of PostScript errors caused by clicking font styling buttons.

By the way, on my machine the WYSIWYG font menu works off the Type >>> Font menu at the top of the window. Where it does not work is in the Character Palette or in the Paragraph or Character Styles popup. It is a minor irritant.

TIP: The size and leading fields work as expected, though you have to tab two and three times, respectively to access them. Hitting the keyboard shortcut for the palette always takes you back to the first field. I use the ⌘T shortcut for this palette, so ⌘T>Tab>Tab takes me to the size field. In other words (with my shortcuts) if I wish to change the point size of selected words, ⌘T>Tab>Tab>27>Return will almost instantly change the point size to 27 (almost before the palette appears if I have it put away) — in about a third of the time it takes to open the palette and double click the field or access the popup to change the size.

Track/Kern fields

These two are virtually useless from a practical standpoint. You really need to learn the keyboard shortcuts for these options. Set them up carefully in PREFERENCES and EDIT SHORTCUTS so they work the way you want them to. To adjust using these fields is an exercise in futility. The numbers used are PREFERENCE specified thousandths of an em. Most of us cannot think in those measurements. With the keyboard shortcuts (which are Option/Alt left or right arrow with the Command/Control key added for 5x adjustments), InDesign does beautiful, elegant kerning tracking adjustments.

New! One thing InDesign adds that has not been available before is OPTICAL kerning or METRIC. METRIC uses the kerning built into your font. OPTICAL analyzes the spaces between letters to determine what looks best. My experience suggests that OPTICAL is an amazing option. I have made a quick font in Fontographer, with no built-in kerning and poor spacing, and watched InDesign do a credible job of spacing the font. It does add a heavy computing hit, however. If you use it, and I do, it will definitely slow down your screen redraw times when you are editing copy. The resulting type really looks nice, however.

The Paragraph palette

This palette (seen at the top of the next page) is very much like PageMaker's Paragraph dialog box or Quark's Formats dialog box. The normal fields of this type of dialog box are here: left indent, right indent, first line indent, space before paragraph, and space after paragraph.

The Tabbing order is different than both former page layout stars. The first difference is that InDesign places the leading field with the point size on the Character palette, where it belongs. So, for Quark users, this palette will have one less tab when going to space before paragraph. The second difference is that InDesign places the right indent second and the first line indent third. This variant is new to publishing software, as far as I know.

This palette, almost more than any other, has been used for quick local formatting to make copy fit pages vertically. However, now that InDesign (like Quark) has VERTICAL JUSTIFICATION, it will be used less. You need to put a little conscious effort into memorizing the tabbing order so

These are the times that try men's soles... Or is it, to try on shoes?#

you can easily add Space Before or Space After paragraph, as needed. Just use the keyboard shortcut for the palette to go back to the first field. Then tab to the field, type in the number, and hit RETURN on the way out. Here you will begin to see the benefits and problems of palettes over dialogs – they open quicker, in a default location of your choosing, but they do not close automatically.

A workaround:
For vertical centering of copy, you will need to make a tight text frame with the copy and then copy>>paste it into another frame as a centered object.

Alignments

Here you begin to see the benefits of InDesign's multiline justification. Their assumption that you will use justified copy more than you ever have before is probably accurate (because it looks so much better with the MULTI-LINE COMPOSER). As a result, they have added JUSTIFIED LEFT, JUSTIFIED CENTER, JUSTIFIED RIGHT, and FULLY JUSTIFIED to your repertoire. Basically, it gives the old controls we had with phototypesetters (QUAD LEFT, QUAD RIGHT, and so on).

Baseline grid

Clicking on the right button will cause your copy to snap to grid. Assuming that your Styles are set up in multiples of your basic body copy leading, your copy will then line up across columns.

Drop caps

Here we come to one of InDesign's strengths. I have never seen such control over drop caps. Again, for many people, this is a real large thing. I would classify it more as nice, but in InDesign's case it is very nice. All you have to do is type in how many lines you want the

letters to drop (top field) and then how many letters you want to drop (bottom field). If you change your mind, change the numbers. The capability simply works. More than that, you can drop inline graphics.

TIP: The ability to use an inline graphic as a drop cap is unique to InDesign, as far as I know. The ability to apply a text wrap around that dropped inline graphic is unprecedented. It is very clumsy (often impossible) to try and edit that text wrap around the graphic after the fact, so I suggest that you carefully set up your default text wrap *before* you place your graphic. However, as you can see to the left, it works wonderfully well. This particular instance has .1 inch to the left and right, nothing on top, and a minus five hundredths at the bottom for its default text wrap.

Paragraph rules

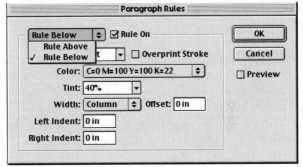

This option is found under the Options pop-up menu next to the arrow on the upper right of the palette. Again, InDesign's version works very well. It will take a slight shift to memorize how their version of Offset works. OFFSET in InDesign is measured from the baseline to the bottom of the top rule or the top of the bottom rule. Other than that, the color, width, and indents work exactly like you would expect. The only other little foible is that the color has to be in the SWATCHES palette to use it. The TINTS popup is normal (assuming that the color is in Swatches).

In General, the PARAGRAPH palette has everything you need in places you expect. It is one of InDesign's more successful 1.5 renditions. All the problems are minor quibbles.

The Tabs palette

This palette has all the features you would expect of a dialog made into a palette. It has the normal four tabs: left, right, centered, and special character. OOPS! What's this special character tab? Simple, you can line up a tab on any character you choose – nice!

1-27	2"x24"
28-102	2'x3'
103-487	3'x12'

Transform \ Character \ Paragraph \ **Tabs** \ Text Wrap

X: 4 in   Leader: <•>   Align On:

0   1   2   3   4

WHY?   **BECAUSE IT**   <•>|<•>|<•>|<•>|CAN BE DONE!

The same is true of the leader options. You can now use up to eight characters to make your leaders. Wonderful! Why? You can make decorative rules with dingbats, but it certainly has no common use. Of course, this is because it is not common. I am certain that I will use it – now that the capability is available. That is the nature of the new paradigm of digital publishing. We are software driven. The problem is that many of us are not controlled at all by taste.

Many of you are already familiar with my position on **nouveau riche design**. This is where a "newly rich" designer shows off by using every new capability found in his impressively powerful software application. Please, don't do it! We have been infested with enough horribly ugly designs of late. Do everything you can to avoid visual assault, in this increasingly ugly culture we live in.

One very nice feature is the vertical line that appears in the text block when you move a tab. It works much like the preferences option in FreeHand and it is very handy here as well. As a matter of fact, it helps so much, that I recommend that complicated tabs be adjusted this way in a sample paragraph before you click the NEW STYLE button at the bottom of the PARAGRAPH STYLES palette (we'll get to that in a bit).

On the popup OPTIONS menu, you have the capability to clear all tabs or to repeat a selected tab across the text block. This is helpful if you need to have repeating tabs that do not fit the default half inch. I can't remember the last time I needed that capability, but it's there.

The Text Wrap palette

This one is very powerful but has proven frustrating – mainly because it doesn't behave the way I wish it would. The largest problem seems to be when you make a text wrap your default. If you do that, the objects placed will have an automatic text wrap. However, I have had considerable problems with modifying that automatic wrap with either the SELECTION or DIRECT SELECTION tool. Usually I have to turn the wrap off and then reapply it with the palette if I wish to modify it. However, this is the only way to make a text wrap around an inline graphic used as a drop cap.

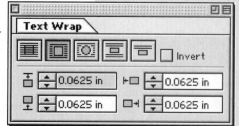

Normal wraps (applied with the palette) work exceedingly well. You can wrap around the frame, around the object shape, make the text jump the object, or cause it to jump to the next column. There is also an INVERT checkbox that lets you wrap text inside a wrapping path.

Path is the operative word. The wrap is simply a path that can be modified normally with the PEN tools and the SELECTION tools. You can use a clipping path as the object shape you wish to wrap around.

The Story palette

Here is a preference masquerading as a palette. This is not to say that it is not important, however. What this deals with is normally called *hanging punctuation*, although

InDesign's Tools and Palettes

Beware!
You really need to remember that you can easily have two different text wraps — one with each selection tool. You will have to watch carefully how the text is wrapping.

InDesign takes it to new heights, heights the other software should have offered years ago. The problem is much like the OPTICAL KERNING option offered in the CHARACTER palette. It takes even more computing power.

What this capability does is hang punctuation and the edges of letters over the margins to give a more accurate optical alignment. Just as the bowls and angles of type characters have to hang below the baseline to look properly aligned, OPTICAL MARGIN ALIGNMENT now enables us to eliminate that optical illusion that the edges of our columns really weren't lined up. Type characters are widely varied and lining them up visually has always been one of the signs of a pro. InDesign has now automated that process with remarkably good results. You need to set this at the point size of your body copy, if you decide to use it (I do).

The Transform palette

Here we are making a transition from type to graphics. This palette deals with very different situations – objects (even text as an object or objects). To the right, we

see a rectangle that has been scaled, rotated, and sheared. You can read the angles and percentages on the fields of the palette.

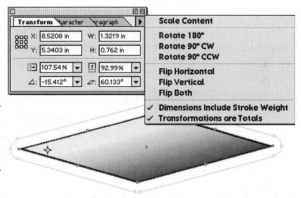

More than that you can see which handle these transformations were measured from. InDesign has the same proxy icon on its palette as PageMaker allowing you to apply transformations from any handle or the center of the object. Several things are missing, though. The PROPORTIONAL button is gone. Usually, however, you can make proportional changes by using a Command/Control+Return/Enter to apply the transformation.

Probably the most useful aspect of this palette is the ability to accurately locate any object on a page, measured from any point, the center, or the transformation point. How many times have you wished that you could measure the size and location of an object from the right side, or the lower right corner? Now you can do that whenever you need to do that.

THE COLOR APPLICATION GROUP

Here we deal with a group of palettes where you'll have to put up with my continual complaints. Actually, I'll try to be nice, but as I've already mentioned several times, InDesign's ability to apply color is severely compromised by its lack of drag'n'drop color. For those of you who have never used it, you don't know what you're missing. There! Hopefully that complaint is out of my system.

Like we hinted when talking about the TRANSFORM palette, InDesign is severely tool driven. By that, I mean you cannot do much of anything without switching to another tool. Thankfully, Adobe has given us easy access with single letter keystroke shortcuts.

 TIP: One of the things you need to get solidly into your memory is this simple fact: all shortcuts change when you are working with type! In truth, only the shortcuts that use typographic characters switch, but that's still very important to remember. For example, in type, the space bar no longer accesses the GRABBER HAND, it types a space (you need to switch to the Option/Alt key to use the GRABBER while working in type). Also, ⇧X no longer switches from stroke to fill, you have to use the mouse. If you feel that you need instant access to any tool or capability, you need to change its shortcut so it uses a function key or one of the non-typographic modifiers (Command, Control, or Option/Alt). I have changed my apply colors shortcuts to Option key shortcuts so I always have access to those commands (even when typing).

As a reminder, you see to the right the tools which control stroke, fill, and which you are using at the time. There are also the buttons for applying the currently selected color in the SWATCHES palette, the last gradient used, or NONE (no color at all).

The Swatches palette

This is the queen of the color application palettes. Basically, nothing can be done, when using color, unless you have added the color, tint, or gradient to this palette. You can see this is done with commands that open actual dialog boxes (gasp!) to produce these colors, tints, or gradients.

 TIPS: These dialog boxes off the SWATCHES palette work much better than the STROKE, FILL, or GRADIENT palettes do. Also (second tip), you will need to think ahead and generate a standard palette of tints you are going to use in the document. If the colors or tints aren't already there, you will be unable to apply them to type, rules, and so on when setting up paragraph styles and so forth. As you can see in the sidebar to the right, I made a complete palette of the colors and tints I was going to use for this book before I started formatting. I may well decide to add a few more gradients as we go through this document, but the tints are already there when needed. Notice that my darkest tint eliminates any worry about tints plugging up from dot gain.

Reading the swatches

In order to understand what you are doing in InDesign when applying colors, you need to be able to read the icons used that tell you what type of color you are using. In Chapter 12 on color usage and separations, we'll discuss the problems you will create if you do not keep track of the color spaces you are using. For now, let's leave it that way. If you don't keep track of the color spaces in which you are working, you will waste time and resources (assuming that you don't run your self or your employer into bankruptcy court).

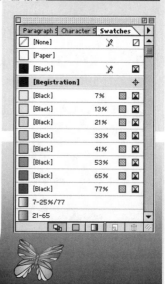

As you can see to the right, InDesign packs a lot of information into each bar. Aspects like the color space used to display the color, whether it is a spot color, tint, or a process color, and whether you can redefine the color. First of all, colors in [Brackets] cannot be redefined for output (although [Paper] and [Registration] can be redefined for viewing on the monitor). Let's start with the top bar:

[None]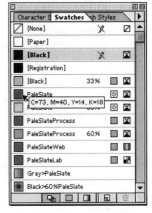

As you know, the crossbar in all cases (icon, tool, or swatch) is red. It is to clearly warn you that there is nothing there. It means what it says, None. As you know, we are dealing with PostScript. The PostScript descriptions have no color or dimension until we specify it – in InDesign's case, color is defined by clicking on a swatch including the specification of [NONE] (not transparent color but none). **NOTICE:** The pencil with the slash through it means that this color cannot be redefined.

[Paper]

This is not white, as you know, or is it? Under normal use, PAPER is an opaque knockout color with no color that reveals the paper through the knocked out hole. **NEW FEATURE:** In InDesign you can actually make the PAPER color appear to be the color of the paper you will be using. Just double-click the PAPER swatch and make the swatch look as close as you can to the color of the paper you will be using. Of course, you can not imitate fiber-added stock, and you have to be aware that it's still just that opaque knockout with which you are familiar once it prints.

[Black]

This, again, is one of those colors never thought about – but it really requires knowledge. First of all, this is process black. Even though it is often treated like a spot color, this is process black (think 70% gray). If you are working in CMYK, you will probably need to create a separate swatch called something like Rich Black. If you are printing it in spot color, remember to specify that the press operator use dense black if it is important. Notice the slashed pencil. This color is yet another that cannot be redefined. By default it always overprints. To the right of the swatch you see the four-sided box that tells you InDesign considers this a CMYK color.

[Registration]

This color prints on all plates and is used for registration marks that must print on all colors. In 1.5, you can now change the color that registration colored objects appear on the screen.

[Black] 33%

Here we have a tint of Black. As you can see from the swatch, it is a 33% tint, process color, CMYK. The little gray square that shows us process color shows up for CMYK, RGB, and LAB color. The only way you can tell which model is being used for the color is to look at the second icon just to the right of the process icon.

Pale Slate

Here we have a custom-mixed spot color, using the CMYK color space to spec it. **TIP:** You can use any color space to specify a color. In general, I would suggest using CMYK if you are going to print the color, and RGB if it is for the Web or CD-ROM. You can see the CMYK mix in the little popup rectangle after holding the mouse over the swatch for a while.

Pale Slate   30%

By now, you should be getting the hang of it. This is a tint of the Pale Slate spot color, using the CMYK lookup tables to render the color on the monitor. Because of the fact that it is a spot color, the color space used to render the color on the screen is really irrelevant. You need to use a printed swatch book to show you what it will look like printed.

Pale Slate Process

DANGER! This is a real problem! This color looks exactly like the spot color Pale Slate on the screen. However, because this is a process color it will print out on the four process plates (cyan, magenta, yellow, and black). That little tinted square is the only warning you will get.

Pale Slate Web

This color may look a little different on the monitor because it uses a different color model – RGB.

Pale Slate Lab

This color may look a little different on the monitor because it uses a different color model – LAB. This is a relatively unused color space, but it does have some real advantages. The primary advantage is that you can adjust the lightness and darkness independently of the hue.

The final two swatches are gradient swatches. You can tell the top one is a linear gradation and the bottom one is a radial gradient. It is a bit frustrating to have to add the gradients to the swatches palette to get any real control over them, but you get used to it after a while. If you only have Illustrator experience, you are used to it already.

Swatch Libraries palettes

InDesign gives you the ability to have entire color libraries available on a palette. At the top right of the next page, for example, you see the entire Pantone Uncoated library. When I first tried this capability, I was really excited (expecting to be able to simply double-click on a spot color to add it to the swatches. I have been accustomed (for

many years) to simply opening a library and beginning to
type the number. However, nothing happened. Then I made the
normal Adobe discovery, nothing
works the way you want it to until

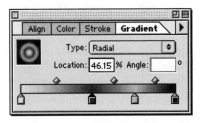

you apply the appropriate keyboard shortcut. In this case that shortcut is ⌘⌥
(PC: Control Alt). You click on the palette with these keys held down. At this
point the library palette transforms into what you wish it was when you opened
it. Type a number and it goes to the swatch, Double click on that swatch and it
is added to the SWATCHES palette.

Here is one place that all the palettes work to our advantage. All of you
probably remember adding PMS colors from a popup menu where every time you
add a color the library goes away. You had to reopen the library every time you
used it. Now it's readily available. Hopefully, of course, for the sake of your printing
budget, you will exercise restraint and set up your colors before you begin your
project. Probably one of the places where this palette approach would be most helpful
would be for Web projects. The ability to have the Web-safe palette at your disposal
is very helpful.

The Gradient palette

As mentioned, this palette is much tougher
to use than the dialog box that comes up when
you use the NEW GRADIENT SWATCH command
on the SWATCHES palette popup OPTIONS menu.
It's confusing to add the colors because there
is no specification for them. In 1.5 there is a
reverse direction button that has been added.

The Color palette

This one, also, should
be forgotten. The NEW COLOR
SWATCH command is far more
powerful and intuitive. This
palette changes the color of
whichever is active: stroke
or fill. It does not add the
color to the Swatches pal-

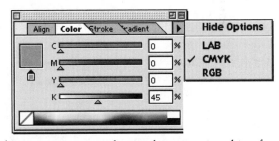

ette. Having unspecified colors roaming around your document is asking for
disaster. **DO NOT EVER USE COLORS IN YOUR DOCUMENTS EXCEPT
FROM THE SWATCHES PALETTE!**

THE GRAPHIC CONSTRUCTION GROUP

As we finish off this examination of palettes, we talk about
palettes that control graphic construction. For the first one, it will
greatly help if you know either Illustrator or FreeHand well.

The Stroke palette

These capabilities are normal for PostScript drawing programs. As you can see on the next page, this palette uses Illustrator's superior stroke generation capabilities. You do not have the ability to create custom arrow-heads or tails, but who ever really does that anyway? The CAPS and JOINS are normal PostScript. The dashed options are over the top (much like FreeHand's ability to create custom arrowheads).

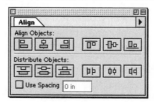

The Align palette

InDesign allows you to align multiple selected objects in any manner you can think of. This palette is obvious and easy to understand. All you have to do is select the objects you need aligned and click the appropriate button. The ability to align perfectly mathematically can save a great deal of time (as compared to hand alignment).

The Attributes palette

Here's a checkbox masquerading as a palette. It will rarely be used. If you are forced to hand construct traps, maybe. If you are working with low resolution printers or coarse registration presses, you may need to eliminate knockouts. If you need the capability, here it is. The only problem is remembering where it was stored.

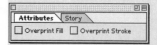

The Library palette

Here is a palette for graphic storage. The local newspaper uses a library to store its repetitive graphics and client logos. Personally I've never found a need. As I mentioned earlier, this one works so well I may change my working pattern and add it to my procedures. If you use libraries (and I'm the first to admit that my needs are different than those who work in large corporate situations) this palette works very intuitively. The ease with which you can save multiple libraries, that can be tabbed into a common palette, make a graphic organizer that could really help.

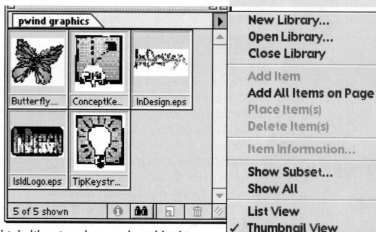

Find/Change

One of the nice little changes in InDesign is found in the Find/Change dialog box. All of us remember the hassle of having to

Find/Change

Find what:

Change to:

Search: Story

☐ Whole Word
☐ Case Sensitive

Find Style Settings

Change Style Settings

Done

Auto Page Numbering
Section Marker

Bullet Character
Caret Character
Copyright Symbol
End of Paragraph
Forced Line Break
Inline Graphic Marker
Paragraph Symbol
Registered Trademark Symbol
Section Symbol
Tab Character

Em Dash
Em Space
En Dash
En Space
Flush Space
Hair Space
Nonbreaking Space
Thin Space
White Space

Discretionary Hyphen
Nonbreaking Hyphen

Double Left Quotation Mark
Double Right Quotation Mark
Single Left Quotation Mark
Single Right Quotation Mark

Any Character
Any Digit
Any Letter

remember those special characters (like ^p for a return) needed to find invisible characters. As you can see above, InDesign has added a popup menu right next to the FIND WHAT: and CHANGE TO: that contains a direct entry menu for all of those special characters. No more fumbling for the User Manual! This is a great help.

Get'em under control!

As you have seen this is not an option with the Adobe interface. My advice is to group the palettes into groups that make sense to you. Set Keyboard shortcuts that you can easily remember to open the palette you use the most in each group. Then keep it consistent so you can open, use, and close palettes as needed to keep as much usable screen space as possible.

Knowledge retention

1. What do you think is the best strategy for palette control?

2. What new alignments have been added to the paragraph palette?

3. Describe a situation where you would use a gradient stroke.

4. Where does a master page item appear when you use the keyboard shortcut to make it editable on the page?

5. What are some advantages of having almost complete control over your keyboard shortcuts?

WHERE SHOULD YOU BE BY THIS TIME?

You should have your palettes set up in functional groups (or at least in groups that you hope will be functional). Practice with tools and simple graphics to get a feel for the program.

DISCUSSION

Discuss with your classmates palette arrangements and methods to smooth production. Consider which software should be used for what tasks and why. Discuss production methods. It might be fun to write them down. At the end of the class, compare what you write now with what you are actually using as you get ready to move on in your career.

Talk among yourselves...

5

CHAPTER CONTENTS

A brief history of our industry to enable conscious choices in graphic design

CHAPTER OBJECTIVES

By presenting the history, both publishing and design, this chapter will enable you to:

1. Describe a basic printing workflow
2. Argue the position of multimedia in publishing
3. Discuss the influence of our marketing economy
4. Describe the differences between various printing technologies
5. Present a thoughtful opinion of the position of Web publishing in our industry

LAB WORK FOR CHAPTER

You now begin to develop practical skills by completing Skill Exams and the slightly more simple Miniskills. The skill exam instructions are found on your CD.

• Miniskill #1
• Skill #1

Graphic History

This chapter is very important!

One of the most common complaints as I go around visiting people I know in the publishing industry is, "I can find people with printing experience, and those who are computer whizzes. What I really need I cannot find — computer experts who know printing and can work fast."

The real problem with digital publishers is that few of them know anything about the industry that actually produces their creative wonders. Worse they do not know the capabilities and limitations of the various technologies. This chapter attempts to give a very brief overview of our industry and where we came from. You may think you know all these things. My guess is that you will be surprised.

THIS IS THE PERFECT WEEK FOR YOU (AND YOUR CLASS) TO TAKE A FIELD TRIP.

If you are studying this on your own, you need to go to some of the printing firms in your area and ask for a quick tour. This works especially well if you have already been working with the company in question.

There is no doubt. You need to see and touch real presses and imagesetters to have any idea how they actually work. If you are fortunate, you will find someone to show you around who really knows what is going on, and can answer your questions.

Make sure that the printers know that you are genuinely interested in learning the capabilities of their equipment so you do not design something that is impossible to print. After you pick them up off the floor, they will be happy to help you get that knowledge.

The

The personal computer destroyed printing as it was known prior to 1990. Even though the stories of printing as it was are fascinating, most of them have little relevance to digital production. So why are we including this relatively large dose of history? Mainly to give you a perspective. To be an effective digital publisher, you must build on the past using its wisdom to help you solve your communication problems. Even if your style and solution to these problems is a conscious rejection of historical printing solutions, you will not be able to convey your convictions without a solid historical foundation. In my experience, most of you (and almost all students entering the publishing industry) have no background in historical printing at all. The modern digital publishing industry is completely overrun by computer geeks with no idea of how to effectively use the production industry that serves you.

You know the old saw: *"Ignoring history condemns you to repeat the same mistakes made historically."* This is part of why we start here. More than that, the history of printing is one of the central factors in civilization as we know it. Until the Web, the knowledge we learned came from books. The decisions we made are still usually based on what we read. The joys of living are still often associated with printed matter (even if it is only a ticket stub souvenir).

Professional graphic communication requires the memory of fine printing.

Our clients and their clients base many of their feelings about a company or organization on historical printed associations. An invitation done in bold, mechanical type is not appropriate and everyone knows it. A quality client does not use cheap paper. We'll get into this in depth later on. The point here is simply to make sure you understand the importance of historical context when using the printed word.

It all started in China, of course

Often it seems as if virtually all the major inventions necessary to civilization came from the Far East, China specifically. This is certainly the case in printing. Their language made the idea of printing much more obvious. Instead of words being made of a certain number of characters, like our alphabet, every Chinese word is a single character.

Almost 2,000 years ago, the Chinese began carving the surface of blocks of wood and stone into the shapes of characters. Because of their skill in brushwork, official signatures were carved this way and used like a rubber stamp for their official signature on all paintings and documents. The concept of building a collection of various characters (words) was the beginning. By making them a consistent size, they were then able to assemble the characters in rows. Once they had the rows put together, all they had to do was cover the surface of the characters with a stiff ink, lay a sheet of paper on the blocks, press the paper into the ink, and peel the paper off. If they were careful not to move the blocks, many virtually identical copies could be made. Printing was born.

The Renaissance: the birth of modern civilization

By the fourteenth and fifteenth centuries, Europe was in a state similar to today. New knowledge was turning everything upside down. All the old standards were questioned and many were found flawed. Like today, there was a tendency to toss out the baby when throwing out the bath water. However, it was an exciting time to be alive. The possibilities seemed endless. We could solve our problems!

The key to the Renaissance was printing

Before the Renaissance, a wealthy noble with a huge library might have twenty or so books. All books were hand-copied (by monks). When you ordered one, the wait was measured in years. Because they were hand-copied, mistakes were inevitable. But the handwriting was beautiful. These books were gorgeous, but they were the equivalent of fine art originals. As a result, these first examples of desktop publishing were very rare.

The library as we know it now was nonexistent. There were no newspapers, magazines, white papers, or brochures. The classics were not

available, except for the Bible (and even that was found only in the church and only seen by the educated priesthood). The Greek and Roman classics were only available in scattered pieces known only to scholar monks (who treated them as heretical and therefore extremely dangerous).

If you needed to learn a particular skill, you were forced to move to the town or city where the master craftsperson lived. There, if you were fortunate, the master accepted you as an apprentice, and you learned via on the job training in a long apprenticeship. Printing completely changed our world.

By the early 1500s, libraries grew to thousands of volumes, as print shops sprang up throughout Europe. Fiction was popularized, the first pulp novels. It became possible for an ordinary person to study masters long dead, or masters that lived far away. Reading became the central skill of education. Science became possible as people could easily share ideas across continents. The idea of the Renaissance man was born – rich, educated, ever curious, always studious.

The birth of printing

Our publishing industry, in the European West, began in the mid-1400s. Several people were experimenting with various printing techniques. Printing production did not exist, but the basic theory was understood. Fine art printmaking was becoming a mature art form.

This press type was the start of it all. Hand assembled character blocks, inked with a roller, were covered with a sheet of paper or silk. The paper was rubbed with enough pressure to pick up the ink. After the paper was peeled off, the next sheet was done the same way

Giving creative people a material like paper was the initial trigger in the late 1300s. The revelation needed was movable type. The concept required standard-sized letters that could be assembled and reassembled at will. By cutting letters into the surface of dies or stamps, molds could be punched. Then the letters could be cast. It became possible to assemble words. With enough letters, pages could be built... books could be printed!

Johann Gutenberg

Johann Gutenberg usually gets the credit for inventing the process instead of the Chinese. For our purposes, it is enough to understand the times and the invention, as we've already covered. There were many developing this craft. However, the identifiable turning point was Gutenberg's 42–line Bible. In other words, he printed a Bible that used forty-two rows of words per page. This came to about 5,500 letters, punctuation marks, and spaces per page.

Even this first book required many letters. While they were printing a pair of pages, they would assemble the next two. As you can see, the number of letters needed was well into five figures. With two persons working twelve-hour days, it took more than three years to produce a couple hundred copies. It was hardly printing as we know it. But it was enough to fundamentally change society.

Gutenberg's press was revolutionary but slow. The design was a modified wine press. The letters were assembled on a tray and locked in place. The tray, or typeform, was mounted on the press under a large pressure plate or platen. The type was evenly inked across the surface of the letters with a very stiff ink. A sheet of clean paper was carefully laid on the type, held in place by a frame called a tympan. Once the ink and paper were positioned, the platen was screwed down with a strong pull on a lever into firm contact. The type had to be all the same height and the pressure even. With good, tight contact, a virtually perfect copy of the type was made.

When the press was opened, the sheet was hung on a line to dry. The form was re-inked, the paper was swung into position, it was rolled under the platen, the lever was pulled, and so on. Working hard, two persons could make around 300 to 1,000 impressions a day.

The major problems were speed and size. It takes 175 pounds of pressure per square inch to transfer ink to paper. The pressure needed to print an 11"x14" sheet is more than 13 tons. Both the press and the type composition needed a great deal of help. The press designs came first. Major advances were made by automating the paper feeding and eliminating the pull-and-release lever action.

Cylinder presses

The cylinder press solved all the pressure problems. By rolling a cylinder over the plate, several things were accomplished. Because a cylinder's contact and pressure point is in a narrow strip, sufficient pressure to transfer the ink could be reached more easily.

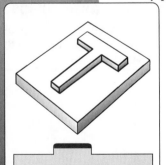

LETTERPRESS FLEXOGRAPHY
RELIEF PRINTING
Background is cut or etched into the plate surface, leaving a raised image. The image is inked and printed.

Cylinders could also be rolled much faster than a pressure plate could be lowered, squeezing the paper onto the ink. Adding inking rollers increased the speed by automatically re-inking the plate. Production reached thousands of pages a day.

At these speeds, weekly newspapers became possible – but just barely. Newspapers became the community lifeline, vital to community life, although production was still very small by our standards. A single page called a broadside, weekly, was a major effort for a couple of people. Mainly, they could not get type set fast enough.

Rotary presses

By the middle of the nineteenth century, the final major advance in press technology was discovered. By using two cylinders rotating in opposite directions, paper could feed continuously. Cylinder presses only rotated through less than one rotation. Then they had to be reversed back to the starting point. This wasted half the time. With a rotary press, 13,000 impressions an hour became commonplace.

It soon became obvious that rotary presses eliminated the need for feeding a single sheet at a time. About the same time, the Fourdriniér brothers invented the continuous paper machine. Paper was produced in huge rolls. A web press feeds rolls of paper, in a continuous stream, through the press. The paper is not sheeted until after it is printed. This concept allowed daily papers to emerge. With speeds of thousands of impressions an hour, huge presses could even print morning and evening newspapers. Magazines and books became much more available because the reduced costs and greater speeds significantly increased printing quantity.

Setting type

The major bottleneck was rarely the presses. In fact, until digital production, presses dominated production. It took many people to keep one press fed with work. (Only with digital production is it possible for one designer to keep several presses busy.) The major problem was type – all those tiny little slugs of lead cast into letters. The technique was tedious at best. Letters were assembled, word by word, line by line. The labor was called composing and the words were composed a line at a time on a composing stick. The composed type was then locked firmly in place in a clamping frame (which became known as a chase). All spacing was done by hand, by inserting tiny blank slugs called quads between letters and words. Spacing between lines was accomplishing with thin strips of lead, appropriately called leading. The entire procedure was what we would call a real pain. Many people slaved away in dirty, dark, hot rooms – a true sweatshop – in what today would be considered barbarous conditions.

Automatic typesetting

The major breakthrough came in 1886 with the demonstration of the first truly automatic typesetting machine at the New York Tribune. Invented by Ottmar Mergenthaler, the Linotype has been called one

Gutenberg's design was so solid that Ben Franklin was using basically the same press.

This replica of Ben's press was photographed in the Smithsonian.

of the ten greatest inventions in the history of humankind. It was the enabling technology for modern periodical literature such as magazines, newspapers, and everything with a fast turn-around. The blockage of handset type was removed and *modern* publishing was born. Our twentieth century marketing economy driven by advertising became possible.

The concept is simple. Rather than assembling letters individually, the Linotype assembled molds or dies, called a matrix or matrices. The type was then cast line by line. The matrix was dropped into position by hitting a key on a board that looked similar to our keyboards today. The matrices were recycled. Teams of typesetters made it possible to cast up to 150 characters a minute. It still took many typesetters to keep up with one press, but a great stride had been made. Print production soared.

A PICTURE IS WORTH A 1,000 WORDS

ALL THE DECORATIONS THAT MAKE THE WORDS PRETTY

The 1400s were a fantastic time, as mentioned. Everything was coming together as Europe struggled out of the Dark Ages. The techniques for graphic reproduction had been in place for many years; in fact, many centuries. The Copts (a societal group in Egypt) had been using woodcuts to print textiles since at least the sixth century. Throughout medieval Europe, textile printing was common. Etching and engraving techniques were well known by metal workers throughout Europe.

The key was the arrival of paper

Frank and Dorothy Getlein, in their analysis of fine art printmaking titled *The Bite of the Print,* (Bramhall House, 1963) are convinced that everything had been in place for some time. The factor that tipped the scales was the arrival of cheap, plentiful paper. The Arabs had paper in the eighth century. The Moors brought it to Spain by the twelfth. Paper mills were up and running, first in Italy, then in Germany during the late 1300s and early 1400s. By the time Gutenberg and the others were experimenting, paper was common and reasonably priced. It was a resource must be used, as far as creative people were concerned.

The best graphics ever

At the same time Gutenberg was developing letterpress, print-making exploded. Some the best printmakers ever were active: Schongauer, Mantegna, Dürer, Holbein, Bruegel, and countless more. The next century brought the master, Rembrandt van Rijn. These people have never been equaled for artistic creativity within the confines of metal and wood carving (except for the Japanese multicolor woodcuts).

Woodcuts — relief printing for graphics

Designs carved in wood were the easiest to add to printing. Many of you have made linoleum cuts in grade school art classes. This is the remnant of an extremely skilled art form. Dürer's woodcuts, for example, raised symbolic storytelling to new heights. The process is simple in concept. You take a block of wood, paint a picture on it, and carve away anything that is not part of the picture. This leaves the image in relief.

The only difficulty with using woodcuts in printing concerned the size and shape of the wood block used. It had to be type high. In other words, it had to be the same thickness as the type slugs being used. The block also had to be rectilinear, in order to be locked into place with the type slugs. These were simple mechanical problems that were quickly solved.

The techniques were developed until the illustrations were being engraved, with exquisite detail, into laminated end-grain wood blocks. For durability, engravings were also done in metal. This type of engraving was also printed as a relief block. The delicacy of detail is almost unreproducible with current equipment. Scanners at several thousand dpi are required.

Engraving and etching — gravure printing

Engraving and etching were also used for another method of printing. Known as intaglio, this technique was the major source of printmaking for fine art. It was not used by the printing industry until much later, due to the virtual impossibility of using type with this technique (until photographic production came into existence).

Intaglio is the reverse of relief printing. Here the concept is to cut the image into the block or sheet of metal. The entire plate is thoroughly inked up with a roller. Then the plate is polished, leaving the ink in the recessed image areas. The plate is then cov-

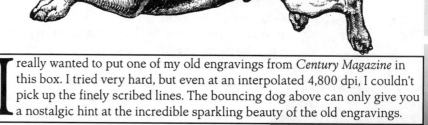

I really wanted to put one of my old engravings from *Century Magazine* in this box. I tried very hard, but even at an interpolated 4,800 dpi, I couldn't pick up the finely scribed lines. The bouncing dog above can only give you a nostalgic hint at the incredible sparkling beauty of the old engravings.

ered with slightly dampened paper and run through a press that squeezes the paper into the image to pick up the ink.

There were many advantages to this technique, especially with etching. For the first time, it was possible to reproduce drawings.

Because etchings were drawn directly on a coated plate, with the image etched through the scratches in the coating, hand-drawn lines could be reproduced in quantity. Rembrandt's etchings demonstrate a fluidity of line and a mastery of line control that has never been matched.

Intaglio is a very high-quality technique. Careful inking allowed very fine lines and dots to be printed. Mezzotints and crosshatching allowed for realistic shading. Lines this fine would break or flatten in relief printing. As a result, intaglio was definitely preferred for illustrations. The obvious problem was that the type was all printed in relief. Movable type in intaglio would leave tiny rectangular lines around all of the letters where the slugs joined together. Intaglio illustrations were bound in as separate pages or glued in on pages left blank (termed "tipping" in an image).

Relief printing allowed for movable type. Because the letter shape was raised from the background, the seams between the slugs did not print. In the case of intaglio, these seams would hold ink and print. Intaglio was not used for anything other than illustration until the nineteenth century.

Stone writing — lithographic printing

In the early 1800s, Alois Senefelder was experimenting with an extremely fine-grained limestone quarried in Austria. His idea was to draw on the stone with etching ground (a mixture of asphaltum and wax) and then etch the background. This created a slight relief that could be printed. It was much cheaper than copper.

This idea was no big deal, however. With the advance to rotary presses in a few short years, his technique would have become merely an interesting sidebar. Limestone makes lousy cylinders. However, after further experiments, Senefelder discovered that coating the background with a water solution of gum arabic made it repel ink. In fact, he learned that keeping the gum damp enabled him to ink up the stone with no etched relief at all.

On a perfectly flat stone (with the image created with a greasy ink and the background protected with gum) he could dampen the stone and ink it up by simply running an ink roller over the entire surface. A sheet of paper laid on the inked stone picked up a virtually perfect image with very little pressure. In fact, I remember printing a very good image in college by merely rubbing the paper onto the stone with the heel of my hand.

Senefelder called this process lithography, from the Greek for stone writing. Lithography developed slowly until two key discoveries were utilized. One, images could be made on thin, flexible metal plates. Two, these images could be produced with a photographic emulsion. However, this did not happen until the 1950s.

Offset printing

The only problem still left was the reversed images. In the early twentieth century, a major discovery was made. By printing the plate first to a rubber blanket cylinder and then to the paper, the reversed image problem was solved. More importantly, the paper damage from all the water was greatly lessened and the blanket allowed lithographic printing on textured paper.

INTAGLIO GRAVURE
ENGRAVED OR ETCHED PRINTING
Image is cut or etched into the plate surface. Ink is forced into the recessed image. The paper pulls ink out of recesses.

PHOTOGRAPHY

Printing developed a rich history of beautiful work. Relief printing, or letterpress, on quality paper has a richness of surface that is hard to describe. The image is slightly debossed, or recessed, into the surface of the paper. Intaglio flattens the paper leaving an embossed, or raised, image. Wood pulp paper did not exist, the sheets used were of a quality that can hardly be found anymore except in handmade watercolor paper.

The problem was the slowness. Type was composed by hand. Illustrations were carved by hand. Sheets were printed very carefully, but very slowly. In addition, the quantity of illustrations was very limited. It took many days, if not weeks for an engraver to transcribe a painting into a printable illustration on a type-high block.

Photography uses a machine to cause the real world to draw its own image.

Photography changed that forever. Photography eventually made the entire page a graphic illustration. Basically, photography uses a machine to cause the real world to draw its own image. It's a simplistic definition, but it shows the difference between hand rendering and photographic reproduction. It takes incredible skill to illustrate realistically. Photographic illustration is a photomechanical process that can be done completely by machine. The skill becomes one of selection rather than creation.

There are many people with good taste who have no illustration skills. As a result, mechanical means of graphic production are extremely popular. This is one of the major reasons why Photoshop is so popular today. Drawing in FreeHand or Illustrator takes a much different skill level than compositing scanned images in Photoshop.

Photography totally revolutionized our industry. No longer needed were entire careers like engraving, die cutting, lockup of letterpress plates, and so forth. It took 150 years to effect the change completely, but the change was total.

Photographic offset lithography

Lithography using photographically imaged plates, offset onto a blanket using rotary presses, took over the printing industry in the last half of the twentieth century. By the 1980s, letterpress was reduced to a trade service for offset lithography. When die cutting, foil stamping, embossing, or other services that required hard physical stamping action were needed, shops sent that work to the few remaining letterpress operations.

In this new technology, all type was set photographically. All artwork was photomechanical. All plates were produced photographically. Roger Black called it "the age of the X-Acto knife." Photographic pieces were cut, moved, arranged, trimmed and cleaned up with technical pens and #11 craft knives. Pasteup ruled the industry.

Graphic History

LITHOGRAPHY
FLAT SURFACE
Chemical difference between image and background. Ink adheres to image, water repells ink on background.

Digital production

Digital production is much more revolutionary now than photography was then. At this point, virtually all design and most prepress is done digitally. However, photography was merely an incredible aid to a difficult process. Digital production is changing our society now as much as printing did in the fifteenth century.

Printing has become technologically democratized. It is now common for top quality work to be done by companies made up of one person. By simply acquiring the appropriate software, hardware, training, and experience, it is possible to produce everything from the same computer console with your own digital press (assuming that you have enough money). This is the reason many of you are studying to learn this career.

An industry in change

Our modern printing industry is a vastly different place than it was a mere decade ago. In 1994, the Graphic Arts Technical Foundation (GATF) listed seventeen different industry segments. Even though GATF claimed to have the latest knowledge of the industry, by the time it published its book, the digital revolution was breaking up those neat categorizations. Even those categories that still remain are being radically altered by the paradigm shift.

The democratization of the craft guild

Printing, before the 1990s, was a guild populated by highly skilled specialists. These wizards practiced a difficult and obscure craft in a rarefied atmosphere outside the understanding of normal folk. Unless a person was part of the industry, communication with the industry was very difficult. A different language was spoken: picas and points, leading, gripper, guides, negs, seps, lineart, stats, Veloxes, Matchprints, halftones, line screen, and so on. If you didn't speak the language, you couldn't join the club. Many companies that produced or used a lot of printed matter hired one special person who could communicate with "those printers."

An economy based on marketing cannot ignore technology requiring yearly upgrades.

Beginning in the mid-1980s, this world was shaken to its roots. All of a sudden, all those things that could only be done in darkrooms or under special lighting by highly skilled masters became accessible to the general public. Predictably, the result was chaos.

For a while, desktop publishing was seen as a joke in poor taste. Everyone lamented the passing of huge industry segments, but it was assumed that digital publishing would fade away because of a lack of quality. Of course, it didn't. The economic pressures were too great. An economy based on marketing cannot ignore a technology that requires yearly upgrades. Digital production is a marketer's dream come true. Once a person enters the digital arena, she is at the mercy of marketing pressures that are unprecedented in the history of humankind.

The printing industry is huge

Virtually every segment of modern society requires printed materials. The advertising industry claims that every individual sees thousands of ads every day. Many of these ads are printed. Just thinking of printed advertisements brings huge industries to mind: magazines, newspapers, product labels, and packaging pop up instantly. A modern discount bookstore has selections that boggle the mind in quantity as well as quality.

Think of lawyers with their legal documents; bankers with their numerous forms and disclaimers; small businesses with letterheads, business cards, envelopes, purchase orders, invoices, shipping receipts. Add to that direct mail, plus posters, bumper stickers, CD packaging and labels, textbooks, software documentation. Then remember the huge packaging industry ... the list is endless and still growing.

Printing is still the fourth largest manufacturing industry compared with industries like automobile manufacturing, appliances, and so forth. GATF stated in 1994 that out of the twenty major manufacturing groups in the U.S. Government's Standard Industry Classification system, we are first in the number of establishments with more than 60,000.

Blue collar to white — a whole new image

As large as it is, our industry has made a paradigm shift. By leaving the guild of wizards behind in their large, expensive niches, much else has changed also. Printing used to be a dirty industry filled with ink and dust and huge piles of paper scraps. Before the modern era, with OSHA, EPA, and industry safety standards, it was very dangerous. It used chemicals that not only stunk, but also ate skin. It was filled with tremendous mechanical devices that commonly ate fingers, if not whole hands. Printing was perceived as hard work done in grimy sweatshops by uneducated mechanics.

Our industry has shifted from a difficult, dangerous craft to office production.

Digital production is an entirely new ball game. It takes place in carpeted, air-conditioned offices with windows. There are pictures on the walls. Most of the participants are educated, often college graduates. Printing is no longer a craft handed down by apprenticeship. It is a technological skill learned from books and specialized training, practiced at computer terminals, and no longer bound to any location.

The tremendous variety

As stated, there are more than 60,000 printing establishments employing more than 1.5 million people, without even considering office production and SOHO shops. These range from one- or two-person store fronts to multibillion-dollar corporations. The industry is dominated by small firms employing from one to twenty-five people. A two- or three-person shop can easily generate several hundred thousand dollars worth of

Graphic History

Skill Exam Rules

You will always see my little friend above when a skill exam or miniskill is suggested. If you are familiar with my teaching style, you already know that the timing and completion of all skill exams is entirely on your schedule (unless you have contrary instructions from your instructor or mentor). The complete rules are found in Appendix A or on your CD-ROM linked off the home page.

printing a year. A company with twenty-five employees can produce several million dollars worth of business. The largest printers gross many billions per year with tens of thousands of employees.

To give some order, let's categorize our industry with three main groups:

- **Public printers:** those used by the general public
- **Traditional industry segments:** those serving other industries like advertising and marketing, producing software production manuals, books, pharmaceutical legalese, and so forth
- **The new completely digital segments (public and traditional):** both those appearing to service the industry and those offering new services unheard of before the 1990s like the Kinko's™, Sir Speedy™, Mailboxes, Etc.™ phenomenon.

Public printers

There are three subcategories in this group:

- Screen and sign printers
- Quick printers and copy centers
- Commercial printers

These three categories have direct contact with the general public. These are the printers most people think of when looking to meet printing needs. If they need "quality custom printing," they look for a commercial printer. If they are motivated primarily by price and quick turnaround, they seek out a quick printer or a copy center.

Screen and sign printers

Screen and sign printers formerly used a totally different technology: screen printing; plus, they did many signs by hand. This is yet another industry segment that has radically changed in the past decade.

Screen printing uses stencils that are adhered to support screens for the production of signs, T-shirts and clothing, uniforms, and many different types of product manufacturing. Screen printing inks are opaque (unlike most printing) and screens are flexible. This allows screen printers to print on metal sheets, wooden plaques, clothing, bottles, control panels, and the like. The opaque inks work well on colored surfaces. Screen printing is relatively slow. Often each piece is hand-printed with a squeegee and screen. For printing done on materials that cannot be fed through a printing press, such as like wood boards, shirts, and the like, screen printing is often the only option.

Sign printers used to be sign painters. Signs were hand-painted by one of the last holdouts of handcrafted tradition. Digital production has largely wiped them out with computerized vinyl cutters. The same software that produces graphics for "normal printing" can be used to produce files that operate plotters with knives that cut type and illustrations out of pressure-sensitive vinyl. In some areas, this technology was first used to produce the sponsor graphics on race cars. It has quickly taken over the sign industry. Not only is the type quality much better, but it was also much cheaper.

SCREEN PRINT
Flat surface. Image is opened into stencil. Stencil is adhered to a support screen. Ink is squeegeed through the openings onto paper.

Quickprinters

Quick and commercial printers in the latter part of the twentieth century shared a common technology – offset lithography. Quick printers handled the low-quality, fast-turnaround clients. The original ads in the late 1960s and early 1970s often revolved around, "Come in, have a cup of coffee, and take your printing home with you." They were built on a new technology – photo-direct plates. These plates were made of paper or plastic. They were produced directly from original camera-ready copy on special copy cameras called platemakers.

What a joke!

Because these plates stretched and could only be crudely lined up on the press, multicolor work was almost out of the question in the beginning. In addition, because all photos and artwork had to be on the original, only very coarse reproduction techniques could be used. Quick printers were considered a joke by many traditional commercial printers. As a result, they quickly took over huge segments of the printing market almost totally unhindered. Most people were not going to pay $100 or more for a 100 copies when the neighborhood quick printer could do acceptable work for less than $5 in less than 10 minutes.

Quick printers worked on much higher profit margins by severely limiting their output to a few standard ink colors on a few standard sizes of a few types of paper. The other enabling technology was the offset duplicator. Duplicators eliminated much of the mechanical perfection found in printing presses in favor of ease of operation and speed of turnaround. A photo-direct plate could be shot and hung on a duplicator in less than 5 minutes for less than $3. Since duplicators ran at 6,000 to 9,000 impressions an hour, a thousand black-on-white letterheads could be produced easily in 15 minutes.

The copier invasion

The electrostatic copier created havoc in the printing industry. Based on an entirely new printing method, a large percentage of printers initially saw it as little threat. By attracting toner to a sheet of paper using electrical charges, these copiers were able to make a single copy for a few pennies. In the beginning they were very crude with pale streaky solids and very low resolution. They were restricted to black toner.

Before very long, industry giants like Xerox, Kodak, and the Japanese brought out printing-quality copiers. Soon there were printing-quality color copiers. Originally, these had the same limitations as early quick print, but they rapidly grew very sophisticated. Copiers added in-line bindery capabilities like collating and stitching. In many ways, they produce better quality than the duplicators: larger and denser solids, more consistent color, and very small setup costs.

Mini #1
A Bookmark

This first little project is simply meant to get your feet wet. It's just a fun exploration of the software, with a chance to make a promo for your company that might actually be useful. It is hoped that you will use this skill to make a bookmark to promote your graphics studio (or whatever it is you call yourself).

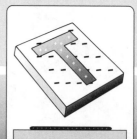

ELECTROSTATIC Laser Printers
FLAT SURFACE
Electrical difference between image and background. Toner adheres to positively charged image, negative charge repels ink on background.

Quick printers utilizing copiers grew like weeds, and were set up to be the first to capitalize on digital production. Much of the new technology is the logical descendant of the copier. They print better, faster, and larger, but the concepts are the same. Digitally, we call the copier a laser printer.

The first digital printers

At present, quick printers can be totally digital. If we still haven't connected, think Kinko's™. The old duplicators are rapidly being replaced by small presses using digitally produced plates to produce the spot color work that is still unavailable on copiers. Since plain-paper copiers and high-resolution laser printers have become common office equipment, quick printers have had to boost design quality, color capabilities, and service to stay in business.

Commercial printers

You are not far wrong if you assume that commercial printers are often kin to dinosaurs. But commercial printing is not dead. Many commercial printing operations are growing faster than they ever have. In fact, this is where much of the excitement is in the new digital paradigm. The thriving printers are focusing on new and exciting quality advances, with digital equipment.

Commercial printers are the top of the heap in printing in terms of quality, versatility, and price. This is custom manufacturing at its best. Every run is custom production, to exacting standards under tight deadlines with uncommon teamwork. Versatility is the key and quality is the byword. A commercial printer might produce virtually anything else you can think of, at a quality most consider perfection.

This is custom manufacturing at its best.

Typographic errors, color variability, or similar problems often result in customer rejection and reprints at the printer's expense. Printing clients demand and receive a level of perfection that is difficult to comprehend outside the industry. On a printed piece with literally thousands of elements, one misspelled word causes total rejection of the job. All of this is done at great speed under ridiculous deadlines.

Why would anyone in their right mind even bother to try? It has often been argued that no printer is in her right mind, by definition, but we'll ignore that attitude. The real reason is usually the terrific sense of satisfaction when an extremely difficult job is done well. Printers are in the business of meeting client needs. Producing a gorgeous printed piece that greatly surpasses the client's expectations is a feeling that cannot be explained. It must be experienced. Be careful though, it can be addictive!

Big iron and high tech

Commercial printers do all of this with an incredible array of equipment. Huge multicolor presses costing millions of dollars are the norm. A medium size press (5-color – 40") is around 12 feet wide, 12 feet high, 40 feet long and weighs in at around 60 tons. Full-color (hereafter correctly called process color) printing requires tolerances of a few thousandths of an inch. Strippers assemble photographic negatives to a perfection obtained with 12X magnifying glasses (called "loupes"). Scanners that have replaced cameras commonly cost a hundred thousand dollars. It is euphemistically called a capital-intensive industry (meaning the machines cost a lot!).

Largely because of equipment costs, the conversion to digital production has been slow and methodical, but the benefits cannot be ignored. In addition, well over 90 percent of all artwork for printing is produced on a computer. Some companies now charge extra for artwork produced traditionally. It is no longer part of the normal workflow and requires old skills that are increasingly hard to find. The result is digital or perish.

TRADITIONAL INDUSTRY SEGMENTS

Printers in traditional industry segments cater to specific industries that produce huge amounts of specialized printing. Here, the concept of custom manufacturing is almost gone. Let's look at one that demonstrates the specialization clearly: business cards. Very early in my career, I received this advice: "The most economical way to deal with business card customers is to hand them a $50 bill and tell them to go down the street to your competitor." It was not told to me as a joke.

The labor required to produce custom business cards means that you must charge $100 per color for 500 cards or you lose money. There are several companies who have capitalized on this fact by providing business cards as a trade service to printers for approximately $20 per 1,000 cards. They do this by limiting color and paper choices and printing either hundreds of designs at a time or by printing on precut paper that is slitted rather than trimmed on a paper cutter. They make very good money and provide a real service to other printers.

Most traditional segments use the same concept. Usually they are built on specialized technology. Often this technology is simply a web press as opposed to a sheetfed press. Web presses print on continuous rolls of paper rather than feeding individual sheets of paper through the press. This allows for several savings. First, they are faster. Second, they can print on thinner and therefore cheaper paper. Third, they can often print both sides at the same time, often in process color. In addition, many web presses can do all of the finishing in-line. This means that they can produce finished product that is labeled, folded, collated, bound, trimmed, wrapped, and palletized. The labor savings alone are considerable.

Web printing is the basis of the following segments:

- Book publishing
- Newspapers
- Periodicals
- Large catalogs and directories

Packaging segments have to feed very thick paper like corrugated boxes and folding cartons. Some have to print on unusual surfaces like bottles. They often use flexography which uses flexible rubberlike plates (letterpress). Recent statistics suggest that nearly 30% of all printing is done on flexographic presses (*Adobe Magazine*, Fall 1999).

Graphic History

Web printing

Some of you may not realize that there are two basic types of web presses and two completely different uses. The COLD-SET web is normally very low quality and very cheap, using 85-line screens and crude registration. HEAT-SET web, on the other hand, has the same clientele and usage as commercial printing. Some of the better printing in the world is presently being done for magazines using heat-set webs.

Some require specialized die cutting, like label manufacturing. Others have artistic considerations with extremely complex production, like the enormous greeting card industry. All of these have gone digital to some extent. Most use at least digital artwork. My last book, for example, was printed directly from PDF files that I FTPed to the printing company. This type of workflow — where the artwork was produced in New Mexico, proofed in Colorado, printed in Canada, with production management in New York — has become commonplace in book publishing.

The training in this book is geared toward work with quick and commercial printers, digital and traditional. However, you can cross-train easily to any of these traditional segments. Just remember, these portions of our industry have specialized needs. If you keep an open mind, you will fit in quickly.

The digital newcomers

There are several blossoming industry segments that have no counterpart in traditional printing. Digital production is the enabling technology for them. There will certainly be others. We looked at these in Chapter 2. We won't spend much more space here, because this is a very quickly changing field.

A closely allied industry is Web design and production. *Electronic Publishing* magazine mentioned, in the summer of 1999 (in one of its industry trends articles,) that the average graphic designer now spends up to 45 percent of his or her time on Web design. New color and multimedia capabilities allow options that have not even been recognized yet. Book publishing is likely to radically change. Digital storage of specialized books that can be printed one at a time, as requested, is just one option.

Short-run color

This brand-new capability, short-run color, has been enabled by digital presses. Process color used to be the dividing line. The technical requirements were very demanding, the equipment was very expensive, and the labor costs were very high due to the skill levels needed. Now, color has been made available to everyone.

Most prognosticators expect this to be one of the fastest growing segments of the printing industry for years to come. Instead of having pieces typeset to avoid the typewriter look, people are now having pieces printed in color to avoid the laser printer look.

On-demand and variable printing

On-demand printing is yet another brand-new capability enabled by digital production. By coupling a powerful computer with a great deal of storage to a digital press with in-line bindery ability, it is possible to produce custom books. We are not talking about short-run publishing here. We are looking at a customer who asks for chapters 1 through 6 and 9 through 11 from one book, chapters 14 and 27 from a second book, with a custom foreword — and wants twenty-five copies. On-demand printing can do this at the current traditional cost of the book.

Additionally, there is the prospect of blending data with templates to print customized mailings for an entire list of clients. A million pieces, all personalized, is now more than a theoretical

Graphic History

possibility. We are not simply discussing personalized phone bills. We are looking at custom brochures based on data gathered by telephone operators. Local real estate companies in my area pay for a general company brochure that is custom-printed in small quantities for individual realtors, with personal pictures and information about the individual realtor, and photos of the houses listed by that person. This same printer is producing baseball trading cards for the local Little League teams.

The possibilities are enormous. Professors can have textbooks custom-tailored to their curricula. Catalog publishers can produce custom catalogs for specific demographics and even very small targeted groups. In the near future, you may call a large retailer like Sears or Spiegel™ on an 800 or 900 number, and have a catalog sent to you that contains only the products you are looking for in the sizes you wear. (In case you don't know, those $10 catalogs you grudgingly pay for from Sears, Speigel™, and Penny's probably cost over $25 a piece to produce.)

CD-ROM/multimedia

This area of publishing is still in its infancy, although you certainly wouldn't know that at my school where students are convinced that this is the best thing since white, sliced bread. The economic pressures are tremendous for this type of publishing solution (even though most early practitioners use it like an advanced video game). With CD-R writing recorders in the low three-figure range, a single person with a personal computer can output a CD catalog at much less cost than traditional catalog production.

Multimedia is the thing that excites students – animation, interactivity, training CDs, video games, and so forth. However, this industry has not grown nearly as fast as software and hardware marketers predicted. I suspect it is because of a simple phenomenon that I have heard best expressed in a quote that I heard attributed to Frank Romano. "CDs will not become commonplace until the industry solves the problem of the three Bs – bedroom, bathroom, and beach." I think he is exactly right.

On the other hand, the easy interactivity offered by Acrobat PDFs cannot be ignored. It is so easy to send a proof, prospectus, or sample via email and the Internet that this type of multimedia is growing fast.

An industry in flux

In general, now is a time of great opportunity. We are still in an exciting period of growth, although digital publishing in general is reaching a maturity long longed for. The benefits offered by the newest updates are not nearly as necessary any longer. It remains to be seen if InDesign becomes necessary, or merely fills a niche of top-end process color production (and process color will never become the normal of the industry).

THE NEW FIELD OF GRAPHIC DESIGN

Graphic design history is a very interesting phenomenon that comes on the tail end of a 500 year history of printing and publishing. Until very recently in human history graphic design really didn't

even exist, although the skills were known, in part. Conceptually, it was not even considered until the later part of the nineteenth century. On a societal level, graphic design did not play a dominating role until the later part of the twentieth century. As we enter the new millennium, however, excellence in graphic design is now an assumed baseline for most companies.

The restrictions of letterpress

Much of this slow development was due to the nature of the craft (prior to 1900 we couldn't even speak of an industry). Almost everything was controlled by the physical limitations of printing technology until after World War II. Only toward the middle of the twentieth century did it become common to photographically etch letterpress blocks. These blocks had to be exactly rectilinear with an exact thickness. The entire process took a great deal of skill and experience, even when done photographically.

What graphic techniques were available were restrained by the difficulty of the materials. Engravings are beautiful, but the beauty of the engraved art on a dollar bill is hard to compare with a monochrome ink Sumi landscape, let alone a fully developed oil painting. Printing techniques, in general, could not be used to enable mass production of fine art images. Graphic elements were relatively rare. Often they were not used at all. Magazines of the mid-1800s are almost entirely type. There was virtually no concept of illustrating a story or adding a graphic for impact. In fact, the New Yorker magazine was considered revolutionary in the 1920s when they developed the first real way to use graphics on a regular basis, other than in advertisements. They took the empty space on their pages and filled it with cartoons — which could go anywhere because they were stand-alone graphics.

Verbal skills dominated. In large part, this was due to the fact that words were relatively easy to deal with. Every document was made up of horizontal lines of type arranged in vertical columns. This is merely fact; there is no quality connotation attached to this fact. Rectilinear construction, left to right, top to bottom, is merely the European method. As most of you are aware, other cultures have very different arrangements. Middle Eastern cultures write right to left, top to bottom. Asian documents are commonly written top to bottom, right to left.

The effective use of normal

Rectilinear construction is neither good nor bad — it simply is. We all learned to read and write in rectangles. Well over 95 percent of everything we have ever read was lined up in horizontals and verticals — left to right, top to bottom. Simply understanding this fact helps us communicate. When we use "normal flow," people read our message more easily. Normal usage is one of the major tools in design, as you will see in the chapters that follow.

Photographic freedom

As briefly mentioned earlier, the first crack in the wall (of rectangular blocks) was photography. Originally a mere scientific curiosity, it was ignored by printers (much as personal computers were ignored in the 1970s). With photography, it was possible to put pictures of real people and reasonably accurate reproductions of reality, both fine art and natural, into printed products.

GRAPHIC DESIGN BECOMES SELF-CONSCIOUS

Composition was wiped out in the 1950s by photographic production as thoroughly as pasteup was in the 1990s with digital production. You would think that rectilinear limitations would have been shattered — not so.

Because most humans follow the course of least resistance, angled text was risky, at the least. In addition, as graphic design coupled with advertising became commonplace, designers started to realize the power of normality. The useful portions of letterpress form were codified into principles taught at design schools. Once codified, these principles caused many design schools to degenerate into legalism. It is very important to remember the following proverb,

> *"Habitual reactions are desired in a reader. They are disastrous to a designer."* — me, 1999

In general, photography brought little graphic freedom. Mainly, it enabled many more graphics to be used. Photographs became commonplace and graphic design flourished. However, the vast majority of pages and page components continued as rectilinear constructions.

A BRIEF REVIEW OF GRAPHIC ILLUSTRATION

The history of graphic design is tortuous, to say the least. You've followed as we went back to the beginning several times to catch another thread in the tapestry of graphics. We're about to do it again. As we have said, the career itself is relatively new, even though illustration goes back a long ways in time.

Starting with the Renaissance again

In the middle of the fifteenth century, books were amazing, hand-illustrated, hand-lettered, works of art. (The original desktop publishing, as it were.) If you wanted a book, you ordered it from the local monastery, with a two-year wait — minimum. The result of this was no books. By the turn of the century (1500), there were thousands of books in print. The novel had been invented. Popular fiction came into existence. Books reached the middle class and self-education became possible. The only problems were the physical limitations of printing processes available. Because everything had to be cut, carved, or cast out of metal or hardwood, printed graphics were relatively rare. Excellence in graphics almost required printed engravings (fine art prints) that were bound into the books as separate pages. Sometimes they were simply pasted onto blank pages in the book (often covered with tissue paper for protection).

The Industrial Revolution

The nineteenth century revolutionized printing much as the fifteenth century changed our civilization earlier. We entered the marketing age as advertising was invented about the time of the War Between the States.

The rotary press and the linotype were the enabling technology for the daily newspaper. By the end of the century, daily papers were common. Magazines were also developed during this period, but they didn't really come to fruition until the twentieth century. They required illustrations and for that photography was needed.

Photographic processes were discovered early in the nineteenth century. The problem was (and remains) the fact that presses are only capable of printing ink or no ink, black-and-white, color or no color. The need was for a method that would allow the continuous tonal changes of a photograph to be reproduced on a press. By the end of the century, that problem was solved with the halftone. We will briefly cover this process in Chapter 11. If you need thorough knowledge read chapters 24 through 27 in my first book, *Printing in a Digital World.* Suffice it to say that by breaking up a photo into small dots that vary in size, it is possible to fool the eye into thinking that those small dots are really a gray.

Editor domination

The fact of the matter was that editors (who were writers, of course) dominated the industry. This is still true to a large extent. Roger Black suggests, in his lamented, out-of-print, *Desktop Design Power,* Bantam 1991, that this is simply caused by the fact that writers are more verbally persuasive than illustrators. This simple fact enables them to dominate meetings, memos, e-mail, and so on.

Editor domination was absolutely true until the 1930s. This time it was a mere concept that changed things – the picture story. The idea was introduced by Tinseltown gossip rags. It was developed into a powerful communication tool by the magazine giants of the time – *Time, Newsweek, Life, Look,* and many others. The idea was and still is that you can more powerfully affect people emotionally with a series of photographs than you can with words.

The graphic designer emerges

The 1930s and the picture story brought in an entirely new career – the art director. This was the first time that graphic design reached the masthead. Formerly, only editors were listed, now, art and creative directors became an integral part of the process.

We've already mentioned how photo offset lithography impacted the 1950s and 1960s. Advertising agencies grew incredibly powerful and transformed our entire culture. Our culture has been developed under market pressures since that time. The arbitrators of our lives were increasingly people whose job survival was based on their success in sales.

We tend to forget that this is a new phenomenon. Everything we use is now marketed. Without mass response, items are no longer available. Marketing relies largely on printed materials. Our industry continues to grow faster than the economy, as a whole.

THE GROWTH OF COLOR

Color, in printing, has always been a problem. Multicolor etchings, for instance, were horribly frustrating. The desired images required breaking up prints into many colors printed with a different plate. This required the paper to be run through the press many times. Every plate had to fit the others precisely – which is virtually impossible by hand.

For this book I have to assume that you have already been taught color theory and learned about RBY, RGB, CMYK, spot color, and hi-fi color. If you have not, we will talk about it briefly in chapter twelve, they are covered much more thoroughly in *Printing in a Digital World* and *Digital Drawing*, my first two books. Here we'll just note that almost simultaneous with halftone development was separation theory. By taking the subtractive complements of light – cyan, magenta, and yellow – the eye can be fooled into seeing full color in a pile of tricolored halftone dots. The theory is marvelous, the practice is a little more difficult.

Recent developments

By the 1970s, printers were commonly producing work that was absolutely amazing. Six, eight, or more colors became common. Marketers were striving for new ways to grab the reader's attention. Printing was becoming almost as labor-intensive as it had been before the industrial revolution, but now labor cost real money.

Jobs often took hundreds of hours simply to assemble the pieces of film and plate. Press technology improved to the point by 1980 that jobs were commonly rejected for flaws that were printed better than the available technology could produce in the 1950s. It became normal to print 20,000 identical brochures, with only very minor color variations and possibly a dozen rejects for dirt or scratches.

Laser scanners

Separations for the first time became the domain of computers in the late 1970s. Digital scans were much faster, much more accurate, and cheaper than the old camera seps. even though they were still received as film (expensive film). The first scanners cost over a million dollars, and the early scans cost several hundred dollars for a full-page separation.

The result of all this was a labor force that was increasingly skilled, and far more specialized. Top-end color printing could not be done without a talented, skilled, and experienced team of professionals. More and more, printshops came to resemble technical laboratories.

NEW CAPABILITIES

Now we are wholly in the new paradigm. We can safely discuss what is available and hike out on a limb to prognosticate the future of our industry. Of course, that future is almost totally digital production. Some of it is recognizable; much of it is brand new. Our industry now has capabilities that were heretofore unheard of. More than that, however, there have been massive changes in our clientele.

Graphic History

A note on digital printing realities

Most of you are using an inkjet printer, usually because it was cheaper. You need to be very careful here. Not only are inkjets normally very inaccurate with color – they usually cannot print PostScript. However, even assuming that you have a professional inkjet, they are incredibly expensive to use. Consumable costs are commonly $3 to $5 per print. Large format inkjet prints are usually charged by the square inch. This is why almost all digital presses are electrostatic. They can commonly output a duplex tabloid sheet for around fifty cents per print.

"... customers want their printing done faster, in smaller quantities, with good quality, often in color, personalized, and at reasonable costs." - Mark Kilgore, *Print On-demand Business*, June 1995

Though this article is from the mid-1990s, these tendencies have increased to become the mainstream. Earlier in the quoted article, Mr. Kilgore talks about the clear hunger for on-demand printing from all sectors of the graphic arts community. Now, we designers tend to assume that we can have a one-off printed proof at no expense, for example. Industry advisors have been talking about the increase in the demand for short-run color.

A run length of one

Most of this is based on the unheard-of capability for a run length of one. This is completely different than the traditional conception of short-run printing which is run lengths of under 2,000 impressions. Most of our industry was based on fixed setup charges. Many companies charged the same for anything 1,000 copies or less. The setup charges were sufficient to make paper a negligible giveaway with runs of this length. Formerly, when customers asked for twenty-five copies of a process poster, or fifteen copies of a vehement bumper sticker, or thirty three-color cards for an anniversary dinner, or the like, they were told that it was financially impossible. Now these requests can be filled — easily and profitably.

A brand new concept: On-demand printing

On-demand printing — that's a cute idea: professional-quality form letters and personalized junk mail. You are still thinking too small. The possibilities are outrageous — and endless:

- You fill out a small form and e-mail it to your favorite mail order house. By return mail, normal delivery times, you receive a 200-page, full-color catalog filled with only those things you are interested in, listing your sizes and your favorite fabrics and colors.

- You have a product line of over 300,000 items to sell to doctors' offices, urgent care clinics, hospitals, day surgery units, ambulance companies, and the like. The entire catalog is 5,000 pages broken into 750 sections ranging from 2 pages to 144 pages. Your sales personnel talk to your clients to get a feel for what sections they need. Catalogs are then ordered with just what is needed: 3 10-section, 130-page catalogs for the ambulance unit; 250 200-section, 1,650-page catalogs for that hospital; 15 25-section, 600-page catalogs for the urgent care facility; and so on.

- You need three posters to advertise your annual charity fund-raiser. The display locations (that have been offered for free) measure 4'x10' with super exposure.

  This list could go on and on for pages. The feature that ties them together is short-run, personalized printing. This is on-demand printing.

Warehousing

One of the major problems with traditional printing was the need to print large enough quantities to ensure a decent price (amortizing the setup charges). This meant that those extra copies had to be stored until they were needed. It was common to print several thousand brochures, distribute 1,500, and trash the rest because a phone number was arbitrarily changed by a new area code. Between the printing and the tossing, cubic feet of storage space were tied up for a year or more. Of course, there are always those 75,000 300-page color catalogs cunningly printed without prices.

On-demand printing warehouses digitally. That brochure is kept as a digital document. You print 1,385 for this mailing; 250 for that store opening; 350 for the new saleswoman with her bio inserted with her photo (in color) — you get the picture by now.

The cost per piece is a little higher (often quite a bit higher). However, the savings in expensive warehousing space and waste is more than enough to cover it. This is true, even for direct mail. The old paradigm of mass mailing is rarely economically feasible now that delivering a brochure to a mailbox has gone from a few cents apiece to several dollars each.

DIGITAL PRINTING IS NOT THE TOTAL ANSWER

Back in the mid-1990s many of us thought we saw the end of traditional printing. This has not come true yet. There is no reason to believe that digital presses will soon produce mass market novels, Juicy Fruit™ labels, or cereal boxes. Almost all of the design and prepress is currently digital, but we will continue to need to know the requirements of the traditional printing technologies. Every technology has specific needs and requirements, advantages and disadvantages.

We will always need to know the printer, and their technology, before we begin designing.

The choice of the publishing technology and supplier will remain the first decision of the designer. Many of the technologies have conflicting artwork requirements in resolution, colors, registrations, and so forth. If we are designing a print/Web package, we may want to start with a Websafe color palette. However, we will have to produce everything in high resolution and then cut it down to the crudities of the Web. You cannot go the other way without wasting hours in nonchargeable time.

Digital printing has already taken over many areas

Some of the digital segments (like sign cutting) have realized such a market advantage that the old methods are almost gone. For others, like quick print, the change is a little more gradual though it does appear to be irresistible. Here, like almost everywhere, the front end is completely digital — in your hands specifically. The digital presses are becoming more and more dominant. Worn out equipment is almost always replaced with digital solutions. This trend will increase.

Skill #1

Arroyo Riders

This first skill exam is deceptively simple. Your task is to lay out the copy exactly as seen in the rough on your CD or Web site. The design flaw renders the project entirely useless. Have fun!

In addition, there are many, like Kinko's™, that have been completely digital for years now. These digital production centers are transforming quick print as we knew it. Most of them are headed for online document reception and Web-based job tickets. Companies like R. R. Donnelley, Sir Speedy™, and others have built huge centralized digital production centers. RRD's center for AlphaGraphics™ (their subsidiary) is built next door to the main FedEx™ hub in Memphis where they can ship their printed materials as late as 3:00 AM. The AlphaGraphics™ franchises send in jobs via modem for delivery the next day. Sir Speedy has a similar setup with multiple centers around the country.

Large-format inkjets

One of the strongest, and fastest growing, areas of digital production is large-format and grand-format color. Here digital printers not only dominate the market, they have revitalized it into one of the fastest growing segments of our industry. Grand-format printers give us new capabilities like bus-side graphics and hundred foot by two hundred foot posters hanging from the sides of skyscrapers.

Inkjets dominate large-format color. There are a large variety of these printers that will output 36 to 72 inches wide and a couple dozen feet long. They will only print 100-line screen, but this is exceptional quality for large posters and small billboards. The substrate used also works great in light boxes for backlit posters (think huge, glowing photographic displays). As a result, large-format inkjets are becoming dominant in the display and presentation fields. Large, gorgeous, full-color trade show booths can be built for very reasonable cost.

Grand-format printers print rolls that are seven to more than 20 feet wide with length only limited by the size of the rolls supplied. The huge skyscraper posters are printed on what appears to be plastic window screen material. The resulting billboard prints are simply stretched over the frames of the billboards.

Top-quality inkjet

This is a new capability. Iris inkjets are one of the best and most accurate color printers on the market. Traditional printing professionals still distrust the fact that the dot structure is gone. The fact is that the prints are gorgeous, continuous tone images. Many shops are using them for in-house proofing.

The new usage is in the world of fine art. More and more, Iris inkjets are being used for limited edition, fine art prints of original, digital art. By printing on 100 percent rag paper, a print can be output that cannot be distinguished from an original watercolor. The remaining problem is fugitive ink. This has supposedly been solved with pigmented inks, but the technology is so new that no one really knows how long the color will last before fading.

FOR MORE "NORMAL" WORK
DIGITAL PRESSES

Let's just talk about printing for a while — good old-fashioned, "I need multiple copies of an original" printing. We have an incredible variety of digital presses. Some do exceptional quality very slowly (like the Iris inkjets). Some produce very good quality pretty fast. Some print excellent quality very fast, but only 1-bit.

Small amortized costs

One of the major advantages with digital presses is the fact that setup charges are greatly reduced (commonly less than $10). Traditional printing required camera shots, negs, flats, rubylith, and so on. For example, we used phenomenal amounts of masking sheets, tape, and X-Acto blades. All of this is gone. With it has gone much of the labor.

As a result, digital printing makes most of its saving in the first few hundred prints. Instead of everything under 1,000 copies being the same, we have $0.75 for one copy, $7.50 for 10, $75 for 100, and so on.

Traditional printing spreads the startup charges thin enough to pass digital, in cost per copy, at around 1,000 to 2,000 copies. By 2,500 to 5,000 impressions, offset is clearly cheaper. Of course that's at present rates. Process color digital presses are getting into the $0.25 per copy range. A Riso digital mimeograph produces at as little as $0.005 per copy per color (nonstandardized spot color). Traditional printing cannot begin to compete against that.

There is a general perception that printing is ridiculously expensive.

If it is true that digital presses will become the equipment of choice for everything up to 10,000 impressions, our industry is in for more shock. What is ignored in a lot of the speculation is the fact that many, if not most, people consider printing to be overpriced. There is a general perception that printing is ridiculously expensive. Very few people outside our industry know how difficult quality offset lithography is. Many people are more than willing to take the slight quality reduction of most digital technology for the return of more reasonable printing bills.

Digital has gotten much larger than anyone thought sooner than they imagined, and that trend will continue. There are five factors pushing digital printing to dominance. They are almost unavoidable. The goads toward change are:

- Economic pressures to cut costs far below the present levels, to get a competitive edge;
- A global economy requiring global marketing;
- A nonmechanical labor force wanting and needing fully automated equipment in the developed countries;
- The pressure to get things done in ever-shorter periods of time to keep ahead of the rush of society;
- The need for personalization in an overpopulated society.

Printing will continue to grow

No one is predicting that printing will go away. In fact, it will become even more prevalent. What will happen is that printing will go the way everything else is going. There will be many more small

printing centers (especially franchises) and traditional capabilities will be in the hands of huge conglomerates. The midsized printers are having the most trouble. Just as color houses with their expensive laser scanners had to change to service bureaus or die, printers will continue to change.

ELECTRONIC MEDIA

Just when you thought the chapter must conclude, we have to cover the new publishing media which is entirely digital. Since the mid-1990s, our civilization has been overrun by first the hype and then the reality of the Web. It has become a normal part of business planning, marketing, and even production. The design industry now commonly produces, proofs, and delivers most or all of their products over the Web. The statistics I saw in early 1999 (I believe it was in a TrendWatch article in *Electronic Publishing*) suggest that graphics designers spend about 40% of their time designing for the Web, on average.

Multimedia

Here we find a place where hype has vastly outstripped reality. Outside of training CDs and video games, there is little viable commercial use of multimedia, at this point. This may change if we develop a multimedia reader as ubiquitous as a Walkman, but no one I know sees that on the horizon. The thing that most of us over fifty fail to remember is that the younger generations was nursed on video and considers it as normal as reading. It is often the only source of education and information.

And we haven't even mentioned video games. If you watch military technology shows on the History Channel, you will quickly discover that the new fighter planes are too complicated to be operated by hand. They are controlled with computers by pilots using joysticks and video data on their helmet faceshields – using the skills learned in video games.

As you can see, the titillating uses of multimedia are far beyond what we can reasonably call publishing. However, there is an area that directly applies to us. For example, when I finished my last book, it was very easy to generate a promotional PDF with internal linkages to be downloaded and viewed. This type of interactivity, in PDFs and on Websites, may not be the multimedia found in the hype. However, it is certainly something that most of you will be creating on a regular basis. You already have the software necessary and the learning curve is almost nonexistent. If you can run InDesign, you can add interactivity to a PDF, almost without thought.

Moving on

Now that you have a basic understanding of our industry, how it works and its history, plus an entry level understanding of the capabilities of InDesign, we are ready to move on to the actual production of documents using this incredible working environment. After a little review of typography and a quick look at file management using InDesign, we will proceed with setting up InDesign to work.

1. What are the practicalities of multimedia?

2. Why were quickprinters often the first digital printers?

3. How large is the publishing industry?

4. What is the place of the graphic designer is modern culture?

5. Will digital publishing eliminate traditional methods?

WHERE SHOULD YOU BE BY THIS TIME?

By now you should be ready to do a little work. Produce Miniskill 1 and Skill 1. If you think they are too easy (and if they are not required for your course), practice with any type of document you desire.

DISCUSSION

Talk with your friends and classmates about where you think you fit in the publishing industry. How do you see your skills being utilized?

Talk among yourselves...

Typography

A brief overview of typography and basic typesetting techniques

CONCEPTS

CHAPTER OBJECTIVES

By presenting the history, both publishing and design, this chapter will enable you to:

1. Describe a basic printing workflow
2. Argue the position of multimedia in publishing
3. Discuss the influence of our marketing economy
4. Describe the differences between various printing technologies
5. Present a thoughtful opinion of the position of Web publishing in our industry

LAB WORK FOR CHAPTER

- Skills #2 and #3

DON'T SKIP THIS CHAPTER,

Unless

you are truly knowledgeable about type. Most students have little idea why their documents look like student work and far less than professional.

This chapter will only highlight the basics of typography. If you need knowledge of typography, I recommend reading *Stop Stealing Sheep*, Adobe Press, first published in 1992. It's a fun read that covers the basics. You can order it through the *Desktop Bookstore*: http://kumo.swcp.com/graphics/bookstores — in addition, there are many tips and typographical ideas to help you set better type.

Type is the core of what we do!

Typography

In many ways, every page prior to this chapter has merely been an introduction to this chapter. Although I have included this basic knowledge in all the books I've written so far, this is the first time I get to talk about it in the context of a tool designed for professional typographic production. Just as FreeHand is the master of type manipulation, and nothing can touch it. InDesign is the master of typographic production. We have never had a digital publishing program that can come close to InDesign's capabilities before. Comparing InDesign to QuarkXPress or PageMaker is almost like comparing PageMaker to Word or WordPerfect.

Even though this is a large overstatement, it does emphasize that InDesign has typographic controls that have not been seen since the best of the phototypesetters. All of the controls are not available, even yet. However, this is the first desktop publishing program where you can be confident that the type you produce will look up to professional standards. Quark has always lacked some of the basics. Even ems and ens needed a workaround. PageMaker did better, but justification controls were always weak.

> *Without professional typography neither your clients nor their customers will take your work seriously.*

However, we are getting the cart before the horse again. First I need to make sure that all of you are on the same page as the rest of us. My experience suggests that very few of you have any idea about typography and what it really is. Typographic knowledge is based on hunches and feelings based upon your experience in observing excellence in graphic design. However, many excellent designs have horrible typography. Most wouldn't know typographic excellence if it bit them.

Now, I am not talking about the anal-retentive diatribes regularly seen in the Letters columns of the major industry magazines like *Adobe Magazine, Publish, Electronic Publishing,* and the others. Anything can be carried to an extreme. Even though I have over twenty years of typesetting and type design experience, most of this type of nitpicking is merely irritating to me. How many times have you seen strong written articles on typographic matters by the national gurus in the magazines where a certain adjustment is declared mandatory when you cannot see the differences in the examples presented. I am here to tell you that, even with my experience, I usually cannot see the differences either.

However, this avoids the basic statement of truth. Without professional typography neither your clients nor their customers will take your work seriously. There is a level of typographic professionalism that must be attained. In our marketing culture, where virtually everything is controlled by advertising and marketing, typographic professionalism is a given.

All of us have had constant exposure to excellent typography since childhood. However, that does not mean that you know how to produce it yourself. Bad typography usually results in a vague first impression of discomfort or distrust by the readers of your digital documents. I am convinced that it is one of the reasons why many have trouble taking the Web seriously. With everything in Times and Helvetica, with no typographic controls, the online reading experience is very uncomfortable. All of us give that sigh of relief when the Web page is printed out in a decent font, chosen by us in our browser preference (even though the column width is far too wide for readability). Bad type is very hard to read, even on an emotional/psychological basis.

Type is not just typed!

One of the major concepts of graphic design (often lost in the shuffle) is the centrality of the copy. The Web's latest buzzword is "content," as our prime focus for an excellent Website. Our entire idea is to communicate the client's product as the solution to the reader's need. More than 95% of this communication will take place through the words you place on the document. (If you don't understand this, you need to read books on advertising and design. Those written by David Olgilvy, Roger Black, Robin Williams, among many others, are highly recommended.) This is why this book emphasizes type so strongly.

The standard proverb is that a picture is worth a thousand words. This is true, but it takes an exceptional picture to express exactly the thousand words necessary to produce the desired action on the part of the reader. These pictures can be created. However, they will take much time and money plus the services of an exceptional illustrator or photographer. Even exceptional designers can rarely pull it off without needing additional explanatory verbiage.

... it takes an exceptional picture to express exactly the thousand words needed...

In reality, writers are much more common than illustrators. The level of competence available in wordsmiths greatly exceeds the accessibility of accurate visual communication among illustrators when communicating ideas or concepts. So, in the real world, you will be dealing with words, but we are talking about typeset, not typewritten, words. I will briefly review some of the basic differences in a little bit.

Typography in general

It would be nice if I could assume that you have already had six credits in typography. However, it is common that students have never had any formal instruction in the basics. Although we do not have the time or the space to teach typography here, we do need to review the essentials. This is yet another place where you need to study (if you have not already done so). I am not talking about some of the overkill found in many schools, but a good solid basic knowledge of type. As mentioned, probably the most fun to read is *Stop Stealing Sheep* by Erik Spiekermann and

E. M. Ginger (Adobe Press, 1993). If you go to the cross-references in amazon.com you can find more. It is certainly an area worthy of study.

You will probably find (or have already discovered) that the longer you work in graphic design, the more you fall in love with type. As mentioned above, it is our major avenue of communication. Often, it comprises all of the graphic design of a piece, with many printed projects that have no graphics. For the next few pages, we are simply going to review terminology and basic typesetting knowledge. This is by no means intended to be comprehensive, but it covers what you will need for most purposes. Your knowledge will increase, almost by osmosis, as you continue your career in graphic design.

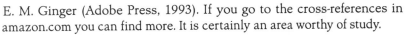

Letterpress terminology

To begin with, most typographic terminology comes from letterpress. This is changing somewhat, for some unimportant words, but most of the present terms will remain. Before you can set type, you must be able to speak the language and understand the concepts.

A typical example is leading (pronounced like the metal). It would be easier to understand (and more accurate) to change the term to line spacing. For a number of reasons, that probably won't happen. Leading came from the letterpress practice of increasing the space between lines of type by adding strips of lead between the rows. These strips came in standard thicknesses: ½-point, 1-point, and so on. In letterpress usage, you could only increase leading and could never have line spacing that was less than the type size. That is no longer true with digital type, but the term remains.

We have gotten ahead of ourselves, however. Before we can continue, you need to know how letterpress type was sized and assembled. The visual aid to the left should help straighten this out. The major fact to remember is that letterpress type was cast metal. The letters were cut into dies and cast into blocks of metal. They all had to be the same height, thickness, hardness, and so on. You had to be able to fit them together into blocks that could be locked into place in the chase. If any letter was a lower height, it wouldn't ink up as you rolled the brayer across the surface of the type. If the rectangles didn't fit together snugly, pieces would fall out during printing. Much of our present type usage comes from factors that were determined by the physical nature of letterpress.

A slug of type always left enough room for the highest ascender and the lowest descender. This was because all type had to fit into evenly sized rectangles to line up properly on the composing stick. Some specialized terms no longer mean the same things. Face, for example, used to mean the actual printing surface of the letter. Now, in common usage, face is used as a synonym for typestyle, font, typeface, and others. The same is true of the word counter. A counter was the recessed area around the letter above which the face of the character protruded. Now it is usually used (if at all) as a term for the open areas inside a P or e or g, for example.

Nevertheless, many terms in our publishing software are from letterpress. For example, the sizing of type remains the same — from top of ascender to bottom of descender, with the capital letters being slightly shorter than the ascenders. This was determined by the necessities of the composing stick, and the slugs of lead that held the individual characters.

Type height measurements are all measured from the baseline, as you can see below. The baseline is the imaginary line that all the letters and

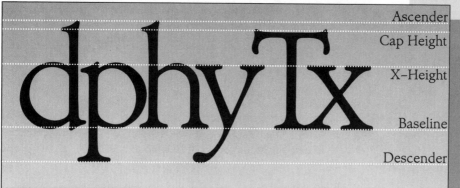

Until the mid-1800s, all type foundries had their own sizes. These sizes were given common names, but there was no universal standard. Some of the names are still familiar. Agate, for example, was a small size used for classified ads (5.5 point).

Around 1875, a type salesman named Nelson Hawkes came up with a measurement system based on one of the more common sizes, the pica. It happened to be 12 points high. In the early 1700s, King Louis XV had established the point as the standard type measurement for French printers. Hawkes decided that 12 points should be called a pica and built an entire type sizing system upon picas and points. It quickly became the standard.

The letterpress point systems did not match inches at all. This caused amazing havoc for traditional pasteup artists and designers. For years, many artists drew all their boards in inches, set all their type in picas, and tried to force things to fit (they often didn't). Picas are going, but points will probably stay.

numbers sit on. The x-height is the height of the lowercase x (the x is the only lowercase letter that is normally flat both top and bottom). Ascenders are the portions of lowercase letters that rise above the x-height, as in b, d, f, h, k, and l. Descenders are the portions that sink below the baseline, as in g, j, p, q, and y. The cap height is the height of the uppercase letters.

The reason that x is specified is that curves have to extend over the lines to look the proper height (as you can see above). Yes, it is an optical illusion. The same is true of letters such as A or V that have points. If the point does not protrude past the guidelines, the letter looks obviously too short. Even your readers, who normally know nothing about type, will sense that something is wrong. Type design has many of these understandings that have become rules. We'll cover some of them as we continue. They are very important because most readers react to type subconsciously. You do not want to upset the reader. You goal is to get the reader to trust you and be comfortable with your message.

Often different typefaces look very different in size, even though they are the same point size. This is primarily due to variations in x-height and built-in leading. This x-height variation is one of the most important factors in picking a type style for your designs. The largest x-heights came from the 1930s and the 1970s. As the new millennium begins, x-heights have become one of the tools we use for stylistic expression. For example, examine this graphic carefully. As you can see, font measurements can and do vary widely. It is a waste of time to

try to make sense of it. Type design is a unregulated industry. All you can do is be aware of the differences, and use them for your purposes, consciously picking type styles that communicate to your readers.

Dealing with points

A point is now normally a seventy-second of an inch, largely due to Apple's screen resolution of 72 dpi. Points are an excellent sizing tool because of the way the human eye works. The smaller sizes of body copy can be clearly differentiated. Type that is one point larger or smaller is almost the smallest increment of size that can be distinguished with the naked eye. Today, and for the foreseeable future, all type is sized in points.

Typographic measurements

Type size: Type size is measured from top of ascender to bottom of descender in points. Capital letters are usually approximately two-thirds of the point size, but a little shorter than the ascender. The x-height is normally around one-third. The most important factor in visual or comparative size is the x-height. Sans serif faces, in general, have larger x-heights.

Leading: Leading was traditionally measured from baseline to baseline. In other words, in phototypesetters (like typewriters) leading was the physical distance advanced to leave room for the next line, measured from the baseline of the original line to the baseline of the following line. To use typewriter imagery: when you hit the carriage return, the roller advanced the distance necessary to allow the next row of type to be typed without overlap. It was simple to calculate leading in traditional typesetting by using a pica gauge.

Here software developers have messed us up. At present, every application has different definitions for leading. No one does it traditionally. InDesign uses one that works, but is hard to figure out in actual use. It measures leading from the baseline of the type to the baseline of the line above. In practice this means you will spend a little time, when setting up your defaults, getting the paragraph styles to work the way you want them to look.

THIS IS TYPESETTING, NOT TYPING

I hope that, by this time, you have realized that type has nothing to do with typing. It is obvious that the terminology is different. However, we have hardly begun. Much more significant than the new language are the actual mechanics of typesetting. The rules have changed! In fact, one of the difficulties in publishing classes today involves a teaching paradox: 1) To get a job, desktop publishers have to be able to type well. 2) Learning to type in a typing class teaches students so many bad habits that you wonder if it is worth it. In fact, the standardized keyboarding classes require many of these typographic errors to receive a passing grade.

At this point, we're going to talk about a group of major differences. By then, we hope, you will be into the new paradigm enough to notice the rest as we finish this section. It is very important to realize that these differences are not minor quibbles. They have a major effect on your ability to communicate with type. They are absolutely necessary for professional document construction and career advancement. *This is my version of the type rules collected by Robin Williams in her great book,* The Mac is Not a Typewriter, *Peachpit Press 1990* (followed by the PC version to stop whining).

1. No double spacing

Typing classes teach that one should always double-space after punctuation. This was required by typewriter character design. All characters on a typewriter are (or were) the same width, or monospaced. The result is that sentence construction becomes hard to see. The virtually random letterspacing makes punctuation difficult to see clearly. A double space emphasizes punctuation and makes it visible.

Typesetting, in contrast, is done with proportional type. This means that every character has its own width that is designed to fit with the other characters. Typeset words form units characterized by even spacing between every letter. In fact, professional typesetting is judged by this characteristic. What is called the *color of the type* is created by this even fit, which is called letterspacing. Professional type should have an even color (no blotchiness) when seen from far enough away that the paragraphs become gray rectangles. Double spacing after punctuation puts little white holes in the type color. Double spacing is no longer needed because the better-fitting words make punctuation a major break. In addition, there is extra white space built into the typeset punctuation characters themselves.

2. Fixed spaces

In general, spaces cause many other problems for people trained in typewriting. On a typewriter, the spacebar is a known quantity. This is because every character in monospaced type is the same width, even the space. This is definitely not true for type. In fact, in type, the space band is rarely the same width as it was the last time you hit the key. Worse, it cannot be predicted without major time-consuming contortions.

This is caused by several factors. The space changes with point size, of course. This is not a problem with typewriters, because they only have one size. More than that, word spacing is one of the defaults that should be set to your standards. InDesign gives you very precise control over word spacing. Not commonly known is the fact that every font has its own spacebar width — there is no standard. Finally, word spacing varies with every line when setting justified copy.

As mentioned, InDesign's multiline justification is a major advance. It automatically helps you to achieve much more even type color. No other mainline publishing software has been able to do this before. However, because it justifies so well, you will be using the four new types of justified copy much more than was formerly common.

These spacebar variations have been solved by using some more letterpress solutions. When type was composed, it was brought out to a rectangle no matter what the alignment was — right, left, centered, or justified. The characters used to do this were blank slugs, called

C&lc

One of the interesting things about type terminology is the strange combo of caps and lowercase. Upper- and lowercase is an old letterpress term describing the method of setting type using two cases of characters, where the capital letters were in the upper case and the minuscules were in the lower case. That's right. What we call lower case letters should be called minuscules. So, Caps is from one terminology and lowercase is from a different technical language. Ah! The vagaries of English strike again! We'll let the proper name for Caps, majuscules, lie for now.

quads, that were a little lower so they would not print accidentally. These quads came in many widths, based on three measurements: em, en, and el. The el space is long gone; it is now called a thin space (if it is even available). InDesign has ems, ens, thin spaces, and hair spaces.

Originally these characters were blanks the width of an M, N, and l, respectively. Slugs with multiple em widths were also used. Eventually, they were standardized. This is something you should memorize. These spaces are now defined as follows: an em space is the square of the point size; an en space is the same height, of course, but half as wide. In InDesign a thin space is an eighth of an em, and their hair space is a twenty-fourth of an em.

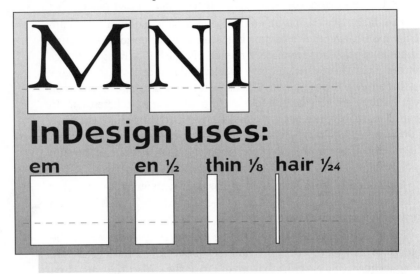

These fixed spaces are used a lot. For example, they should always be used for custom spacing, because the spacebar can vary nonproportionally if you change the point size. Another fact to bear in mind is that numbers and punctuation are normally an en space wide. This means that an en can often be used as a blank when lining up numbers (an em for two numbers) — unless your font uses lowercase numbers which are proportional. You will use ens a lot if you are stuck setting financial statements in annual reports (often at three in the morning). I have used ems. ens, thins, and hairs a great deal in this book to keep the hanging indents lined up on the curved margin on the right pages.

3. Tabs

Actually, custom spacing should normally be done with tabs. They come in four kinds in InDesign: left, right, centered, and special character (as we demonstrated in Chapter 4). All tabs can be set up with leaders. These leaders can be lines, dotted lines, or any set of up to eight repeating characters. Get used to the idea that the spacebar should only be hit once. In typesetting there is no legitimate use of the double space. Clients can, and will, bounce them as typos.

4. En and em dashes

The next major change we need to discuss is dashes. Typewriters only have one: the hyphen. Type has three: the hyphen, the en dash, and the em dash. All three have very specific usage rules.

Hyphen - En Dash – Em Dash —

Hyphen: This is the character used to hyphenate words at the end of a line and for compound words. A hyphen is used in no other places.

Em dash: This dash is an em long. It is a punctuation mark. Grammatically it is stronger than a comma but weaker than a period. Other than that there is no standard anymore. American English is a living language in constant flux. These changes have accelerated in recent years. In many cases, there are no rules anymore. Em dashes are used more every year. In many ways they are very helpful, but traditionalists tend to hate them. In general, all you can do is flag any doubtful use and go with your customer's opinion, right or wrong. Typewriters use a double hyphen for the em dash. This is an embarrassing error to professionals. In fact, it is one of the sure signs of amateurism.

En dash: This dash is an en long. It is used with numbers, spans, or ranges. For example, pages 24–39 or 6:00–9:00 or May 7–12. It is a typo to use a hyphen in these cases.

Finally, do not think you will not be caught. As you can see in the samples above, hyphens are about half as wide as an en dash. They are often higher above the baseline than en or em dashes. Also, they are often slanted with little swashes on the ends, whereas en and em dashes are normally rectangles.

5. No underlines

The next difference has to do with the physical nature of typewriters. Because they only have one size of type, there is no way to emphasize words except for all caps and underlining. Underlining is necessary here. In typesetting, underlining ruins the carefully crafted descenders. In addition, the underlines that come with the type are usually too heavy and poorly placed. More importantly underlined type is usually a typo. Usually, it must be converted to bold or italic.

When copy to be formatted is received from nonprofessionals, underlined type is normally set in a boldface — unless it is the name of a book or periodical, in which case it is set in an italic font. If you decide that an underline is an appropriate solution in a headline, please use a narrow box or a hand-placed line, as in the following example:

TYPING NOT TYPING

The goal of typesetting is to make clean, elegant type that is read without distraction. Underlining is almost as bad as outlines and shadows as far as professionals are concerned. They ruin the unique characteristics of the font. At times they serve a useful design function, but this kind of modification should be used very discreetly — and always intentionally.

6. No ALL CAPS

As just mentioned, all caps is the other way to emphasize words on a typewriter. Typesetting has many more options. There are italic, bold, small caps; larger size, extended, different fonts, and so on. This is not the major problem with using all capital letters, however.

Studies have shown that type in all caps is around 40 percent less legible than caps and lowercase or just lowercase. Using all caps also makes a word much longer than the same word set caps and lowercase. Because our major purpose is to get the reader to read our piece and act on the message, you should never use all caps (unless you have a good reason). For example, caps can be used very effectively to de-emphasize a line of copy. All caps in six-point type was a standard method used to keep people from reading the small print on unscrupulous contracts.

This is an area of major disagreement in the design community. I have given you my experienced opinion. Many currently use all caps for heads. In fact, it is taught as correct by some professors. There is some indication that, in areas like billboards, all caps make no difference. However, I would rather be safe than sorry, plus caps and lowercase usually looks much more elegant. Capital letters, in general, are much cruder and more boxy than their lowercase counterparts.

By the way, all caps reversed is even less legible. In fact, text set that way will not be read unless you force the reader graphically with size, color, or some other such ploy. Sometimes this can be used to the client's advantage. For example, you will regularly see the anti-smoking warning on cigarette ads set small, all caps, reversed out of a gray box.

 WEB USE: It is true that reversed type works well in presentations and on Web sites. However, you cannot print that reversed type from the Web sites so you are adding to the frustration of your viewers (who normally print anything they actually want to read).

7. Real quotes and apostrophes

Here is another place where typewriters are limited by the lack of characters. All typewriters have is inch and foot marks (technically they do not even have that, but use prime and double prime marks). Quotation marks and apostrophes look very different. This is another typographical embarrassment when used wrongly (and they often are).

Inch/foot' "
Open/close quotes' ' " "
Apostrophe '

Typography

8. Kerning and tracking

Here is another typesetting capability that cannot even be considered by typists. We mentioned letterspacing earlier. Letterspacing has a peculiar meaning in digital typesetting, much like leading. This is caused by the fact that with hot type you could only space the slugs apart by inserting slivers of metal. Digitally, anything can be done — and often is.

Tracking is the official term used to replace letterspacing now that we can move letters either closer together or farther apart. In reality, either term can be used and understood. The actual procedure simply inserts or removes space around every letter selected or affected. In typical software programmer style, InDesign uses a digital invention called Range Kerning which is measured in % em and applied to selected type.

Although Range Kerning is used all the time by typographic novices, it is despicable to traditional professionals. Quality typefaces have the letterspacing carefully designed into the font. Changing the tracking for stylistic reasons or fashion changes the color of the type at the very least. At worst, it can make the color splotchy. It always reduces the readability, *which is certainly a mortal sin.*

Kerning is a different thing altogether. Here the problem is with letter pairs. There is no way to set up the spacing around letters to cover all situations: AR is a very different situation than AV; To than Tl; AT than AW. Literally thousands of different kerned pairs are needed to make a perfectly kerned font. Most of them can only be seen at the larger point sizes. Some pairs kern together and some kern apart.

Quality fonts have kerning designed into about a thousand letter pairs. Most cheap fonts have about 128 kerning pairs. In addition, all professional publishing programs allow you to adjust kerning for individual pairs. InDesign gives you keyboard shortcuts. ⌘–left arrow and ⌘–right arrow (PC: Alt–right/left arrow) move letters 1 percent of an em. Adding the Control key moves the letters 5 percent of an em. The best way to show the basic difference is seen in the illustration to the right.

Normal: Edges of character slugs touch	Awkwardly
Tracking: All letters are moved equally	Awkwardly
Kerning: All pairs are adjusted	Awkwardly

As a graphic professional, you are expected to kern everything over 14 point or so — certainly all headlines and subheads. It is entirely normal to spend 15 minutes to a half hour getting the letterspacing perfect for that logostyle or headline. In fact, in FreeHand and Illustrator, it is not at all uncommon to kern the best you can and then convert to paths and modify some of the lettershapes so they fit even better.

9. Use returns only at the end of paragraphs

It seems stupid to have to mention this, but it has become a real problem once again. The culprit is HTML and text copied off the Web.

Every line will have a return at the end of it. If you have a lot of copy you need to use Edit>>Find & Replace>>Text. Search for line breaks (^N) and replace them with spaces. Then search for paragraph breaks (^P) and replace them with spaces or returns as needed. The only returns left should be the returns at the ends of paragraphs. If you need a return without ending the paragraph (a line break), use the soft return (Shift+Return/Enter).

10. Be careful with hyphens

Because typeset line endings are automatic, so is the hyphenation. You can turn it on or off. Hyphenation in InDesign is done by dictionary, which is the best method. Always make sure that you add the proper hyphenation when adding words to your user dictionary by typing in the appropriate discretionary hyphens. Look for bad line breaks caused by unhyphenated words. If necessary, add discretionary hyphens using ⌘⇧ Hyphen (PC: Control Shift Hyphen). These must be used to cause words to break where they should. Proof very carefully: clean-ed is not acceptable (or the many others of its ilk).

Another problem is that automatic hyphenation can create hyphens for many consecutive lines. Here there is sharp debate. Most of us agree that two hyphens in a row should be the maximum (a three-hyphen "stack" looks odd). InDesign allows you to set that limit.

Yet another problem comes when you run into something like two hyphens in a row; then a normal line; then two more hyphens. The final problem comes when the program hyphenates part of a compound word. **BE CAREFUL WITH HYPHENS!**

11. Eliminate widows and orphans

As Roger Black states, "These are the surest sign of sloppy typesetting." A widow is a short line at the end of a paragraph that is too short. What is too short? The best answer is that the last line must have at least two complete words and those two words must be at least eight characters total.

Bad widows mess up the type color. They allow a blank white area to appear between paragraphs that stands out like a sore thumb. There is no way to eliminate them except by hand. The best way is editorially. In other words, rewrite the paragraph! However, graphic designers do not often have such editorial authority. In that case, you must carefully adjust the hyphenation, point size, glyph scaling, or word spacing(in that order). Changing the tracking always messes up the type color.

You must be gentle or your corrections will stand out worse than the widow. The point size should never be changed more than a half point, for example. Always make your changes to the entire paragraph. Extremely short paragraphs cannot be fixed, except to "break for sense." This means placing soft returns so that each short line makes sense by itself (as much as possible). This is especially true with headlines and subheads. Widows can make headlines look like they are balancing on a point — which causes visual tension, makes the reader uncomfortable, and may cause the reader to go elsewhere for a more friendly, relaxing read.

InDesign does not know what a widow is.

Typography

Like most publishing software, InDesign thinks a widow is an orphan at the bottom of a column and an orphan is a paragraph fragment at the top of a column. Both of these are orphans. A widow only concerns that short line at the end of a paragraph. Do not confuse widows with orphans. Widows are a paragraph problem. Orphans are a column problem.

To repeat, an orphan is a short paragraph or paragraph fragment left by itself at the top or bottom of a column. A classic example is a subhead left at the bottom of one column with the body copy starting at the top of the next column. The absolute worst orphan is a widow at the top of a new page. Other horrible typos are: widow at the top of a column; subhead at the bottom, as mentioned; a kicker separated from its headline; and a subhead with one line of body copy at the bottom of a column. These errors must be eliminated at the proofing stage. This is what we mean by massaging a document into shape. Corrections like these are among the primary factors that cause people to react to a design. If they are missing, the design is classed with amateur productions like school and bureaucrat output.

12. USE REAL SMALL CAPS

Small caps are a specialized letter form. Correctly speaking, they are little capital letters, a bit larger than the x-height, that are designed so they have the same color as the rest of the font. Here you have to be careful, again. InDesign creates small caps by proportionally shrinking capital letters. This makes them appear to be too light. The best method is to use fonts that have custom-designed small caps (they usually have lowercase numbers also). If you have an expert set with your font, InDesign will use the real small caps automatically.

REAL SMALL CAPS: INDESIGN'S SMALL CAPS

There is one place where small caps are not an option. This is with times. The appropriate typographic usage is not 9:00 A.M. or 9:30 AM or 9:45 a.m., but 9:53 AM. As far as I know, AM and PM are the only two words where small caps are required.

This has been a small review of type usage

The Chinese showed their wisdom again by considering calligraphy to be the highest form of art. Once you understand type, you will see its beauty. Well-drawn type is absolutely gorgeous. After a while, you begin to understand why some of the best graphic designs are simply type. Excellence in typography is invisible to most readers (on a conscious level), but it adds grace, elegance, and trustworthiness to your designs.

Three categories of people produce words on paper — typists, typesetters, and typographers. We have been discussing the first two. Typographers make typesetting an art. You should now have an inkling of how difficult that is. They are some of the finest artists in existence. They are working with graphics that are so "normalized" that excellent type is a major effort. It can take 1,000 hours or more to design one font.

SOME CLASSICS

Dashingly
CASLON

Dashingly
BEMBO

Dashingly
GARAMOND

Dashingly
BASKERVILLE

Dashingly
CHELTENHAM

Dashingly
CENTURY SCHOOLBOOK

Dashingly
BODONI

100,000 TYPE STYLES ...

Now that we have briefly discussed typesetting, we need to quickly review the typefaces themselves. There are many classification systems for type. For the purposes of this book, there are five classes: serif, sans serif, script, text, and decorative. It would probably be acceptable to combine script and text or even script, text, and decorative, but these five categories have served me well over the years.

Bringing it into perspective

Out of the 100,000 typefaces mentioned earlier, only 1,000 or so are used all the time by many people. Out of those, there are about a hundred or so serif fonts that a majority use for body copy and another hundred for heads and subheads. There are a huge number of decorative faces. Most of these are unsuitable for serious work. Many are totally illegible on a practical level. Probably 30,000 are multiple-derivative, differently named copies of the 200 popular fonts. So it isn't as scary as it sounds – quite. However, you will have to learn to recognize several hundred fonts by sight. It will help a lot to learn some of the history. That way learning Baskerville will cover that style plus its three or four dozen derivatives.

First, we must define a serif

A serif is a flare, bump, line, or foot added to the beginning or end of a stroke in a letter. I'm sure you already know this, but do you know their importance? They seem totally insignificant, but they certainly are not. They strongly influence how we react to type. In fact, on a subconscious level, serifs can be one of the most powerful influences on the reader's perception of the product. Most people are totally unaware of the effect type designs have on their lives.

Reading has many habitual associations. The type read during or about an occasion takes on the flavor of those events. Many of these typographic reactions are very personal. For example, you may find that your favorite script font happens to be the font on the restaurant menu

the night you became engaged. No matter what, to be functional in modern American society, we must read, and we do it constantly. Each of us reads thousands of pieces every day.

Reading has many habitual associations.

In our homogeneous, franchised society, most of us see the same things every day. The result of all of this is that virtually every person in the United States has similar reactions to various type styles. However, there are large differences between the habitual viewers of Fox, MTV, and Disney when compared to the habitual viewers of HGTV, A&E, and the History Channel. This has greatly accelerated as we enter the twenty-first century.

The dominance of serif

Almost every good book you have ever read was set in serif type. Virtually every textbook was also. All body copy before the 1950s was serif. Because of these things, serif typefaces are perceived as warm, friendly, nostalgic, and easy to read. Designers began to use these connections consciously during the 1950s and 1960s. As a result, serif faces are used almost exclusively in ads promoting quality, stability, good value, integrity, and warmth. They are also used to reinforce family values, patriotism, and the emotional content of character traits considered positive by our culture. Serif faces produce these types of reactions in the reader (at least subconsciously). The only exception would be the youth cultures like snowboarders or extreme jocks who, in cultivating rebellion and adrenaline rushes, have made sans serif their "normal" type classification.

Sans serif is relatively new

Even though sans serif faces have been around since at least the nineteenth century, they were never popular until the 1950s. Up until then, they were used extensively only by groups like the modernist, Bauhaus movement in Germany during the 1930s, where geometric type was promoted as modern. Futura, Bauhaus, and Kabel are classic examples of this style. Most people saw them as plain and unadorned or aggressively modern.

In the late 1950s, Helvetica became extremely popular. It was designed by Max Miedinger in 1957 and was quickly accepted as a new standard type style by many in the business, scientific, and advertising communities. Most logos from that period (like CBS, Exxon, and many others) were created with Helvetica Black or a modified Helvetica. Sans serif faces, in general, became de rigueur for scientific publishing. It is likely that many of you have bad memories from science textbooks.

Businesses of the time saw sans serif faces as modern, clean, cool, unemotional, and businesslike. Recently, there has been a fad among the avant garde computer byteheads of setting body copy in sans serif. They use distorted, condensed versions, but they fit the stereotypical usage pattern. Their usage is more a rebellion from convention, which fits nicely into the gestalt of sans serif usage.

Again, graphic designers have consciously reinforced these reactions. At this time, sans serif faces can be used effectively to produce these feelings and responses. The usage was almost unanimous until desktop publishing brought in designers with no design education. So the reactions are predictable enough to be very useful. Sans serif faces are clean and mechanical. Serif faces, in general, are more elegant and "beautiful."

Typography

Skill #2

SERIF POSTER

Design a poster for a nostalgic poetry reading at Carnegie Hall using only serif fonts for the graphics.

Classic Sans

Strongly
BAUHAUS

Strongly
FUTURA

Strongly
KABEL

Strongly
UNIVERS

Strongly
GILL SANS

Strongly
FRUTIGER

Strongly
CORINTHIAN

The Times/Helvetica problem

One of the more interesting phenomena of digital publishing is the use of Times and Helvetica. Although these are very well-designed typefaces, their excessive usage resulting from their specification as the default fonts in so many nonprofessional applications and operating systems has completely changed their perception in the mind of the "typical reader." At this point, most serious graphic designers avoid these two fonts like the plague. As a result, the only place people see them is in output by people who are untrained in publishing and simply use the software defaults — think schools, bureaucracies, the IRS, collection agencies, and the like. Because of this uncaring usage, Times, Times New Roman, Helvetica, Geneva (Apple's system font), and Ariel (a Microsoft version of Helvetica) have been virtually ruined for serious use by designers.

The importance of readability

We mentioned that serif faces are considered more readable. This is probably due more to their overwhelming use as body copy than any other factor. However, there is good reason to believe that the serifs do provide more distinctive letter shapes. The serifs also help the eye follow the line of type across the column, making body copy easier to read. Whatever the reasons, serif typefaces are clearly easier and more comfortable to read.

Studies have shown, though, that sans serif faces are more legible (as opposed to readable). What this means is that for short bursts, sans serif type can be grasped more quickly. As soon as several lines are read, this effect is lost. The eye becomes tired, wanders, and loses the ability to easily find the beginning of the next line. You can compensate for this effect by increasing the leading. Typically, people just quit reading sans serif body copy. Normally, you should pick a serif for body copy and a sans serif for heads and subheads.

For things like billboards, sans serif is often the best choice. (Especially with billboards, where the rule is a maximum of eight words.) The difficulty is finding a sans serif that is warm and friendly with trustworthy overtones.

What about the rest of the typestyles?

What about all the type that is neither serif nor sans serif? First of all, proportionally there isn't that much of it. Decorative is the term for the miscellaneous grab bag, but most of it is either serif or sans serif anyway. Decorative type is defined as typefaces that are so highly stylized that they cannot be read in body copy sizes. For that reason some people call this category display. Display is the term used for the large, splashy ads in newspapers, as opposed to the classified ads.

You need to be very careful in the use of these fonts. Legibility is the obvious problem, but that can usually be solved by size and location. Simply making them 36 points or larger is often enough. Some of the more complicated and/or abstract faces must be used several inches tall. Often they work only for posters and billboards.

It goes beyond that, though. Circus type and western or Victorian type are commonly so fancy that they defy classification. Decorative faces can have shadows, fills, outlines, inlines, or any combination of these attributes. Sometimes they are three-dimensional.

The good thing about decorative fonts is that they have very specific historical connotations. Fonts are available in art deco, art nouveau, Victorian, and almost any other artistic or decorative style of the past several centuries. They are the best (and usually the easiest) method of promoting an instant, emotional, stylistic reaction from the readers to your design.

Typeset handwriting

There are two other general classifications that must be considered. Script and text fit nowhere and must be dealt with separately. Basically they are both handwriting. Script is modern handwriting. Text is medieval handwriting. Text is also known as Blackletter. Blackletter was used in Germany until the Second World War.

The 1950s saw an explosion of script styles. This was primarily due to the fad for hand-drawn headlines brought about by photographic pasteup. The problem with scripts is making the letters match up. This is one place where you have to watch the tracking very closely. The letter forms are designed to overlap precisely. If the tracking is too loose or too tight, they miss each other.

Most script must be hand-kerned to fit well.

Because script and text are so difficult to read, both of these categories have very restricted usage. In fact, they are limited to products where people are extremely highly motivated to read them, like invitations, greeting cards, and the like. Often scripts or text fonts are the only acceptable option for clients desiring a design. Occasionally you may find a use for them as headlines or banners or other such items, but you must always be aware of reading difficulty. Use all the tricks you can muster to enhance readability, such as emphasizing with white space, large sizes, extra line spacing, and so on.

Too tight Too loose Correct

Italics and obliques

One original standard for type is the carved type in Roman columns honoring emperors' great deeds. They are still the classic standard, and the reason why many old-time pros call vertical faces "Roman." You should check out fonts like Trajan, Augustinian, and their ilk. The problem with these carved letters was that they were all caps. Lowercase letters crept in as people wrote the words. As they wrote faster and faster, miniscules (what we now call lowercase letters) developed out of the handwriting of the day. This was first carved into a font in Italy in the early Renaissance. In Venice, a man named Aldus Manutius developed a font based on the handwriting of his day, which he called "Italic." It became very popular, but because of the slant of the letters, it was not as legible — and still isn't.

In this day and age, every normal vertical style (sometimes called roman) has a matching italic: Diaconia Roman foxy, *Diaconia Italic foxy.* As you can clearly see in these six words, italic is a very different

CHAPTER SIX

Typography

Skill #3

SANS SERIF POSTER

Design a poster for an avant garde poet reading his work at UC Berkley using only sans serif fonts for the graphics.

font. The *a*s, *f*s, *x*s, and *y*s show the most obvious differences. One of the aberrations of the digital age is a new phenomenon of fake italics called oblique. These are not true italics, but merely slanted roman characters. Obliques drive type purists nuts!

REMEMBER, LEGALISM KILLS

The factors discussed so far in this chapter have to be considered, but they cannot become rigid rules. If you have a good reason, ignore the rules. Make sure you do it on purpose, though. The relationships described here are real and they work on a practical, predictable level. You ignore them at your own risk. Some fields, like the early snowboarding culture, try to require that you break all rules (but that's just another rule). Many have strict requirements, often unwritten. For example, accounting firms will occasionally ask for something special. But, even then, they usually approve only small formal type, caps and small caps, huge leading, centered designs (usually Copperplate). The main thing is to be conscious of what you are doing and why. As the designer, you are responsible for every mark on the sheet. If you cannot think of a good reason to use it, delete it!

Your task is to control the reader's eye, directing it to the message.

Some guidelines

Here are some techniques to help you control readability:

- Lines of text more than ten or twelve words long make it difficult for the eye to track back and forth. You should use columns. Lines less than five words usually have to have soft returns added for readability.

- Indents at the beginning of each paragraph create a visual cue that a new thought is being introduced.

- Drop caps tell the reader, very effectively, where to start the story or articles. **TIP:** This is the only place they should be used, or you risk confusing the readers.

- One of the most important elements to control is contrast: serif versus sans serif; light versus bold; large versus small; simple versus ornate; and so on. **TIP:** Make sure you use enough contrast. Wimpy contrast merely irritates the reader.

- You need to consciously and carefully guide the reader's eye through the document.

Much of this is obvious stuff, once you become aware of it. Common sense plays an extremely important part in design. If you look at the piece and you have to concentrate to read it, readers certainly will not bother. Examine what you are doing, carefully. You will find that you have solved many problems without having to call in "expert" advice.

Typography

1.   Why are sans serif fonts relatively rare?

2.   When can you use a double space?

3.   What is the only required use of small caps?

4.   What is InDesign's method for leading?

5.   What are the problems with setting headlines in script typefaces and how would you solve them?

WHERE SHOULD YOU BE BY THIS TIME?

You should have at least a couple of skills or miniskills completed. You should also have at least two theory exams completed. By now you should be working relatively freely in InDesign and your illustration programs. The slowness caused by your lack of experience will only be eliminated by more practice and exploratory work.

DISCUSSION

Talk with your classmates about favorite typestyles. Why do you think you like them? How do your tastes in type compare to the mass market norm (if there is such a thing)? Discover the large differences in taste among your classmates (at least there better be – unless you are all groupies for the same rock group).

Talk among yourselves...

Importing

An introduction to document assembly showing how and why we use various formats and how to fix them

CONCEPTS

CHAPTER OBJECTIVES

By presenting normal formats for both print and Web, this chapter will enable you to:

1. Simplify your workflow
2. Pick the most appropriate format
3. Describe the proper use of LZW compression
4. Describe the differences between the common formats
5. Describe appropriate word processing formats

LAB WORK FOR CHAPTER

- Continue your work on skills and miniskills
- Submit finished theory exams
- Locate a real project for approval by the instructor
- Miniskill #2
- Skill #4

Importing

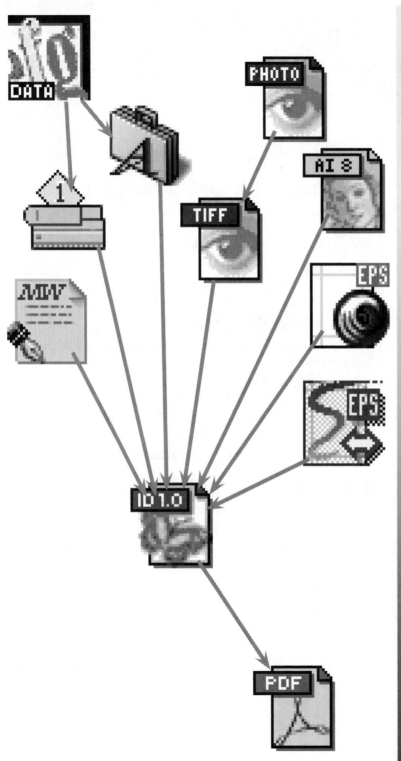

The building of
digital documents

One of the most frustrating things to teach is the matter of file compatibility, file formats, and document assembly. Most of the common mistakes students make involve these issues. They are always asking, "Why won't this open?" "Why can't I see this in the Open dialog box?" "Why do I only see a box with an X through it?" "I try to place the copy but it is not there!"

The basic problem is language

This is the simplest explanation. Start by imagining that PageMaker speaks English, FreeHand speaks German, Illustrator speaks French, Quark speaks Bulgarian, Photoshop speaks Russian, Painter speaks Chinese, Word speaks Italian, WordPerfect speaks Spanish, CorelDraw speaks Ubangi, and so on. The next complication to add to this scenario is the fact that almost no one speaks more than its native language. Continuing the analogy, we find that this is indeed true, although InDesign has made great strides.

What this means, on a practical level, is that Quark cannot open a FreeHand file. FreeHand cannot open a PageMaker file. When I wrote my first book, none of our publishing programs could open any other application's documents. What a mess! InDesign can now read Illustrator and Photoshop, but you probably shouldn't do that.

Digital Esperanto: Universal communication

In the 1950s, there was a huge push for the world to learn Esperanto. It never came to anything, but the principle helps us here. Esperanto is an invented language that no one speaks as a native tongue. Its goal was to provide an easily learnable language that could be used to cross all language barriers. The Esperanto effort was wiped out mostly by arrogant or lazy Americans who refused to learn it. As a result, everyone else has been forced to learn English or not trade with us.

The digital equivalents of Esperanto are the various universal formats. The most common is ASCII text. ASCII is understood by virtually every program, but no application speaks it as its native tongue, because ASCII is too clumsy. Nevertheless, ASCII is by far the most universal tongue. It is what we normally call a text file.

The problem with ASCII is simple — it can't do much. You can use it for raw HTML coding, for example, but not much else. The major lack is the inability to add formatting. Most of us have probably tried to use ASCII text in another program. It is never a problem to import it. The problem is the shape it's in when it arrives. Usually there is a hard return at the end of every line. There is no font assigned, so it comes in to your program in whatever your default font is. There is no bold, italic, tabs, or anything like that. ASCII is simply raw copy.

The closest equivalent to the crudity of ASCII that we use regularly is seen in articles copied off the Internet and pasted into a document. It's very frustrating. It can take a half hour to clean up the transferred copy, before it can be used at all. However, we are getting quite a bit ahead of ourselves. Before we go on we need to talk a little about word processors and their use.

Importing

WORD PROCESSING

All of us have used a word processor at one time or another. More than that, most of us use a word processor regularly. As we have mentioned, a word processor has replaced our typewriter. That is what a word processor is — a glorified typewriter. The problem is that most of us use the word processor equivalent of the 1958 Buick or the Disney channel. Everything is mucked up and covered with chrome or animation in the samples given. In the case of most word processors, everything is mucked up by pretensions to page layout.

It has become very hard to find a word processor that just writes, quickly and easily with great editing power. In fact, most of you probably use Microsoft Word™ which is a system-devouring resource hog posing as a word processor. For those of you who can remember, what we really need is something like Word 4 or less with drag'n'drop editing. This is why I use Mariner Write. There are other small, fast, powerful word processors out there. I strongly suggest that you get one.

Word processing formats

The word processing world fits into the scenario we described in the first couple of paragraphs. Every word processor speaks its own language. Worse than that, each version has its own version of the language. The newer versions can speak the older languages, but the older versions cannot speak the newer. There is no large difference between Word 4, Word 5, Word 6, and Word 98 files, as far as importing copy to use in publishing is concerned. However, it is likely that you can only read a few of them. I remember when my school changed from WordPerfect™ 5 to WordPerfect 6. At the time, we were using PageMaker™ 5 in our lab. Because the rest of the school is PC only, we kept receiving files with a *wpd* extension. The problem is that we had no way to import a wpd file, let alone a WordPerfect 6 file. Every copy file we received had to be saved in WordPerfect 5 format and renamed with a *wp5* extension. But, we are still getting ahead of ourselves.

Filters

To deal with all of these different languages, software has developed translators. In former days, applications had huge numbers of translators. PageMaker, for example, had well over fifty. These translators are called filters. These are not like Photoshop™ filters which apply complicated mathematical formulas to the selected pixels. In reality, these are translators. These filters can read the foreign format and translate it into a format that can be read by your software. We will run into these filters again when we talk about graphic formats later in the chapter.

As far as we are concerned, in this book, InDesign™ has relatively few filters. For copy, it can only read some Word and WordPerfect files, some Excel™ and spreadsheet files, recent PageMaker files, and recent QuarkXPress™ files. The problem with these formats is all the extra baggage that comes with them. I converted a Word file today that had two pages of copy and one hundred thirty one pages of Word

baggage (including a list of the directories on the hard drive the file was created on and a lot of code). Plus I can only handle Word 4, 5, 6, 7, 97, and 98. You may have a different list on your PC, but certainly you can see some of the problems here.

Rich text format

What is needed is a text format that keeps the formatting and is supported by almost everyone. Actually there is such a thing. It was created by Word in ancient times, and called Rich Text Format. This has become the universal word processing format. All word processors can save in Rich Text Format. Plus, all professional graphics programs can import Rich Text Format. When you accept a job from a client, you should probably get in the habit of asking that all files are sent to you in Rich Text Format.

Now, I have no doubt that many of you are willing to take the performance hit caused by using Word. Many of you will be involved in workflows that use Word and Word Perfect. There is nothing inherently wrong with this. All I am saying is that things tend to go smoother using Rich Text Format to transfer the copy.

Formatted copy

As we will discuss a great deal next chapter, the power of page layout is found in its style palettes. InDesign uses paragraph styles and character styles. But styles also include graphics styles in the case of FreeHand and Cascading Style Sheets on the Web. The basic idea of a style is simple. Professional publishing software has the ability to set up a document with defined styles to keep everything consistent. In InDesign you will set up styles like headlines, subheads, body copy, bulleted lists, captions, italics, emphasis, and so forth.

These styles save a designed paragraph as a style so you can apply that style to any other paragraph with a click on a palette (or better yet, a keyboard shortcut). Character styles do the same to selected copy instead of paragraph blocks. So, our definition of formatted copy is this: typed words in paragraphs that have predefined styles applied to it. These styles can be applied in several places. Most commonly they are either applied as they are written in a word processor, or they are applied after import in the page layout software (in both cases, with keyboard shortcuts).

Secretarial formatting

There is a major problem here. You probably noticed it when we were talking about typesetting last chapter. This problem is very simple yet very hard to eradicate. Basically, people who are taught to type or keyboard are taught typewriting. In fact, as these people are learning, normal typesetting procedures like *no double spacing after punctuation* are considered errors. Beyond that, administrative assistants and secretaries, in general, are taught nothing about design issues.

In fact, without a great deal of additional training, most secretaries and typists are incapable of producing formatted copy that will work in a professional environment. If they are capable, they are normally too valuable to be wasted on strict keyboarding. In many cases, it is usually better to simply ask secretarial typists to type in the words with a return at the end of every paragraph. It is often difficult enough to get them to avoid returns at the end of every line.

If you decide to train one of these keyboardists, you'll have to spend quite some time explaining word processing paragraph concepts and how the needs of publishing differ from secretarial work. The essentials are simple, though: there must be only one return in a paragraph there should be no styling of bold or italic; there should be nothing typed in all caps; and bold or italic words should be underlined (if they are emphasized at all). If typed correctly like this, you can be resize and reformat this copy easily after importing. If there are extra returns, styled words, or lines in all caps, reformatting becomes a laborious task at best. One of the major strengths of desktop publishing is the ability to reformat copy freely (as we will discuss in Chapter 8).

Regrettably, it is often necessary to spend many minutes (if not hours) removing all the secretarial formatting before copy can be flowed into a page layout with any degree of freedom. All the multiple spaces have to be deleted, changed to single spaces, replaced with tabs, or indents. Copy set in all caps must be retyped to C&lc. The list of problems goes on for quite a while: using a tab for the first line indent; centering headlines with multiple tabs; using multiple tabs instead of hard returns to go to the next paragraph in a bulleted list; lining up each line in a bulleted list with a hard return at the end of the line then multiple spaces in the front of the next line in the paragraph; and so on.

However, a word processor in the hands of a trained operator can save a great deal of time by preformatting everything. Imported text simply flows into place. All the indents, tabs, headlines, subheads, and so on just appear as planned. The designer merely has to message the type to perfection and add the graphics and sidebars. Word processors provide the raw material for the graphic professionals to manipulate. The problem is that these trained word processors are usually only available in large operations like magazine or newspaper publishers.

 We need to mention publishing realities here for those of you who are just learning publishing skills. For many reasons, your customers expect perfect work. Until recently, it was very difficult to even find printed materials with any typos in them, at all. The advent of amateur publishers has changed that radically. It in now common to find typos in formerly clean magazines, like *People, TV Guide, Newsweek*, and so forth. However, most of your clients expect, and demand, "Madison Avenue" perfection. It is the standard we are judged by. A single typographical error (called a typo) can mean a reprinted job and a major loss of money and credibility. Proofing is extremely important. At least three people should proof everything. You will normally not find your own mistakes. That is why you made the mistake in the first place — you couldn't see it. If you missed it the first time, you will usually miss it the second.

Keyboard selection shortcuts

This is one place where it really pays to read the documentation. Virtually every application has a different set of type selection

Importing

Mini #2

DIRECT MAIL POSTCARD

Here you create a 4"x6.25"postcard, direct mail marketing, to a very targeted list of counselors, social workers, and therapists who are thought to be excellent prospects to attend this series of seminars— four days in the high cool mountains of southern New Mexico — networking with the best in the country in the field of antidepression therapy with presentations from a wide variety of speakers.

shortcuts. You need to learn the ones used in your word processor. With programs lacking built-in word processors, like Quark and InDesign, text editing is really limited to correcting typos. We will cover InDesign's shortcuts next, but in reality, most of your editing will take place in the word processor you use. It is more important that you know the ones in your word processor.

In every program the shortcuts are a little different, but they really save time when you learn them. In InDesign, the basic commands are typical: a double click with the text tool selects a word and a triple click selects the paragraph. Beyond that, ⌘⇧right or left arrow selects the next or previous word; ⇧ right or left arrow selected the next character right or left; ⇧ up or down arrow selects the line above or the line below; ⌘⇧ up or down selects the paragraph before or after. Repeating the command extends the selection. PCs use the Control key instead of ⌘. For a complete list refer to your QUICK REFERENCE CARD that came with your software. Similar shortcuts are available in the word processor you use.

Drag'n'drop editing

Many word processors offer drag'n'drop editing. InDesign does not. This (and editing speed in general) is why you will normally be editing your copy in a word processor. This capability enables you to press–drag selected text and drop it in the new position without needing the Clipboard. This can greatly speed up editing when all the words being moved are visible on the screen. If you have to move the selected type to a different page, the clipboard works better.

Spell and grammar check problems

I went two town in my knew car to sea a show.

The proceeding sentence would cause no problem for a spell checker. A spell-check command will not flag wrong words that are spelled correctly. A spell checker is no substitute for careful proofing by the three persons recommended earlier. It does eliminate many errors, but it also misses many.

Another thing that helps is to spell check in your word processor and in InDesign. All spell checkers are a little different. Some catch initial caps on sentences, some catch double words, some catch transposed letters, some check proper names. All have a different set of features. So, the operative principle is spell check in your word processor, and then spell check again in InDesign (after everything is formatted).

Word processing: a final comment

Remember that word processors are not WYSIWYG. Now you can work in a preview mode that approximates what you will get, but you will not have the page, margin, gutter, and paragraph controls you need. The graphics will not be there. The latest versions are much closer to WYSIWYG, but the typographic controls are still missing. Plus you will be radically reformatting everything after import into InDesign, anyway.

Word processors are designed for the business community rather than the printing industry. As a result, their abilities are geared for business at the expense of professional type. These programs are very powerful, but they are to be used for writing, not for design decisions. Be very careful about using features such as tables in your word processor, for example. They do not transfer — at all.

Many word processing abilities are centered around communication by letter. For example, most word processors have a mail merge capability. This means that mailing list databases can be combined with form letters. In addition, they commonly have e-mail (electronic mail) capabilities. These capabilities are no help, and they are often a hindrance in generating usable copy for you to use in InDesign.

Dealing with secretarial copy

Many jobs will come with a disk containing the copy. For the moment we will assume that it is in a format you can read and import. Often though (unless all of your copy comes from in-house), the copy will have been input by a secretary with no training in printing requirements. It will be filled with multiple spaces and returns. Copy that should be italic will be underlined, or at the very least have quotes around it. The tabs will be made with multiple spaces. Centering will be done with the space bar. The list is almost endless, as I mentioned earlier.

You will have to eliminate all of these typos before you can format your copy. Most often, you will do this in your word processor, but it can be done (slowly) in InDesign. Your word processor may be different, but you will have to use a special code to search for and replace many of the invisible characters. InDesign uses the same ones that were used in PageMaker: ^p is a hard return; ^n is a soft return; ^t is a tab; ^m is an em space. There are others, but these will usually get you where you need to go. There is a complete pop-up list in Find/Change in InDesign.

Here is a procedure that will eliminate most common secretarial typos in a few brief steps:

1. Use the find and change command to change all double spaces to single spaces.

2. Use find and change command to change all double returns to single returns.

 TIP: Steps one and two may have to be done several times. Many typists center headlines by using the space bar. This could use ten to twenty spaces. Each time you run the command, you will halve the number of spaces until there is only one left. The same is true of returns. Often spacing, or moving to the next page, is accomplished by adding many extra spaces or many extra returns. These will all be in the wrong places when you format the type for your document.

3. Select all to select the entire story. Then format everything to No style (on the PARAGRAPH STYLES palette).

4. With everything still selected, select Normal or Plain from the Type Style menu. This will eliminate all underlines and improper styles. (This is not available in InDesign, but formatting everything to Body Copy accomplishes most of this for you. You really should do this step in your word processor.)

Importing

Please don't be upset with me!

Some brain dead troublemakers really believe that I am putting down secretaries. Nothing could be further from the truth. I realize that they run most offices and make most of the important decisions. My only problem is with the people who taught them how to type or to use their word processor.

5.   With everything still selected, format everything to body copy. This is why the style is called body copy, because the vast majority of the copy is set in this style. Doing this will enable faster reformatting because all that will have changed are the heads, subheads, and special paragraphs. Plus it will make your text as small as it will ever be to give you a clearer idea of how many pages you are going to need.

These procedures will eliminate all the foreign formatting, which is probably littered with typestyles and fonts not found on your machine. In addition, the formatting that was used probably contrasts greatly with your approved layout. Word processors never format in multiple columns effectively, for example.

Now you are ready to format everything with your style palette. Edit your styles after eliminating all the imported styles from the palette. Often the fastest procedure is to eliminate all styles and then copy styles from a template you have set up properly. (This could be done as step three.) InDesign allows you to SHIFT SELECT all the styles you need to eliminate. Eliminating all styles automatically changes everything to no style.

The only problems remaining should be with tabs. Many secretaries have no idea how tabs are used in setting type. You will commonly have to replace all tabs with a space (using FIND/CHANGE) and retab everything by hand. In general, indents and tabs are not effectively taught in secretarial word processing courses. Furthermore, these controls are usually very clumsy in comparison to those in professional page layout programs.

Although this process may seem like a real hassle, it is much faster than anything else. Ideally, your copy will come in properly formatted. In reality, this rarely happens except with in-house copy or regular clients. Even then you often have to train them. **A general guideline is this**: If the copy was not keyed in by a trained typesetting professional, all formatting probably should be eliminated before you go to work — simply to save you time.

GRAPHIC FORMATS

There is nothing as universal as ASCII graphically. However, there are three formats that are close. If you receive graphics that are not in this format, you need to get them changed to these formats.

In our industry, where PostScript is required, EPS is universally read. EPS is short for Encapsulated PostScript. Simplistically, an EPS file is a PostScript file written in a universal language that any professional publishing program can read. The PostScript code is encapsulated in code markers.

The second format that almost everyone can read is TIFF. TIFF stands for Tagged Image File Format. This is a file language for bitmaps: 1-bit, 8-bit, 24-bit, and 32-bit. In addition, all nonprofessional applications understand TIFF. In fact, the only place where TIFFs are a problem is on the Web.

The third format that is becoming universal is PDF. InDesign works transparently with PDFs, importing and exporting them with no special steps. All our software currently supports PDFs.

The import/export process

When you need to move a graphic from one program to another there is a simple two-step process. First, you have to export a copy of your document from the originating application in one of the variants of the universal formats. Second, you have to open a new or old document in the receiving program and import the exported graphic (InDesign calls this step "Placing").

Most of the Big Seven also support drag'n'drop for graphics. Here you can simply select, drag, and drop the selection into the window of the other program. This does have some limitations. Some drag'n'dropped graphics become editable (which is often dangerous), and sometimes they are added to the Links palette and sometimes they are not. In general, I suggest the normal, traditional procedure of exporting/importing. It avoids many problems.

Normal beginner mistakes

The most common problem with beginners is trying to open a graphic instead of importing it. EPS graphics cannot normally be opened. Even if you are allowed to open the EPS, you will not be allowed to edit the graphic. Even if you can edit it, opening a graphic does not import it into your page layout document for publishing.

Imported graphics should not be edited in page layout. They can be resized, flipped, skewed, rotated, or transformed as a whole. One-bit TIFFs can be recolored. However, imported graphics should only be edited by returning to the creating application, making the changes, and then reexporting and re-importing. InDesign's Links palette makes this procedure relatively painless.

The second problem has to do with resizing bitmap graphics. Unless you are very careful, resized bitmaps do not fit the pixel grid any more. As a result, resized bitmaps are usually blurred. Many people claim to do it all the time. However, they are also usually the persons who complain about the quality of computer halftones.

SCREEN/PRINTER ACROBATICS

GRAPHIC FORMAT STRUCTURE

One of the major difficulties with graphics, in general, is their sheer size. Text-only files run in dozens of kilobytes. Graphic files are much larger. Full-color bitmaps are commonly dozens of megabytes.

One of the results is that exported graphics are normally at least two-part files. In one case, the DCS EPS has five separate files (or more) that are linked to each other. If the full-resolution graphic was rendered on the monitor, screen redraws would take virtually forever. In addition, the monitor cannot display all the information because of its extremely low resolution (72 or 96 ppi).

What is imported?

All graphic formats have a screen preview. This is a low-resolution image that interprets the high-res image as well as it can at monitor resolutions. When you import a graphic to another program, only the preview can be seen. The high-res image is not used until the document is output to a printer, imagesetter, or press. This causes all kinds of problems:

- The inexperienced are constantly frustrated because the screen image does not look like they expect. After all, it was *gorgeous* in the originating program. The obvious reason for this has already been mentioned. The imported image looks bad on the screen because it is a low-resolution bitmap. It has to be low-res to make screen redraws tolerable. InDesign does a much better job with this than most programs, but it is still a problem.

- Because the image on the screen is only a low-res preview, the high-resolution image has to be available for the document to print. We'll discuss this problem in a bit, under Link Management. Many assume that because the image has been imported, it is in the document, and the original can be deleted. This is certainly not the case. In most cases the low-res preview is the only thing in the document. The high-res image is only linked to the file.

- When the document prints, the printer or imagesetter searches for the original high-res file. If it does not find it, the printer either quits in disgust or simply says, "The heck with you — I'll just print the low-res screen garbage." It is very important to make sure that the imported file (or a copy of it) is contained in the same folder as the final document. You might get away with it if everything stays on your computer. If you transport everything to another computer (as is usually done), all linking is broken. Printers and imagesetters are instructed to look in the same folder as the final document. If they do not find the high-res original there, the output is messed up — one way or another.

- When a scan is placed into a drawing program for tracing purposes, the preview is so crude that tracing is very difficult. Often it helps to make a black-and-white version of the scan. These tend to be more visible in the preview. Previews are always crude, however. For tracing purposes, a high-resolution preview helps a lot. As you remember, in InDesign this is accomplished in PREFERENCES>>GENERAL>>IMAGES: DISPLAY>> FULL RESOLUTION IMAGES. It can seriously slow down redraw, though.

Platform glitches

Here you have to understand what is going on with the previews as well as the originals. The Wintel world has dozens of formats. Many of these are not even understood by most PCs. For our purposes, EPS and TIFF still work well. TIFF is especially portable.

TIFF works because the screen previews are also TIFFs. Our professional programs read these well, in most cases. EPSs are another story entirely. Here the problem is the previews. DOS EPS uses Windows Metafile, and Mac EPS uses PICT. These are both file formats that the other platform refuses to recognize. Generic EPS usually does not have a preview at all. As a result, EPSs brought to another platform usually only show a box with an X through it. This box is the size of the frame holding the graphic.

The problem, of course, is that you cannot see the cross-platform graphic on the screen. It will print fine, but it is very difficult to properly arrange a graphic if you cannot see it. Most illustration software allows you to control the type of Preview used. Make sure you are using a format that can be seen on the platform and in the software in which you will be assembling the document.

 TIP: When working cross platform, you have to regress to using the old 8.3 naming conventions. Wintel still requires the dot three extensions to know what type of file is being dealt with. (Even if Windows 95 and 98 not longer seem to require that, they simply make the required extension invisible.) However, to open a PC file on a Mac the dot three extension for the format is required. To open or use a Mac graphic on a Wintel machine, it must be saved in a PC version of the format, the extension must be there, and the name will be truncated to seven letters followed by a tilde unless it is eight characters or less. This can cause severe problems when trying to make cross platform CDs, for example.

This kind of digital acrobatics is irritating, but it works. It is relatively easy to open and convert PC graphics to Mac graphics. On a Mac you can simply change the name to add the dot three extension to open or use a graphic. (It doesn't always work, but it works most of the time – if you have any idea what the originating software was.) The opposite is not usually true. Cross-platform work must be planned and practiced. Wintel machines required specially purchased software to read Mac files. Every PC is different. Once you know a particular PC machine's foibles, cross-platform graphics are simple to deal with.

Specialized and nonprofessional formats

There are a huge variety of formats, especially in the PC world. In most cases, the PC formats do not matter to us. You will have to ask your PC clients to save their files in EPS or TIFF. Nothing else translates well without contortions. There are utilities such as DeBabelizer and MacLink Pro that translate them. However, in almost all cases, it is better to save them in a usable format when they are created.

Beyond this, programs outside the Big Seven often generate dialects of the standard formats. CorelDraw EPS, for example, often cause problems. The best solution is usually to save into Illustrator format from CorelDraw (dot ai extension). Then open the file in Illustrator and save as an EPS from there. Off-brand TIFFs often have to be opened in Photoshop and simply resaved to make them usable. This is normally needed with Painter TIFFs, for example. If the graphic was not made in one of the Big Seven, you should open and resave it simply as preventative maintenance. This will rewrite the code to PostScript compatibility.

Importing

 CROSS PLATFORM WORK

All of us have to work cross platform. The primary thing to remember is that almost no Wintel machine can read a Mac formatted disc. Therefore you will have to use DOS formatted disks. Never work on a disk from another platform. First of all, removable disks are usually slow. Second, they are not very durable. Third, your machine can crash or the removable driver can be damaged as your computer struggles to work and to translate from one operating system to another – all at the same time.

FORMATS YOU NEED TO KNOW

Now we need to go through the formats and discuss their idiosyncrasies. I am not going to cover all formats, only those you will see on a regular basis. Each format is the best choice for certain things. The problem is remembering each one's strengths and weaknesses. As publishing professionals, this is relatively easy. In print, if it is not EPS or TIFF, fix it. On the Web, if it is not GIF or JPEG, fix it (PNGs are not widely supported at the time of writing this book in early 2000).

PICT

PICT is short for picture. This is Apple's internal format created by QuickDraw. This is a common output of digital cameras because it JPEG compresses so well. Because it is virtually universal on the Mac, it allows you to freely move images from program to program. In fact, the clipboard usually converts COPY/PASTE graphics to PICTs. It can handle up to 32 bits per pixel. This means it can handle CMYK files. Because it is such a complex format, other platforms almost never support it. The PICT format always saves four channels and defaults to 72 ppi.

PICT is a metafile format, so it can also handle vector documents. However, these are certainly not PostScript. In fact, printing a vector PICT on a PostScript printer results in all sorts of anomalies. It gets so bad that double lines might print as patterned lines, for example. In general, PICT vector files fall into the "general nonprofessional" category. This is where many of the cheaper drawing programs fall short. Many of them only produce PICTs.

PICTs are best for monitors. In fact, they are the best choice here. As a result, they are used almost exclusively for multimedia. In other words, when you are producing presentations, CD-ROMs, or any other materials that will be shown on a monitor, PICT is often the format to use. It can handle the JPEG compression used for QuickTime video. RGB only uses three of the four channels, and the fourth can be used for all kinds of masking and special effects. Remember, monitors are only 72 ppi, so do not waste your time and storage space by creating these PICTs at high-resolutions.

TIP: In general, it is usually best to open PICTs in Photoshop and save them into a "proper" format. The problem with this is usually the low resolution of most PICTs. Beyond this, it is always necessary to open the QuickTime™ PICTs produced by digital cameras in Photoshop and SAVE AS a PSD image. If you do not do this, the JPEG compression of Quicktime will quickly add artifacts to your image.

EPS(F)

ESPF is the full acronym for Encapsulated PostScript Files. It was designed to store PostScript vector information. It can save vector, bitmap, or both kinds of graphics; but it is clumsy for bitmaps because it has no compression scheme. The F is usually dropped. This is primarily because the DOS extensions can only use three letters.

EPS was invented by Altsys (writers of FreeHand and Fontographer) to be used for their graphics. It is still the only universally usable format for printable vector graphics. With bitmaps, many avoid it because of its size. However, it prints beautifully and can carry designer-specified angles, dot shapes, and other occasionally critical information. EPS bitmaps (from Photoshop) or EPS graphics with embedded bitmaps have the same resizing and file size problems as all bitmaps.

TIFF

The TIFF format was developed very early by Aldus (creator of PageMaker). It is used a lot by many platforms, including DOS, Windows, UNIX, and Mac. As a result, it is the most common format and the best for cross-platform usage.

One of the major problems is that TIFF has been around so long, and has been used so much in the PC world, that there are many TIFF dialects. This is primarily because TIFF is so flexible. For example, in Photoshop, TIFFs can have up to sixteen 8-bit channels. Other programs cannot use this data at all.

TIFFs also support the LZW (lossless) compression scheme. This means that they can be reduced in size with no data loss. It's basically very simple. A typical lossless compression takes an entire area of the same color and says, "fill this area with this color." This saves a lot of space when compared to, "make pixel one gray, make pixel two gray, make pixel three gray, make pixel four gray, etcetera."

 TIP: You have to be careful about LZW compression. It can add to file size for continuous tone images. It should only be used for images with relatively large areas of flat color. When in doubt, do not compress. Also DOS LZW and Mac LZW are not entirely compatible. If you need the compression on the competitive platform, it is usually best to save uncompressed and then open the file and compress on the platform where page layout takes place.

 TIFFs now can also contain a clipping path. InDesign supports this (but you have to do it by hand: Object >>> Clipping Path). If you want the clipping path as your frame be sure to check the Import Options box before you import and then check the Use Clipping Path as your Frame option. And also remember that InDesign can edit that clipping path frame, if necessary.

PDF

This is the new format of choice for most of us in print publishing. It's a streamlined, cleaned up PostScript, in essence. In many workflows this is the final output that is sent to be printed. It's still a bit too large for most uses on the Web. InDesign can import and export this format

with ease and comfort. It offers a wide variety of compression options: downsampling, JPEG, ZIP, and others. The major problem is that you really need to make sure you keep track of where the PDF will be used. There is a huge difference between a PDF generated for prepress use and one generated for use on the Web. Web versions are so compressed that they are horrendously ugly when printed. You must keep track of the font embedding options also. The default for Screen Optimized PDFs is to have no fonts embedded, for example. You will have to set up your own custom Distilling setups.

GIF

The GIF is an example of a specific-use format that you use a lot but it is not professional printing quality. GIF was developed by CompuServe and is the primary format for Web graphics. It only supports 256 colors (8-bit) maximum, but it supports LZW. All of these attributes make it popular over modems because of the small file size. It can also save in 3-bit, 4-bit, 5-bit, 6-bit, and 7-bit for increased size reductions. It remains the best file format for the Web in most cases, even though a lot of software companies complain about the licensing fees for LZW. ImageReady and FireWorks now do lossy GIFs, which are marvelous.

RIFF

Raster Image File Format (RIFF) was developed by Fractal Design for use in the Painter, Sketcher, and ColorStudio programs. It supports multiple layers, and 32-bit color, and has options for compression. Almost no one supports it, but it works very well in Fractal Design's software. You should save in TIFF, PICT, or EPS when exporting for use in other programs. Or you can open it in Photoshop and save it in any format you need.

IFF

The Interchange File Format (IFF) is an Amiga system format, 24-bit, using the RLE compression formula. It is used almost exclusively for Amiga video, which has a very good name in video production. However, Amigas are only available used, so you will probably not see this one much unless you work with a lot of animators.

TARGA or TGA

These formats has the same usage and compression scheme as IFF, but it is tied to the TrueVision, TARGA, and VISTA video boards. It does save up to 32-bit color and is used almost exclusively in the PC world. It is used to transport images to professional video systems. You need to make sure to use DOS conventions in naming the files.

BMP

The BMP format used by Microsoft Paint and other Wintel programs. It is 24-bit, using RLE compression. It is used almost exclusively by PCs and is supported by none of our professional software except Photoshop. Usually BMPs are 96 dpi, so they are almost useless.

Photoshop

PSD files are common because everyone has a copy of Photoshop. The important thing to remember is that in most cases layers and transparency are lost when you try to publish anything from Photoshop. As was the case, years ago, with FreeHand and Illustrator, you now need to always have an original PSD file and then export a TIFF, GIF, JPEG, EPS, or whatever version when needed to actually publish the image.

PhotoCD

This is not a format. It is a CD storage system developed by Kodak. It has become popular primarily because it has reduced the cost of scans to the single-digit range, for the first time. Each file is saved into five different pixel sizes ranging from 128 x 192 to 2048 x 3072. You can have a film processor scan your photographic images onto a PhotoCD for about a dollar an image. The quality is more than acceptable for commodity color. There is a new Professional version with higher resolution, now that Kodak has recognized that our industry is interested in good-quality cheap scans. Those scans typically cost $15 for the blank CD and a couple of dollars per scan. The original consumer TV push has been resurrected recently, so be prepared for an assault of amateur files using this technology.

JPEG

This is really not a file format, but a lossy compression scheme. Lossy means that data is lost. With care, luck, and practice it is not too noticeable, but compressions of up to 10 to 1 are possible. The problem is that JPEG has many variations. JPEG was used originally for video and is a built-in part of QuickTime. It is often the best way to put 24-bit photos on the Web. It has almost no use for print publishing. If you receive one for print, you are usually better to open it and resave as a TIFF.

PNG

The is the touted new format for the Web with 24-bit color and tight compression. However, PNGs don't do as well as their hype and they require a 5.0 browser. In other words, they won't be in common normal use until 2002, if then. It's the native format of FireWorks, for example.

So why should I care?

PRACTICAL EXPORT/IMPORT

You should care because you will be importing and exporting constantly. As was said several times already, no one program can do it all. You will be scanning halftones and seps in Photoshop; making illustrations in Painter, FreeHand, and Illustrator, plus a host of others; and importing (Placing) everything into InDesign for assembly. Every graphic you create or use will have an original document and an exported version for import into page layout.

 TIP: Be careful concerning that last statement. Many programs now offer the capability of working in the final format you will be using. DO NOT DO IT! For many reasons, some of which we will mention in passing, having editable graphics (with no

original standard for that graphic) is a very dangerous practice. You will do well to get in the habit of always having an original in the native format of the creating software and then exporting a copy in the specific format you need or desire.

Often there will be several intermediary files in various formats. For example, a regular routine in common use is this:

1. Scan into Photoshop: clean up and save as a TIFF.
2. Open and trace in Streamline, which creates a new file in an old Illustrator variant. Sometimes you can actually use the autotrace tool in Illustrator or FreeHand. FreeHand's tool has gotten very good, especially in FreeHand 9. However, Streamline is still the best and recommended for difficult traces.
3. Open to generate the final illustration in FreeHand or Illustrator.
4. Export as an EPS.
5. Import into InDesign for final positioning.

Obviously, we may want or need to open in both FreeHand and Illustrator. (I often temporarily pass through Illustrator 8 just to use their wonderful Brush tool , for example.) You may use Dimension or some other 3D illustration tool. The point is that for many illustrations, we need to create five files. All five of these files are not necessary in the final folder. The TIFF and dot art file can be tossed (after you are sure you no longer need them). But you need to use all of them (if you use this technique) to quickly scan and trace a logo for use in your document.

The workhorses

Watch out! There is a little heresy here. Three of the professional programs will cover almost all "normal files" — Photoshop, PageMaker, and FreeHand. FreeHand covers about a dozen and a half formats as does Photoshop. Virtually every graphic file you ever receive will be in these three dozen formats. PageMaker has forty-one filters that cover more than eighteen word processors on both platforms.

The format problems you will have to deal with will come from the "oddball" programs such as Canvas, CorelDraw, SuperPaint, or whatever your source has not been able to give up yet. It is not that the programs are weird. They are excellent programs. They have simply not been blended into the mainstream of PostScript publishing, so far. This is one area your sales personnel and customer service representatives (CSRs) need to check: what file formats are you going to receive?

Dealing with size issues

A major problem in all print publishing is dealing with the sheer size of the files. PostScript illustrations help, unless the designer goes crazy complicated. To a certain extent, these files can be handled with removable cartridges. JAZ cartridges will hold almost two gigabytes. If DVD formats ever get sorted out, it will hold several gigabytes. But even here, the file size builds to the point where storage can be a problem.

One common solution is compression. We have mentioned this possibility in passing. TIFFs use LZW lossless compression.

Several of the other formats use RLE. JPEG offers incredible size savings with the compromise of quality caused by lossy compression. These only apply to individual files and only to specific graphic formats. In many cases, dedicated compression software is the answer.

What is compression?

The basic idea is to find patterns in documents that can be described more briefly than the original code. This is easiest with files such as black-and-white bitmaps. Here black and white areas can be described as a group. Even flat tint screens can be described as an area. There are numerous complicated compression schemes. The details do not matter to us. The concept is to describe a file with fewer words, which makes it smaller.

There are several dedicated compression programs. The leader and normal standard on the Mac is StuffIt Deluxe. On the Wintel side it is WinZip. The decompression utility is given away free.

Compression is very useful for several scenarios. For long-term backup storage, self-extracting archives save a lot of space. They also prevent idle destruction by the curious who are just looking around. Self-extracting archives also work well as installers of files kept on locked floppies. In fact, this is the only real use for floppies, as hard use wipes out a floppy in about a week. Compression, in general, is the only solution when you cannot afford adequate hard drive space. Finally, online and modem use requires any amount of compression available, because they are so slow.

The biggest problem is that Wintel can't read *dot sit* files (the StuffIt extension) and Macs can't normally read *dot zip* files (the WinZip extension). If you create SELF EXTRACTING ARCHIVES (*dot sea*), they can be opened anywhere on the same platform by simple double-clicking. In many cases you will have to make a Zipped file for Wintel and a *dot sea* file for Macs.

The PDF solution

Actually the best solution for most of this is to make a PDF. There is a lot of compression available here. In most cases, it makes special compression software irrelevant.

SUMMING IT UP

PLAN AHEAD!

The primary fact you need to burn into your synapses is this: determine your needs before you start drawing, and certainly before you begin document assembly. Preplanning is more important in digital work than it is most places. In few fields can you get into so much trouble so quickly. The nice part is that everything can be redone or undone. However, deadlines can get trashed very quickly. By figuring out what you need and how to get there most efficiently, many of your problems will be solved before they occur.

For virtually every part of your document there is a best format to use. Sometimes this is just common sense. Sometimes it is controlled

by the desires of your service bureau or printing firm. The main thing you need to keep in mind is that your choice is important.

- For copy, use either Rich Text Format or Tagged Text. Tagged Text is where your typesetter basically codes the copy like it was formerly done in phototypesetting before WYSIWYG. Tagged Text is a coding style that can be learned (I think there is a PDF on your installation CD) for those of you in a heavy production setting. It is worth doing if you have a specialized operation where some people key in copy, others edit, and others assemble documents. It will not work with nonprofessional copy set by secretaries. You simply do not have time to train all of them. Just ask them to send in their copy in Rich Text Format. Then check the copy very carefully.

Tip for Mac users: I keep an old machine with Word on it simply to Convert Word files to Rich Text Format for the rest of our machines. Microsoft products cause so many security hassles, virus problems, and file complications that I just keep the Word machine offline and sneakernet things over there for conversion. My entire network runs much faster with no Microsoft on it. I also use this old machine to test Web pages with a copy of Explorer.

- For vector graphics, EPS is still usually better although PDF has emerged as an option. For non-PostScript applications, PDF may be the only option.
- For bitmap graphics, TIFF is almost always the best option. The only exceptions are things like duotones, tritones, and so forth which have to have correctly specified screen angles. For them and for graphics that need to have a special screen frequency that is different than the basic document, EPS is the only option. Some workflows prefer EPS, DCS, or PDF for bitmaps. As usual, contact your service bureau or printer before you start so you can work the way that works best for them.

In general, plan ahead and include your final output device's capabilities heavily in your planning. You will not believe how many problems this will solve for you. Remember, demanding that a machine do things it was not designed to do will cost you a lot of time and money (if the project is ever completed successfully). Using proper formats is a large part of this.

1. What is the problem with TIFFs from nonprofessional software?

2. What does it mean when a placed graphic only appears as a stroked transparent rectangle with an X through it?

3. What is a RIFF file and how do you make it usable?

4. What is the problem with InDesign's copyediting abilities?

5. What are the advantages of a PDF workflow?

WHERE SHOULD YOU BE BY THIS TIME?

You need to have done several tutorials, skills, miniskills, and hopefully started (at least) on a real project for a real client. Ask your instructor where your weak points are and listen carefully so you can make plans to remedy these lacks in your skill set.

DISCUSSION:

You should be networking with your classmates and finding out their skills and weaknesses. It is quite possible that you will find a future business partner or a subcontractor among them who can supply what you lack in certain areas. Publishing is a team sport, you might as well get started now.

Talk among yourselves...

8

CHAPTER EIGHT

Basic Text Styles

CONCEPTS

1. **Style**
2. **Body copy**
3. **Hanging indent**
4. **Head**
5. **Subhead**
6. **Pull quote**
7. **Paragraph rule**
8. **Kicker**
9. **Leader**
10. **Callout**
11. **Local formatting**

CHAPTER CONTENTS

Presenting the professional setup and use of the styles palettes, both paragraph and character styles

CHAPTER OBJECTIVES

By presenting a basic set of styles for your PARAGRAPH and CHARACTER STYLES palettes, you will learn how to:

1. Gain global control of your documents
2. Save formatting time
3. Maintain consistency within your documents
4. Develop a personal pair of default styles palettes
5. Set up NEXT STYLE chains in your word processor for writing

LAB WORK FOR CHAPTER

- Continue your work on skills and miniskills
- Submit finished theory exams
- Begin working on your approved real project
- Miniskills #3 and #4
- Skill exam #5

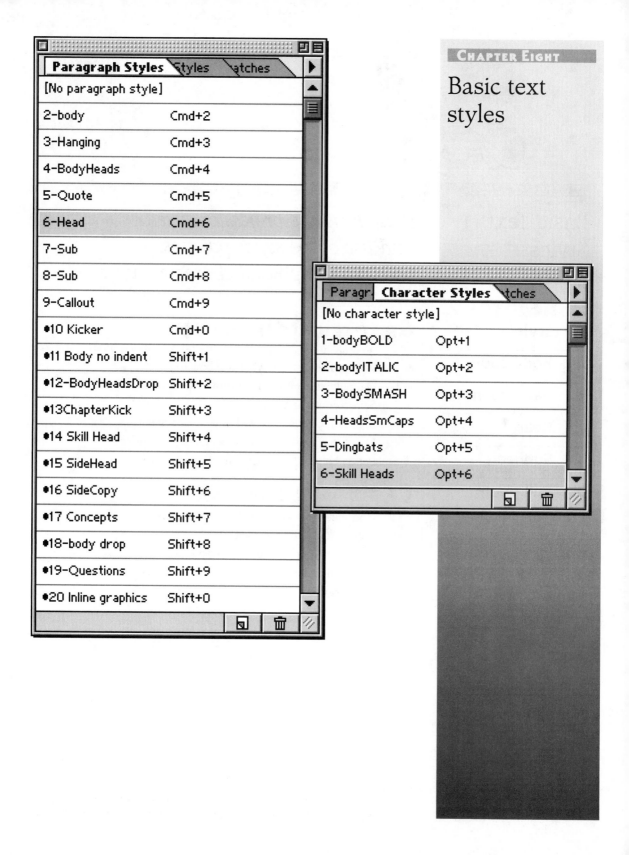

Basic text styles

Paragraph Styles | Styles | atches

[No paragraph style]	
2-body	Cmd+2
3-Hanging	Cmd+3
4-BodyHeads	Cmd+4
5-Quote	Cmd+5
6-Head	Cmd+6
7-Sub	Cmd+7
8-Sub	Cmd+8
9-Callout	Cmd+9
•10 Kicker	Cmd+0
•11 Body no indent	Shift+1
•12-BodyHeadsDrop	Shift+2
•13ChapterKick	Shift+3
•14 Skill Head	Shift+4
•15 SideHead	Shift+5
•16 SideCopy	Shift+6
•17 Concepts	Shift+7
•18-body drop	Shift+8
•19-Questions	Shift+9
•20 Inline graphics	Shift+0

Paragr | **Character Styles** | tches

[No character style]	
1-bodyBOLD	Opt+1
2-bodyITALIC	Opt+2
3-BodySMASH	Opt+3
4-HeadsSmCaps	Opt+4
5-Dingbats	Opt+5
6-Skill Heads	Opt+6

Words are the main thing we do

So far I've mentioned several times why word processors are not professional software, even though they are an essential part of the production process. A certain percentage of you will end up working for firms that are large enough to have a typesetting department. For the rest of us, I've spent a lot of time explaining the shape our copy will be in when we receive it — and how to fix that expeditiously.

In addition, much of the copy will suffer from typos, obvious grammatical errors, and inaccurate content. This is one of the main reasons why you should read the copy early in the design process. This is normal, do not get upset — fix the problems and become a hero.

A word on what we fix

In many if not most cases, we do not have editorial control as graphic designers. What this means, in practical terms, is that you repair only the horribly obvious grammatical errors and all the spelling. The rest you simply warn the client about. If he tells you that is the way it is supposed to be, bite your tongue, and do it the way he wants it.

Part of this is because we speak a living language. What this means, again in practice, is that things are constantly changing. In this day and age, usage is changing extremely rapidly. In many cases, there is no absolute wrong or right. The only sure guide is this: that the customer is always right — but it's part of your job to make sure that the customer knows the alternatives (so she isn't embarrassed).

The customer is always right — after he has heard the options.

When you are paying the bills, you get to do it your way. Until then, it is done as the client requests. Our task is to present the copy readably, with no errors, as the customer approves, on time, and within the budget. Having said all that, our tools are awesome.

THE CORE OF THE PROCESS

PARAGRAPH AND CHARACTER STYLES PALETTES

Styles palettes are the enabling concept for page layout fluidity. Styles palettes are a collection of specialized typographic defaults that can be accessed at the click of a mouse or stroke of a key. You can set up styles for headlines, subheads, body copy, hanging indents, bylines, captions, tabular matter, or whatever your heart desires or imagines. Just keep your style list as simple as possible.

For most beginning designers this seems like a little thing, but believe me, it is not! The major advantage of using PARAGRAPH STYLES is reflow. If you decide that you just don't like Baskerville for this project and want to use Caslon, simply change the relevant style and the entire document changes automatically.

Another problem solved elegantly by the use of styles is the situation where you end up with 16.5 pages of copy in a saddle-stitched booklet. The number of pages has to be divisible by four in saddle stitching, so you are forced to cut to 16 pages or stretch to 20. With a Style palette, you can simply cut the leading of the body copy by a half point and save several inches (every 72 lines saves half an inch if you cut the leading a half point).

Based On

To make a good thing better, any style can be based on any other style. This means that when you change the first style, all the styles based on that style change also. The only things that do not change are the specific changes in the derivative styles. In most documents, all the headlines and subheads are tied together and all the body copy, hanging indents, bulleted lists, bylines, captions, and so on are tied together.

If all the heads are based on Headline and all the copy is based on Body Copy, then an entire document can be reflowed by simply changing those two styles. This saves a lot of time on one- and two-page documents. You can imagine how much time it saves in 100-page booklets.

Next style

To increase the power when writing (usually in your word processor), any style can be set up to change to another when the Return/Enter key is struck. Again, this sounds like a little thing, but think about it. Every head, subhead, and specialized style in this book automatically returns to Body Text when the return is struck. This happens, on average, three times a page. It takes 3 seconds to pick up the mouse and click on the Style palette. This is almost page 175, so approximately 500 seconds, or almost 10 minutes, has been saved so far with this simple default.

In the sample that follows, all you have to do is set up the four styles before you begin. A MEETING style that changes to a TOPIC style that changes to a SPEAKER style that changes to a LOCATION style which has a NEXT STYLE of MEETING. You will have to create the styles and then set the NEXT STYLE option. Once this is set up, you merely select the style for the first meeting and everything else formatted automatically: Meeting to Topic to Speaker to Location to Meeting and so on. All you have to do is keep typing and the returns cause the change to the new style.

The white type in the paragraph rule, the size–length–color of the rule, the indents, the spaces before and after paragraphs, the font changes, the size changes, and all the rest were all specified in the four styles used. If you analyze the styles used in this book, you will quickly see how much variety can be built into a style. You can genuinely make writing, or importing and formatting, a semiautomatic procedure.

Basic Text Styles

Meeting: 8–9 AM

TOPIC: GENUFLECTIONS

Minister of Procedure, Sir Hillary George
THE EAST VERANDA

General Session: 9–NOON

TOPIC: ANNUAL BUDGET

Chaired by Basil Rottenbothem
MAIN BALLROOM

Formal Luncheon: 1–3 PM

ENTERTAINMENT: THE ROLLING STONES

Hiz Oner, The Mayor
MAIN BALLROOM

As you can see, having a set of styles set up like this will save a great deal of time the next opportunity you have to set up a conference brochure. This entire book is formatted with the two styles palettes. Much of the type styling is virtually automatic. All I have to do is remember the shortcuts when I have to start back with one of the heads. Using a well set up style palette in my word processor, I can write and format as fast as I can type.

Copying

This is another powerful use of the style palettes. For every new chapter, I simply import the copy from the word processor with its very different styles that have the same names as the style palette I am using. Then I copy the styles from the template; and the chapter reflows in the new format. A quick check for widows, orphans, and similar typos, applying the character styles where needed, and the chapters are done! All it takes is opening the PARAGRAPH STYLES palette's OPTIONS menu and using the LOAD PARAGRAPH STYLES... command. In 1.5, I don't even have to import the styles; the existing styles automatically change what was done in the word processor.

Because of their ability to reformat documents globally, the PARAGRAPH STYLES palette is indispensable. You should always use it unless you are setting only one or two lines of type (in which case, you are probably in FreeHand, Illustrator, or Photoshop anyway). Styles enable consistency.

SETTING UP YOUR DEFAULT STYLES

The largest problem with using the styles palettes is simply the time it takes to set them up. Most designers have a mental block with this sort of thing. Some think *"this is women's work"* to use an old chauvinism, although women designers are just as guilty as men (and at this point there are more female designers than male). Somehow there is this idea that formatting copy is done by underlings, as if it were some sort of production busywork that has little to do with *"true design"* – whatever the heck that is.

GROW UP! If you leave this part of design to underlings, all of your projects will look like they were done by amateurs (and it will be true). Also, your underlings will get all the good experience and you will end up working for them! For the truth of the matter is that the styles palettes are what set the tone and layout of your design. In reality, you should set up the style palettes for your underlings to use, so you can control how the project looks.

The styles palettes are what set the tone and layout of your design.

The second large reason why the styles palettes are not used more is simply because many designers set up a new set of styles for every project. Because they have no palette continuity from project to project, it takes them an inordinately long time to set things up, so they give up in frustration. You really need to see the consistency of all projects.

The basic styles

When we talked about type we mentioned the *normal* practice of using a serif face for the body copy and a sans serif font for the heads. I imagine that you saw that, knew what it meant, and passed it by without conscious thought. It is now time to spend some conscious effort on that concept. My experience suggests that most people do not know what goes with those two commonly used terms.

Body copy styles

When we talk about body copy, we are talking about everything that is formatted in the basic serif font family used by the bulk of the readable words of your manuscript or word processing file. There are several styles, that are used in almost every document, that need to be on every PARAGRAPH STYLES palette.

- **Body Copy:** As mentioned, this is what the majority of everything will be set in. The basic readable materials.
- **Hanging body:** This style is used within the body copy to deal with lists of concepts, ideas, and so forth. Hanging body styles include bulleted lists, numbered lists, definition lists, and so forth. They are one of the most important factors in readability and used for recapturing the readers' attention (who use these lists as a synopsis). These paragraphs are a bulleted list.
- **Quotes:** There often needs to be a special style to handle long quotations of materials with different indents and often a different alignment. However, it is usually in the same font and size as regular body copy.
- **Captions:** It has been conclusively proven by many people that captions are probably the most important part of your copy. They, too, are usually based on the style of your body copy because of its readability.
- **Bylines:** Using a standard style, based on your body copy, is an excellent method of maintaining consistency.

CHAPTER EIGHT

Basic text styles

Mini #3

QUËRCEL TROUBADOUR INVOICE

You will build a simple invoice using nothing except the Styles palettes for all of the fields that need to be filled according to a given rough layout.

- **Forms paragraphs:** These are paragraphs, again built on body copy, that contain the tabular setups necessary for filling in information needed by the client. We'll discuss this in more detail as we go.

- **Body heads:** These are small subheadings that are really modified body paragraphs with several explanatory body copy paragraphs between (as in *Body copy styles* above and *Headline styles* below).

As you can see, you will be using a couple of these in every project. The rest are determined by the type of job you are dealing with today. Keep these styles in the back of your mind as we go on to the styles needed for headlines and so forth.

Headline styles

Here again we have several styles that need to be in every document. These styles are more concerned with legibility rather than readability. We mentioned this in Chapter 6 when we stated that sans serif fonts are easier to grasp quickly, but they are very poor for reading in large doses. So we need to discuss a little about the purpose of the headers.

Headlines are used to grab readers' attention as they page through your final printed materials. As such, they are normally brief, focused topic statements about the material that follows. I am aware (and I agree) with David Ogilvey's position that headlines can actually be quite long – in the context of advertisements that are presented as tightly focused posters in a magazine spread. In most cases, however, the heads are used as mentioned here, in the first sentence. Again there are several styles that are used in almost all documents.

- **Headline:** This is used as the opening attention grabber for a story, article, chapter, poster, ad, or flyer.

- **Subhead 1:** This style has the same basic purpose as the headline, but it is used to indicate the beginning of a more important section with the story, article, chapter, poster, ad, or flyer.

- **Subhead 2:** These headers of lesser importance are used as lead-ins for important points in ads, posters, and flyers. They are also used as lead headlines for subsections of the sections delineated by the first level subheads.

- **Subhead 3:** This level of headlines is really only used in books, longer articles, and stories.

- **Kicker:** This is a small introductory statement leading into a relatively important headline or subhead.

Of course, this does not cover it all. If you do newsletters, magazines, or books, you will probably need one or two Pull Quote or Callout styles. You will probably need headline and body styles for your sidebars (these may even be in a third font family upon occasion). You may have special column headers or chapter heads or questions or footnotes. Most documents have need for a couple of special styles, like the program meeting styles demoed two pages earlier. The key is to leave room in your standard PARAGRAPH STYLES palette for these special styles.

Local formatting

One of the biggest temptations to new designers is to attempt to fix small problems, or create specialized paragraphs, by going directly to the CHARACTER or PARAGRAPH palettes and the formatting options found there. This is called local formatting because it only affects the paragraph(s) (or the copy in the paragraphs) selected at the time. There is a time and place for this. Local formatting is appropriate for eliminating widows and orphans and for adjusting vertical justification. The problem is that locally formatted type is not reformatted when either of the STYLES palettes are adjusted. So, the rule is this:

Use local formatting only for final cleanup.

All local formatting should be done last, if possible. Its appropriate function is massaging the copy into its final configuration. Even then it should be done very sparingly. Extensive local adjustments can make simple reflow a nightmare costing an amazing amount of extra time and aggravation. Our world is stressed enough without self-inflicted pressures.

Styles used everywhere

As usual, all I can do is share what I have learned and show you the standard palette I use. Again, as with keyboard shortcuts in general, the important thing is to design a standard set of styles palettes that will meet your needs without thought. To rephrase, it is possible to have a set of styles that apply to virtually all situations. All it takes is a little thought and some planning.

If you look at the lists above, you quickly see that there are four styles that are used in every project: body copy; hanging body; headline; and subhead 1. In addition, there are five more styles built off body copy and four more built off headline, plus a few others.

InDesign's keyboard shortcuts

InDesign has so many shortcuts that there are many options that are simply not available because they are already in use. Recognizing this, the Adobe team wisely chose to use the numerical keypad with modifier keys for its styles. In other words, when setting up styles you can pick any numerical keypad number plus a modifier as its shortcut. To get specific, shortcuts will be ⌘/Control 1–0; ⌥/Alt 1–0; and ⇧/Shift 1–0. According to the USER MANUAL, it appears as if you can use multiple modifiers also, but that doesn't work on my machine. I might be doing something wrong, but then thirty styles is a lot to memorize. Plus, we just showed that there are really only a dozen or so that are regularly needed.

 TIP: The important thing to remember, when setting up your styles, is consistency. In my case, for example, ⌘6 always gets me Headline; ⌘3 always gets me the hanging indent; ⌘7 always produces a second level subhead; ⌘9 always supplies a

pull quote. This is true for every document I produce. If I am doing a poster, my main head is ⌘6; my body copy (limited though it is) will be ⌘2. After I key in the copy, it is a matter of a few seconds or a couple of minutes to reflow and set up the entire poster. Changing 2 Body and its subsets to 24 point, for example. The key to quickly flowing production is simple – now I think headline and my hands hit ⌘6 (without conscious thought).

CONCEPT: The simple trick I have learned is to number the styles. This seems strange, but hear me out. I learned this in PageMaker where the shortcut was determined by its place, alphabetically, in the Style Palette. If I didn't number the styles, the shortcuts were constantly changing because the alphabetical position constantly changed as I added or subtracted styles. If I added Byline it bumped ahead of Hanging body, for example. Now (in InDesign) I find that numbering the styles help me to remember the shortcuts.

A BASIC SET OF DEFAULT STYLES

Here are the styles found in my default style palette:

First is always No Style

2 Body copy	⌘2
3 Hanging	⌘3
4 Miscellaneous body	⌘4
5 Quote	⌘5
6 Headline	⌘6
7 Subhead 1	⌘7
8 Subhead 2	⌘8
9 Callout	⌘9
•10 Kicker	⌘0
•11 Body No Indent	⇧1
•12 Body Drop Cap	⇧2
•13 Miscellaneous body	⇧3
•14 Miscellaneous body	⇧4
•15 Sidebar Head	⇧5
•16 Sidebar Copy	⇧6
•17–•20 Miscellaneous	⇧7–⇧0

Paragraph Styles	Styles	Swatches
[No paragraph style]		
2-body	Cmd+2	
3-Hanging	Cmd+3	
4-BodyHeads	Cmd+4	
5-Quote	Cmd+5	
6-Head	Cmd+6	
7-Sub	Cmd+7	
8-Sub	Cmd+8	
9-Callout	Cmd+9	
•10 Kicker	Cmd+0	
•11 Body no indent	Shift+1	
•12-BodyHeadsDrop	Shift+2	
•13ChapterKick	Shift+3	
•14 Skill Head	Shift+4	
•15 SideHead	Shift+5	
•16 SideCopy	Shift+6	
•17 Concepts	Shift+7	
•18-body drop	Shift+8	
•19-Questions	Shift+9	
•20 Inline graphics	Shift+0	

You've noticed that I added bullets in front of the style names for the Shift styles. If I didn't do that, styles 10 through 19 would jump up to before 2 body. You may want to use another character like a tilde, but the concept is important. Also, you can notice that many of my names are abbreviated. In truth, by now I could simply use numbers for the names (they are that automatic for me). When you use a standard palette like this, looking for the miscellaneous styles is simple – because they are always in the same place. For the longer documents (like this book, for example) you will quickly memorize most of the twenty. For all of my documents, styles 2, 3, 6, 7, 8, •15, and •16 are the same. The sidebar styles actually serve as a sans serif body copy set (for me).

Hopefully it is obvious that styles 3 through 5 and •11 through •14 are all based upon 2 Body copy. Styles 7, 8, •10, •15, and •16 are all based on 6 Headline. I can change the fonts for the entire document by simply changing 2 Body and 6 Headline – talk about global document control!

In addition, 4 is usually 4 Caption or 4 Byline (although you can see that I made it my body copy font headlines in this case). If I use both, 4 Byline becomes •14 Byline with the ⇧4 shortcut instead of the ⌘4. It is *not* important that you use my set up. It is important that you find one that works for you. If you always use the same basic palette, you will find that the shortcuts are quickly added to your publishing design repertoire.

THE BASIC UNIT

Paragraph control

Remember, a paragraph is defined by the Return key. Every time the Return key is hit, a new paragraph begins. This is one of the major characteristics of typesetting. If you need to make a line break without ending the paragraph, you must use the soft return (⇧Return or Shift Enter). This is how you *break for sense*. On very narrow paragraphs, you might have to place a soft return at the end of every line to make it read easily (you'll probably have to go to flush left alignment also). If you hit a hard return instead, all the space-before and space-after choices will affect every line. The first-line indent will also apply to every line.

Alignment

The next thing to be dealt with is alignment, orientation, or justification. We have seven choices: flush left, flush right, centered, justified left, justified centered, justified right, and force justified (all). These determine how the paragraphs will sit within the column. Many customers request justified copy because they think it is incredibly neat that you can have both edges of a column line up automatically. In some cases, you need to remind them, gently, that justified copy is often less readable. This is particularly true if you are using relatively narrow columns.

However, as we have mentioned several times, InDesign justifies copy so well that readability is no longer the issue. In fact, there have been several studies that have shown that justified copy is more readable. This is probably due to the consistent line endings, which may allow for easier eye movement from the end of one line to the beginning of the next line. This is the limiting factor in readability.

Tabs

One of the more important things about styles is tabular formatting. A frustrating thing about desktop publishing is that tabs normally

Basic Text Styles

clear out every time you strike the return, especially if you go to a different style automatically. Only if you set tabs in a style can you access them at will. Bulleted or numbered lists are painful without style sheets.

Readability

Justified copy can be hard to read if the column width is too narrow. Other things that make reading difficult include: type size too small; leading too small; tracking too tight; line length too long or too short; tiny x-heights; decorative fonts; weak color; colored backgrounds; sans serif faces; condensed typestyles; all caps; reversed type; underlines; among others. We've covered most of these before.

The main point is simple: the reader is looking for an excuse to ignore your work. Everyone is so pressured and stressed, lacking sufficient time to do what we are supposed to do, that much reading material is eliminated at first glance. Readers feel that they only have time for important stuff. If something is hard to read, they will skip on looking for other articles or ads that matter to them.

Most of us have the following scenario taking place in our homes every day. We bring in the mail. We separate it immediately into three piles: read, file, and toss. The read pile is read immediately after sorting (sometimes before, especially if the letter is from a friend). Bills and notices get looked over and filed. Everything else is thrown away. Magazines and catalogs are sorted into the same piles. Many of us actually stand over the waste basket trying to throw everything away. We simply do not have the time to read everything we receive.

The reader is looking for an excuse to ignore your work.

This is important even with fiction like novels. As I was writing my first book, my wife was trying to read a rather large book with a compelling title, stirring cover illustration, and intriguing back cover synopsis. She loves to read for relaxation. She complained every day for over a week that she didn't know if she would be able to finish the book. It was just too hard to read. It had very wide columns. The type was small, old fashioned, and stylized. The leading was so tight that finding the beginning of the next line took an almost conscious search. She claimed the book was excellent — it was just too hard to read! A week later she tossed the book in the trash — unread!

Indents and tabs

One of the major differences between nonprofessional word processing and typesetting is indents and tabs. Nonprofessionals usually simply use the factory defaults.

Left and right indents

The left and right indents work much as you expect (as long as you remember that they are measured from the frame edges or column sides). They can be used to leave a consistent space for sidebars or graphics. An indent on both sides is the most common method of indicating a long quotation.

First-line indents

Here is a concept many have trouble understanding. What many miss is that the first-line indent is measured from the left indent location. This is what you are supposed to use instead of an opening tab. It seems stupid of me to mention this, but many still do it wrong.

Hanging indents

The first line indent concept just mentioned is important because that first-line indent can be either positive or negative. A normal positive first-line indent is set off to the right from the left indent. A negative first-line indent is set off to the left of the left indent.

The first line can be as large negatively as the left indent is positively. In other words, a left indent of one inch and a first-line indent of minus one inch would start the first line exactly on the margin, but every other line in that paragraph would be indented one inch.

A hanging indent uses this feature to produce bulleted or numbered lists by setting a tab for the first line that matches the left indent. This is basic for many of you, but many still have a great deal of trouble with it. The following examples illustrate (first) with a simple negative first line and (second) with a tab at the left indent.

➡ **Negative first line** – As you can see, this looks a bit strange because you are used to seeing all the lines in a paragraph line up to the same margin or having the first line indented to the right a little. This is why hanging indents are necessary. First of all, they are much neater and tidier. We normally like to see things lined up on the left side. Secondly, a hanging indent greatly emphasizes the bullets or dingbats so that the eye is drawn to the paragraphs involved. As mentioned earlier, bulleted lists are one of the better devices used to attract readers.

The next example shows a genuine hanging indent. To do this, a left tab is placed exactly on top of the left margin, leaving the negative first line.

➡ **Hanging indent with a tab at the left indent** – A hanging indent uses this feature to produce bulleted or numbered lists by setting a tab for the first line that matches the left indent. This time everything is neat and tidy.

Tabs

 CONCEPT: All alignments, indents, and tabs are in relation to the column. For tabs to work as you expect, the alignment almost always has to be flush left. All tabs are tied to a paragraph. Without the automatic wrapping tabs of FreeHand, you have to hit

 Mini #4

PROGRAM POSTER

Construct a convention program schedule in poster form using supplied copy, logo, and map of the facility.

a hard return after every line to get the words to line up correctly. This means you may have to have two virtually identical styles — one with rules and space before or after paragraph, and one without for portions of the tabs that wrap.

Leaders

One of the aspects of tabs that many forget is leaders. This is where a repeating character leads into the tab. You normally associate these with pieces like menus, where a row of dots connects a name with a price. There are many types of leaders. Any character can be used to repeat (InDesign allows us to use up to eight characters as a repeating pattern). Here are four obvious examples.

This is a dot leader produced by a repeating period:

Green Chilé Chicken Alfredo.......................$8.95

This is a line leader produced by a below-line rule (an em long):

Black Beans w/Carne Adovada_____ $11.95

This is a arrow leader produced by Shift+Period (>):

Buy now! >>>>>>>>>>>>>>>>>>> Last chance!

This is a decorative line produced by ⇧ (Option 5 in Diaconia):

⇧⇧⇧⇧⇧⇧⇧⇧⇧⇧⇧⇧⇧⇧⇧⇧⇧⇧⇧⇧

These are just the beginning of leader use. Let's do a quick review. Those of you who know these things can skip ahead until you see a tab set up you don't recognize.

The best use of leaders you need to remember is probably form design. Almost anywhere that repetitive fill-in blanks are needed can be done with leaders. Again, a few examples: This is the identical tab setup as the preceding line leader example. The only difference is that there is no price at the end of the line this time.

```
Transform  Character  Paragraph  Text Wrap  Tabs  Story
↓ ↓ ↓ ↓ X:[    ] Leader:[ ] Align On:[    ]
0        1/2       1        1/2       2        1/2       3        1/2                1/2
```

Name _____

Address_____

City _____

State and Zip _____

_____

The next illustration shows a similar setup with double lines and a blank space between the columns — the right tab at 2" has a line leader; the left tab at 2.125" has no leader, and the right tab at 4.25" has a line leader. This is a style used very commonly for invoice headings. It comes in handy for such things as City/State/Zip, home and work phones, billing and shipping addresses, and so on.

Once you understand the principle, you can easily create forms without having to resort to dedicated table generators or drawing programs. You can have many leaders on the same line. With paragraph styles, it is easy to have different setups for different purposes. The only limiting factor is the time it takes to setup the tabs. Sometimes it is simpler to merely add lines with the line tool (but they do not flow with the copy). This is one place where creativity helps a great deal.

| Transform | Character | Paragraph | Text Wrap | **Tabs** | Story |

Leader: Align On:

```
0        1/2       1        1/2       2        1/2       3        1/2       4
```

#1 _____   #2 _____

#3 _____   #4 _____

#5 _____   #6 _____

#7 _____   #8 _____

Another helpful arrangement looks like the following:

| Transform | Character | Paragraph | Text Wrap | **Tabs** | Story |

Leader: •   Align On:

```
0        1/2       1        1/2       2        1/2       3        1/2       4
```

Yes< • • • • • • >No

Up< • • • • • • >Down

Yesterday< • • • • • • >Tomorrow

Good< • • • • • • >Bad

Intuitive< • • • • • • >Legalistic

Uses for indents and tabs are limited only by your creativity. Simply keep this hint in the back of your mind: **THE SOLUTION TO THIS MIGHT BE A TAB.** In addition, file it next to this thought: *there is no excuse for hitting the spacebar more than once.* However, in some cases, another paragraph tool comes in handy.

Paragraph rules

No, this is not a slogan spray-painted on a blank wall. It is a powerful tool for adding lines in appropriate places. You have the option to automatically add a line above or below a paragraph.

The rule(s) are added when the return is hit at the end of the paragraph. These rules can be almost any width, any color, and almost any length. They can be the length of the line or the width of the column. They can be indented left or right, either positively or negatively; in some cases up to the width of the pasteboard (this enables rules that cross the gutter and the other page of a center spread or even cross a single, double, or triple foldout). Here are some examples (each line is a separate paragraph with a different rule setting).

Sample line w/double rule

Sample line w/double rule

Sample line w/double rule

Sample line w/black above and white below

Sample line w/single rule w/white type

These options for paragraph rules are certainly interesting. You should take the time today to duplicate them. If you cannot figure them out, ask your instructor. If you don't have an instructor, email me at graphics@swcp.com or check out http://kumo.swcp.com/graphics/pneumatika. However, we began with rules used instead of tabs. Here are some examples of these.

NAME:

ADDRESS:

CITY/STATE/ZIP:

PHONE (WORK & HOME):

THESE ARE FIVE PARAGRAPHS WITH A HALF-POINT RULE, WIDTH OF COLUMN, OFFSET SIX POINTS ABOVE THE BASELINE (WITH 6 POINT TYPE), AND A RIGHT TAB AT ONE INCH AND A QUARTER.

Here's a solution to another common problem: a half-point rule above the paragraph, width of text, with negative 1" indents left and right, 6 points above the baseline, centered (using 6-point type in all caps). This particular setup has countless uses. It can also be used for forms that use tiny names just below the blank line (simply change to a flush left alignment). This is one place where all caps is required for it to look good.

AUTHORIZED SIGNATURE

HELP!

A 10 POINT, 21% BLACK ABOVE PARAGRAPH RULE WITH A .7" LEFT INDENT.

Be open to the possibilities

I have been trying to give you a feel for the power available with paragraph formatting. It goes far beyond the ability to cut and paste. STYLES give you immense control over the appearance of the copy. The major professional design problems with word processors lie almost entirely in their inability to produce (or clumsiness in producing) professional-quality type – kerning, exact leading control, tracking, baseline shifts, paragraph rules, and fancy leaders are all beyond the power of most word processors.

Nevertheless, the editing ability of word processors is formidable. In addition, many word processors can preformat paragraphs in styles that can be further improved, automatically, by page layout software. Again, this takes a trained typesetter. The person in your secretarial pool probably cannot handle it without specific training (as I have mentioned many times *[I just don't want you to be surprised]*).

STYLING TIPS

What I want to do here is give you some design tips to use when setting up your set of standard styles. I will go through those that I use, explaining the hows and whys as I go. Again, my solutions will probably be different from yours. You must come up with your own styles. If you do not work on this now, you'll pay with extra unpaid labor later.

2 Body copy

I should be able to assume that you have this under control. Normally this will be 10/12 flush left or justified left. All the other alignment options are much more difficult to read. With a poster, flyer, or advertisement, you may well use centered or justified center. But if you do, be careful to break for sense. In other words, make each line break fall between phrases or concepts to aid readability.

- The standard for body copy is 10/12 with the point size varying from 9 to 12 point. The leading will be determined by the amount of line spacing built into the font used and the x-height. The larger the x-height, the more leading is needed. Many publishers demand 10/12 no matter what.

- Invitations and the like (using script fonts) are normally set at 18/24 because of their severe legibility problems. In general, formality means increased white space. Script make this worse with their extremely small x-heights and unusual letter shapes.

- For posters and flyers, body copy sizing needs to be multiplied by the reading distance. The norm of 10/12 is for normal reading distances of around 18 inches or 45 centimeters. If you expect the readers to be reading from 3 feet or a meter away, you will need to double the point size, at least. If they will be reading it at 18 feet, than you must enlarge the body copy point size by twelve times.

- Longer line lengths or heavily stylized fonts require increased leading. Formality also needs extra leading – plus a lighter, more elegant typestyle.

Basic text styles

Specing form

When specifying type for others (or receiving instructions for formatting) there is a convention that is used. For example, "14/15 left" would be 14-point type with 15 points of leading. It would be said, fourteen on fifteen flush left. When talking about type, you should always size with this size on leading convention.

- Historically, you used either a first line indent or extra paragraph spacing, not both, Now, however, it is common to see a first line indent with a couple of points of space before paragraph. You need to be careful though. If your design style requires that lines of type line up horizontally from column to column, you will not want to add space before or after your body copy paragraphs. You never have the same number of paragraphs per column so they will not line up.

- There is no right or wrong about first line indents. The norm would be somewhere between 12 points to a half inch. However, for highly stylized copy. I have seen first line indents of half the column width with the first letter of the paragraph bumped up to two or three times the normal point size.

3 Hanging body

Here the norm would be to have the left indent the same as the first line indent of 2 Body copy. The negative first line indent should be between half the left indent and all of it. In other words, the bullet should hang somewhere between the left column margin and halfway to the left indent.

- With numbered lists it is often desirable to add an additional tab. With a negative first line indent that is identical to the left indent of the style, you can then add a flush right tab an eighth inch to the left of the left indent. Doing this makes for better number alignment when you go from 9 to 10 or 99 to 100, for example.

- To make your hanging indents work the way you desire, it is normally necessary to change 3 Hanging body to a flush left alignment.

- Watch your lists carefully. Often these paragraphs are so short that you have to break for sense to get rid of the large amount of widows generated. Extra care needs to be taken for readability.

- If your bulleted and numbered lists are crucial to reader understanding, you may want to make them larger, bolder, and/or in a different font than your body copy. They are very important.

Miscellaneous body

Quotes: These are usually indented left and right to the same amount as the first line indent, but this is certainly not written in stone. Quotes are also usually set justified when the body copy is flush left and often set flush left or centered when the body copy is justified. The main thing is to make them different enough.

Bylines: The name of the author of the article is set in many and various ways. Most common is same font as the body copy, flush right, often italic. You may also want to have an entirely different paragraph style at the end of the article with an indent that allows room for a small picture and a short bio to go with the name and credits. The little bio can add a gentle warm fuzzy to help leave the reader with a good taste in his mind about the article.

Captions: This little item has changed greatly in the years I have set type. Originally captions were commonly set small and italic. Current research suggests that the caption is commonly much more important than the headline in attracting readers. Current thought makes captions a little larger than body copy, flush left, with a synopsis of the points the article is making about the picture. In other words, because the picture is illustrating the article (why is it there if it is not?), the synopsis helps the reader decide whether or not to read the articles. Remember, if it is not important to the reader, he or she will be angry if you trick them into reading an article that has no relevance to their life.

Body heads: These lesser subheads are now largely made irrelevant by the Character Styles palette. Before character styles, it was clumsy to make words bold in a paragraph. Not only that, but the words made bold were now locally formatted and therefore unreachable by the styles palette. Not only that, but the bolding was usually accomplished with styling from the bold or italic buttons or the keyboard shortcut. These styling shortcuts commonly attempted to select a PostScript font that didn't exist (so what you intended to be bold was actually printed in Courier). InDesign has solved all of these problems by not only having a CHARACTER STYLES palette but also by only allowing you to select font styles that are truly available, in the CHARACTER palette. *It is important that you set substituted fonts to be highlighted in the Preferences.*

6 Headline

This needs a lot of contrast with the body copy – in size, color, and/or type style. Typically the heads are sans serif and the body is serif, as you well know. However, heads should be a black sans serif and copy needs to be a book serif (lighter than medium, darker than light). The normal size for headlines is 24 to 36 point. In general, they should be reasonably short and pithy. In other words, they need to give the reader a clear idea of what is coming in the copy following.

The alignment needs to be closely watched. If the body copy is flush left, the heads need to be flush left. If they are centered over flush left copy they will typically look off center. If the body copy is justified, the heads can be either left or centered. The main thing is ease of reading and logical consistency.

7 Subhead 1

This needs to be the same basic setup as the headline but about 25 to 33 percent smaller.

8 Subhead 2

This is smaller yet and almost always flush left (even if the heads and first level subheads are centered). Also if the 6 and 7 styles are black, 8 subhead 2 is often bold in the same sans serif. These second level heads do not need nearly as much contrast as the larger, more important heads. As you can see, for this book I have reversed them out of a gray bar.

9 Callout

Pull quotes or callouts are one of the more important typographic features in long articles and books. They are type used as a graphic to recapture the reader's attention (in case it is wandering). Occasionally

Basic text styles

Skill #5

ONE COLOR BOOKLET

This skill exam includes drawing skills as an option to increase your grade. You have the option of using any program that can produce a professional quality, printable EPS or TIFF graphic to add to your basic documents. This requires you to develop the layout and to assemble the resulting documents.

they get extremely graphic, but the norm would probably be 50 to 100% larger in italicized body copy. They often use paragraph rules above and below to set them off, as I have done in this book. If they are actual quotes, it is a common device to make the quote marks extremely large (400 to 1,000% of the point size of the pull quote). By the way, the only difference between the two names is that pull quotes actually quote part of the surrounding copy.

Sidebar styles

There are no real rules here, but let's give it a shot. First of all, sidebars, by definition, contain peripheral information. In other words, they contain data that is interesting and nice to know; but they are often tangential to the main thoughts and concepts of the body copy. This means that they should be deemphasized a little. We still want the body copy to be primary.

The best way to do this is to put the sidebar in a tinted box. Contrary to common, nonprofessional thought, a tint box tends to make items less important. The tint back ground lowers contrast so the type is harder to read. To make a tint box primary, you will need to place a background image over the entire page – then the light, bright tint boxes will stand out. Or you can startle with unconventional placement – like I did above.

As far as type is concerned, you want a font that contrasts with the body copy at least. Depending upon how you intend to use the sidebars, you may wish to pick typestyles that contrast with both the main body and its heads. As I mentioned earlier, in my books I try to set up my sidebar styles so I can use them for emphasis within the main copy also. I use the same font as used in my heads, with a plain, light, or medium version of the font for my sidebar body copy.

The key to remember is that the tint in the tint box will mess up your type. Even at 150 linescreen, the tiny little dots will blur the edges of your characters. So you need to pick typestyles that will not be damaged by those dots. This is why I usually use sans serif for my sidebars. When coupled with the fact that my sidebars are usually very brief, this works well. If your sidebars are going to be long, even a parallel story with your main body copy, maybe you should try something like Century Schoolbook or even a strong contrast like Rockwell or Serif Gothic. Because of the lessened contrast you can use much blacker type than normal. In some cases, an actual Black or Display weight printed at a 70% tint works well.

CHARACTER STYLES

In addition to its paragraph styling power, InDesign offers a very powerful CHARACTER STYLES palette. This palette enables you to format selected text. It is meant as an addition to the PARAGRAPH STYLES palette. One of the main reasons it is so nice is that you can change only what is needed.

For example, I have a **Bold style** (I use Option 1 for the shortcut) that does nothing but change selected words from whatever they were to Diaconia Bold. It does not change the point size, leading, or anything else, just the font. I have an *Italic style* that just changes the font to Diaconia Italic, nothing else. In these cases, I just change the font and nothing else.

The main thing enabled by the CHARACTER STYLES palette is global control of local formatting. If I change the Character style, everything formatted with that style is changed also. I have built up six character styles for various purposes, mainly when I need to temporarily go to a different font, type color, or point size for some purpose. By doing all of my *local formatting* with the CHARACTER STYLES I retain global control over the formatting.

Before character styles, all local formatting resulted in removing the type that was custom formatted from style palette control. Then, if I made a global change to the STYLES palette, I would need to go back and find every locally formatted piece to change it to the new settings. Now all I have to do is change the PARAGRAPH STYLES and then change the relevant CHARACTER STYLES.

Styles you'll need

I have found four character styles that I always need. First come a **1 Bold** and a *2 Italic* style to modify anything based on 2 Body copy. You will constantly need to add at least italic styling to words in your body copy paragraphs. Third, I have a style that I call **3 SMASH** that formats to an entirely different, sharply contrasting font for major emphasis within a paragraph. I find that I also use a style to make certain lines formatted in one of the headline or subhead styles to a small caps version of the headline font. As I mentioned earlier, I have created a true small caps version of my headline font for this book (using Fontographer). So, my **4 HEADSSMCAPS** character style enables me to switch to small caps whenever needed.

You will also notice that I have used the ⌥ key (Option/Alt) as the modifier with all of my character styles, with the style numbered to retain consistent order (and to help me remember the shortcut). This gives me ten character styles, which is far more than I have ever needed. So I have twenty paragraph styles and ten character styles to memorize. I find that I use most of them enough so they are relatively easy to remember. If I forget, I quickly open the relevant palette and I can see what the shortcut will be by the number before the style name. In my case, with paragraph styles, 1–•10 is the Command key; •11–•20 is the Shift key; and 1–•10 on the Character Styles palette use the Option key.

Remember, that consistency is the most important thing. You need to have the same styles with the same names for all of your documents. This way they can easily be remembered and applied without conscious thought. It does not matter at all if you use the same styles as I do. You need to come up with a set that will work for you. Observe yourself as you work and add styles as you use them. Consciously try to set them up in a way that is logical to your mind and memory. Do the best you can to keep the same styles in all documents and you will find your formatting speed doubles or triples. You can use mine to start with.

TO SUM UP...

You will never be competitive professionally, either in speed or in consistency, until you begin formatting everything with your STYLES palettes. If you have never done this, it will be a major adjustment. If you have only done it a little or occasionally, it will be a major revelation.

This is where you really enter the world of digital publishing. Between you and me, *those illustrators* really believe that they are the most important part of publishing. Just let them keep their delusions. The person who makes a document work is the person who does the formatting. No matter how good the supplied layout, it will not work without excellence (and speed) in formatting.

In fact, STYLES palettes could be considered a major portion of the new paradigm of digital publishing. Traditional publishing used specialists for everything, with the formatting done by lower level craftspersons. In the new paradigm, the formatting is done by the designer.

The amount of time

It will take you a while to make style palettes your habit. You need to decide to generate no documents without using the style palettes. In many cases, it will seem to slow you down. In fact, as you start this process, it will slow you down — temporarily. Style palette formatting does not save you much until it becomes a subconscious habit. **YOU WILL DEFINITELY HAVE TO WORK AT IT.**

To learn what you need for your personal set of default styles you will need to set everything with styles: business cards, flyers, ads, programs, brochures, bookmarks, books, newsletters, signs — every document you create for at least three months (six months would be better).

Yes, it is true that once this becomes a subconscious part of your working style, you can do the simple stuff without the styles palettes. But you will find (when you need to globally change the fonts) that you will wish you had formatted with styles. The basic concept is very simple: STYLES palettes may take a little longer starting a document, but they save huge amounts of correction and editing time over the months and years. If you haven't tried it, you will be amazed.

1. What is the major advantage of basing all of your styles on one or two core styles?

2. Which styles should you base your subsidiary styles upon?

3. What is the problem with *local formatting*?

4. Why do you want default styles palettes?

5. What are the advantages of numbering styles?

WHERE SHOULD YOU BE BY THIS TIME?

You should have done several tutorials, skills, miniskills, and started on a real project for a real client. Ask your instructor where your weak points are and listen carefully so you can make plans to remedy these lacks in your skill set.

DISCUSSION

You should be networking with your classmates and finding out their skills and weaknesses. It is quite possible that you will find a future business partner or a subcontractor among them who can supply what you lack in certain areas. Publishing is a team sport, you might as well get started now.

Talk among yourselves...

Basic Text Styles

Basic Layout Techniques

CONCEPTS

1. **Gutter**

2. **Gripper**

3. **Sidebar**

4. **Mill order**

5. **Signature**

Presenting more of the basic setting and design considerations for every job

CHAPTER OBJECTIVES

By presenting the basic set up options for your new documents, you will learn how to

1. Determine an appropriate page size
2. Determine appropriate margins and gutters
3. Maintain consistency within your documents
4. Produce interest through layout
5. Define the true purpose of consistency

LAB WORK FOR CHAPTER

- Continue work on skills and miniskills
- Submit finished theory exams
- Continue work on your approved real project

Basic layout techniques

Product WATCH

as self-contained AVI movies. The $99 Digital Photo Maker from Dazzle Multimedia (888/436-4348, www.dazzle.com) is a small device that lets you capture and export video on a USB-equipped Mac. The package includes two simple editing applications, Dazzle PhotoStudio for still photos and Dazzle VideoImpression for video.

Two for One Now you can have USB and FireWire and still keep a PCI slot free. The $159 OrangeLink FireWire/USB Board — Orange Micro (714/779-...micro.com) is

---

news

(800/835-9433, www.tek.com) has launched a site called Creativesite.com where artists and photographers can post examples of their work.

multimedia

Macromedia Weaves Web Upgrades

FIREWORKS MAKES NICE WITH ADOBE APPS

by Frith Breitzer

Macromedia (415/252-2000, www.macromedia.com) may be learning that the best way to compete with Adobe is to ...'s own game. With ...media's

Fireworks vector graphics as Illustrator files. You can import Adobe Photoshop files with layers and editable effects, and the program now works with third-party Photoshop plug-ins, such as Alien Skin's Eye Candy.

In addition to improving integration with Adobe products, Fireworks 3 lets you export SWF files for use in Flash 4, Macromedia's popular vector animation software. You can also preview rollovers and gamma differences between Macintosh and Windows displays.

Weaving HTML The integration theme carries over to Dreamweaver 3, an upgrade to Macromedia's HTML authoring program that works with native Fireworks and Flash 4 files. In addition to importing the files directly, you can launch Fireworks or Flash from within Dreamweaver to edit the files. When you quit Fireworks or Flash, the modified graphic gets placed in the Dreamweaver document. In this feature, Macromedia may be anticipating the next version of Adobe GoLive, which will likely boast improved synergy with Adobe's other products, including InDesign, Photoshop, ImageReady, and Illustrator.

Other new Dreamweaver 3 features include local and remote file synchronization, the ability to define styles without using Cascading Style Sheets, and the ability to edit tags within the document window.

Dreamweaver 3 and Fireworks 3 are expected to ship by the time you read this.

Vio Grand

Applied Graphics Technologies and Vio Worldwide Ltd. have announced an alliance that will result in the creation of a global digital media asset management service. The service, M-Cast, will allow users to build, update and access a database of their digital media assets efficiently and economically from anywhere in the world over Vio's secure network. With corporate brand owners and their graphic arts service providers in mind, M-Cast brings AGT's Digital Link asset management technology and database experience together with Vio's Digital Graphics Network. M-Cast users will pay a monthly service fee, and they will also pay to store their assets on a cents-per-MB per month model.

Vio is also entering into a relationship with Kodak Polychrome Graphics. The two companies are coming together to promote the benefits of remote proofing. To that end, one free year of Vio's global managed network service will be bundled with any Kodak DCP 9300/9500 desktop color proofer purchased before the end of 1999. The Vio bundle includes Vio's two-channel ISDN service, worldwide access through a Vio toll-free number and 300MB of free file transfer per month. After using the 300MB allowance, users will pay only $.40/MB to transfer files. (AGT, www.agt.com; Kodak Polychrome Graphics, www.kpgraphics.com; Vio, www.vio-dgn.com)

Free software is cool

Nikon announces a scanning software upgrade for its Super Coolscan 2000 and Coolscan III film scanners. The NikonScan 2.5 package takes color management to a new level, increases ease of use and adds Altamira Genuine Fractals 2.0 LE scaling technology to the bundle. NikonScan 2.5 ships "in the box" with all new Super Coolscan 2000 and Coolscan III models, and previous users can download the new package free of charge from www.nikon techusa.com. Although the Altamira software is not included in the free download, the site links to the Altamira Group Web site for information on the product. (Nikon, www.nikonusa.com)

Objects-oriented

Whether you're looking for an image of a birthday cake or dental floss, it can probably be found in Corbis' first royalty-free image catalog completely dedicated to objects. Objects Collection 1 includes every image from its 16 Objects Collection CDs. Each image comes with a handmade clipping path, which allows it to be dropped into a layout without a halo effect. A comping disc lets you search for a specific image quickly and easily, but it might be more fun to spend some time thumbing through the print version, enjoying the images. (Corbis Images, www.corbisimages.com)

...-Jet Printers

...ING STIFF COMPETITION ...announced two new ink-jet ...w.epson.com). The $279 ...x replaces the Stylus Color ...k at up to 9.5 ppm and pho-...h Stylus Color 760, $199 after ...ext at up to 7 ppm and color ... Both printers feature USB and ...connections. Epson offers a $159 ...odels that allows connection to ...tworks.—MACWORLD STAFF

Font Savior

A new technology from DiamondSoft promises to standardize the way applications save font information within documents and enable accurate automatic font activation. Font Sense technology allows print publishers to realize a seamless workflow: to open a document in any application, have the correct fonts activate with it and print it without problems. Font Sense makes this happen by saving a precise font specification with documents. This includes information such as the name of the font, its foundry and its version number. In addition, it also contains information about the font's outlines, width tables and kerning tables. With all this information available to it, Font Sense knows to activate the correct font. Font Sense technology is built into Font Reserve 2.5 and Font Reserve Server. (DiamondSoft, www.fontreserve.com)

The page in back is a layout from *MacWorld Magazine*, January 2000.
The page in front is a layout from *Publish Magazine*, November 1999
Both of these samples show the use of a multicolumn grid to promote visual interest.

A general overview of page layout

In this chapter we move on to the heart of graphic design. This is where designs become reality. Illustrations are nifty — sometimes spectacular — but they don't communicate specific messages very well. The copy contains the meat of the matter, but it won't be read without excellence in design to capture the attention of the reader. Even copy and illustrations put together are a waste without an overall design and consistent direction.

This chapter takes you through many of the decisions you must make to start page layout, step by step. It's a conceptual analysis of how to produce documents, plus lots of tips and warnings. In a program like InDesign, these procedures are absolutely essential for professional production speed and accuracy.

GETTING STARTED: BASIC SETTINGS FOR EVERY PROJECT

Many parameters have to be covered for every document. We've already covered a lot of this in passing while discussing Preferences and Defaults. You might want to consider setting your measuring system to inches or millimeters, for example. You should work in whatever measurement system works best for you. To repeat, the point is to set it up so it works best for you.

Size

Often document size is a given. Magazine and newspaper sizes are determined by the publisher, for example. If you have any options, make sure that you design for an economical cut out of the paper stock you choose. If you only have 23"x35" sheets available, 9"x12" pages are a horrible cut. Instead of having eight 8.5"x11" sheets, you can only get four 9"x12" sheets. If you can locate 25"x38" stock, however, 9"x12" works well.

Here are some interesting cuts out of 23"x35": 7.5"x11" gives nine out; 11"x11" gives six out; 7.5"x16" gives six out; 5.5"x17" gives eight out. You can get a four-page, 4"x9" rack brochure out of a standard 8.5"x11" sheet. If you come up with some really wild cuts or folds, check them out with your printer or bindery before you show them to your client. There are some terrific folds that have to be done by hand — but, handwork costs a fortune! A quick conversation with your bindery can save you lots of money and uncounted heartache. There are times when that custom hand-folded job is the perfect solution. Usually, forcing the bindery to do a lot of handwork is one of the quickest ways to a blown budget

One of the major things you need to do is pick a paper and find out what parent sizes are readily available in your area. I can't speak for sizes available outside the United States. Here almost every paper is available in 23"x35". However, for projects where you want or need to get outside 8.5"x11" module, there are papers that come in 25"x38", 19"x25", 20"x26", 26"x40", and several other parent sizes. Check your paper suppliers' catalog to find out what is available.

Basic Layout Techniques

This is especially true when you find a gorgeous color or texture in your paper supplier's swatchbook. No distributor can afford to carry every color of every product line in stock. Many of the prettier colors and weights are only available as a mill order. Mill orders can require a minimum of five to fifteen cartons and a three-month wait. I'm not saying that you shouldn't use these gorgeous papers. I'm saying that you need to plan ahead to budget both the time and the money necessary for a mill order. Often it is a wonderful solution for your client's need for a standout brochure or presentation folder. Without planning, it can be a budgetary disaster.

 TIP: I know this seems stupid, but it is a common problem. One of the first things you need to do when you get set up as a professional designer is to contact some of your local paper distributors. You need to get a copy of their catalog and swatchbooks

Calculating number out

This seems like a simple problem, but many simply have not seen it done. You divide a number into the width and the height of the parent sheet to come up with appropriate size measurements for a custom-sized project.

23" by 35"
the most common parent sheet size in the States

As we all know, 11" goes into 23" twice, and 8.5" goes into 35" four times. Two times four equals eight out — or we can get eight 8.5"x11" sheets out of a 23"x35" parent. However, 8.5 only goes into 23" twice and 11" goes into 35" thrice which gives us only six sheets out.

Often it is easier to divide the width and height by whole numbers to determine unusual sizes. For example, 23 divided by 3 equals 7.67", and 35 divided by 6 is 5.83". So, a little flyer or postcard set at 5.5"x 7.25" would give me 18 trimmed out of a 23"x35" parent even with a full bleed.

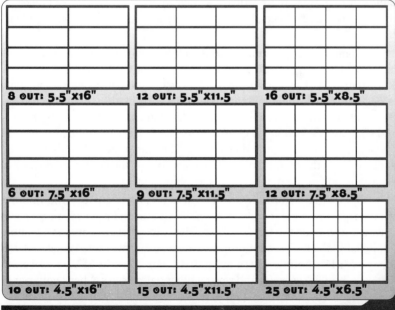

8 OUT: 5.5"x16" 12 OUT: 5.5"x11.5" 16 OUT: 5.5"x8.5"

6 OUT: 7.5"x16" 9 OUT: 7.5"x11.5" 12 OUT: 7.5"x8.5"

10 OUT: 4.5"x16" 15 OUT: 4.5"x11.5" 25 OUT: 4.5"x6.5"

of the papers you intend to use. This is a relatively major effort, and do not believe the hype of the salesperson. Every printing process has different paper requirements, and it is important that you pick a paper stock that will work well and easily. In addition, there are tens of thousands of different papers. One of the major things you can do as you establish your style is pick paper stocks that you like, that fit your sense of style. Picking your standard papers is as important as building your personal font list.

In the graphic at the bottom of the previous page, you can see some simple mathematical cuts of a typical 23"x35" sheet of paper. They are merely meant to give you something to think about. The 12 out: 5.5"x11.5" cut makes a beautiful 5.5" square four-page sig for a little booklet or brochure. It also makes an excellent 5.25" square booklet, full bleed. The 6 out: 11"x11.5" gives an eight-page signature of that same booklet, and the full 23"x35" sheet gives you a 24-page signature. Neat, huh?

If you don't remember what a signature is, let's give a quick reminder. A signature is a sheet of paper with multiple pages arranged on it so that, after it is folded and trimmed, the cut pages end up in the proper order.

Bleeds

Again, in an advanced page layout book like this, I should not have to mention bleeds. I should be able to assume that you know about them. In fact, I did just that until I remembered all of the "advanced" students I teach who have certainly heard about bleeds, but in truth do not know why we need them or how to produce them. So, I've come back to this spot in the book again to try to clear up the mess.

A bleed is needed when you produce a design where you really need the ink to go exactly to the edge of the paper. To produce a bleed, you must make everything that reaches the edge of the page an eighth inch oversize and then trim the piece back to finished size after printing. That's an eighth inch, nine points, or a little less than four tenths of a millimeter (.375 mm to be precise).

You may discover that the printing company you are using asks for a different bleed. For my last book, *Digital Drawing*, Webcom wanted a quarter-inch bleed because it fit their digital imposition better. However, that is very unusual. You will almost never go wrong in making the bleed exactly an eighth inch.

Bleed production problems and tips

The most common problem is seen when the submitted artwork goes exactly to the trim (the edge of the finished size). If you do that, you force your printer into four bad choices:

1. They can either print it as submitted, leaving little slivers of blank paper on one of the four sides on almost every finished piece.
2. They can enlarge everything by 102%, or so, which changes the appearance and messes with the margins.
3. They can bounce the job back to you to be fixed, which can blow your deadlines.

Basic Layout Techniques

4. They can fix it themselves, which can be a couple of hundred dollars of nonbudgeted expense out of your pocket. (You don't really expect the client to pay for your stupidity, do you?)

The second major problem shows up when you have forgotten to tell them that there is a bleed when getting your estimate or price quote. This causes the previous problems one and three. Plus, a bleed requires oversized paper to enable trimming back to size. Commonly, a bleed bumps the paper costs up 25% or more. For letter-sized pieces you can only cut six-out instead of the normal eight-out from a 23"x35" sheet. The only other solution is to print it as submitted and cut it undersized. An eighth inch on all sides means your precious 8.5"x11" is cut back to 8.25"x10.75".

The worst scenario, as far as you are concerned, is to have the service bureau or printing company fix it for you. First, they charge from $75 an hour to $250 an hour for the privilege. Secondly, they will now assume that you are yet another of those incompetent desktop geeks who are the bane of their existence. Thirdly, because their focus is production, the way they modify for bleeds will almost certainly change your design in ways you find horrifying.

Finally, there is that subtle area that will probably catch many of you smug ones who are belittling all of the others in your mind. If you make the margins too small, not allowing for gripper and or image area considerations, the printer will be forced to print it like a bleed

The dotted line is the actual trim size of the document.
BLEED   **TRIM**

regardless. They will have to print on oversized paper and trim it back to size. This can completely eliminate all of your profit on the project and even make a sizable dent in your savings, if the project is large enough.

Margins

Again this seems to be too obvious, but many ruin their job here. The most common amateur mistake is to make margins too small (which we just mentioned under bleeds). Every sheet of paper has to have a gripper left. The gripper is that blank portion of the sheet needed for the press to physically grab the paper and pull it through. Ask the printer what their gripper is, it differs for almost every press.

On digital printers, you need to be very careful to stay inside the maximum image area. You can assume that you need to leave .375" margins, minimum. On digital printers and presses, you often need to leave half-inch margins (especially on letter-sized printers). Anything less than that is often priced as a bleed because your project will have to printed on oversized paper and trimmed back to size.

TIP: If you are having your project trimmed after printing, you need to be careful to take cutter inaccuracies into consideration. Most power cutters are only accurate to ± 1/16". Many of the older ones can barely manage ±1/8". This is one of the major reasons why bleeds are set at an eighth inch.

In addition, margins are often a large part of style. If you are trying for the elegant look of an old book, for example, you will need huge margins. There are many formulas, but here's one you can try: 100% top, 125% outside, 200% bottom, and 150% inside (for example, 1" top; 1.25" outside; 2" bottom; and 1.5" inside). Many clients will not allow the margins required for the style, "Look at all that empty paper. I can't afford to waste that space!" You might want to keep some old books of the style to help persuade.

Conversely, if you need to convey cheap bargains – yard sale flyer, grocery store ad, and so forth – you need very small margins, gutters, and a lot of rules and boxes. You need to fill every open white space, making the page look like everything is crammed in to save money.

Columns

Be very careful with your column choices. It is easy to bore your audience to the point of reader rejection. Symmetrical layouts are the worst, unless you need to be formal and reserved. Two or four columns tend to divide in half. It is hard to make the reader's spreads look like they flow as one consistent unit. They are really only useful in extremely formal setups. Even then they should be handled with care.

An extremely common setup is six, seven, eight, or more columns. These are used as grids that can be readily divided into different column structures within the same page to keep things interesting. A six-column grid can have stories that are six single columns, three double columns, two triple columns, a double and a quadruple, and so on. Just set up your guides and make the text blocks as needed.

Generally, the more asymmetrical and the more open you can lay out the piece, the better. Of course, you can go crazy and make things totally illegible. Modern style tends to be chaotic, splashy, and overly complex (think Disney™). But your innate taste and discretion should keep these tendencies in check. The basic concept is that we have all become extremely used to "normal" layouts. In fact, these factory default layouts tend to put your piece in the "bureaucratic camp" or worse. Plus, we are all graphically jaded. As a result, it is necessary to go a little out of the ordinary to allow the reader to even see the piece – boring layouts are invisible and the readers simply skip over them.

TIP: Be very careful of using cheap clipart. Art from sources like Word™ or CorelDraw™ is instantly recognizable, and subconsciously causes most readers to reject your work as bad quality, bureaucratic, official, or any number of similar horrible epithets. My personal recommendation is Artville or Dynamic Graphics clipart. All of us use clipart. The important thing is to purchase high quality art, with unlimited use, in current styles. This needs to be a standard yearly line item in your budget. You should plan on $1,000 or more, if possible.

The problem, of course, is that wildly different designs are not read either. There are some exceptions, like the current grunge fad; the graphics for *The Practice*; a lot of MTV, Fox, or ESPN2; and so on. Take a look at some of the Web sites or marketing for the Xtreme sports. However, most of these designers frankly admit that their work is illegible. They are selling rebellion, and the very illegibility and destruction of the norm is what calls their readership to their work. It wouldn't work for more conservative products. (And our dirty little secret is that most of these rebellious images are from companies that are unreliable financially — there are not many MTVs, *Wired* magazines, or shows like *The Practice*.) You need clients who pay well and on time. Most of them are more than a little conservative.

Gutters

Gutter is one of those terms that you have to watch. It means different things in different places. Sometimes it means the interior margins of a reader's spread. Most often it means the vertical gap between two columns. Column gutters provoke many strongly held opinions. The general rule is that a gutter should be larger than a pica (.167") and smaller than the margins. For most purposes, one-quarter inch works well. The guiding principle is that gutters need to be small enough so the columns of a story hold together as a text block. Yet the reader must be able to easily read down the column without jumping the gutter to the neighboring column.

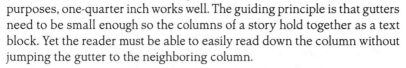

If confused, they flee!

If there is any tendency to read straight across, from column to column, your readers will get confused. If confused, they flee (turn the page to something else). If you decide that you need narrow gutters, you should separate the columns with a thin (or light colored) vertical rule. The only problem with rules, boxes, and borders is their tie to cheapness and low quality, as mentioned earlier. In general, for readability, the use of vertical rules necessitates wider gutters than normal.

Smart, curly, or typographer's quotes

Automatic typographer's quotes are one of those things that sounds good in principle but works less than perfectly in practice. It is important that you learn to access the characters without the *smart quotes* option turned on. The problem is the real use of inch and foot marks — 8.5"x11". They can get curly without you noticing. Curly inch marks are a far worse typo than straight quotes. If you have to enter measurements, it is usually better to shut off typographer's quotes and enter them by hand. The keyboard access on the Mac is: for double quotes Option[and Option Shift{;

Basic layout techniques

Japanese Paths

Japanese gardening has developed a standard set of rules for laying paths or brickwork.

• **The basic concept is to never let a group of stones be cut in half by a line of mortar. A mortar line should never extend more than two stones before it is blocked by another stone.**

• Another standard rule is to always place pieces in odd-numbered groups. Even-numbered groupings are always divided into at least two portions by the brain, thereby destroying the unity of the design.

• These rules also work exceptionally well for groupings of any kind, such as: columns, short newsletter stories, photo montages, catalog pages, and so on.

for single quotes Option] and Option shift}. The PC keyboard is different. InDesign has a keyboard shortcut that allows you to toggle typographer's quotes on and off. You should use it (although it's not completely reliable).

Guides

Guides are the equivalent of the non-repro blue lines drawn in traditional pasteup. They enable designers to line up graphic pieces to help keep their designs neat and tidy. More than that, it is assumed that text blocks will line up with each other; that graphics will line up to an assumed grid; that headlines and subheads will relate to that inferred grid. Many designers get very tense if you do not line up the bottoms of the columns as well as the tops. Version 1.5 now has vertical justification, but this causes spacing problems, however subtle.

TIP: Especially when you are learning your craft, shut the guides off on a regular basis. Until you get used to the fact that these lines appearing in your design on the screen do not print, you will tend to leave room for them. As a result, many of your white spaces will be too large. This is a terrible problem with programs that surround text and graphics with non-printing lines, like InDesign and Quark. Proofing helps a lot, but simply turning off the guides and frame edges occasionally will tend to keep you on track.

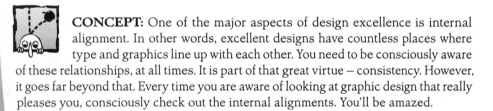

CONCEPT: One of the major aspects of design excellence is internal alignment. In other words, excellent designs have countless places where type and graphics line up with each other. You need to be consciously aware of these relationships, at all times. It is part of that great virtue – consistency. However, it goes far beyond that. Every time you are aware of looking at graphic design that really pleases you, consciously check out the internal alignments. You'll be amazed.

"Snap-To" controls

All professional programs except paint applications have snap-to commands. In all of them, the principle is the same. When you move an item within a specified distance of a guide (or grid or ruler), that item jumps to exact alignment with the guide, ruler, grid, or whatever. Many designers seem to think this is the greatest thing since white sliced bread. Others (like myself) aren't so sure. In fact, often *snap-to's* really get in the way. Some use them very occasionally when creating something with a tight, regular, repeating grid structure. However, the biggest problem with digital design is the computerized, overly perfected images. Snap-to guides are one of the main culprits.

If you use snap-to's a lot, be careful to introduce randomness in judicial quantities. It is extremely easy to produce lifeless boredom with page layout set on autopilot. If you are compulsive about vertical justification, where both the tops and the bottoms of column line up on a grid, then snap-to rulers are for you. You can easily set up these programs so type baselines snap to a ruler based on your leading. Vertical justification can add inconsistent paragraph spacing. Be careful to keep your brain from slipping into neutral as the text flows in so automatically.

Finally, if you cannot move your graphic or text block into precisely the correct position – if it keeps jumping around , out of your control – it is snapping to something. Turn off the relevant snap-to and you will be able to move it exactly into position. It will also help a lot if you enlarge to 400% or more. Sometimes you think things are jumping and you are just moving them less than a pixel. In other words, the low resolution screen image can jump even when things are lined up perfectly. You will be surprised how often InDesign's 4,000% enlargement comes in handy. Even in FreeHand, where you can enlarge 25,600%, I regularly use it all.

Auto leading

Automatic leading is line spacing based on percentages. Like all things automatic, it gives good results, on average. However, average is a mythical figure. The average family now has 1.7 children. Which family is that, and what does a .7 child look like? Always be very careful of averages. They are one of the main reasons for mediocre design.

Autoleading is based on the fact that normal body copy is 10/12 (spoken "ten on twelve" or 10-point type with two extra points of space between the lines). Auto lead is factory defaulted to 120 percent which makes 10/12. However, it also makes 40/48, which is ridiculous. Forty-point heads often have to be set 40/35 or less to look good. In fact, if you are setting heads or subheads in all caps, the autoleading should probably be 75% (if you use it).

In addition, auto lead is based on the largest character in a line. If you add an in-line graphic (or anchored graphic), the line containing the graphic will increase its leading to allow for the image. This can leave huge and unsightly gaps in your copy. Word processors can add this extra leading whenever you use superscript or subscript. Fixed leading, or leading with a specified point size, will cause the image to overlap the lines above and/or below. There is no right or wrong here. You simply need to be aware of the problems and control the leading to produce what you desire.

Master pages

Some might think that this fantastic ability requires at least a larger subhead, or something. Really, all master pages do is place repeating elements automatically. Adobe suggests the concept of a background image, and it's not a bad one. Unless you have a large project or a repeating task like a monthly magazine, master pages are only used to place automatic numbering markers for page numbers.

InDesign allows for multiple master pages, plus you can have parent/child master pages where the child is based on the master (just like in Styles). I don't know how many master pages are available. All I know is that it is far more than you'll ever need, no matter what. This might be important if you design a 200-page monthly magazine or a huge daily newspaper, but most of us do not. In fact, multiple master pages are really only helpful to designers who work with projects that repeat monthly, such as newsletters, magazines, reports, and so forth.

Basic layout techniques

An apology

I realize many of you are wishing I would give you more specific instructions. The problem with that is I would just show you how I would do it. For most of these options, there is no right or wrong. All I can do is pose the questions, and give the basic parameters. You will have to decide how to set things up so you can communicate most effectively with your client's readers.

That being said, I use master pages more every year. They are indispensable for newsletters, magazines, programs, annual reports, or any kind of multiple-page book or booklet. I am using two, plus a child of one of them, for this book.

Automatic page numbering

InDesign does page numbering in a method more reminiscent of a word processor than anything else. There is a menu command under the Layout menu — LAYOUT >>> INSERT PAGE NUMBER. You simply use that command wherever you want with an insertion point flashing in the text block you desire. If you do it on a master page, the page number will appear on all pages where that master page is applied (or its child). If you insert a page number on a normal page, the number will be on that page only. It will always be correct, no matter how many pages you add, delete, or rearrange. The main advantage to this method is that it is easy to remember.

Version 1.5 now offers automatic "continued from" and "continued to" numbering. However, you shouldn't do that regardless, except under duress. All studies suggest that the vast majority of copy continued on another page is not read. Something like 10% to 25% of readers actually go the continued copy — **AT BEST**. You are far better off to make it strict policy to redesign as necessary to eliminate any continued articles. On those rare occasions where it is necessary, you'll normally have to go to the online help to remember, anyway.

Table of Contents and Index

Here are two more capabilities like master pages. If you need them, they are critical. If you don't — yawn! With InDesign, these capabilities require a specially purchased plug-in. Virginia Systems produces one called Sonar Bookends InDex, http://virginiasystems.com, that is extremely powerful. There is a hope that future releases will include something like it. Tables of contents are normally created from information stored in the Style palette. Indices are created by hand flagging the entries and then automatically gathering them into an index. Sonar Bookends InDex reportedly provides extremely powerful options. Ole Kvern has given us a script for Tables of Contents, but it is very limited.

These features are geared toward the publishing end of our industry — books and magazines. They are specialized abilities that most of you will rarely use. When you are looking for software, make sure that you have the features you need. However, the most important feature is ease of use for your specific projects. If every job is different, you need flexible software that makes spontaneity easy. If most of your jobs are repetitive, you need automation and specialized features. Buy the plug-ins that will save you enough production time to pay for themselves.

Tables

Like all professional page layout software, InDesign has trouble with tables. Tables are intrinsically complicated items to set up, even though they are commonly needed. At this point, the best available is a plug-in called PowrTable from PowrTools Software Inc. (http://www.powrtools.com). It is an updated version of Adobe Table (from the same company, but it was bundled free with PageMaker). For those of us who have a copy of Adobe Table, it still works as good as it ever did. Either the plug-in or the stand alone software make EPSs that can be imported into InDesign as a graphic. I assume that PowrTable is much more embedded and integrated, but Table works fine for me.

Basic Layout Techniques

Sidebars

In general, sidebars are a wonderful idea. As mentioned before, sidebars contain interesting data that is not essential to the document. They add reader interest. They add graphic interest. They alleviate boredom. They contain graphic and typographic aberrations that are added merely for aesthetic reasons.

Some design considerations

Sidebars need to have definite, sharp contrast to normal body copy. You can do this with different fonts, different alignment, tint boxes, borders, or all of the above. Sidebars (for all of their impact) must be lesser than normal body copy. Tint boxes or background graphics lessen contrast enough to be very helpful here. Sidebars are also stored at the sides of the page (duh). In this position, they greatly help in making newsletter or book pages asymmetric and visually more interesting.

The sidebar should be the frame that shows off the normal copy. My sidebar location in the page gutters of this book give the body copy you are reading a lot more impact. By now you probably don't even see those center tints, type, and graphics, but they are still working! Compare this textbook with one that doesn't have such a graphic device and the difference will be obvious.

A FINAL WORD ON CONSISTENCY

We've called this a major virtue in digital publishing, and this is true. On the other hand, I am not referring to rigidity and absolute rules. While it is certainly true that there are a strong set of normals in graphic design, no design will be effective unless you break some of those rules. The key comes in clearly acknowledging how your readers are reacting and the making specific breaks to the norm to increase their understanding by making specific points.

The callout or pull quote style, for example, is a severe break in the normal flow of the text. It is used to jolt the reader's eye into seeing the specific concept that is most important to the editorial sense of the story at that point. If used too often, they become part of the norm and are seen no more (on a conscious level, at least). Devices like pull quotes work best when they are found sparsely.

The same is true of drop caps. If they are used as intended – to indicate the starting point of an article, section, or chapter – they are very powerful. If they become a mere graphic ornament following every major subhead, the impact is lost.

Styles and the basic format settings are used to provide that consistent base from which the graphic devices stand out to make

those important specific points. One of my personal problems, for example, is what I would euphemistically call an evolving consistency. Brooke, my copyeditor, is always having to rein me in. If she doesn't, the basic style of my books gradually change every chapter until the last chapter is radically different from the first.

This is why I basically pooh-paahed master pages. It is not that they are not wonderful tools of design and consistency. It is simply that a forty-eight page booklet with twenty master pages is not going to be very consistent. You must add master pages only when made necessary by the content.

This is a very delicate balance. Graphic design is a very delicate thing, even though we are often using sharp contrasts with massive visual impact. Too much or too little can quickly destroy the flow of communication. This is the key:

All that matters is clear communication!

Knowledge retention

1. How can a bleed ruin your budget?

2. Why are Style palettes crucial to page layout?

3. Why would you use many, very narrow columns?

4. Why are tables so difficult to construct in normal page layout?

5. What is an appropriate use for a sidebar?

WHERE SHOULD YOU BE BY THIS TIME?

Nothing has changed since last chapter. You need to have done several tutorials, skills, miniskills, and hopefully started (at least) on a real project for a real client. Ask your instructor what your weak points are and listen carefully so you can make plans to remedy these lacks in your skill set. You may want to go to the specific project chapters (14 through 17) for more advanced skill exams. Ask your instructor first, though (unless, of course, you are studying on your own).

DISCUSSION

You should be networking with your classmates and finding out their skills and weaknesses. It is quite possible that you will find a future business partner or a subcontractor among them who can supply what you lack in certain areas. Publishing is a team sport, you might as well get started now.

Talk among yourselves...

10

Design Terminology and Procedures

CONCEPTS

1. **Thumbnails**

2. **Roughs**

3. **Line**

4. **Shape**

5. **Volume**

6. **Symbols**

7. **Texture**

8. **Morgue**

9. **Contract proof**

Presenting terms, questions, and a basic production procedure to avoid creative block

CHAPTER OBJECTIVES

By presenting the basic terms and production procedures, you will learn how to:

1. Communicate with other designers
2. Avoid creative block
3. Meet client needs
4. Communicate with the readers
5. Improve your work ethic

LAB WORK FOR CHAPTER:

- Miniskill #5
- Submit finished theory exams
- Continue work on your approved real project, ideally your second, third, or fourth real project

Paper
Products

FROM ABYDON MILLS

Looking for
peace & quiet?

The
idea of covering design in a book like this is pretty ludicrous. This is the subject of four-year degrees, with a generous portion of genuine on-the-job experience working for real clients on real projects. However, it must be done, because this book is about training in graphic design production.

We need to quickly review design terminology. These terms cover basic concepts we all need to deal with in our daily work. They enable us to talk with each other in a language that conveys certain things to everyone in the design field. They also give a quick checklist to help determine how we are doing what we are doing.

Every project you produce needs to keep track of these concepts. In the beginning you will have to consciously remind yourself of many of them. More than that, you will need to find someone who can help you remember to keep track of all these things. The sad thing I have discovered is that even those of you with several years of experience often have no idea why you do the things you do.

The majority of desktop publishers are self-taught, learning at random through experimentation. There is definitely benefit in this procedure. It has enabled old boundaries to be broken and new methods of communication to develop. However, much is also missed.

The self-taught, random method of learning is also responsible for many of the incredibly stupid designs of recent years. It is responsible for the amazing proliferation of typographic errors, incomprehensible layouts, illegible fonts, "professionally ugly" graphics, and wasted marketing dollars.

Before getting into terminology, we need to cover some aspects of graphic design that are either unknown or inaccurately taught. First of all, this is not fine art. I remember the second day of my first painting class, where my professor stood up in front of the class and pompously pronounced that "in the world of art, good is defined as what you like." To a large extent this is true, because fine art is an attempt to express a personal vision of reality. Even in most areas of fine art there are problems with this view, however. In our world the prime virtue is accurate communication not our personal sense of style.

Our personal design taste does not matter much, if at all.

Secondly, superb graphics are often seen as a magic result of mental alchemy, mysterious and incomprehensible. Again we are confusing our output with fine art where the best is often produced by people like Van Gogh and many, many others, who were certifiably insane. In graphic design, the best work is often the result of subconscious associations that we call creative, but it cannot be incomprehensible to the reader without becoming nonfunctional and counterproductive.

Third, many design schools push the concept of the "big idea" that will solve all marketing problems, make the client ecstatic, and the designer both famous and rich. This "masterpiece" approach causes more misdirection than excellence in design. It gets designers looking in the wrong direction for practical production purposes. This is the commercial version of the "art for art's sake" attitude that decimated fine art in the last part of the twentieth century. In most cases, the "big idea" is the incidental outcome of a life's work of competency and excellence. If you seek for that big idea, and focus on it, your work tends to become amazing rather than obvious, complex rather than clever, and forceful rather than convincing.

Subjectivity rules!

Probably the most difficult aspect of design is the simple fact that everyone sees things differently. This means that there are very few hard-and-fast rules. This is why the field is so difficult. When you are discussing a design with another designer, the most common reaction is something like "That doesn't work" or "That really pops!" The problem is that these words can be understood only experientially and subjectively, by those with trained eyes.

DESIGN TERMINOLOGY

Needless to say, this type of conversational approach is less than satisfactory to the neophyte. It doesn't help the experienced professional much either. Fortunately, there are many terms that are much more precise. As we cover them, think of them as a vocabulary exercise. It is simply learning a new language (which really doesn't have many words). More than that, they give us common definitions for words we are already using.

The basic procedure in design is to continuously fix the largest problem until you run out of time.

What is needed is a method of identifying problems. As we help each other to effective design solutions, we can allow the designer to come to his or her own conclusions about the solution. This can only be done by accurately pointing out problems with commonly understood terminology. The basic procedure in design is to continuously fix the largest problems until you run out of time. Professional competence means you bring your designs to where the remaining problems are invisible to anyone else.

It is completely without value (as well as nasty) to exclaim, "Gad, that is horrible!" However, when you are asked, it is very helpful to make remarks like, "That background is too close in color and value to the product. It makes the product hard to see." Or, "I think one of the main problems is that the font does not match the historical style of the rest of the piece." Or, pointing to a product benefit list and saying, "The contrast seems weak. I agree it's an important point. You should hit it harder. I think you need to change the font or the point size or the color or something." The idea is to help each other correct all of the large mistakes.

You have known most of these since you were little, but let's review, because there are some differences in professional design. Remember, as we go through, that we are looking for a terminology that helps us to isolate areas of a design that are not working or are ineffective.

Line

This most basic term, for example, is not the one-dimensional object you learned about in high school physics that only has length (no width or height). In graphic design, lines have infinite variety: thick, thin, light, dark, angular, curved, complex, simple, smooth, textured, hand-drawn, descriptive, or simply organizational. The main attributes of a line are length and direction.

Shape

This is even more complex. There are entire drawing systems based on the three basic simple shapes of the triangle, rectangle, and ellipse. It is said that any shape can be made of combinations of those three basic forms (though that is stretching things to their absurd limit). Though it can be argued that a rectangle is simply a very wide line, all the other shapes vary in width and/or height. Shapes differ from lines primarily in how they are used. However, the shape is often the easiest identifiable unit that can be discussed in a graphic design.

Volume

Here we add the illusion of an apparent third dimension — depth. Simple volumetric relationships can be created with simple layering techniques. Others require an understanding of perspective. If you do not understand perspective, get a small book at the art store, library, or online. It is essential basic knowledge. 3D illustration is becoming more common all the time (although its use is mostly fashionable and of little communication value).

Symbols

These are shapes that have additional meanings not directly attached to the shape. For example, what we call stars look nothing like stars. Five-, six-, seven-, eight-, and nine-pointed stars all have specific symbolic meanings that go way beyond their simple shapes.

Symbols are often used as logos. However, there is a real danger here. In a society as large as ours has become, symbols mean different things to different people. The swastika is no longer the quaint sun symbol of ancient India or the southwestern pueblos of the United States. The rainbow means very different things to the Jew, the gay activist, and Jesse Jackson's followers.

Many readership groups can only be reached by using their currently fashionable symbols, but you have to be sure the symbol is current and that you are using it correctly. We are all familiar with that warning bell that goes off in our mind when someone tries to patronize us with slang or symbology improperly used.

Texture

This is difficult to define, but easy to recognize. Some textures are graphic techniques that indicate how a surface would feel: hard, soft, smooth, furry, slimy, oily, scratchy, and so on. Other textures are stylistic. For example, Rembrandt's crosshatched shading has a very different feel from the crosshatchings found in the engravings on paper money. Textures can be dense, loose, light, fluffy, and many others.

In general, realistic textures are only found in scanned or bitmap images. One of the reasons why PostScript illustration usually looks like computer drawings is the smooth, matte, unreal texture that is the normal output of these programs.

Color

This is so complex that I devoted an entire chapter to color in my first two books. It will be the major focus of my future book on Photoshop. Yet, I have not even begun to cover its actual use as a component of design. Color is very tricky. It is extremely easy to add color that lessens contrast and therefore impact. However, well-designed color can cause a strong reaction. Color is often one of the main indicators of fashion. It can have strong emotional content (although the Japanese use of white for death and funerals shows how tricky that can become).

ARRANGING THE PIECES: BALANCE

Basically, all designs need to be balanced. At the very least balance needs to be controlled. A lack of balance makes readers uneasy, irritable, even fearful. There maybe times when this is exactly what you need — when you are designing a poster for a new horror flick, for example. However, these are rare exceptions. In general, everything has to be balanced.

Balance is concerned with the visual weight of the pieces of a design. A piece top left needs to be balanced by a piece bottom right; an area on the left needs to be balanced by an area on the right; and so forth. A large light area can be balanced by a small dark area. A grayscale design can be balanced with a tiny spot of brilliant red. Darks are stronger than lights. Large is stronger than small. Shapes are stronger than simple rectangles. Color is weaker than black and white.

Symmetry

Coupled with balance is the concept of symmetry, which has to do with a image reflected across an axis. In other words, on a symmetrical image, both sides (as divided by the axis) are identical but flipped. Normally, the axis is vertical.

When talking about type, symmetrical designs use centered or justified text blocks, or they use equally sized text blocks on opposite sides of the axis. You could even use flush left on the right side of the axis with an equal-sized flush right block of type on the left side — leaving the two sides facing each other.

Asymmetry

Asymmetrical design foregoes the balance of equals by replacing it with conceptual balance. Currently, asymmetrical balance is by far the most common sort of layout. The question to ask is, "Does everything

Design terminology and procedures

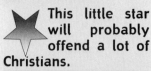

Be careful!

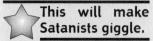
This little star will probably offend a lot of Christians.

This will make Satanists giggle.

Here in Albuquerque, we have seen some major brouhahas over this simple little sun symbol used by the local pueblos carved into building facades in the 1920s.

hold together?" A work can be built of widely varying pieces with huge differences in size, color, texture, shape, and line. Yet an asymmetrical balance can be maintained that pulls the pieces together into a powerful and focused statement. Zen monochrome ink landscapes are often 75% to 95% blank sky, but the feeling of space is compelling and awe-inspiring because the emptiness is exactly balanced by small intense brushwork of trees, rocks, and mountains.

Once the three concepts of balance, symmetry, and asymmetry are tied together, we can talk about two basic styles of arrangement, formal and informal. They are used for very different purposes, and much of this usage is culturally based. Formal designs are a very small proportion of the pieces produced. This is more true the farther west we go in the United States. Our culture has become very loose (some would say impolite). As a result, our communications tend to be informal, so we do not get accused of snobbery, arrogance, or elitism. In the Southwest, where I live, formality is considered an insult.

Formal designs

Formal designs have developed a strong set of normal usage. Norms govern much of what we do in design. Most of the control we exercise over our readership comes from habitual subconscious reactions that we trigger by normal usage.

Formal designs are almost always centered compositions; that means the pieces are either centered or have an exact balance symmetrically with a vertical axis. They usually use small point sizes with a great deal of leading. This often seems extreme. For formal invitations using script faces, 16/24 is not uncommon.

Typefaces are normally light. Book is often the best choice because it is a little lighter than medium and often more elegant. Typestyles are chosen for their elegance. Either classic examples of excellent design or type from the late 1800s or early 1900s are chosen. You should be careful of extremely stylized or "heavy" faces. Formality is always restrained. Think of the British stiff upper lip. White space (empty area) is used lavishly.

Formal layouts tap off the fine art world for its images. There is a much greater use of beautifully drawn illustrations (as opposed to photos). If photos are used, they must be extraordinarily good "art" prints. There is also a large body of work that may be called semiformal. These use formal type conventions and graphic styles with flush left alignment.

Informal designs

In this day and age, informal layouts are the most common by far. In general, they are asymmetrical but balanced. As mentioned, almost all work must be balanced. Purposely unbalanced work

Looking for peace & quiet?

is very disturbing, yet even there an asymmetrical organization must exist to evoke the intentionally created reaction.

Asymmetrical balance is a subjective thing. When a piece is balanced, it is obvious to any professional. The comment will be, "That works!" Getting to that point is a little tricky. Large light pieces can be balanced with small dark pieces. That is obvious. What many do not realize is that small intense areas can be balanced with large empty areas. Large areas of grayscale (type and graphics) can be very effectively balanced with a tiny intense area of color.

White space

Blank paper is one of the design elements used in design. It must carefully controlled. It is usually referred to as white space, even though it is only white if the paper is white. The empty spaces are just as much a part of a design as the drawn elements. You are required to control them. Elegant pieces have lots of white space. Discount ads have almost no white space (it's part of the style). When you look at a warehouse-style grocery store ad, you will have to search for any white space.

This is one area where you may have to fight with your client. Many clients are loath to leave any white space because they are already upset by the "high cost of printing." You may well have to tactfully explain the effectiveness of white space. In a vast sea of tightly filled ads on a newspaper spread, an ad with a great deal of white space stands out much more than just another bold burst of typographic shouting.

Your layout choices will greatly affect the first reaction of your readership (or surfership). This must be one of the first design decisions you make on a project, along with the font choices. Until you have a lot of experience, this is not one of those areas where you can spontaneously slip into an arrangement that makes the reader react as you hope they will.

GUIDING THE READER

One of the most important aspects of graphic design is guiding the reader's eye through the piece from start to finish. Our purpose is communication. A client is paying us to communicate a message to a customers about a specific product. There are many methods and techniques that can help us realize that goal.

Contrast

Probably the most useful method of directing the reader's eye through your design is contrast. There are

Design Terminology and Procedures

The Quality Lighting Group

invites you to join them

as they celebrate

the opening of

their brand new

interior design gallery.

• • • • •

February 30, 1999

15721 Le Grande Boulevard

in downtown Yuppietown

11:00 am to 7:30 pm

• • • • •

Wine, cheese & door prizes

Formal layout

countless contrasts that can be used: light/dark; large/small; simple/complex; thick/thin; chaos/order; complementary colors; and on and on. Through the careful use of contrast, we can make one item pop off the page and grab the reader's eye (hopefully without offense).

The most common mistake with contrast is cowardice. Inexperienced designers usually do not have enough nerve to push the contrast far enough. Inadequate contrast is merely irritating, at best. Normally, it simply looks like a mistake. You usually see this most commonly in font choice — the bold is not bold enough, the plain is not light enough, the style differences are not clear.

Thick Thin

Frantic Calm

Large Small

Serif Sans

Chaos Order

Rhythm

This design attribute is produced by some sort of repetition, either obvious or subtle, that causes the reader to expect and look for the next piece in the pattern. A good example is a bulleted list. After a couple of bullets, the reader looks for the next one. In addition, the repetition of bullets down the side of the column is probably what attracted the attention in the first place. Rhythm must be used with care. Too much rhythm simply becomes texture and disappears into pattern.

Unity

This is a technique that must also be used carefully. Too much unity becomes bland, trite, and invisible. What we are looking for is unity of content; the more common word among designers is consistency. The illustrator at my first professional position in graphic design carefully showed me that decorative illustration must be unified in technique and palette but absolutely diverse in detail. For example, a painted bouquet of flowers had to be consistent in technique, consistent in color, consistent in every way, except that every flower needed to be different in shape and color combination.

Another use of unity concerns shape construction. Adjusting the position of shapes until the curves and angles of one flow into or point to the next brings the two shapes into oneness, visually. In fact, you will normally find that pieces that *work* have this kind of relationship between the shapes. This internal alignment is an important factor to look for when proofing or critiquing a design.

Cultural usage

It is imperative to be aware of the culture of the reader. In European cultures or derivatives like the United States or New Zealand, reading order is left to right, top to bottom. Therefore, an American reader will normally, and habitually, try to start at the upper left corner of the design and read through to the bottom right. You will have to work hard to force a reader from these cultures to start anywhere else.

Different cultures react differently. For example, readers from Middle Eastern cultures would tend to read right to left, top to bottom. Asian readers would be prone to look from top to bottom first, then right to left. This is simply a function of how their language is written. You need to be aware of these things. I have had students who finally began to learn only when they realized that they were always starting at what we in the West call the back of the book.

WE KNOW WHAT WORKS

The centuries of printing experience and decades of advertising and marketing have given us a great deal of knowledge about what works and what does not work in graphic design. Huge amounts of money have been spent on market research to determine who reads what, and why; what historic styles cause which responses; what typestyles are more readable, and why; which layouts are effective; and so on.

Beyond all the studies and statistics, the fact remains that good design is always a subjective judgment. It is easier to identify the reasons why you do not like something than to identify why you do. This is the reason for the previously mentioned procedure of continuing to fix the largest problem until you run out of time.

Even though you are dealing with subjective reactions, there is much you can do to increase the effectiveness of your work. When you set out to design a page, think of the purpose of your design. For any design, someone is paying the bills and someone is receiving the message. You need to be clear about who these people are and design accordingly.

The basics are constant

Our job is communication. We do this primarily with words. This is why so much time in this book is spent on typographic matters. However, the same design principles apply as we deal with logos, illustrations, product shots, and so forth. We communicate a *message* about a *product* to help our *client* explain to the *reader* why a desired *action* is appropriate.

Graphic design is about communication and little else matters.

In the case of a logo, the product is the company itself and the message is "Trust us!" With a product shot, we are simply looking for accuracy. But the task is always the same. It is the designer's job to convey the message effectively. This is true no matter how much the project covers, no matter how complex the document or Web site, and no matter who the readers or surfers are.

Graphic design is about communication. Everything is subordinate to the message. The most important thing about the message is: will it be read? If it is not read, the message doesn't matter.

Design terminology and procedures

Mini #5

PROCESS POSTER FOR QUERCUL TROUBADOUR

The size will be tabloid, full bleed, process color. You will need to scan, trace, and save as a PostScript illustration EPS the QT Logo. You must use the Quizno Chapel and the mule photos converted to EPS or TIFF.

There are many other books focusing on the intellectual design process. One of the best is Robin Williams' *The Non-Designer's Design Book*, Peachpit Press, 1994. Many of the other books are concerned with design for design's sake. Almost all avoid production realities. The five principles discussed here are a basic starting point, applied before design can begin.

The important thing to remember is that these principles help very little without adequate production skill. If you cannot meet the deadlines, the best design does not matter. The problem in digital publishing is that the designer and producer are usually the same person. We have taken over the publishing industry (with all of its responsibilities, of course).

These general guidelines contain questions that must be answered for every design: logo, corporate image, brochure, poster, or whatever the client needs. They should be considered before you start and all along the way.

A FIRST PRINCIPLE OF DESIGN

DESIGN FOR YOUR READER, NOT YOUR ARTISTIC GRATIFICATION

The best design does not call attention to itself. It should not be noticed. It is very bad if the reaction is, *"What a great design!"* The message should be easily available to the reader. The product should be obvious. It merely has to be made attractive. An appropriate reader reaction to your work could be, "Hey, this really looks like something I need," or, "I better check this out. It may solve my problem."

Here are three goals to keep in mind regarding readers:

- Attract the reader. It won't happen by accident.

- Make your work easy to read and visually accessible. The surfer or reader is subconsciously looking for an excuse to skip your design, flipping to the next item in her inbox or pile of mail, or clicking a link and moving on.

- Give the readers the desire and ability to act. Give them something to do now, something to get that meets their need or at least their want. "**ORDER NOW!** Just click the Order button." "Drop by our shop and say hi."

Some designs attract through beautiful layouts or dramatic impact, yet totally fail in leading the reader to a desired action. You wouldn't believe how many times readers are enthusiastically ready to respond to a piece, but cannot because the designer forgot the address or telephone number! I have seen many instances where even the logo and company name was forgotten.

A SECOND PRINCIPLE OF DESIGN

IT'S THEIR MONEY, IT'S THEIR CALL

Your clients are the ones paying the bills. Even though the reader is the most important person in the design solution, you're serving the client. They often know their market better than you do. The fact that they are still in business (when most businesses die within six months) tells you that they have something going for them.

You must stay within their budget. If the client likes brown, don't insist on blue unless you are convinced that it will cause a better reader reaction and can give reasons why (tactfully). Get all the information you can from the client. Ask as many questions as the client allows:

- What is the budget?
- What is the due date or deadline?
- Who is the audience, or what are the demographics?
- What does the client want the reader/visitor to do?
- Who are the client's known competitors?
- What messages have worked in the past?
- What is the existing graphic identity?
- What corporate image is being pursued?

Find out what goals the client wants to achieve with the project. If the client has not formulated them, help get them in writing. (Yes, this is an additional source of income.) You are getting paid for your expertise, so offer suggestions. Remember, though, because the clients are paying the bills, they also have veto power. Don't let your ego get in the way. Your job is to serve the client and his customers.

Don't assume clients are creatively deficient.

Considering yourself as the design extension of the client often helps you to walk in their shoes. In a very real way, we designers are hired guns. We are brought in to do what the client is unable to accomplish. Don't make the assumption that they are creatively deficient. Often they simply do not have the time to spend in design. We become their creative ability for their concepts (but don't tell them that!). We are literally hired specialists. Our clients have very different concerns than we do. You should focus on their needs and how to meet those needs. This is a service industry, not a gallery offering design *objets d'art*. Our task is to enable the client to communicate a message to her customers.

A THIRD PRINCIPLE OF DESIGN

PAY ATTENTION TO DETAIL, THE GOAL IS PERFECTION

Once you get involved in actual production, make sure you clean up all the details. Nothing affects the reaction to your design more than typographical errors or sloppy mistakes (such as strokes that don't meet, elements that do not align, or widows).

It is always difficult to see your creation in an objective, fresh way; that is why it is virtually necessary to have someone else proofread for errors, consistency, and detail in your layout. Most professionals have at least two other people proof their work. If you made a mistake the

Design terminology and procedures

AWARDS

One of the temptations in graphic design is the pursuit of awards. It takes a great deal of maturity to realize that the award-winners are rarely successful graphic designs. They are very gratifying to your sense of self, but awards are rarely given for designs that successfully attract new business to the designer's clients. In general, award-winning artists get all of their strokes from fellow designers. In most cases, I would not want to hire them to increase my business.

first time, you are probably going to make the same mistake when you proof your own work. (That is why you made the mistake the first time – you didn't see it!) You cannot proof too much or too often.

The proofs the customer sees should be perfect. One typo per page is too much. Many budgets have been destroyed because the designer left mistakes on the proof. The client was thus given a golden opportunity to employ the old "since you have to make these changes anyway" routine. It is almost impossible to charge for client changes when they know you are making changes already to correct your own sloppiness. This is a common cause of very poor client relationships. Much of your repeat business can come from the quality of your proofs – you are always building or maintaining your reputation.

Always, one final check

Just as important as proofreading is taking the time to run out final laser proofs before sending the file for final output. It doesn't matter how urgent the deadline is. It is extremely common to create new errors when correcting proofs. The worst case is a job that must be reprinted, at great cost to your client or maybe yourself. Always check out this final laser proof and send it along with the disks to the service bureau or image assembly department (with appropriate comments written on the proof, if necessary).

... the time to iron out production details is before you start designing.

Keep in mind that the service bureau or printing company cannot (and usually will not even try to) read your mind. In fact, their focus is completely different than yours. They need a job that will print easily and flawlessly. If you give them any leeway, they will always choose the easiest production method (which is rarely the most beautiful or the most effective). The only solution is to give complete and accurate instructions with your laser proof. Remember, the time to iron out production details is before you start designing. It can cost you a small fortune to change your plans after production has started and you discover that your nice plans won't work with the equipment available.

A FOURTH PRINCIPLE OF DESIGN

KNOW YOURSELF AND YOUR EQUIPMENT

You cannot do more than the constraints of your time frame, budget, or abilities. More than that, you cannot do anything that your imagesetter refuses to print. You cannot match opaque screenprinted spot colors to process color printed matter. As the designer, you interpret what is possible within the given needs. Evaluate your strengths and weaknesses. Then you will be able to design according to your abilities.

Illustrate, if you are a good illustrator. Shoot your own photographs, if you are a competent photographer. Don't attempt to create four-color process artwork if you don't understand how to trap it and print it. You will be much more successful if you do what you do well. Ask for advice when you need it. It is a sign of strength and confidence to know and admit when you need help — and seek it out.

 TIP: Study constantly to learn the capabilities of both your equipment and your software. Work to expand your own abilities and polish your skills. Fill your brain with all the design data you can. Then the ideas will flow relatively easily. If you relax in your pursuit of creative and artistic growth, what ideas you do have will be increasingly dull, repetitive, and uninspired.

Be sure to design within the limitations of your equipment, as well. A 75 MB, CMYK separation is going to be a little difficult on your old Performa with 24 MB RAM. If the only printer available for final output is 600 dpi, process work is pretty much out of the question. In fact, working in process color puts large demands on you, your software, and your hardware. Common sense helps a lot.

I'm not saying that you shouldn't push the limits. What I am suggesting is that unless you know your limits, you won't know what can be pushed. The sad fact is that most designers today are not pushing limits to extend their capabilities. They are flailing about in random rebellion, confusing unusual with inventive, loud with effective, and rejection of the past with a view of the future. It is virtually impossible to be innovative without a solid knowledge of who you are and where you have come from.

A FIFTH PRINCIPLE OF DESIGN

BE COMPASSIONATE TO THOSE WHO MUST PRODUCE YOUR DESIGNS

It is easy to design documents that are complex enough to choke an imagesetter. Remember **K.I.S.S.** (Keep It Simple, Stupid!). You should add complexity only when you know it is necessary. Dense (very complicated) designs are usually difficult to read. If complexity is called for, pay special attention to the readability of your type.

 TIP: You really need to spend time getting to know the capabilities of your production providers. All shops have certain things that cause them severe problems. For example, the RIP with my first digital press at school cannot handle Quark or Illustrator files. Call them and ask them. First of all, they will be pleased. Secondly, they probably already have a handout to give guidance to those who ask.

A major portion of a designer's career is ensuring clear communication with your production staff. This is true whether they are the next department down the hall, a service bureau across town, or even a printer in another country (like this book). You must include all

Proofing helps

To help you see problems with your layouts, try looking at your proof upside down or backward (use a mirror). The real problem for many of us, when proofing, is actually seeing the layout without necessarily reading the type. We get so focused on the type that we miss the reading order. I back several yards away from the proof myself so I can see what is seen first by the cruising reader of my project. I am often very surprised by what is immediately visible and therefore seen first.

necessary files and fonts. Give them a marked-up laser proof with full instructions so they will know what you expect. Send a practice file to new suppliers to iron out production problems before the deadline panic.

Talk to the rest of the team

The importance of this cannot be overstated. Publishing is a team sport. Talk to them, be polite, make friends with them. Make certain you make friends with the receptionist and your personal contact. They can be the key to the survival of your designs. You should know who will output and who will print your work. You need to know the shops' capabilities. This is still true if you are working in-house. Have your questions answered before you begin to design. You should design a checklist to note down the answers to all of the following questions, plus any others you consider necessary:

- Do you need camera-ready art, native files, composite negs, or PDFs, and how do you want them delivered?
- Do you go direct-to-plate? If so, how do you proof?
- Who are your contact persons?
- Are the financial arrangements understood and available?
- Where can money be saved by making design changes?
- Who is responsible for the proof?
- What linescreen and dot gain?
- Will you see a blueline, color-key, laminated, digital, or soft proof?
- Is a press check possible or necessary?
- When will the work be finished, and when will it be delivered?
- What is the rush charge policy?

Professionals are helpful

Industry professionals are happy to answer these and other questions because they know that planning early pays off. If you work with them in-house, they'll be tickled to find out you care. If you have to go outside, thoroughly go over your documents with the service bureau and/or your printer. It is time well spent. If they won't talk with you, find another company. You will learn much that can save you time and trouble. Often a simple change can save you a great deal of money.

This is not easy work

It may be sandbagging to let you get this far, but here goes. Many people get into desktop publishing because they *like to draw.* This is not sufficient. This will give you an enjoyable hobby, but it will not sustain you in this very difficult career. Professional design is impossible without constant study, undying curiosity, and an insatiable drive for excellence. Most of us are not designers in an attempt to get rich. We are designers because that is what we do whether we get paid for it or not.

Graphic design is one of the most difficult and complex careers. It can be argued that fine art is even more difficult, because there you have to invent the rules in addition to developing skills. However, graphic design makes that look easy when you consider that first you have to figure out who is making the rules, what the rules are, and who determines which set of rules will be used in a particular situation. Then you have to make yourself conform to the rules someone else made and produce designs that they are proud of.

Fine artists please themselves. Graphic designers have to please themselves, the client, the reader, and the production staff, in reverse order, all at the same time.

In addition, you need a great deal of printing knowledge, Web knowledge, typographic knowledge, software knowledge, hardware knowledge, business knowledge, design knowledge, and much more — coupled with the ability to remember all of this and have it on tap to use.

Design responsibilities

As a graphic designer, you are responsible for every mark on the paper. You need to have a reason for everything. That reason can rarely be whimsical, and it has to increase accurate communication. All of this has to be done in an environment run by people who rarely understand creative necessities. In fact, that last statement is not only true, it is also a good thing. When designers gather together and pat each other on the back, design quickly degenerates into the pit called *art for art's sake*. We commonly need others, like our clients and readers, to keep us in line.

If you can't think of a reason for it, trash it!

There is no room for the egomaniacal in graphic design. This is a service industry, mainly for meeting marketing needs. Properly viewed, we are hired guns who provide creativity, for a fee. Our services are as valuable and at least as difficult as the services offered by doctors and lawyers. It has been accurately said that the only equipment a doctor or lawyer needs is a phenomenal memory. Designers, in contrast, have to tread where others fear to go.

More than that, designs are such an integral part of the personal expression of our character that critiques can be taken as offensive attack far too easily. It helps a great deal to remember that you are offering your creativity for the client's use to serve that client. In most cases, she couldn't care less what you want. What she wants is her ideas and concepts delivered clearly, accurately, and beautifully — the way she would if she could.

HOW DO I GET STARTED?

As mentioned, design is incredibly difficult. The possibilities are endless and there are no rules. Whole schools of design are based on breaking all the rules; the current crop is but the latest variation on a recurring theme. It's usually told as a joke, but we really are expected to read our clients' (and readers') minds. On top of everything else, the deadline pressures are often unreal. Because of all these things and much more, creative block is a real fact of life for the designer.

Design terminology and procedures

TIP: One of the skills you must develop is the ability to start over early and often. When your design seems to getting bogged down and you can't solve the design problems you are running into, when the design doesn't flow smoothly and effortlessly, often the best solution is to dump the document and start over. The second time you produce a design, it will not only go much faster, but many of those nagging problems plaguing you the first time around will be solved in the redo.

Fortunately, there is a simple methodology that makes design blockage highly unlikely. Though there are no laws, it is certainly true that norms rule. We have already covered some of those norms, and we will touch on many more. You now know you must train your eye to see and recognize both historical norms and current fashion.

Our cultural history and marketing economy have made it certain that almost all our readers will react according to very definite habits. Because we are all exposed to most of the same general influences, we have predictable reactions. We have discussed some of the reactions to type and layout, but we also have predictable buttons that can be pushed with color, form, texture, smell, and the like. For example, there are certain curves that will attract the attention of most human males.

Design, in general, is like that. Though legality virtually eliminates creativity, many things can enhance the creative process. Even though we do not completely understand where creativity comes from, we can set up an environment in which it is more likely. There is much discussion concerning whether creativity is a learned technique or an innate gift, but it is clear that we can develop rudimentary talent into strong, competent skills. The technique is simple:

Ask questions and get moving!

Is this simplistic stupidity leading to weak and poorly thought out design? No, it is a basic technique used to generate superior ideas and concepts. Much if the mystery surrounding creativity is solved by simply getting to work. However, there are important things to consider as we do this.

The creative process

First, you have to understand how ideas are generated. Basically, you add huge amounts of data to a large pot and wait for the dumplings to pop to the surface. How this works we are not sure. The most common word used by the geniuses of our civilization is inspiration. It is clear that new concepts and structures are an intuitive outgrowth of an educated or trained mind. Creativity generally builds on a basic curiosity and hunger for facts. It then assembles those facts through methods which are predictable only in that they will almost always result in ideas.

In our field, that hunger for input revolves around printed materials, graphics, signs, paintings, Web sites, and visual stimuli in general. Graphic designers normally have an almost compulsive desire to feed their mind with images. You should read every book you run across on design, go to every gallery within reach, read magazines and look at the ads. Tear everything apart in your mind and try to improve the designs. Designers do this continuously (often compulsively).

Most clients don't want incredible creativity.

If you don't have this compulsive curiosity, it's quite possible you need to focus on production instead of design. Creativity cannot be faked. It can only be recognized, and often not by the creator.

What most clients truly need is reliable production of projects within budget and on time. This does not take creativity.

However, many creative designers allow these production pressures to stifle their creative processes. Creatives often allow themselves to be overwhelmed by production necessities. You need to see this as simple immaturity and ignorance. To survive in this wild and wonderful world, you need a plan. You can be creative on a deadline.

A BASIC TECHNIQUE FOR CREATIVE OUTPUT

1. START WITH QUESTIONS

What questions do you ask? That is simple — when you receive a new project, find out everything you can. We have mentioned many of these questions in our basic principles. But they are just the bare beginning.

If you have the opportunity, ask the client directly, question the service provider directly, and if you are a part of a design team question them or brainstorm. However, even if this is an interior mental process, it must be done.

The first thing you must determine is what you are communicating — more appropriately, what are you supposed to be communicating? Ask any question you can think of to get at that fact. Ask the client. Do a market survey. Research the benefits of the product. Find out what the competition is doing. Ask your client what has worked in the past. Get a customer profile. Determine the budget, mailing requirements, deadlines, taboos, and customs. Get intimately involved with the project, mentally and emotionally (if possible).

Once you have learned about the product's history and future, the message, and the designated readership, find out all you can about your client. What are her favorite colors? Who does she admire? What is her circle of friends? What is her reputation? Find out if she is part of her readership's culture or if she is marketing to strangers.

- Who has editorial authority?
- What are you selling?
- Who are you selling it to?
- What kind of people buy or use the product?
- When does it have to done?
- Why is the product held in the hands of a nearly naked female?
- Why is this product needed, wanted, or desired?
- What are its advantages and disadvantages?
- Is this a new product, concept, invention, or execution?

Limitations and strengths

It is extremely important that you determine several key factors early on. These are absolutely necessary to help you determine what you can offer and what is inappropriate with the resources available.

- **Budget.** Clients are often hesitant about this area. You must earn their trust. This is imperative data for later decisions.
- **Equipment.** This is so important that equipment purchases are often budgeted into your price quotes. In fact, for many of us, this is how we purchase equipment.
- **Deadlines.** Many design decisions are forced upon you, even before the creative process starts, by the required completion date.
- **Subcontractors.** Portions produced by others have deadlines, too.

These four factors will have a huge impact on enhancing or limiting your design. There is no sense even thinking about process color if the client needs 10,000 letter-sized copies and only has $1,500. Even if you have the budget, being forced to use duplicators often eliminates tight-register projects.

In contrast, if the client is willing to go with the best suppliers (service bureau, printer, and bindery), things can be done ridiculously fast with extremely impressive quality (especially if you have a good, ongoing business relationship with the suppliers so they'll fit you into their schedule).

When you have asked the persons involved all that you can think of, begin meditating on the questions and the answers. It helps to run through a personal list of questions that you ask yourself. At this point try to avoid solutions. You are merely assembling data. You are not looking for ideas at all, at this point.

Conclusions made before data is collected are usually in error.

Remember, there are no rules carved in stone. You are trying to produce accurate communication using every means at your disposal. This structure helps to channel your rampant creative urges toward the specific project you were hired to design.

2. GET PHYSICALLY BUSY

As the data reaches mental overload, begin the physical process by organizing your work area. Look over the supplied materials; read the copy; clean the area while focusing on the project. As you do your necessary busy work, think in terms of preparing for a flood of ideas and how are you going to capture them.

By this time, it is easy to see that your mind will be whirling with data. You need something to focus on. This is not a time to try to produce ideas. There has not been enough time to process the data. You will discover that first impressions are often very weak ideas. You very much need some processing time.

Organize your area and the project!

This basic step is often forgotten in the pressure of work and deadlines. Messy work areas slow you down. Not reading the job ticket allows you to design without ever orienting to reality. Running out of supplies in the middle of a project is frustrating at best. Plus this work is excellent busy work to keep your hands occupied without mental effort. This allows your subconscious to continue at full speed with the data processing that is the natural result of all the questions you just asked.

Organize your computer!

If you do not set up your files and folders (documents and subdirectories) BEFORE you begin production, you will regret it. This is one area where preplanning saves an inordinate amount of time. Unless you plan where to store your pieces, someone will have to spend hours organizing things when you finish. This may work if the final organizer is you – it is disastrous if it is someone else.

Many companies have standard filing systems. If so, this goes quickly. If you have to create a system, make it easy to understand. Please do not think of this as a waste of time. It is actually the first step to organizing the data you are digesting internally.

Organizing focuses on the task at hand.

Read the copy!

Why is this being stressed so hard? Because it is so rarely done! It should seem obvious that reading the copy is the best way find out what is going on in a document. Yet many designers are so caught up in the graphics that they ignore the copy. My experience suggests that nearly half the graphic designers never read the copy. This simple step really helps.

1. You will find and correct errors before you even format the copy.
2. You will be able to get questions answered before you waste time on wild goose chases.
3. You will download, to your mind, the most important data for idea generation. If your ideas do not help the copy communicate more clearly, they are probably a misdirection, at best. Use the copy to generate the concepts.

Graphic needs

Often the photos are supplied. If not, you need to get them shot. Once you have read the copy and the questions have been answered, the graphic needs of the project are usually obvious. It becomes a simple matter of budget and skill availability. Only create the graphics that fall into one of your primary skill areas. Your job as designer is to describe the need and find someone to fill it. You do not have to do everything. In fact, that is a foolish policy.

Only create the graphics that fall into one of your primary skill areas.

There is nothing wrong with top-quality stock art or stock photography. Most clients do not have the budget to create everything

REMEMBER, one day soon some person other than yourself will have to figure out your filing system. What will they do when you call in sick, when they see it at the service bureau, or whatever? K.I.S.S. – Keep It Simple, Stupid! Make the folders' names obvious and consistent. If working with DOS (or cross-platform), make a printed index of all the eight-dot-three subdirectory and document names. Update the file additions daily. Index them with clearly labeled explanations of file content.

from scratch. Remember, your job as a designer is to solve communication problems, not to demonstrate your illustrative prowess. Top-quality stock art is far superior to inadequate original art (even if it is yours).

Only use art that helps the message.

Normally, only the best, most creative graphic designers can use illustrators well. Unless the graphic designer knows clearly what has to be done for a given project, subcontracted artists can easily sway design focus with their graphics. Often the message gets lost. This can be a problem with stock art also. Make sure that you know what you need for the design, and do not accept or use anything that changes the direction or focus of the message.

Get the pieces ready

At this point, with graphic production assigned to illustrators able to produce graphics in the needed style, it is appropriate to scan and trace supplied lineart and to send the supplied photos to the scanner for halftone creation. Of course, you cannot get the photos scanned if you do not know what size you need, but often that can be determined very early in the design process.

Make sure that the copy is usable. If it is on disk, make sure your import filters can read the files, convert them, or get them converted. If you do not have hard copy, print some out at this point (how did you read the copy if it was not printed out?). You may have to OCR the printed copy in some cases.

While you are doing all of these organizational tasks, ideas will begin popping to the surface. Do not get sidetracked by working on those ideas yet. Just quickly jot them down (we'll discuss methods in a bit), and keep on with the organizational necessities. It will help you more than you now know to get all of these things done before you allow yourself the treat of creativity and the fun of design. Just keep organizing. By the time the cleanup and setup process is complete, you will almost always have plenty of ideas to flesh out.

3. IDEA GENERATION

The next step involves finalizing your ideas; creating the necessary graphics; choosing the type, color palette, and document size; and settling on a style (as well as a set of STYLES).

Often the ideas that started coming during organization require research. In addition, the idea quality might simply not be satisfying. Then you go to the library, search stock photo catalogs and stock art indices, rifle through your personal morgue where you have all those samples stored of materials you like. You need to locate good reference materials.

Research and morgue perusal can trigger solutions when ideas don't flow fast enough. Then the search for ideas becomes an extension of the organizational process. No matter how the process develops during a particular job, the key is to make visual notes. No matter how good the idea, it's a waste if you cannot remember it. You need to record your visual ideas.

Visual notes

Thumbnails and roughs (or quick design sketches) have been commonly taught to artists and the design community for centuries. When the computer arrived, many designers dropped the practice. It is so easy to design directly on the screen that thumbnails were seen as a waste of time. Everyone wants to work directly. Recently, however, the original value of the practice has been realized.

The problem with sketching on a computer is that it is too perfect. In most cases, once you have your drawing application open, you don't sketch a border. You simply drop one in with the rectangle tool — it's perfect. In fact, it is unnaturally precise. The corners are all perfectly square. The edges are all parallel. The lines are too straight. In all ways, it is a mechanical shape. Computerized sketching tends to lead to boring design. In fact, it could be successfully argued that it is impossible to *sketch* on a computer in the first place.

The value of hand sketching has been rediscovered

We have rediscovered that quick hand sketches produce glitches and bumps in the shapes that are important. In fact, these "aberrations" are often what your mind sees as the true shape. That misshapen corner allows your mind to see the shape as a four-sided shape with no square corners and no parallel sides that is much more interesting than the sterile rectangle. These visual clues are totally missing from computer sketches.

Thumbnails

My use of thumbnails is a bit different from the traditional. My thumbnails are visual notes in personal shorthand. They are very fast sketches (usually done in a few seconds) that give me only enough data to remember the idea if I decide to develop it into a rough.

As I am organizing, I jot down ideas as thumbnails. These thumbnails are meaningful to me, but no one else can decipher them. They are small (less than an inch square). They are so quick that others see them as scribbles. Because they are done so fast, all detail is missing, but the overall layout is captured. This is proper procedure. Many designers ruin an excellent idea by developing detail to great lengths but leaving the overall composition with no balance or direction. Thumbnails help to avoid that problem.

Roughs

When you are done organizing, gather the thumbnails and pick out the ones you think will work the best. Develop these into roughs. A rough differs substantially from a thumbnail. Primarily, it is done to size; at minimum it is done to scale or proportionally. In other words, make a much more finished sketch the same size as the finished project, if possible.

An idea production sample

Let's quickly look at the example I used in *Digital Drawing*. By the time I got to the place where I was ready to proceed with the logo production I had four thumbnails. I chose the thumbnail at

Design terminology and procedures

Be careful!

Unless the client requests to see your thumbnails and roughs (AND PAYS YOU FOR THE PRIVILEGE), do not show them to the customer. Unless your clients are visually educated, they will see different things in your rough than you do. You will set up false expectations and cause yourself all sorts of avoidable problems.

the lower right. I liked the way it looked and somehow it seemed to express what the paper mill wanted to convey with its line of bags, boxes, towels, and chipboard (in my mind).

You do not want to spend any money on materials for roughs, so they are produced with the tools at hand: pencils, markers, watercolors, and the like. Try to use the actual paper you are going to print on. However, this can cause problems with bleeding unless you are using pencils. Do not spend more than a half an hour on a rough. Most times, a slightly more careful thumbnail is all you need to firm up your ideas.

Roughs can be scanned in and placed as templates in the actual digital documents used for production. In the rough seen here, I thought the triangle and type were too crude to be used for anything other than a proportional template. I scanned it and placed it into the background and locked the background layer, so the image could be used to keep things in proportion. When I was done the rough was simply deleted.

However, the tree in the rough had a nice loose feel that I thought would help keep the logo friendly. It had some problems, but they were easily fixed in Photoshop. I spent about ten minutes cleaning up the image and adjusting it to the vision I had in my mind. As you can see, I added some delicate detailing; cleaned up the ground; added a few smaller plants and debris; balanced the tree vertically; and made it more solid in appearance. The final result had what I considered to be the basic look of a tree that might be used for pulp.

The next step was to place the cleaned-up tree into a new PostScript illustration document, lock it in a background layer, and then trace it (this one was autotraced). As soon as it was traced, I joined it into a composite path to make the holes transparent. Then I deleted the tracing TIFF and placed the TIFF of the rough into a background layer. After lining it up with the trace, I locked the background layer so I wouldn't keep on selecting it accidently.

Then, using the rough as a guide, I added the type and the triangle. As you can clearly see at the top of the next page, the image in my mind had little to do with the actual type scribbled out in the rough. You'll have to take my word that the final result is a faithful rendering of the idea I saw in my mind. If this were a real project, I would probably do more with the font choices. These are just ones I had open on the computer while writing that book. For a real client, I would have gone through my library of several thousand fonts to make a choice that was more in keeping with the client's traditional usage — but then, as the client doesn't exist, that seemed to be a waste of time. This final version of the graphic would traditionally be called a comp (short for comprehensive). It should be output on a color-calibrated proofer and shown to the client for approval.

The same procedure is followed when designing larger projects. Here is what I went through as I started this book. I did a few small thumbnails and I liked the movement of the one seen upper left. I liked the movement. At the bottom right of this page you can see the slightly more detailed thumbnail I used to firm up the idea. At this point I opened an InDesign document and started assembly.

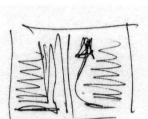
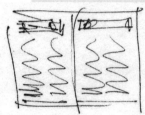

Reduced Scan of thumbnails

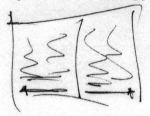
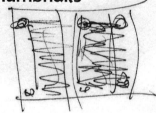

Picking a style

While working with these visual notes of your ideas, you will begin to get a feeling for style. This is one place that often needs a historical context. For example, if the project is a picture story booklet for senior citizens advertising life in a managed care high rise, it might be helpful to consider the layouts from *Look* and *Life* in the 1940s and 1950s. If the task is a reminiscing article on Jefferson Airplane, a good place to look would be the style of the early Rolling Stone. If the client needs an ad for the Smithsonian, it is simple common sense to look at that magazine for layout ideas.

It is important to choose a style that will appeal to the chosen readership. A no-holds-barred, professionally ugly, nail-'em-to-the-wall approach will probably work with the snowboarding set. It

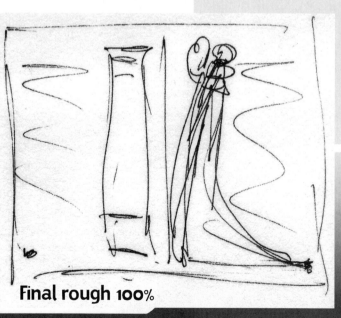

Final rough 100%

will spell disaster if you are producing a fund-raising brochure for the Prairie Star Buffalo Restocking and Wild West Nostalgia Fund. If you have no personal experience with the readership, a little research is in order.

Typography

Some of the first choices to be made as a style is chosen are the fonts to be used. This is an absolutely critical decision that will greatly affect readership. The fonts must be consistent with the style. Art Nouveau fonts do not work well for a financial prospectus. Geometric sans serifs rarely work for brochures concerning support groups for abused women. Flowery scripts would probably not be effective for an ad for a jock shop retailing licensed sports items.

As mentioned many times already, the font choices are among the most important choices you will make concerning the general *feel* of the piece. More importantly, it almost entirely controls the first reaction when reading actually begins. In an environment where you have only a few seconds to get the reader's interest, an appealing font choice can help a great deal.

Color

Early in the questions phase, you and your client were forced to come to a decision concerning the amount of color that could be budgeted. As you finalize your layout and style decisions, you should pick an actual color palette. This is true even if you are working in process color. Although you have millions of colors, a limited and structured palette is much more functional and manageable. More than that, it helps you develop a specific look for your project, greatly helping with that prime design virtue — consistency.

When you pick a color palette, include as much of the spectrum as possible. With process, that means you'll need a basic yellow, red, and blue, plus an appropriate gray and a brown, purple, or green that works with the others. This will enable you to put together a color scheme that is coherent, but not really limited. With choices in all the primaries, it becomes easy to develop a full-color look that remains consistent.

With two-color spot, this usually means picking secondaries or complements that cover a wide spectrum. Instead of black, use a deep slate blue, complementing it with a leaf green or a rust. Deep purple works well with lighter greens or orange-browns, and it pops with a deep yellow or mustard. With the expense of spot color (and traditional production), you might as well avoid black. It only costs a small additional mixing charge to use two spot colors instead of black and one spot. The color variations and impact added by that small change are immense, however.

Remember that the key to making all of these things work is contrast. Without enough contrast, you will never make it work. If you hit it too hard, you can always pull it back with judicious use of tints. However, hitting it too hard is almost never the problem. Normally, the problem is timidity. The real problem is that hesitancy on the part of the designer often translates to untrustworthiness of the client as far as the reader is concerned.

Talk with the creative production crew

As soon as you have the style finalized, communicate your decision to those producing the pieces of the project: artists, writers, and photographers. The more they know about what you need (and the sooner they know it), the better the results will be. With creatives, holding too tight a rein causes stilted and contrived artwork. Allowing too much freedom gives license that can produce beautiful art that has no bearing on your content or style.

Let them know what you need — no more, no less.

At this point, it is time to gather everything into a neat pile. Put all of your logos and PostScript graphics in a folder (originals and exported graphics). Put all your scanned photos in a separate folder (high-res halftone or sep or the low-res FPOs if you are going to be using an image substitution scheme with your service bureau). Go stretch your back, drink a cup of coffee, or whatever you do to relax and clear your mind. Now you do the actual work the client hired you for: the production of finished documents.

4. PRODUCE IT EFFICIENTLY

Once you reach this stage, document assembly becomes a relatively simple exercise in production. You are enabled to produce the documents with minimal hitches, glitches, and redoes. You simply build on your decisions and assemble the project.

It is important to stay light on your feet (mentally). Production always raises questions that were forgotten in the excitement of creation. No matter how tight the rough is, things never fit exactly as planned. Even after a long professional career, a designer's final documents commonly look much different from the roughs and layouts. You are still in creation mode, but the process is much easier because all the pieces are in hand and the stylistic decisions have already been made.

Defaults

The first thing that has to be dealt with is the defaults. Everything we have discussed in the earlier portions of this book must be adjusted to this specific project. You must get the documents under your control.

The first step of composition is to take control.

Setting up a functional set of custom defaults takes a fair amount of time. The temptation is to skip over this step. *Do not do it!* Sure, quick half-hour jobs often do not allow the luxury. Even normal one- or two-hour jobs don't seem to require it. But all it takes is a serious copyfitting problem for you to realize what a fool you were for not setting your defaults. This is where those old proverbs like, "A stitch in time saves nine," come into play. You will relish the default habit once you create it.

You should have your basic defaults already set up, but you'll need to adjust fonts, sizes, leading, tracking, font width, hyphenation, linking control, amount of autoleading, indents, tabs, paragraph rules, leaders, colors, text wrap, margins, columns, master pages, automatic page

numbering, typographers' quotes, table of contents entries, line width and color, fill color, guides, and more. Yes, the entire list has to be reviewed. You do get very fast at this after a while, but that skill must be developed and encouraged until it becomes a habit.

Save your document(s) to the proper folder

The first step when you start your new documents is to save them. Before you can even open the new file, you usually have to choose the number of pages, the page size, the bleed, the margins, and the resolution. After saving, you adjust your defaults and preferences. At this point you also want to create your master pages. This is when you have to set up your text boxes and linkages. It is worth your while to spend careful time developing your master pages before you start composing.

Styles palettes are not optional.

The second step is to set up your palettes – Styles palettes (both paragraph and character) and color palette. The Styles palettes are your major organizational tool – as I have said repeatedly. They give you global control of all the type in the entire document. The color palette is also essential for efficient production.

Import and flow

At this point, almost all of your work is done. All that remains is final assembly and massage. By massage, we mean the gentle kneading and shaping of the type and graphics until everything fits the way it should fit. If you have prepared properly, this should be an almost effortless exercise. Here's a suggested order for final assembly:

- Import your text and flow it into position.
- Make necessary formatting corrections using your style palettes.
- Import your graphics and locate them.
- Size the graphics and adjust the text wrap to produce the best-looking, most readable type.
- Adjust the style palettes to make the type fit the required spaces.
- Print a proof.

A strong reminder!

We cannot emphasize enough how important it is to proof the document thoroughly. Sloppy proofing is one of the surest signs of nonprofessionalism. It is the cause of countless problems with client relationships. Everything should be proofed by three people minimum. You can be one of the three, but you cannot be the only proofer. One thing is certain: if you made the mistake in the first place, you will probably miss it when you proof it. If at all possible, turn it over to a professional proofreader.

Client approval

At this point, everything comes to a screeching halt until the client reads, proofs, and signs off on the proof. This is one place where you do not want to be Ms. Nice. Without a client signature on the proof, any production problems can (and probably will) be made your responsibility. You will be forced to either pay for or absorb any correction costs. These unbudgeted expenses can easily run into thousands of dollars, so be forewarned!

The customer is always right?

Of course not! What we have to keep foremost in our minds is that it doesn't matter whether the customer is right or wrong. Our job is to serve him. Our task is to convince him that we are professional and that we really care about his business. It does not matter if he's wrong, if we treat him like he is, he is gone. That may solve the problem (since he is no longer our client), but it is a poor way of doing business.

A service industry

Publishing is referred to as a service industry throughout this book. Our job is to please the client. We are manufacturers of custom products. We normally cannot just make millions of copies and throw them around, hoping to sell a high enough percentage to stay in business. The best Web site has to attract hits and keep them, or its design costs are a total waste of time and money.

We sell custom products for individuals. Even though you may be dealing almost exclusively with large corporations, it is the individuals in the corporation that matter. If we do not make the individual who ordered our services happy, that person will find a designer who will. It really is exactly that simple.

THE REALITIES OF PRESSURE

DESIGN IN A PRODUCTION SETTING

There has been an adage in the industry for many years. You can have any two of the following three qualities: fast, excellent, and inexpensive. In others words, you can have fast and excellent, but it won't be inexpensive. You can have fast and inexpensive, but it won't be excellent. You can have excellent and inexpensive, but it won't be fast.

The problem is that the adage is no longer true. Our industry is extremely competitive. Many publishers now meet all three of those parameters. It used to be considered cute to have a large sign over the door saying, *"If you wanted it yesterday, you should have brought it in tomorrow."* You cannot blow customers off with cute sayings anymore. Rush jobs are a major portion of our income. Ridiculously fast deadlines are one of our major opportunities to win customers who remain loyal because of our service.

There is a very common cartoon, printed in various poster sizes, found in many offset litho shops, showing a printer collapsing on the ground in gales of laughter, choking out, *"You want it when?"* In this age, those attitudes will send your customers down the street faster than you can imagine. Your clients have serious problems. Your task is to help them solve their problems.

Sometimes it's impossible

However, sometimes you can't. Most clients are smart enough to realize that 30,000 copies of a 200-page, perfect-bound book will not be done tomorrow. What you have to realize, though, is that there are companies that will give it a real good shot (and your client has probably heard of them). Digitally, many things are possible that were not possible ten years ago.

Deadlines

Our industry is run on deadlines. Many of these time limits are ridiculous. We know it. The customer knows it. It does not change the fact that the deadlines are real. If you are producing an event program, complaining about the deadline will not move the event back a day. If the SEC has a March 1 deadline for receipt of that annual report, March 2 is not good enough.

It is common to blame the client for delays. It is common for designers to lose work because they blame their clients for deadlines. Instead, they should figure out what can be done as soon as the job is brought in. This is one of the main reasons for the questioning process. One of the things you are looking for is possible production problems. You can do a great deal to help customer relations by simply explaining reality to your clients whenever possible.

An excellent designer is prepared to do whatever it takes.

That's a scary thought. What if you are asked to work the weekend? What if you have to come in a little early or leave late? Are you willing to be reliable help to your employer? If you have your own business, have you decided to be a dependable service to your clients? This goes way beyond the normal requirements of showing up every day, on time, ready to work.

The proper attitude

We cannot continue until we cover what you should expect to offer an employer or your clients. They do not owe you anything beyond honesty and integrity (even these are sometimes in short supply). When you are hired or sign the contract, you will be given a list of company or client expectations – sometimes written, sometimes verbal, sometimes through the grapevine.

Your job is to meet those expectations. If you cannot, do everyone a favor and find a place where you fit. Every position has pluses and minuses. You want to find work where the positives meet your needs and the negatives are inconsequential. It is not the employer's job to change the company to satisfy your desires. The client can't afford to care about your creative needs. Their concern is financial survival.

Owners and managers make the big bucks because they have the big headaches. If you want the money, you get the pressure. It is a decision you have to make. You will never be a welcome employee if you are always complaining about reality. Your task is to meet your employer's needs by satisfying the company's customers.

Publishing is a team sport, even though this team is often made up of a constantly changing group of separately employed or self-employed subcontractors. All of us need to work together. Many students are almost horrified to learn that they cannot take anything all the way through production. Sooner or later, you have to hand off your baby to someone else. The likelihood is that you will be working on something started by someone else anyway. If you cannot communicate with each other, how can you possibly communicate with the client's customers?

The key is communication.

How many times has this been said so far? Experience shows that it cannot be repeated often enough. There must be good communication between the sales staff and the client; the sales staff and the designer; the designers and the client; the image assembly staff and the pressroom; image assembly, the client, and the press room; the client, designer, and ISP; designer, programmer, and ISP; and so on.

The job ticket

The first major communication tool is the job ticket. This is the way the sales staff communicates with the rest of the shop. In your own firm this is how you keep track of your promises to the client. It is extremely important that these forms be filled out accurately and completely. Not only are the complete job specs required, but also the complete client name and address, former job numbers, and the appropriate contact person(s) with both phone and e-mail.

Just as important as filling out the job ticket is reading it. Most jobs that have to be redone were messed up because someone did not read the job ticket. Do not take anyone else's word for what you need to do — read the job ticket! This even covers the bosses' instructions. You make them look good if you discover that what they told you does not match what is on the job ticket. You can save the company thousands of dollars.

Customer proofs

The next most important communication tool is the proof. We've mentioned them throughout. However, we need to examine them from the customer relations viewpoint. The most important proofs from a legal and public relations standpoint are the customer proofs. These are sample prints, PDFs, or a Web page that show the client what the final product will look like, what it will contain, and how everything is organized.

Three proofs are usually necessary. This differs a little in print and Web. In print, the first is a laser proof of the artwork, color if necessary. This art or copy proof must be signed off by the client before you proceed to the expense of a color contract proof. In some cases, it is better to have an artwork proof that has FPO graphics. You might not want to spend the time color-correcting separations if the customer has not even approved the photos yet.

Online proofs

On the Web, proofs go in stages. One of the real advantages of working online is that Web sites can be updated at any time. In fact, they should be redesigned, updated, or simply changed about once a month or so. Therefore, Web proofs tend to be ongoing e-mails with a link to the page, saying something like, *"I changed [x], what do you think?"* Web graphics should just be attached to an e-mail for proofing.

Often, what we are calling the art proof takes the place of what used to be called the comprehensive or comp. The comprehensive was accurate enough to enable the client to approve the artwork (without spending any more time or money than necessary). In many cases, all the budget will allow is a digital color print of the final artwork and the hope that the client doesn't make too many changes.

It is important to make sure that the customer realizes that signing the art proof means that he approves of the graphics and the copy on it, including all typos, spelling, and grammar. If you do not have that, you will find it very difficult later to charge for customer alterations. Supposedly if the client changes his mind, about copy or layout, he should be charged for the time and materials it takes to make those changes.

Without a signed art proof, you have no evidence that he ever liked the artwork in the first place. This is one reason why you need such thoroughly proofed samples before the customer sees them. Clients are rarely professional proofers. They will not see typos or obvious printing errors. It is very bad form to use their lack of expertise to point the accusing finger when something goes wrong. *"But you signed the proof ... "*

Getting customer approval

The signed proofs become legal contracts. You promise to produce the work as proofed. The client promises to accept and pay for the work as proofed. The service bureau and printer promise to duplicate the proof with the printed materials. There are ways to ease the approval process. The primary method is by doing thorough proofing yourself. As a general guideline, you are in trouble if you have more than one correction per four pages. Any more problems or typos than that and you will be considered less than professional.

... you are in trouble if you have more than one correction per four pages.

The basic problem is that clients are used to "Madison Avenue," just like the rest of us. Their baseline assumption is perfection, because that is what they are used to. When's the last time you saw a typo in a national slick magazine (see the sidebar on the next page)? Many clients feel the same about artwork charges as they do about dental bills – and it does not make them happy. Many of them are looking for an excuse to prove that they know as much design and printing as you do. You will find that customers will use your mistakes to leverage a reduction in the charges. What is the simple solution? Do not give them anything to pick on. Give them a technically perfect proof.

The customer is always right!

The old saying, "The customer is always right," is not a joke. It is a truism. In other words, it is so obviously true that it seems stupid to mention it. This is where we started this little section, but we have not covered it yet. By definition, the customer is right because our job is to serve the client. Our task is to bring their requests into reality.

There will be many times when you are asked to do something very difficult. Remember that to develop skill, you have to be stretched. If everything is easy, you get bored, relax into bad attitudes, and begin to dislike your profession. Some of your clients' most ridiculous requests are your best opportunity for growth. Learn to relish the challenges.

You do not have to like your clients. You do have to respect them. In a very real way, the success of your business depends on the success of their business. Often clients are headstrong, arrogant, or egotistical. Some of this is necessary; some of it is simply obnoxious. It is not your job to tell them that their arrogance is simply a projection of their insecurity (even though this is usually true). They are in business to make a profit and your job is to help them. They need help, not hassles.

Business relationships are not social relationships.

Even if you do like your clients (and that is always pleasant), you should not expect a social relationship to develop. Friends that you hang around with tend to make poor clients. There is a tendency to give them favors, put their jobs on a higher priority, and do many other things that jeopardize your relationships with the rest of your clients. The friend who allows you to keep business on a businesslike basis is a rare friend. I hope you have many.

BUSINESS ETHICS

There are many lists and several books concerning business ethics and trade practices. For example, there is the excellent *Graphic Artists Guild Handbook: Pricing and Ethical Guidelines*. They put out the tenth edition in spring of 2000. We find their prices extremely high for our locality, but it is easy to make a percentage adjustment. At least they offer an objective standard to base your pricing upon. Don't restrict yourself to books. Ask your employers for a copy of the list they use. In general, these books and lists are concerned with legislating morality, which is always tricky at best. The basic tenets are always the same: honesty, integrity, keeping your word, and fulfilling written agreements. In this day of constant litigation and adversarial relationships, it is extremely wise to have written contracts.

This is a major pain, but it is really not optional. Contracts are not about limiting people and keeping them in line. The purpose of a contract is clear communication and mutual agreement. Little is more disheartening than to do exactly what you think you were asked to do and get screamed at for your incompetence. People simply hear wrong, believe it or not.

Your word may be good, but that does not help if clients think you promised something else. This does not count those who are looking

A word on typos

One of the most serious changes in the past decade is the general lowering of standards by the newcomers to publishing. Too young to be conscious of industry standards, and too ill-educated to know grammatical excellence, the modern digital publisher is often embarrassingly crude to those of us who have been around since the 1960s or earlier. More than that they embarrass themselves and ruin their budgets because of the quantity of errors left in the final produced pieces. Remember, the client can demand a reprint for a single typo or layout error.

to pick a fight to avoid payment. Those people exist also, and contracts help keep them in line. The best thing is a standard printed contract. The *Graphic Artists Guild Handbook: Pricing and Ethical Guidelines* has many of these, of almost every possible variety. That way personal friends and disliked clients get the same treatment. It is all in the interest of fairness and communication.

When in doubt, write it out!

Another reason this book cannot be a complete guide to industry practices is the flux things are in. This chapter closes with a series of areas to think about concerning your business and/or your employer. Chances are things are still changing rapidly.

- How are roles defined?
- When will quotes and proposals be ready and what will they contain?
- What proofs will be provided?
- Who pays for which alterations?
- What are all the deadlines and delivery charges?
- Who stores the materials?
- Who owns the materials: the output and the digital files?
- What is the payment schedule?
- What kinds of rights are being purchased (copyright questions)?
- How will disputes be settled?
- Who is paying for production?
- Who is responsible for production?
- Who handles outside services and how are they billed and paid for?

As you can see, it gets very complicated. The likelihood is that your new employer already has a working set of guidelines in use. If the company doesn't, the book recommended is an excellent resource. It is part of your necessary knowledge.

I thought this was a chapter on design

It is. One of the first things you have to learn is that design is not an abstract, conceptual process done in an ivory tower of creative and artistic elitism. Design is a service we provide for those who shape our culture. Much like the unknown craftsmen in medieval society generating artwork for the nobility, we serve business and its marketing needs. Even nonprofit, political, and educational operations now need design to market their services.

We are a marketing economy. If you do not get that straight in your mind, you are headed for trouble (or at least disappointment). Our task is not some abstract goal of excellence or artistic perfection. We are charged with helping clients communicate with their customers. **SERVE YOUR CLIENTS!**

1. Why is design so involved with customer relations?

2. What is the advantage of using thumbnails?

3. What is the usual mistake made with contrast?

4. Why do you need to control the reading order of your document?

5. Why do you always fix the largest mistake first?

WHERE SHOULD YOU BE BY THIS TIME?

By now you should have almost earned your "A". You should be in the beginnings of a *production mode*, and you are rapidly coming to know what you are good at and what you need help with — your design strengths and weaknesses.

DISCUSSION

Discuss all of your projects with your classmates as you approach the proofing stage. Begin to develop the skill of discerning what is genuinely part of your design style and what is hindering communication with your client's readership. Help your classmates come to the same place (but only if they ask for help).

Talk among yourselves...

CHAPTER ELEVEN

Graphic Usage

CHAPTER CONTENTS:

Knowledge needed to add graphics to your documents in a form that is printable, or that is small enough for quick downloads

CONCEPTS

1. **Lineart**

2. **Continuous tone**

3. **Linescreen**

4. **Halftone**

5. **Separation**

6. **Screen angles**

7. **Moiré**

8. **Scanning resolution**

CHAPTER OBJECTIVES

By presenting the basic terms and production procedures, you will learn how to:

1. Prepare your scans for printing
2. Pick an appropriate linescreen
3. Compensate for dot gain
4. Avoid most printing problems
5. Improve the look of your finished document

LAB WORK FOR CHAPTER

- Continue work on skills and miniskills
- Submit finished theory exams
- Continue work on your approved real project – ideally your second, third, or fourth real project

There are far too many terms to be covered with a simple list of concepts. These words are also defined in the Glossary in the back of the book.

Terms: camera ready, dots, pixel, dot, color depth, dithering, diffusion dithering, stochastic, loupe, halftone cell, flexography, waterless printing, heat-set web, emulsification, nouveaux riche design, dot range, highlights, shadows, specular highlights, dot gain, generation, EPS, TIFF, screen preview, link, export, place (import), bounding box, cross-platform, compression, lossless, lossy, self-extracting archive, duotone. tritone, quadritone

Making it printable

Here we come to an area where many designers sit up and howl (or maybe just scream in pain). For here we have to talk about some semi-complicated theory that causes many people conceptual problems. The basic question is, "Why do I need 1,200 dpi or more to print photos?" Or second, "Why are my photos so dark and ugly?" Or third, "What are all of these bull's-eye shapes in my pretty background?"

Essential knowledge for the advanced designer

This is one of the major areas of ignorance among those of you who have been doing this for a while. I am really not sure why this is so, but my suspicion is that most of you have never been inside a printshop or service bureau except to drop off a job with a hope and a prayer, trying to get out the door before they tell you that there are major problems with the way you work.

Nearly two-thirds of all jobs are unprintable as received!

This does sound kind of harsh, but the reality is still that nearly two-thirds of all jobs received by the output personnel are unprintable as received. Almost 100% of the problems are caused by ignorant, lazy, or arrogant designers. Of course, the most common problems concern fonts and font usage which we will cover in a bit. And with OpenType, there is some hope that this will be solved.

However, the major source of unacceptable printed quality is found in the area surrounding dots, linescreen, dot gain, dot range, banding, and so forth. These areas are all part of the same conceptual darkness about practical production matters experienced by most designers, whether self-taught or school trained.

For some reason, resolution and printability issues have remained part of that black magic achieved by wizened practitioners in the darkened dungeons of the stripping department (which has now been euphemized into image assembly). The problem, of course, is found in the new paradigm where we designers are now responsible for all of those decisions formerly made in that incomprehensible environment of high resolution, process color, commercial printing.

WE ARE NOW THEM!
OF COURSE, WE ALWAYS WERE, IF WE HAD ANY SENSE.

For that reason, no matter how advanced you think you are, you need to read this chapter carefully. Unless you have actually worked in a printing firm or in an image assembly position, most of this knowledge will probably be unknown to you. Even if you did, you probably just did what you were told without comprehension. Even worse, much of what you may think you know is probably actually in error. Check it out! Maybe you actually have this knowledge under your belt, but that puts you in the top 10% of all designers. The contents of this chapter are excerpts from materials I have written for *Image Manipulation* by Radiqz Press, 1998 (as yet unreleased), with the publisher's permission.

Graphic Usage

Lineart and continuous tone

As we study this, we need to be constantly aware of the type of art we are dealing with. Lineart in a traditional definition was black and white camera-ready artwork. All color was added by the prepress department as directed by overlays showing color breaks given by the designer. Traditionally it was called inkwork.

However, there are many graphics that are much more than just black and white. We are not talking about spot color here (which is just a variant on lineart). Currently, the lineart production place is taken by PostScript illustration using FreeHand or Illustrator. Although these programs can do amazingly complicated lineart, the artwork produced remains drawn shapes with hard edges that are colored individually. The graphics InDesign produces are also lineart, by this definition.

The other type of artwork is called continuous tone. This is artwork that varies in color. This type of artwork — which includes photos, pencil drawings, watercolors, paintings, and most fine art — continuously varies in color. When scanned into Photoshop, every pixel is a different color (even in supposedly flat areas like empty blue sky). Even if you are using grayscale, it is still continuous tone.

The problem is that continuous tone cannot be printed without going through contortions. The tinted areas of PostScript illustrations need the same transformations. This is where the rubber meets the road, and where most designers lapse into ignorance, at best — arrogance, rudeness, and nastiness, at worst.

REMEMBER, ONLY THE TRULY INSECURE FALL BACK ON ARROGANCE TO COVER THEIR LACK OF COMPETENCE.

PRESSES AND PRINTERS ALWAYS REQUIRE DOTS

Most of the reproductive processes (with the exception of photographic prints and some of the new digital presses), are unable able to print areas that vary in color. More than that, even digital presses cannot print dots that are different colors from the same printhead, plate, or toner.

This is the key concept you must remember. Presses and printers use dots that are a constant color. They might be all black or all red or all cyan, but for any given printhead, only one color of ink is possible. To rephrase, every different color of ink or toner requires a different print head.

The varying colors and the appearance of continuous tone on a printed product (or a monitor) are an optical illusion. This illusion is created by using dots that are so small the human eye blends them into tints, shades, and continuous tone.

There are two basic types of dots

Before we can go on, we need to discuss the two basic types of dots. The conceptual difference is simple. Can the dots vary in color or not? Those that cannot are better called dots. Those that can vary in color should properly be called pixels. Pixel is a shortened form of picture element standing for the smallest part of a digital image.

The number of different colors that a pixel can express is determined by its color depth in binary numbers. Color depth is an expression of how many bits of data are assigned to each pixel. If one bit is assigned, there are only two possibilities: on or off. If 2 bits are assigned to a pixel, there are four possible colors; 3 bits = 8; 4 bits = 16; 5 bits = 32; 6 bits = 64; 7 bits = 128; 8 bits = 256; and so on. These numbers represent possible colors. For example, a four-bit monitor would have sixteen colors available, a 6-bit GIF has sixty-four colors.

A two-bit screen would have four colors — maybe white, green, red, and blue. These colors would be it. Each pixel would be one of those colors and nothing else. There would be no grays, no yellows, no browns, nothing else.

But what would happen if the screen was drawn in a checkerboard pattern of red and blue? Probably some sort of purple, depending on the hues involved. This technique of generating the illusion of additional colors by using patterns of pixels is called dithering. Dithering can be in defined patterns (think uglier than s***) or in an apparently random arrangement called diffusion dithering.

For clarity's sake, I will attempt to remember to use the following codes to help you separate dots from pixels. Basically, scanners and monitors use pixels. Printers and presses normally use dots. The problem is that everyone calls any type of resolution whether using dots or pixels: dpi (which obviously stands for dots per inch).

Here are the codes we will be using (assuming an accurate proofing process) with thanks to Blatner and Roth's *Real World Scanning and Halftones*":

- spi = samples per inch for scanner pixels
- ppi = pixels per inch for monitor pixels
- dpi = dots per inch for printers and imagesetters
- lpi = lines per inch for halftone screens on plates, masters, toner drums

These codes are not important, in themselves, but my hope is that they will help you separate the vast difference between pixels and dots.

THE HALFTONE REVOLUTION

As we mentioned in Chapter 5, photography triggered the search for the ability to print shades of gray. In the later part of the nineteenth century a technique to solve this problem was developed. This was first seen, commercially printed, in Century Magazine in 1887. The technique produced, what came to be called, halftones. A halftone broke a continuous tone image into tiny little dots that vary in size. However, these dots are smaller than the resolving capability of the human eye. Therefore they blur together in our minds and we see the illusion of continuous tone.

There are two basic ways to vary the tints that are apparently created by the dots. (Remember that, in halftone dots, a tint is a percentage of area covered — in a 15% tint, 15 percent of the paper is covered with ink or toner.) The most common, at the present time, is the

IF YOU LOOK AT THIS FROM 15 FEET AWAY OR MORE, THE DOTS WILL BLEND INTO A SMOOTH GRAY.

Graphic Usage

original technique that varies the dot size, with dots that are in a rectilinear grid. This is the halftone technique. It has been used since the 1890s. Only since the mid-1990s has there been an alternative.

This second, alternative method varies the dot location and frequency. Here the dot size remains constant. This is commonly called the stochastic technique. In appearance, it resembles the technical pen technique of stippling or the old intaglio method called mezzotint (but the stochastic dots are often much smaller). This is a brand new capability made possible by the extremely fast computers that are now commonly available, and can only be produced digitally.

Most commonly, what we call stochastic is really diffusion dithering. True stochastic requires great computer processing power to precisely place extremely tiny dots. Cheap inkjet printers all use some form of diffusion dithering. We will talk briefly about using Photoshop's diffusion dithering capabilities to solve problems with low resolution printers. There is a third method used in a couple of digital printers (it may never see common usage), that varies dots in both size and location.

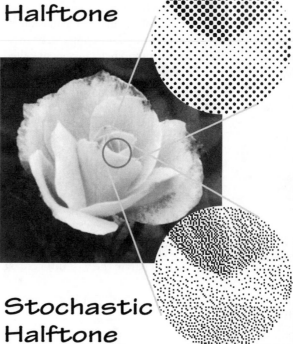

Round Dot Halftone

Stochastic Halftone

For now, what you need to know is that printers and presses require dots. There are only a few (very expensive) digital color printers that use pixels (the Xeikon variants, Canon's CLC series, Xerox's DocuColor series, and a few others). More than that, all digital or traditional printers (except for low resolution proofers like dye sublimation) need what are called hard dots. These dots are a specific size and a uniform density. It is very important that they be predictable in size and location, and that they can be calibrated to produce tints that are accurate to plus or minus a half a percent or less in color.

This example should give you a much better feel for how these dot structures appear when magnified. As you can see, the dots have very hard edges and destroy all fine detail. Notice that halftone or stochastic makes no difference. At the dot sizes used, all we see is smooth gray gradations. In fact, if you move back from this illustration about 15 feet, you will see that both of these enlargements look the same.

Once the dots are formed, the image cannot be enlarged without making the dots visible to the naked eye. If they are reduced in size, the dots can easily get so small that they will not reproduce, and the image will get muddy, blotchy, and ugly.

Pixels are very different from dots. First of all, they do not vary in size, they vary in color. Pixel size is determined by the scanner, monitor, or software. We mentioned this earlier. The color variance is determined by the color depth (or number of bits assigned to each pixel). They do not vary in frequency. More importantly, pixels cannot vary in frequency — they are always part of a rectilinear grid of specified dimensions.

Pixels are used by scanners, monitors, and in digital files in general. Paint programs, like Photoshop, define images by their pixel dimensions. An image that is 300 pixels square would be two inches square at 150 ppi, one inch square at 300 ppi, and half an inch square at 600 ppi.

Usually you can't see pixels (and do not want to), so here is a demonstration (it's the same rose). As you can see, the pixels are on a regular grid. Each picture element is assigned a position on that grid or map. This grid is commonly called a bitmap. This may be because the first bitmaps used one-bit pixels on their grids. However, a bitmap is simply a description of the color of the individual pixels with each pixel having a specific location defined by the grid. This location is usually measured from the top left pixel. So the third pixel from the left on the second row would be mapped as 2,3 (or 3,2 — who cares except programmers?).

All of these pixels are fixed elements. They cannot be moved. All you can do is change their color. If you change the color of the shape to the background color and redraw the shape 10 pixels to the right, it appears to have moved. It has not. It's much like movie marquees with moving lights. The lights do not move.

PRINTED HALFTONES: LINESCREEN USAGE

As mentioned earlier, printers and presses require dots, and the vast majority of those dots (except for the cheap inkjets and some of the most expensive imagesetters) come in regular patterns. These regular patterns are called linescreen. The name comes from the original screens, which were made of plate glass with tiny parallel lines scribed into the front and back surfaces at right angles to each other. (*Yes, tap them and they were reduced to a pile of glass dust.*)

Linescreens are measured by the number of lines per inch. This is a physical measurement; for instance, a 133-line screen has 133 horizontal lines and 133 vertical lines. The term is in such strong usage that no one even questions the fact that lines haven't been used for many decades. Linescreen now refers to the grid size that holds the dots — expressed as the number of dots per inch or linescreen, as in a 65-line screen having 65 dots per inch.

First of all, notice that these dots produced by the halftone screens are very close together. The number of lines per inch is commonly 150 for the normal "slick" magazines you read. For ultra-premium art reproduction printing, 300, 500, and even finer linescreens are used. Second, notice that linescreen is much coarser than the dpi ratings of digital printers. Printer dpi start at 300 and continue up to 4,000 to 6,000 dots per inch. So, the question becomes, "Why does traditional linescreen need so few dots per inch while digital dots need many times more?" Hold on, the answers are coming.

Lines per inch

There are two reasons why we use the dot sizes commonly available. The first (and most powerful) factor is the capability of the human eye. At normal reading distance (around 18 inches), dots that are a seventy-fifth of an inch (75 lpi) or smaller are blended into smooth colors. We might notice a grainy texture at 75 lpi. Even this disappears at 133 line or higher. With anything more coarse than 75 lpi, almost everyone can see the dots with the naked eye. There are always one or two students in my classes who can see 85-line dots easily, and always a couple of others who cannot see even 65-line dots.

The second factor controlling dot size is the technology of the printer or press. For example, for years newspapers were limited to 65-line screen. They were printing with letterpress on unsized newsprint paper with relatively liquid ink. If the dots were any smaller than 65 lpi, they soaked into each other, plugged up in the shadows, and disappeared in the highlights.

What we need to do, briefly, is consider all the linescreen ranges in common use. It is important that you understand which printers use which linescreen and why. You also need to know what linescreens are used where and why. This knowledge will greatly help the production of your printed designs. In fact, you must know the output linescreen before you start assembling your document. It will affect the length of gradients, the detail of photos, and much more.

Zero to 25 lpi: Billboards (grand format inkjets)

Sometimes these very coarse screens (0 to 25 lpi) are used for purely graphic reasons by designers, but in standard production, only billboards use them. Remember, the use of 75 lpi is based on the 18 inch reading distance. 75 lpi @ 18" is the same visual quality as 37.5 lpi @ 3', or 19 lpi @ 6', or 10 lpi at 12', or 5 lpi at 24', etc.

Billboards are normally read at 100 feet or more. On top of that, they are usually read by someone flying by at highway speed. To help visualize, 150-line at 1.5 foot is roughly equivalent to 15-line screen at 15 feet. Billboards are commonly 4-line to 12-line. But, as you can see, their resolution capabilities are superior to those glossy photos in *National Geographic* or *Smithsonian* magazines. (Traditionally printed billboards make wonderful wallpaper, if you can still find them. All you normally

have to do is call the local outdoor advertising company. Ask them for outdated printed signs that they are tossing. A 20 foot Clydesdale makes a wonderful mural.)

25 to 50 lpi: Graphics

Linescreens of 25 to 50 lpi are rarely used except for graphic effect. They could be used very effectively for posters and flyers when forced to use 300 dpi printers. They rarely are, but this just seems to be the result of design school training, and the general belief that finer screens are better. Any linescreen is neither better or worse. It is just a choice you make as a designer relative to the publishing technology you intend to use. Quite often, a linescreen of this size is the best solution for screen printed graphics on shirts or towels.

These coarse screens can be very effective. In addition, they are very easy to deal with. They usually produce very small file sizes. They print beautifully and even low-res printers can render them clearly. The photos look great from a distance of five or six feet, and up close you want your readers to read the words anyway. Try it on your next poster or flyer!

50 to 75 lpi: Cheap copiers, flexography, and screen printing

This is the area inhabited by cheap copiers, 300 dpi laser printers, consumer inkjets, cheap package printing, and most screen printing. As you will see in the discussion of halftone cells, 400 dpi printers (or less) are only capable of photo reproduction in this range (50 to 75 lpi). These dots are still easily visible to the naked eye, disturbingly so. Only the uneducated eye can ignore the low quality of continuous tone art rendered with these large dots. But, they work fine for a poster hung high on a wall.

In this low-res area, you really need to go to bitmap Photoshop images converted to diffusion dither. The random dots actually look quite good this coarse. For work produced on low-res machines, like a 400 dpi Risograph, diffusion dithers at 200 dpi produce dots about a half point in diameter that print beautifully. You will have to experiment to find what works on your particular machine.

Of course, the consumer inkjets are all doing this automatically (take a look under a 6X loupe or stronger). This is why even the 1,440 dpi inkjets are forced to use diffusion dither screening. These inkjets use much smaller dots for their *photographic look*, but now you know why printshops blanche when you bring one of these *photo* prints in to make a 1,000 copies. These stochastic dots cannot be copied because they are far too small.

Screen printing has changed a lot in recent years. Screen printers are limited to this range partially by the size of the holes in the screens they use. Currently, 120- and even 133-line screen printing is possible, but don't believe it until you see samples from the company you intend to use. Screen printers are also limited by the surfaces on which they print. Clothing causes trouble with dots that are finer than 50 lpi. The fabric weave can be more coarse than that. Even here you will occasionally see 100-line artwork on relatively smooth materials like T-shirts, sweatshirts, and soda cans. Again, talk to your supplier.

Flexography seems like a newcomer on the printing scene. In fact, the technology has been around for many years. Formerly, this rather crude technology could only print solids. Now it can print screens fairly effectively (in some cases, up to 133-line screen and process color). The amazing fact is that flexography has captured 18% of the world market and totally dominates the packaging industry (according to *Adobe Magazine*, Autumn 1999). The operative advice here is the same as always, but much more necessary. Talk to your supplier and give them what they ask for.

85 to 120 lpi: Newspaper and quickprint

As mentioned earlier, in the days of letterpress, newspapers used to be limited to 65-line. Now offset printed newspapers normally use 100-line. Some older papers with outdated equipment (usually the last remnants of letterpress) still cannot handle anything finer than 65- to 85-line. This is due to the poor quality of paper and the relatively liquid ink used. When designing newspaper ads, be sure to call and ask what the paper requires. You may be pleasantly surprised. You may be disappointed. Some of the special color sections are printed on better paper with even finer screens.

Most quickprinters are proud of the fact that they can print 100-, 120-, or even 133-line images. Most should stick to 85-line. Again, this is due to the equipment used. Quickprinters have been built around the duplicator (think AlphaGraphics™, Sir Speedy™, and all the corner store printing franchises.) A duplicator is a cheap, mass-marketed press and its resolution capabilities are fairly crude.

Plates contribute to the situation. Most quickprint plates are exposed on platemakers using plastic or even paper plates. These specialized cameras are designed to save money, not to increase quality. The quality of the lens optics is relatively poor. Many of the lenses do not even focus well. Their sharpest focus is still "soft." The plate materials are yet another factor. The paper and plastic used cannot normally hold dots smaller than 100 lpi (if that).

Digital quickprint

A newer problem involves digital plates. Many of these plates are output on plain-paper laser printers. These 1,200 and 1,800 dpi printers claim 133 lpi. In fact, due to the nature of toner melted onto

paper or plastic, these printers often give very mottled screens at anything finer than 85 lpi. (However, much of this is due to the fact that many so-called 1,200 dpi printers are truly 300 or 600 dpi printers interpolated to 1,200 dpi, correctly expressed 300 x 1,200 dpi.)

Nevertheless, digital plates have transformed quickprint in one major way: traditionally camera ready artwork could not contain halftones. (They had to be added with stripped-in film halftones.) Now the digital plates output beautiful 85-line and 100-line screens, including the halftones. They can even do a decent job with short gradients, though any gradient longer than a couple of inches usually bands badly. We'll talk about banding in a bit. As usual, talk to your supplier, look at samples, and print some practice pieces, if possible.

Finally, there are the quickprinters that have gone entirely digital. By using black and white copiers, like the Docutech and many others, they can now do many things that were not possible with the old duplicators. However, most (if not all) of these digital presses are limited to 85 linescreen. Some of them can do a reasonable job with 100 line, but again ask for samples and a loupe to examine the actual dot structure.

In most cases, 85-line screen will give better results. All the equipment used by quickprinters can handle 85-line screen well, with no effort. Trying to print fine linescreens on quick-print equipment is analogous to trying to road race the family sedan. It can be done — with extreme care, a lot of work, and many special parts. However, neither the printing nor the racing can match the real thing.

133 lpi and up: Commercial printing

This is where the printing professionals live: 133 lpi and up. Many are quite snobbish about it. You need to remember that there is nothing wrong with coarser screens. They have their place. In some situations, those large dots are a real advantage. However, for reading, 133 and up is where it's at. For many years, 133 lpi was the commercial printing standard. Recently, with technological advances, 150-line screens have become the norm. Much of the improvement is determined by two main factors: equipment and paper. Equipment (presses mainly) has gotten good enough that 150-, 175- and 200-line screens are no big deal. If the shop is set up to handle them, these fine screens give superlative results. All it takes are good materials, a relatively dust-free environment, and excellent personnel.

Magazine publishing has made a similar turn. The heat-set web presses used to print full-color magazines have developed to the point where 150-line images are common. The change from 133- to 150-line has been gradual, but much of what you buy at the newsstand these days is 150 lpi.

The finer linescreens have been encouraged by the fashionable trend to use ultrasmooth, coated papers. These sheets hold the ink on the surface of the paper making it much easier to control the dot size. The negative side is the slick look. Some of us, who have been designing for many years, have been relieved by the recent turn toward uncoated, fiber-added stock. In all cases, the look of the final product is controlled more by the quality of the artwork than by the size of the dots that render that artwork.

Excellent designers produce beautiful printed pieces – even on 300 dpi B&W non-PostScript laser printers.

The upper limits and practical considerations

The upper limit is primarily a function of the technology. Offset lithography is normally limited to around 200-line screen. At this point, even quality lithographic presses have enough emulsification to limit dot size. However, many printers brag about being able to print 300-line screens. One printing firm, in Phoenix, has developed litho processes that allow 300 to 500 linescreen with outstanding results.

Gravure uses no water, so emulsification is no problem. These presses function comfortably in the 150 to 300 lpi range. Their limitation is primarily the grain structure of the plate and the ability of the resist to prevent the acid from breaking down the dot edges. Also, the plate can deform if the dots are too small.

Waterless printing is limited only by the grain of the plate. Some waterless jobs actually use the granular structure of the aluminum in the plate for the dot. These measure around 600 to 700 lpi. In fact, 400–600 lpi is not uncommon for these top-end waterless printers.

Printers working in hi-fi color are using stochastic dots that are roughly comparable to a 1% or 2% dot at 200 linescreen (as small as 4 microns). As a result, most of these printers are also using the new waterless technology. However, none of these top-end options are common. They are very expensive and rarely necessary. They tend to be used for detailed maps like seen in *National Geographic*'s offerings or for fine art prints.

Quite often, it is undesirable to print with too small a dot. When you push the limits of the available technology, there is a tendency for the larger (shadow) dots to plug up. As a result, 300 lpi can have much less shadow detail than 200 lpi, even though the midtones are sharper. In addition, the finer the dot, the higher the cost. Ultra-fine screens require better equipment, better facilities, better personnel, and more time.

In most cases, screens finer than 175-line are not cost-effective. In fact, unless you are printing on super-smooth, cast coated stock, the ultra-fine screens might easily muddy the image. This is the same problem mentioned when I recommended 85 linescreen for quickprint. A quickprint press operator using a duplicator might be able to print 133-line screen – but, can the duplicator handle the ultrasmooth paper necessary to benefit from those tiny dots?

As a desktop publisher, you need to understand the client's needs and the printer's capabilities. You need a stable of suppliers that can produce what is needed, in the most cost-effective manner, at the highest practical quality.

The first decision in design is: "Who is going to print this?"
The second decision is: "What am I going to print it on?"

THE PROBLEMS WITH DIGITAL DOTS

PRODUCING THE ILLUSION OF VARIABILITY

As you now know, digital dots fit a tight grid called a bitmap. In addition, these dots do not vary in either size or location. There are a couple of new printers that use dots like pixels (that is, they vary in color), but this is not the normal situation. As a result, digital printers have had to come up with what are called halftone cells to produce the illusion of variability.

These cells are made up of groups of dots. Each cell corresponds to a single linescreen dot. There are several problems with these cells. To start, they use the bitmap we keep referring to. This means that our formerly well-shaped linescreen dots become jagged assemblies of squares. This is more of a surprise to traditional printing professionals than anything else. They still cover the required percentage of area to make a tint. The dots that constitute the cell are so small that the irregular dot shapes are invisible without magnification.

A larger problem is the way the dots vary in size. Traditional photographic dots gradually changed with virtually infinite variability. Halftone cells are limited by the number of dots available within the given cell. If the halftone cell is three pixels square, there are only ten levels of gray (3x3=9 plus one for all white). This means that, with a 10-level halftone, I only have 0 percent, 11.1 percent, 22.2 percent, 33.3 percent, 44.4 percent, 55.6 percent, 66.7 percent, 77.8 percent, 88.9 percent, and 100 percent tints to work with. This ruins the halftone by posterizing it.

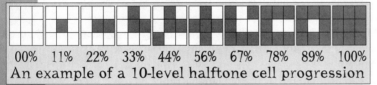
00% 11% 22% 33% 44% 56% 67% 78% 89% 100%
An example of a 10-level halftone cell progression

The only way you can achieve more levels of gray is to use more dots per cell. For example, the following cell sizes produce these gray levels: 3x3=10; 4x4=17; 5x5=26; 6x6=37; 7x7=50; and so on. The problem is that the human eye requires at least 100 levels of gray to see smooth gradations. In fact, over 200 levels of gray are required to show detail in areas like dark hair. This requires cell sizes of 10x10 to 16x16, or 101 to 256 levels of gray.

Decent halftones require at least a 12x12 cell.

This is why digital printers require so many more dpi than linescreens need lpi. If you have an 85 lpi screen with 101 levels of gray, you need 850 dpi, because each dot on the linescreen requires

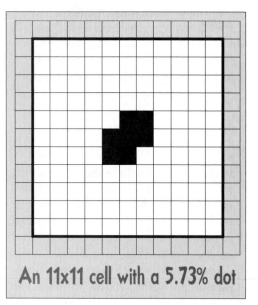

An 11x11 cell with a 5.73% dot

10 digital dots. A 150 lpi screen with 256 levels of gray needs 150x16 = 2,400 dpi. As you can easily see, a 300 dpi laser printer is not going to get you far.

Graphic Usage

Here's the hill

From the beginning of the chapter at 50-line screen.

For any reading situation, 300 dpi halftones are less than acceptable. They are defaulted to 50- or 60-line screen. Simple division shows us that 300÷50 = 6 and 300÷60 = 5. This means 5x5 = 26 levels of gray and 6x6 = 37 levels.

Even with 37 levels of gray, all the detail is gone. This happens because at 37 levels, each level has to cover almost 3 percent. Much of the subtle detail in a photo is the result of gray levels that vary by half a percent or less. Dark hair, for example, might fall entirely between 73% and 79%. This means that all of the detail will have to be rendered by the dots in this range. If you only have 60-line screen (26 levels), the levels would be 72%, 76%, and 80%. This would mean that the hair just mentioned would all be rendered by these three dot sizes. They could all be 76%. No matter what, neighboring hairs that were 75% to 77% would be the same color (76%), and the detail would be gone. The hair changes to an area that looks like dark gray felt.

With enough dpi in the printer, PostScript resolution allows for up to 256 levels of gray (up to 4,000 with PostScript Level 3). This means that each level is four-tenths of a percent (.4%) from its neighbor. With that small a difference, even the subtlest details can be rendered. Of course, this assumes that the dot size of the linescreen is smaller than the detail. A half-point dot has obvious difficulty rendering quarter-point detail.

Printer resolution requirements

Now you know why digital printers require such seemingly ridiculous resolutions. When you divide it out, it quickly becomes apparent why 300 dpi printers are limited to the standard 53- or 60-line screens; 600 dpi printers can barely handle 85-line screen (with 50 levels of

gray); 1,200 dpi plain paper printers work best at 85-line though 1,200 dpi imagesetters that output film can output 100-line or even 120 line. However, as you can see, 120 line at 1,200 dpi only gives 101 levels of gray.

The formulae are simple.

- Dpi ÷ lpi = the horizontal dimension of the halftone cell
- Dpi ÷ the horizontal dimension of the halftone cell = lpi
- Lpi x the horizontal dimension of the halftone cell = dpi requirements of the printer

Professional output is normally 2,400 or 2,540 dpi. This allows 256 levels of gray at 150-line screen This is one of the reasons why many industries are switching to 150-line from 133-line. The 150-line composite negs allow easy production of 150-line plates. Increasingly, the plates are output directly.

The higher resolutions cause more problems due to the size of the files necessary. Let's simply state, at this point, that 200-line plates require huge amounts of memory and very high imagesetter/platesetter resolutions. 200x16 = 3,200, so, 3,200 dpi is required. A 10"x10", 3200 dpi, 24-bit file would be (10x3,200x24)2 or 589.824 billion bits of data, or over 93 gigabytes (if my quick math is accurate).

Not many of us have hard drives large enough to hold this. We aren't even counting Photoshop's requirements (like at least three times the file size for RAM and up to twelve times the file size in empty hard drive space).

Practical considerations

So, the final question in determining linescreen becomes, "When do I use what?" The answer is obvious. The linescreen used is determined by the capability of the hardware that will be used to print your project — not the printer you use for proofing at your desk.

The linescreen used is determined by the capability of the final output hardware.

The first choice you should make when beginning to design a project is the printer, service bureau, or printing firm you are going to use to print the project. Everything in your project must be designed within the capabilities of your printer, imagesetter, or press. We will talk next about the adjustments you need to make to enable printability. We will start with that most common form of printing, grayscale. You must do this well before you can do color well.

EXCITING B&W COLOR? CHECK OUT A REMBRANDT ETCHING

GRAYSCALE IS ROUGH ENOUGH

Often, one of the more difficult concepts to grasp is color. In printing, every color costs almost the same as any other color. That is the positive side of it. The negative side is that every additional color plate costs almost the same as any other color. Sorry it sounds so cute, but it is an important point.

What I am saying is that there are an almost unlimited number of colors available to print. But each additional color costs nearly as much to print as the first one did. For a rough example: if a grayscale document costs $100, then red and black will cost around $200 and red, blue, and black will cost $300, and so on (plus the cost of the paper). It is very easy to reach twelve or more colors and extravagant expenses unless the designer uses skill instead of his ego. The most common solution is process color which we will cover in the next chapter. However, even with CMYK there are four colors of ink to pay for.

Most jobs are limited

The theme of this book is realistic design— for real world publishing and the majority of your potential clients. In the real world, most jobs were formerly one or two color. Process color is becoming increasingly common, but it is still expensive. Most jobs do not require the expense. As spot color costs rise (due to the emergency shortage of press operators), increasingly the choices are grayscale or process, at a ratio of about three to one. Most of the time, you'll have one color to work with: black. I want to suggest that you can make grayscale pop off the page, grab the reader by the throat, sell the desired message, and produce an appropriate response.

Needless to say, you want to do all of this tastefully and tactfully with a sense of style and grace. Like I said earlier, every one sees thousands of messages per day and your work has to pierce the clutter and the consciousness of the reader you are pursuing. Fortunately, it is much easier to do that in a single color than you might think.

If you can't design persuasively in grayscale, your color work will be unbearably weak.

Especially while you are learning, it is usually better to design in black and white adding color conservatively to an already strong structure. You can clearly see the structure of a design in black and white (B&W). Color can be marvelously subtle, but it can also be muddy in concept and incoherent structurally. Any color is weaker than black or stronger than white. Creating entirely in mixed colors always weakens contrast, at the very least. It also tends to loose focus. And I haven't even mentioned the huge numbers of people who are either partially or completely color blind (certainly 10 percent of the population or more).

Traditionally, all artwork for printing was done in black and white to make it camera ready. Even now, most of your proofing will be done in B&W on a laser printer. Working powerfully and competently in black and white is a saleable skill that will help you throughout your career. Yes, this is one of those fundamentals you hear so much about in all fields.

B&W design helps keep the structure of a project strong. Computer screens cause many problems because it is so easy to add strong, complicated, and often unprintable color at the click of a mouse.

Even if you get the chance to design a high budget, multicolor piece, always proof it in black and white. Look at it carefully. Hang it on the wall and walk off 20 feet. Squint at it (to blur it) so that you are looking at the layout without being seduced by details that the reader may or may not notice. Many designers look at the work upside down or in a mirror, for the same reason.

The single color majority

... back to our portion of reality. Since most of your jobs will probably be single color, let us figure out how to do them well. It only takes a good copy of a Chinese monochrome landscape to realize that black and white (and a few grays) can move your emotions more strongly than most color photos ever could. In fact, unless carefully controlled, color merely reduces contrast and lessens impact, as I mentioned. Blue and white is much weaker than black and white.

Black-and-white pieces can be extremely "colorful." Of course, there is a problem with starkness, but the human brain has a phenomenal capability of blending multiple objects into apparent grays (as we have already covered).

Graphic Usage

What Rembrandt did with fine line cross hatching, you can do with simple screen effects. Every photo that you see printed – color or grayscale – is screened. Every tint screen is made up of the same size dots as those used in the halftones. It is the only tool a printer has to produce the illusion of continuous tone artwork.

You do get much more control with the computer. Digital control of individual gray levels is impossible with a traditional camera. However, digital halftones require much knowledge and experience. If you do not know how to create a crisp halftone adjusted for dot gain, you need to contact Radiqz Press and get on the list for my PDF book called *Image Manipulation*.

Even flat tints can have great impact. A screened box in back of your type can separate it from the rest of the text. It makes a natural setting for sidebars (those additional pieces of information placed on the edges of your article for the more serious readers).

Screened boxes do not produce impact!

Screens in back of type lower the contrast and make type harder to read. However, they make excellent devices to separate different sections. Use the screens to set apart the areas of lesser importance so the primary content areas pop off the page easier.

Beware looking like a novice!

One of the digital jokes in the industry is the piece done by a desktop novice with screens and boxes and lines and ... Screens should be used like color in general, for specific purposes, with restraint. Color can have great impact when used tastefully and carefully. A grayscale page with one red spot is extremely dramatic. A little color has much impact. A lot of color often merely lowers contrast and confuses the reader by interrupting the flow of the copy. Colored headlines and subheads often have less impact than black ones unless they are much larger.

Yes, color is important, but learn to work in black and white first. Then you can add color carefully. Forget color entirely if you lack taste or style. The world needs less garishness not more.

PRACTICAL ADVICE:
TIPS ON HALFTONE PRODUCTION

Remember that the printer or imagesetter produces the actual halftone screen. InDesign or Acrobat merely send the necessary PostScript code to enable the RIP to produce appropriate halftone dots. Producing screened photos or scanned artwork that print well involves several factors that are not immediately apparent. First and most important is that a halftone laser printed in your hand is going to print very differently when it gets on the press (unless you have direct digital output). In fact, if the laser

proof looks good it will normally look terrible when printed traditionally. This true for a number of reasons. The major reason is that little phenomenon called dot gain. Or there can be holes in the dot structure.

Dots everywhere

For a halftone print to look good, every area of the picture has to have dots. If the highlights go blank (paper color), the picture will look like it has a hole in it. In addition, all of the highlight detail will disappear. If the shadows print solid, they won't look like part of the picture. They will appear to lie on a different plane than the surface of the photo. In addition, the shadow detail is often lost in those flat black areas.

The goal is to have a 3–5% black dot in the highlights and a 3–5% white dot in the shadows – after it is printed. This is usually spoken of as a 3–97 or a 5–95 dot range. When you scan your photo, you need to find the brightest highlight and put a dot in it and the darkest shadow and put a dot in it. Be careful not to put a dot in the specular highlights. These are the places where the sun is reflecting off chrome or something similar. Specular highlights need to go to pure white to look natural. However, the actual highlights need to have that dot. It's easy to provide, using the curves adjustment techniques found in my first book, *Printing in a Digital World* (or in *Image Manipulation*).

Dot gain

The next problem is that offset presses, inkjets, screen presses, flexographic presses, and so on do not work very well. Printing is a very difficult process. We expect 9,000 to 13,000 perfect images an hour – the color remains consistent, everything is square all at 3 to 4 sheets per second! Most of the printing has been lithography. However, even the digital processes have problems in this area.

Let's just talk offset litho for a while. As you know, the plate is coated with water then a greasy ink. That whole mess is offset on a rubber blanket which in turn rolls it onto the paper all at 3 to 4 sheets a second. It goes even faster if the paper is in rolls instead of sheets. Printing is a craft, not a science!

The ink has to be wet enough to transfer easily. As a result, it soaks into the paper. It spreads a little. In fact, with a cheap press or duplicator on uncoated paper, it spreads a lot! Even with the best presses on extra glossy coated paper the size of the dot gains around 5 to 10 percent or more. At a 10 percent dot gain, a 10% dot becomes 11%, a 50% dot becomes 55% and a 90% dot becomes 99%.

The problem is greatly multiplied with uncoated stock and/or old presses and duplicators. Uncoated stock has a dot gain ranging from 15% to 40% depending on the condition of the press and the absorbency of the paper. With the lower figure, the dot range on the plate has to be 5 to 85. With 40 percent, the range often has to be 10 to 60.

Your halftones must be adjusted for dot gain.

We haven't even mentioned factors like ineffective sizing on the cheaper sheets (of paper). This causes the ink to bleed into the surrounding areas. Simple, physical pressure from the large steel rollers carrying the image can squeeze the dots, spreading them out over a larger than specified area. Toner scatter (around the edges of the dots and shapes) makes even electrostatic dots hard to control.

Graphic Usage

Reproductive capabilities

Commercial printers use presses. A good press can produce a 3 percent dot at either end with a premium cast coated sheet. Part of this is because a press has much better water and pressure control. Part of it is because high quality presses have many ink rollers that mill the ink (grind or pulverize it) to very fine particles. In addition, presses usually have much more experienced operators (primarily because these presses often cost seven figures or more – a million dollar process press is on the cheap end). They usually run 133 line screen, minimum.

Quick printers usually use duplicators (or old, worn-out presses). Many duplicators use the ink to carry the water to the plate. This means that they have to use a stiffer ink (with varnish in it). This also results in emulsification where the water and the ink turn to a sludge. (Emulsification is usually connected with soap, but here we are talking the physical blending of oil and water.) This sludge bleeds into the nonimage areas around black solids and is repelled off the tiny dots. As a result, duplicators do very well to hold seven percent dots at either end. In fact, it usually takes a very good duplicator with a good press operator to enable a duplicator to hold a 15% white dot in the shadows.

Duplicator dot gain normally runs around 25 percent or more. In many shops, speed means more than quality and the dot gain suffers. Top quick printers produce excellent work (though forced to use coarser screens). They normally run 85- to 100- line screen. Be leery of claims of 120 linescreen by quick printers. It is theoretically possible, but practically unattainable since 120 linescreen on a duplicator almost always means muddy screens and large dot gain.

Generational shifts

Most of you have seen what happens when you make a copy of a copy of a copy of a copy, and so forth. The edges are destroyed on the image, all the grays disappear and the entire image gets much more contrast. The contrast increase also messes up our halftones. Every generation causes loss at both ends of around 3 percent.

To demonstrate, if I shoot a negative of a laser print I lose 3%. When I make a plate from that negative I lose another 3%. When I print off that plate, the paper image loses another 3%. So, composite negs out of an imagesetter save 3%. Outputting plates directly with a platesetter saves another 3%. Printing directly with a digital press saves an additional 3%.

I wish it were all this tidy. The figures I have given you work theoretically. In reality, they can vary quite a bit. For one thing, they do not add up so tidily – 3+3+3+3=12. But those numbers do give you a solid feel for what you have to do when producing screened halftone scans. The main thing to remember is that every generation increases the contrast

and causes dot loss at both ends of the grayscale. Every shop is different. Usually, all you have to do is ask, "What is your dot gain?" If they cannot tell you, find another printer.

Miscellaneous problems

One has to do with the abilities of printing personnel. Many quick print operators are taught to run their ink very heavy to compensate for the fact that duplicators can not run very dense solids. Even large bold type gets washed out unless they pump up the ink flow. Of course, running the ink thicker means you need more water to keep the background clean — more ink, more water, more sludge. This gives the huge dot gains in the 40 to 50% range. Often screens are almost impossible.

A more common problem is plain paper, laser prints used as camera ready artwork. Here the problem is the toner. Toner particles are attracted into clumps and then ironed on to produce the halftone dots. In addition, computer output is dealing with square pixels. They may be very small squares; but square they are, not round. There is also random toner "noise" from particles scattered around the dots, as mentioned previously.

To put it nicely, plain paper laser halftones are a blotchy mess. The dots are not smooth circles but ragged approximations of circles. Generational changes smooth things out, but greatly increase the dot gain. The only solution is to use curves to lighten the shadows enough to pre-adjust for dot gain. However, it is better than plugged shadows. You must lighten them enough so the result, after printing, is around 95%.

Electrostatic presses (think printing quality copiers and laser printers) can work with no dot gain at all, if properly calibrated. This is the only technology that can work with no dot gain. However, this rarely happens. In addition, those copier operators at the corner copy shop won't have a clue what you are talking about. However, by carefully running your own tests, you can quickly finds out what that Docutech at Kinko's is capable of.

Some observations on fine screens

I would suggest that you examine the coarseness of your screen. Printing establishments are usually compulsive about printing at the finest screen they think they can handle. Often they can't print as fine as they think they can, without quality compromises. It is true that fine linescreens produce halftones that look much clearer and sharper than coarse screens. They also plug easier in the shadows and drop the highlights. Many cheap books would look a lot better if printed at 100 line instead of 133 line.

At school, I was having a horrible time with my 1,200 dpi laser halftones on plain paper. We were printing on student ravaged duplicators that are twenty years old. The shadows were plugging terribly and everything looked mottled. The solution turned out to be reducing the line screen to 85 line and adjusting the dot range of the TIFFs to 10–70. Now they are certainly more coarse. However, the printed results have clean midtones, the crisp highlights, and good detail in the shadows. The clients are much happier.

Preadjusted halftones look flat proofed!

This is where it pays to work with one printer. That way you can develop a solution that produces excellent halftones, quickly and easily. Permanent relationships with your print suppliers will help you a great deal to improve quality. As you have (or will) discover, every printing firm has different dot gain, different capabilities, and different personnel. These techniques are important.

Your design work will require mastery of these single color techniques. You will learn that a 25 percent dot gain means that tint blocks using an 80% gray are impossible. Again, this is not a great problem. There is an easy solution (70% gray). Remember, designers are graphic troubleshooters and problem solvers. If you learn that now, your entire career will benefit.

If that single color is not black, you will have to work more. Everything has to be hit a little harder. This is also true if you are using colored paper. All of these things cut contrast and reduce impact. It is no real problem. You simply have to be aware and compensate. Designers love to solve problems, you know. Often the biggest problem is simply being aware there is one.

Single color jobs are just as much fun to design as the four-color monsters. In fact, you often have much more freedom because the budget doesn't hit the client so hard in the pocket book. Only pride requires huge budgets and unlimited options. Forget about simple. Buy an original photo by Ansel Adams – and realize the potential.

Target dot ranges

I will give you some rough approximations based on my experience with a wide variety of printing equipment on many different shops. The only thing I am sure of is that these are merely ballpark starting points. You will have to keep track of the output from the presses you use. They will also vary with the stock used. A number one premium uncoated offset comes close to cheap, thinly coated matte (and usually looks much better). Some uncoated stock is so absorbent that screens are almost entirely unprintable.

Talk with the people who will actually be printing your project; but don't believe everything they say. Many press personnel honestly believe that everything they get on a plate is 5–95. Be careful not to burst their bubble. Dot gain normally runs from 15% to 35% at quickprinters. It will usually be closer to 10% even at top quality process shops on coated stock.

In general, dot gain means that every dot grows by that percentage. This is not strictly true, but it works well enough conceptually. The following table should give you a rough idea:

Starting dot	10%	20%	30%	40%	50%	60%	70%	80%	90%
10% Dot Gain	11	22	33	44	55	66	77	88	99
20% Dot Gain	12	24	36	48	60	72	84	96	100
30% Dot Gain	13	26	39	52	65	78	91	100	100
40% Dot Gain	14	28	42	56	70	84	98	100	100

Graphic Usage

This theory has to be modified by reality, of course. The midtones gain the most. The physical nature of a press produces pressure of the plate on paper that actually squeezes the dots so they spread out. This effect is most noticeable in the midtones. Actually, these figures are not off by much. The midtones (from 30 to 60 percent) should be lightened a little more to compensate for the larger gain there. (This is easily done with the MODIFY>>>CURVES control in Photoshop.) It is certainly true that every shop and every job in that shop runs a little differently. You can usually assume that the midtones will gain more than the shadows, but you cannot count on that. With some printers, even the 60 percent dots go solid.

Reality check

If you have a duplicator that generates a 40 percent dot gain, everything that is 65 percent or darker goes to solid black with no detail. This is one reason why cheap printers often produce photos of black people that show eyes and teeth as white spots in a solid black shape that used to be a face. If you do not compensate for dot gain, the printed photo will look horrible, dark with no detail. More and more, halftone production is your responsibility.

Even in a book on InDesign and advanced publishing procedures, we need to cover these facts. Many (if not most) of you will be producing your own halftones with your own flatbed scanner. If you think you can avoid these things, you are a fool. Again, if you do not know these techniques you need to purchase my first book, *Printing in a Digital World*, or my PDF book, *Image Manipulation* (when it's released) from http://kumo.swcp.com/graphics/bookstores

Dot gain is usually expressed in a dot range from the highlight to the shadow. In an ideal world, the plate would be 5–95 so that the press could produce 3–97. This is rarely the case. The good news is that competent printers (by definition) know precisely what their dot gain is. More than that, they know what the dot gain is for each press they own. Each press is different. The printer for my first printing textbook asked for the halftones to be adjusted to 5–85. I did what they asked, and it worked as predicted. The point is that dot gain is important and you need to keep on top of it. To a large degree, it is controlled by the skill of the press operator and the quality of the press or printer.

No matter what is said here, someone will get upset. The only consistent thing about dot gain is that everyone deals with it differently. The important thing is to know that it exists. When you bid out a job, ask your supplier for their procedures, and ask how they want you to handle it.

Final comments

Halftone production techniques are very important. I recommend that you either get a copy of *Image Manipulation*, Radiqz Press (when I get time to finish it), or *Real World Scanning and Halftones*, Peachpit, 1993. Of course, I think mine is better (that's why I wrote it). At the very least, halftones need to be checked thoroughly. At this point, heed a few words of warning. If at all possible, create your halftone at the finished size. This is seldom mentioned by other writers, but it makes things flow much more smoothly. Most simply make the halftone oversize and then crop or scale it in page layout. This is a makeshift approach, at best. Changing the size of imported halftones often softens them, at the very least. It always increases the load on the RIP at output time. Many service bureaus and printing firms have time limits on their negative or plate output. If your project goes over that limit, you can end up paying for that extra time — out of your own pocket, at $1 to $3 per minute.

Halftone production is (and will remain) a craft, not a science. Be very careful of automated solutions to halftone production. There is no such thing as an "average" picture. Examine every photo carefully before scanning. Some pictures have textures that can never be sharpened. Some artwork is so light that everything has to be darkened. Others are so dark that the brightest highlight is 40%. Sometimes you can simply change that beast to a 7-85 like the others. Other times, lightening the highlights in that manner ruins the picture. Sorry, but you are going to have to think and decide for each scan. This is why you are getting the big bucks.

Pencil drawings cause all kinds of problems, for example. Here the highlights have to go to white, but extreme care has to be taken so the delicate light detail is not lost. Also the darkest areas of a pencil drawing are 60% or so. This means that after dot gain, the darkest areas are 60%. You may end up adjusting the scan to 0–40 to make the drawing look right.

Some of the worst things to scan are old engravings. You almost always have to scan and rescan until you get the best you can. Scanning as lineart with very high resolution sometimes works (using an amount of 500% in Unsharp Mask). Other times you have to scan grayscale, use Gaussian blur to get rid of most of the fine crosshatching, and then sharpen very carefully. In most cases, their detail is so fine that you will need an optical spi of over 1,200 to pick up those hairlines.

Even photos vary wildly. We will cover finer color correction decisions, like balancing neutral grays, in the next chapter when we cover color. Basically, you need to remember that a steeper curve (in the Modify>>>Curves dialog box) increases the contrast, and a flatter curve eliminates contrast. Often you have to select certain areas for an increase in contrast and others where detail must be eliminated. Just don't beat the poor photo to death. Remember, you are usually only getting $10 to $20 for that halftone. This basically means that those halftones need to be produced in 10 to 20 minutes, or you are losing money.

THE PROBLEM OF BANDING

One of the major new problems with digital output is banding. This is when a gradient fill, or an area that gradually changes color, shows bull's-eye rings or parallel bands when it is output. On the Web this is caused by too low a color depth (too few bits per pixel). In print, banding is caused by too few levels of gray (a halftone cell that is too small).

You need to understand how PostScript produces the illusion of a smooth gradient fill. The easiest way to understand this is with a blend. In the following sample, the top box is blended from white to black in 256 steps. In the bottom box, there are five steps. The five-step box demonstrates severe banding. So here we see one obvious solution to the banding problem: use more steps in blends.

However, many times this is not enough. First of all, you must realize that all gradients in PostScript use layering of multiple shapes to produce the illusion of smooth color changes. The reason gradients look smooth is the same phenomenon we talked about with linescreen. If the bands are narrow enough, the eye blends them smoothly into the illusion of a graceful transition from one color to another. The problem is that there are not infinite bands available.

The same thing happens with halftones with smooth gradients over too great a distance. The number of bands in a gradient is equal to the levels of gray produced by the halftone cells multiplied by the percentage of color change. White to black, or 0% to 100%, uses all the available levels of gray. A gradient from 30% PMS345 to 50% PMS345 would only use 20% of the available levels of gray. A tint band, or level of gray, becomes visible to the naked eye when it is a point wide or wider.

Banding is caused by insufficient colors.

Banding results when there are not enough different colors, color variations, or levels of gray to span the distance of a gradient with bands larger than a point. On a monitor this would be bands two pixels wide or more. To make it more real, if I have a gradient from 20% green to 30% green output on a 1,200 dpi printer at 100 linescreen, then I have 10% of 145 levels of gray or fourteen bands of color. If my gradient is 2 inches long, there will be seven bands per inch and each band will be more than one-eighth inch wide — easily visible.

There are several ways to solve this problem. One is to increase the resolution of the printer. At 3,000 dpi, there are 900 levels of gray, or ninety bands for this gradient. This would make the bands almost invisible at forty-five to an inch. However, there are very few 3,000 dpi printers and not many can print this many levels of gray. PostScript Level 3 does it better than has ever been available.

Second, we could go to 25 linescreen. This would make the halftone cell 40x40 or 1,600 levels of gray. This would solve the problem (if we can print that many levels of gray), but the dot size becomes easily visible.

Third, we can change the gradient from 15% to 35%, which would give us 20 percent of the available levels and double the resolution to 2,400 dpi, which would give us plenty of gray levels so that we could have 50 or more bands per inch. We've had to change the design a little, but the elimination of the bands is usually worth it.

Banding is a simple mathematical problem.

The point I'm making is this. Banding is a simple mathematical problem. The solutions are also mathematical. A good designer will not have this problem – design around it!

The solutions to banding include:

* Increase the output resolution
* Decrease the linescreen
* Increase the percentage of color difference

Remember, these are all things you need to control in your designs. No one can fix a bad design on your part except yourself. At least, no one can fix it without added expense out of your pocket or profits (unless you are fortunate enough to have a client that doesn't care about things like staying in a budget).

CHANGING GEARS:
WHICH GRAPHIC FORMATS WORK?

Once you have a properly prepared scan or graphic, we arrive at the next major problem with graphic usage. For many of you, this is an area that you follow blindly because someone, at some time, told you that this is the way to do it. Most of you have no idea why.

We covered this thoroughly in Chapter 7. Here is the down and dirty, *what you will actually use* version.

Graphic formats you will use

Until very recently, there was nothing as universal as ASCII graphically. However, there were two formats that are close. In our industry, where PostScript is required, EPS is universally read. EPS is short for Encapsulated PostScript. Simplistically, an EPS file is a PostScript document written in a universal language that any professional publishing program can read. But there are cross-platform issues, as mentioned in Chapter 7.

The second format that almost everyone can read is TIFF. The acronym TIFF stands for Tagged Image File Format. This is a file language for bitmaps: 1-bit, 8-bit, 24-bit, and 32-bit. All professional programs understand TIFF. The only problem is that TIFF has been around for so long that the anarchy of the DOS world has produced almost countless dialects of TIFF.

The new hope for universality is the PDF format. It remains to be see how far this goes. InDesign is the first major move in that direction. If MacOS X uses PDF for all its system graphics, another major boost to the format will fall into place.

When you need to move a graphic from one program to another there is a simple two-step process. First, you have to export a copy of your document from the originating application in one of the

variants of the universal formats. Second, you have to open a new or old document in the receiving program and import the exported graphic. The Adobe family calls this function Place.

The latest versions of the Big Five also support drag-and-drop. Here you can simply select, drag, and drop the selection into the window of the other program. For many reasons, I have problems with this procedure, but it is now possible.

Format use stated with bullets

- **TEXT:** Use Rich Text Format whenever possible. It is the most universal format that includes formatting.
- **LINEART:** Use EPS or PDF. At this point, EPS is more universal, but PDF is better cross-platform.
- **CONTINUOUS TONE:** Use TIFF. In some cases, with clipping paths (or with custom screen angles like duotones) Photoshop EPSs work better. Some service bureaus and printing companies still demand DCS. But in most cases, the simplicity of TIFF works best.
- **WEB LINEART:** Create in FreeHand or Illustrator, rasterize in Photoshop, ImageReady, or Fireworks and save as a GIF — using the lowest color depth you can tolerate.
- **WEB CONTINUOUS TONE:** Use JPEG or one of the new lossy GIF possibilities with ImageReady. PNGs are just not ready for primetime yet.
- **PRINTING:** Use PDF as much as possible.
- **SOFT PROOFING (proofing on a monitor):** Your best bet is PDF. But you surely needed calibrated monitors on both ends of the proof sharing.
- **PRESENTATIONS:** Interactive PDFs are probably the best solution, but HTML also works very well. Almost everyone has a browser and Reader. If you think that your readers will want to print pages, use PDF.

Proper import procedures

For years, the most common problem was trying to open a file instead of importing it. Formerly, EPS graphics could not be opened. Now both FreeHand and Illustrator allow the creation of editable EPSs. Even if the software allows you to open the EPS, however, you should not be allowed to edit the graphic. Likewise, even though TIFFs can be opened, the mere act of producing your TIFF tossed a lot of the data contained in the original PSD file. The basic idea was to have a graphic that cannot be ruined by people without authorization — with a high quality original in case changes are needed.

InDesign allows a great deal of editing on imported graphics. This is a very dangerous procedure. What is eliminated is the separate original to return to if something disastrous occurs (and it will, sooner or later). It is far better to have an original in Freehand, Illustrator, or Photoshop for a backup (hopefully with an additional copy on a removable in a safe place).

So the proper procedure for managing graphics is to import them by Placing. Using the Clipboard causes huge problems by avoiding link management capabilities all together. In addition, the CLIPBOARD is restricted in the formats it supports. Copying and pasting can literally ruin the graphic.

Drag'n'drop is simple and easy and I suspect that it is only old paranoia that causes my hesitancy. InDesign considers drag'n'drop to be the same as PLACING. The only real problems are that IMPORT OPTIONS cannot be set when dragging and dropping, and that some attributes of the original might be lost (if InDesign does not happen to support everything produced by the originating software).

When importing by placing, graphics should only be edited by returning to the creating application, making the changes, and then re-exporting and re-importing. The best setup was PageMaker's HotLinks with FreeHand which made this a relatively automatic procedure.

InDesign follows a more normal procedure currently. Using the LINKS PALETTE, you click the EDIT ORIGINAL button at the bottom of the palette. The originating program opens the original. After you save the changes, a warning triangle appears in the links palette. You can then update the link. It does work very smoothly, however. The before release rumor of a simple double-click to open the original with an automatic update after saving was sadly wrong.

The second problem has to do with resizing bitmap graphics. Unless you are careful, resized bitmaps do not fit the grid anymore. As a result, resized bitmaps can be badly blurred. Many people claim to do it all the time without problems. However, they are also usually the persons who complain about the quality of their computer halftones.

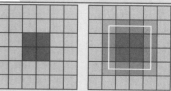

If we try to resize the red square on the left, to the yellow square on the right, the pixels become a mixture of the colors by percentage, for a pixel can only be one color. This blurs the edges.

Dealing with file size issues

As we have been discussing, a major problem is dealing with the sheer size of the files. PostScript illustrations help, unless the designer goes crazy complicated. The PDF workflow has also helped a lot. To a certain extent, these files can be handled with removable cartridges. MOs will hold more than a gigabyte. Currently, the best solution is probably the pocket-sized, multi-gigabyte Firewire hard drives. But even here, the file size builds to the point where storage is a severe problem.

Another solution is compression. We have mentioned this possibility in passing. TIFFs use LZW lossless compression, but it doesn't work well with continuous tone. Several of the other formats use RLE. JPEG offers incredible size savings with the compromise of quality caused by lossy compression. These only apply to individual files and only to specific graphic formats. In many cases, dedicated compression software is the answer. This is especially true when transporting files across the Web.

There are several dedicated compression programs. The leader and normal standard on the Mac is StuffIt. On the PC the standard is WinZip. At this point, there are several competitors. Most of them work the same way. They commonly add an icon to the menu bar in Finder that allows any file, folder, or drive to be compressed, decompressed or archived. Probably the handiest use for storage is the self-extracting archive.

This is a file that is compressed with a small application added to the file that allows anyone to decompress it. Even though the compressed archive is a little larger, it can be given to anyone. They can decompress it simply by double-clicking.

If you need to send files over the Web, your recipient will commonly ask you to compress your files in a self-extracting archive. This can cause major problems. Macs don't Zip files well. PCs don't Stuff files well. As some of you know, I sell fonts online. Because I create on a Mac, I have constantly had problems with my PC versions of the fonts, especially the TrueType versions. For some reason, the Mac compression software usually corrupts the fonts when they use Zip compression. A PDF does Zip well, but the customers have no way to open a PDF and extract the fonts. Just a word to the wise, be careful and test cross-platform exchanges procedures. Don't assume everything will work simply because the software manufacturer claims it will.

Practical usage

Compression is very useful for several scenarios. As mentioned, anything except a PDF needs to be compressed for Web transmittal. For long-term backup storage, self-extracting archives save a lot of space. They also prevent idle destruction by the curious who are just looking around. Self-extracting archives also work well as installers of files kept on locked floppies. In fact, this is the only real use for floppies, as hard use can wipe out a floppy in about a week.

Outside sources

I've mentioned several of these things briefly in passing, but we need to add enough for it to sink in. In the everyday workflow pressures, most of us will not have the luxury of using custom-created graphics for all situations. To rephrase, stock art and photos are a simple fact of graphic design. You will use them. The important thing to realize is that mass marketed art is not blasphemy or even heresy. There are excellent choices available. I mentioned Dynamic Graphics and Artville. There are many others. Just remember this horrifying fact.

If it's cheap, it's junk!

You definitely need to plan your stock purchases. It should be a line item in your budget. You will probably need to spend hundreds of dollars per year. You also need to keep it current. Nothing is worse than fashionable art from a couple of decades ago. Imagine platform shoes and a 'fro.

You will also need a wide variety to cover all of your clients. In my case, I tend to need a lot of educational images. Your clients may need business situations, heavy construction, electronics, computers, physical sciences, or whatever.

Finally, you will do well to purchase top quality EPS stock art. These pieces are completely editable. More than that, each part of an image is often on a separate layer that can be removed from the image and used by itself. It is much easier and faster than trying to select the model and her flying hair against the background of leaves.

Summing it up: Plan ahead!

The primary fact you need to burn into your synapses is this: determine your needs before you start drawing. Preplanning is more important in digital work than it is most places. In few fields can you get into so much trouble so quickly. The nice part is that everything can be redone or undone. However, deadlines can get trashed very quickly. By figuring out what you need and how to get there most efficiently, many of your problems will be solved before they occur.

Knowledge Retention

1.   What are the three basic graphic formats?

2.   What is the most common use of 8-line screen?

3.   Why is dot gain important?

4.   What does a 7–70 dot range mean?

5.   Why are halftone dots essential?

Where should you be by this time?

By this time you should have earned well over half your grade. You should be working comfortably in InDesign, with your defaults working smoothly. By now you should be noticing which operations you use a lot and should be starting to remember the relevant shortcuts. You should have already noted and changed those shortcuts you use from other software that are different in InDesign.

DISCUSSION

You should be discussing definite strategies for your hardware and software purchases. One of the real problems is maintaining your skill level. This means that you will need your own computer. The basic advice is simple: "Sell your car and get your computer." Having a computer at home to build up your skills will increase your income so you can quickly afford a better car.

Talk among yourselves...

CHAPTER TWELVE

Color Usage

CHAPTER CONTENTS

Knowledge needed to add color to your documents in a form that is printable, and predictable

CONCEPTS

1. **Color space**

2. **Primary colors**

3. **RBY**

4. **RGB**

5. **CMYK**

6. **Separations**

7. **Moiré**

8. **Spot color**

9. **Hi-fi color**

CHAPTER OBJECTIVES

By presenting the basic terms and production procedures, you will learn how to:

1. Compare color spaces
2. Use full spectrum color spaces
3. Balance neutral grays
4. Avoid most color printing problems
5. Improve the look of your finished document

LAB WORK FOR CHAPTER

- Continue work on skills and miniskills
- Submit finished theory exams
- Continue work on your approved real project, ideally your second, third, or fourth real project

There are far too many terms to be covered with a simple list of concepts. These words are also defined in the Glossary in the back of the book.

Terms: color space, primary colors, reflected color, tungsten or incandescent, color temperature, 5,000°K, hue, saturation, value or brightness, neutral gray, tint (fine art), shade, electromagnetic spectrum, secondary colors, complementary color, permanent color, fugitive color, additive color, full-spectrum, color reproduction, registration, subtractive color, separation, process color, tint (printed screens), screen, standard color, Pantone Matching System (PMS), swatch book, commodity color.

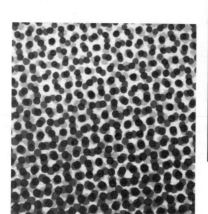

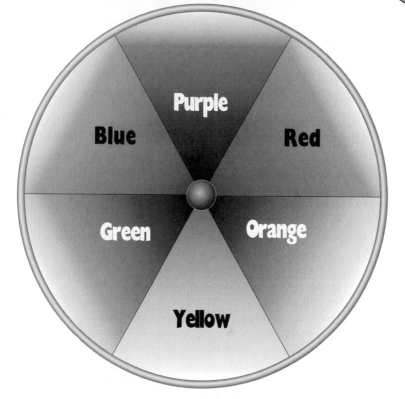

Beyond black and white printing

As you have already seen, black-and-white design is complicated enough. Color increases the complication to an entirely new dimension. For this reason, it will be wise for you to work in black and white as much as possible to develop your skills. More than that, you will find that even your color pieces should be proofed in grayscale to see the structure of the design more clearly. Color usually lessens your contrast and confuses your eye, as I have said several times already (indicating its importance).

Remember that there are sizable portions of your readership who are color blind. Statistics would suggest over 10 percent. Your pieces have to work even if reduced to grayscale. Add color only when it is required by your client and/or circumstances. We'll just mention the cost increases created by more color – every additional color adds the same costs as the first color. That is: two-color is almost twice as expensive, three-color is three times as expensive, and so on.

Having said that, we must acknowledge reality. One of the primary results of the digital revolution is a vast increase in color usage. It has become increasingly easy to work in color, proof in color, and print or publish in color. The problem with this is the same one that arises over and over: many new desktop publishers know little or nothing about commercial printing or web publishing necessities. This is the uniqueness of this book.

You need to thoroughly understand that the colors used in digital publishing come from several color sources and theories, none of which are reproducible in the other output. In other words, reality in not reproducible. Fine art cannot reproduce reality, and fine art cannot be reproduced. Monitor color cannot be calibrated (as far as general web use is concerned) and it certainly cannot be reproduced by printing inks without substantial color shifts. Printing color cannot be viewed on the screen (unless you spend a lot of money for the software and hardware to calibrate your monitor, printer, scanner, etc.).

WHICH COLORS ARE YOU USING,

COLOR SPACES OR COLOR SYSTEMS?

Color space is the term used to describe the colors available in a given color theory using primary colors. A color system is a standard set of colors – a classic example being the sixty-four standard colors found in the Crayola system (which are extremely useful). There is a color space for TV, a color space for printing, a color space for fine art, and so forth.

The problem is that the different colors existing in the various color spaces may not be available in other systems of color. To work with publishing, it is necessary to be familiar with three color spaces plus several color systems. I know many of you know some of this, but a brief review is in order. Bear with me please, the likelihood is that I will cover several areas you are not sure (or completely ignorant) of.

Color Usage

RBY color

The first of these three spaces is the one you learned in elementary school. As you all know from early childhood, there are three primary colors: red, blue, and yellow. You were told that any color could be made with these three. As you found out (if you played with color at all), that this is not so. I still remember the frustration of trying to generate a strong vibrant purple by mixing red and blue.

The red, blue, yellow (RBY) color space was the first one you learned. It claims to be all encompassing, but it is not. Unfortunately, color does not lend itself to neat, tidy analysis. Actual physical production of colors can be immensely frustrating. The only way you can produce the illusion of reality is by carefully adding the hundreds of pigments together.

The problem with the RBY color space is simply that there are no true RBY primary pigments. The theory works well when trying to predict what colors will result when mixing cobalt yellow and ultramarine blue, for example. However, the practical use of the color space has nothing to do with mixing primaries. It simply becomes a way to describe how the various fine art pigments are going to interact.

The complexity of color vision

It's amazing that we can see at all. The eye sees in that second color space we mentioned – red, green, blue (RGB). What we see as specific colors are in fact the reactions of our optic nerves to mixtures of electromagnetic waves. How that really works is of mere scientific interest. What is important is the realization that a red rose is much more than that.

Most people are not aware that a red rose is a different color every time you see it. Our eye sends signals to our brain. Our brain places that input in a category that says "red rose." Our mind literally changes our perception to make it match our past experience of roses from that bush. Unless you train it differently, your brain sees what it expects to see. One of the most difficult skills for a fine artist is training your eye to "see" reality instead of your mind's construction of reality.

It is important to note that there are major differences in color, every day, all day long, even with an identical rose. We are not talking about the color of the petals fading in the bright sun. The rose in the yellow light of sunrise is very different from the same rose in the bluish light of noon. A rose at noon with a clear, dark blue sky at 5,000 feet above sea level is very different from the same rose with lots of brilliant white clouds. The light at sea level is that fuzzy, murky haze that coastal dwellers call clear sky, and the rose is yet a different color.

Reflected light

Many things affect the color we see. First we must talk about the reflected color. That rose will change color if a woman in a brilliant yellow dress stands next to it. It will look different next to a white wall, a blue pool, or a red brick wall. We are not talking about how the brain perceives color differently when seen against different color backgrounds.

What you need to realize is that the light reflected off the yellow dress colors the rose yellow on that side. The same is true of the light reflected off the walls. If there is a green bush on one side and a brick wall on the other, our poor rose will have greenish tints on the bush side and reddish ones one the brick side, all colored by the bluish ones on the top from the blue sky and the intense white ones from the direct reflections of the sun. Plus the shadows are all blue because they are light by the blue sky, not the sun.

This is what the impressionist painters, such as Degas, Monet, Renoir, and Cezanne, were after at the turn of the century. They tried to solve the color reproduction problem by adding dots of the reflected colors in the appropriate places. They could perceive color much better than most of us can. Even then, however, the accuracy of their color was affected all of these complexities.

Light color

The next major factor to consider is the color of the light. We have already alluded to this by mentioning that our rose looks different in the yellow of sunrise, the glare of noon, or the diffuse light of a hazy sky. Artificial light sources are even more problematic. Incandescent lighting is very yellow. This tungsten lighting is named after the material used to make the filaments in the light bulbs. Fluorescent lighting is normally very blue or green, though it is possible to find warm fluorescents that are tinted pink. The pink tint mixes with the blue light to make something that is less harsh. It's weird color, though, and simply doesn't look natural. The greenish tint of fluorescents is what makes people look dead (or very ill) in its light.

Printers try to deal with this by using a concept called color temperature. This concept uses a temperature scale that begins at absolute zero (that place where all molecular activity ceases). This is 273°C below zero. If we place what is called a black-body radiator into a furnace and begin heating it, we can watch it go through color changes as it gets hotter. As the heat increased, the color changes, passing from red, orange, yellow, through white to blue white.

All you need to know is that printers need lights with a predictable color. The standard used by printers for viewing printed color pieces is special fluorescent lighting at 5000°K. This is an average white light. It is very close to the white light from the sun, which is around 5,400°K. A light source of 7,500°K is recommended for checking press output for color uniformity. The bluish tint to the light aids the human eye in the detection of minute color differences and color misregistration.

Any printing company that is serious about quality color reproduction will have a 5,000°K color booth with the walls of the booth painted a specific neutral gray. Often, all of the lighting in the press room will be 5,000°K. This is not because the color looks better under this lighting. It is because a standard is needed when jobs are printed in multiple facilities in different areas of the country. Designers also need a standard for color comparison. Color will always look the same in a 5,000°K light booth, no matter where it is.

This color temperature has a very strong influence on printing. For example, studies have found that an identical process color piece will tend to print very blue if printed in Ohio, New York, and so forth. The same piece printed in Tucson, Las Vegas, or San Diego will have a distinct reddish bent. More than that there are differences between the day shift, evening shift, and night shift. The day shift prints warm, the evening shift prints most accurately (though it would certainly vary as the sun sets if there are windows), the night shifts tends toward the blue.

Wise designers do the best they can to design so their work shows best under the light source their readers will be using. Needless to say, this is a guessing game at best. A fascinating test (that can be dangerous for the clumsy) is to take a printed process color piece and carry it through several different light colors. My old, traditional commercial printing lab at school, for example, had a section that was tungsten, another was fluorescent, the stripping section was yellow, the darkroom was red, the press area was 5,000°K, and outdoors at 5,000 feet the ambient color is around 6,000°K. Observing carefully, it was possible to see the colors change before your eyes as you walked through the different light colors. Some students could see the changes and some couldn't. Of course, some simply fell down.

Color terminology

Of course, color (like all areas of design and publishing) has its terms that are unknown to the layperson. Some of these will be familiar to those of you with fine art training. Some are specific to printing. Again, the goal is communication with our peers.

There is no room here for such undefinable frivolities as blush, mauve, lime, peach, and so on. These names are simply fashion and mean different things to different people. For example, I could easily mix fifty or more colors that could be called apricot yet were very different from each other. What we are looking for is a language that can be understood by anyone who is not color blind.

Artists are taught to break color down into three parts – hue, saturation, and value. Printers tend to substitute the word brightness for value (as they are commonly uneducated about color). Software programmers (as usual) just do what they are told and have no idea how the words are used in the real world.

Hue

This is the name of the color: blue, red, yellow-green, and so forth. There are only six hues plus white and black – red, orange, yellow, green, blue, and violet (or purple).

Saturation

This is the intensity of a color, or how far it varies from neutral gray. For example, grass green in the spring is more saturated than forest green in late summer. Saturation should be used instead of terms like dull or brilliant, because these terms could include value variations.

Brightness or Value

Brightness or value refers to the lightness or darkness of a color. The same hue of green may be a dark green or a light green. This is different from the saturation changes that would be referred to as dull green or intense green.

Perspective using value

Most perspective problems in landscapes that are caused by color are value problems. Distant objects of the same hue and intensity must have a much lower value to be seen in the proper place in the distance of your image. Of course, distant objects also become much bluer as they are covered by the haze of the air.

If you are having trouble getting an object to lay at the proper distance in a drawing, quite possibly it is too dark, or too saturated.

Any color can be described in terms of hue, saturation, and brightness or value (HSB or HSV). A neon red, for example, could be described as an extremely saturated, extremely bright red. Barn red could be referred to as an unsaturated, very dark red. The hue could be the same for both.

Two more terms that further define value may also be of interest when talking to fine artists. These terms are used by fine artists when mixing pigments. A fine art tint is a hue with white added. A shade is a hue with black added. White and black cannot be added in a true full spectrum color space. This only works in a color space made up of huge amounts of different pigments like RBY. A tint of red is pink. A shade of red is maroon. A shade of orange is brown. Pastels are tints. Jewel tones are shades. All of these terms are useful when trying to explain a color to another person.

Red, Yellow, Blue

The artists' color wheel

The color wheel is a diagrammatic illustration of the color space that was taught to you in grade school. What you need to understand is the relationship of colors. It does not help very much to understand that each color is a certain wavelength on the electromagnetic spectrum. It may be of interest to a color scientist, but that has little or nothing to do with what designers use in color.

The wavelengths of visible light are measured in billionths of a meter and cover the range from 400 to 750 millimicrons. The color change here is linear, starting from invisible ultraviolet through violet, blue, green, yellow, orange, red, and invisibly ending with infrared. This is the spectrum we see in a rainbow. In fact, the interesting thing about double rainbows (which we see frequently in the high desert) is that one of the rainbows has red inside and the other violet. The rarer triple rainbow usually has a band that goes from violet through red and back to violet again.

The fascinating thing about a color wheel is that though the spectrum is linear, the color relationships are circular. In other words, red does not end things. Instead, it blends through violet-red, and red-violet, to violet, and then continues. In addition to being continuous, some color relationships seen in the wheel work in a circular fashion. Of course, there are specialized terms to describe these relationships.

Purple
Blue
Red
Green
Orange
Yellow

We have already mentioned one of these relationship terms: primary colors. The three primary colors here (of pigment) are yellow, blue, and red. With these three you can theoretically make any color. All three together make black. You can mix any two primaries and produce the color between them on the wheel. These are called secondary colors. This is true even though red is at one end and blue at the other end of the spectrum. If you mix them you get violet or purple (even though highly saturated purples cannot be mixed).

Complementary colors

A complementary color pair is a primary color and the secondary color on the opposite side of the color wheel: that is, red/green; blue/orange; and yellow/violet. Again, all these colors have the same relationship with each other. Two complementary colors of equal saturation and value will produce a vibrating edge between them: harsh, garish, exciting, compelling, maximum color contrast. This is true even when the colors a low in both saturation and value as between a maroon and hunter green. Just make sure you are using complementary hues.

More interesting is the fact that when you mix a primary with its complementary secondary you get neutral gray. This again boggles the mind, because the same neutral gray is produced no matter what the complementary pair is. Purple and yellow produce the same gray as red and green. Assuming you have theoretically pure hues. Of course, the complement is made up of a mixture of the other two primary colors and all of the primary color mixed together give you black — so it makes sense once you think about it.

Available pigments

Theory works fine until reality smacks you in the face. The theoretical colors available can almost all be seen by the human eye. Finding pigments is another story. This is why artists' paints have so many color pigments. Most pigments are muddied by their complements or a neighboring primary. As a result, most common pigments tend toward brown or muddy green. However, because of all the different pigments available, artists can reproduce almost every color in nature except for the most saturated.

Additionally, fine art pigments are often very poisonous. I remember working on a gouache painting (opaque watercolor) several years ago. I absentmindedly shaped the tip of my brush with my tongue when using cobalt yellow and got extremely sick for several hours. In fact, many of the fine art pigments are poisonous, to one degree or another.

Finally, the better, purer, more saturated colors are all extremely expensive. Common colors like barn red (which is iron oxide or rust) might cost $3.60 per artists' studio tube. It is very low in saturation and brightness. The same tube filled with the best cadmium red could be up to $20. A pound of printers' ink runs $5 to $10. A pound of cad red medium could be as much as $300 or $400. Originally, ultramarine blue was ground lapis lazuli. Because lapis is a semiprecious gem, a tube of ultramarine

Color Usage

Rainbow tip

As an aside, when you are drawing a spectrum, a rainbow, or whatever, do not make all of the bands equal in width. For the proper look the yellow band must be much narrower. It is really not much more than a yellow line between the red and orange bands on the one side, and the green-blue-violet bands on the other. Brilliant bright blue is also a narrow band about twice as wide as the yellow. A working percent spread might go something like: red 8, orange 10, yellow 3, green 10, bright blue (cyan) 5, royal blue 6, purple 7. Of course ideally the orange will blend through from red to yellow, as will the green from yellow to blue. If you are using distinct bands try: R10, O9, Y2, G7, B10, P6.

blue would cost several thousand dollars a tube (if it hadn't been removed from the market several years ago as it passed the $1,000 mark). Obviously, printers had to find a better solution.

Printers' color printing problems

When printing color, economics play a huge role. Every separate pigment requires a separate plate and an additional printing cylinder. In practical terms, every additional plate costs about the same as the cost of the first color to produce (disregarding paper costs). So, a fine art painting that used thirty different colors of paint would cost thirty times as much to print (plus the cost of the paper). Even if such a thing could be done (and it cannot, under normal circumstances), the economics would prevent it. The only place we find such a thing is in classical Japanese woodcut prints, for which dozens of plates were used.

The solution involved using a different color space – cyan, magenta, and yellow (CMY). With the addition of black (because the cyan is weak) printers can produce a full spectrum printed space that give a convincing illusion of reality using only four colors. These four colors use cheap pigments that only cost about 60% more than black (which is by far the cheapest pigment). Black is simply soot.

Permanence

Before we pass on to the other color spaces, there is one more consideration to be touched. Those who come from the world of fine art are horrified to find out how nonpermanent printing colors are. To fine artists, permanent colors are pigments that will last for several centuries or more. In fact, in fine art, permanent means 200 years with no visible fading, at barest minimum.

Except for black, no printer's ink is permanent by this definition. It is possible to specifically order permanent inks and pay premium prices. However, this is rarely done. Printing inks are considered permanent if they retain their color (indoors) for a year. Outdoors, in the bright sun, they fade after a month. The reds go first, followed by the yellows. After a year, many process color pieces are reduced to cyan and black. After several years, even the cyan disappears.

 TIP: This is an area you should check out if you buy contemporary fine art prints. Most of them are simply printed with normal process printing ink – CMYK (and are therefore almost worthless as investments). Not to mention most are printed on wood pulp paper. If you want permanence, get it in writing, certified – permanent ink and museum grade paper.

This is really not so horrible. First of all, printers' inks fade very little if kept indoors away from bright light and/or ultraviolet light sources. Secondly, exactly how many printed materials are kept for more than a year? Most of our production is almost instantly disposable. Even critical color work, like a fashion catalog, is only good for a few months. Premium coffee-table books are another, very different story. Permanent color ink can be one of the reasons why they are so expensive.

There is an attribute of pigment that causes severe problems. This is fugitive color. A fugitive color is only good for about a month. In bright light, some colors fade severely in a week. Severely fugitive color like the neons (more correctly known as Day-Glo™) will fade in a matter of hours if not protected. If your client is concerned, suggest the use of permanent inks (warning about the expense, of course).

THE COLORS OF LIGHT: RGB

Humans see color through the rods and cones of the retina in the eye. The rods measure value. The cones, however, are more complex. There are really three different kinds of cones. Some are sensitive to red, some to blue, and some to green. That seems really strange to those of us used to the color wheel mentioned earlier.

This second color space is the first that you will need to thoroughly understand in this industry. The color space our eyes use is called RGB by our industry, for the three primaries used: red, green, and blue. These are the primaries used by light and light sources. They are called additive color. They are additive because adding all three primary colors gives white light. White light contains all the colors.

This is the color space used by monitors and scanners. This is where you live in the GUI, or graphic user interface, lived in on the desktop. Everything seen in the environment on your computer screen is RGB. RGB is a full-spectrum color space like RBY or HSV. However, RGB is the first color space we have discussed that is severely limited. Many colors that are seen in reality are not available in RGB color. In fact, only about 60 percent to 70 percent of the colors seen in the real world can be duplicated by RGB. The human eye sees trillions of colors. Digital RGB is 16.7 million.

This is normally not a problem. When in the color space, it seems as though every color is available. This is because it is a full-spectrum space – there is a good representative sampling of all six hues, most of the values, and quite a bit of the saturations available in reality. However, if you bring a TV with a video of your garden into your garden, you'll see a vast difference – and not just brightness and saturation differences. Many of the hues will be different on your screen.

In fact, if you visit your local electronics superstore, you'll quickly see that every TV reproduces the colors differently, not only in brightness and sharpness either. Some TVs will show that shirt as blue, some as purple, some as teal. For the first time in our little discussion, we have run into the bane of our industry, accurate color reproduction. Accurate reproduction of color is a virtual impossibility, even on a theoretical level. You need to burn that into your consciousness — right now. Things will get worse.

The white triangle is comprised of the colors of light. The black triangle is comprised of the colors of ink. Any two black points make the white color between. Any two white points make the black color between them.

THE COLORS OF INK: CMYK

Now things get complicated. First of all, we are no longer dealing with light. The problems of printing full-spectrum color were severe. Most of the problems originally involved the number of colors needed. Japanese woodcuts often used thirty to sixty colors and even they were not remotely realistic. After a full-spectrum space for printing inks was discovered, the main problem became registration. This is the ability to place two or more colors in exact alignment with each other, image after image after image. Process printing tolerances for registration are a half dot, or about a three hundredth of an inch. Any more than that and the colors shift.

To understand how this works, we need to leave additive color and reenter the space of subtractive color. RBY is subtractive. Subtractive color uses primaries that, when added together, produce black. These primaries absorb light. When added together, they absorb all light, leaving black. Printing uses the complementary opposites of light.

This is the major full-spectrum color space you need to know for printing. It was discovered that reproductive camera shots of color originals using red, green, and blue filters created negatives that could be printed in the subtractive primaries to reproduce the original colors. These subtractive primaries are cyan, magenta, and yellow (CMY). This process is called color separation. The following shows you how CMY colors are related to RGB when starting with white light and white paper:

- Magenta — The color seen when all green light is eliminated.
- Cyan — The color seen when all red light is eliminated.
- Yellow — The color seen when all blue light is eliminated.
- Black — The color seen when all RGB is eliminated.

Process color

Process color uses the separation concept to print full-spectrum images. There are some real problems, however. Even though process color covers the entire spectrum, it misses many colors. Remember, RGB only covers 60 to 70 percent of all colors, and CMY covers a little less than that. This is further confused by the fact RGB cannot reproduce some CMY colors, and CMY cannot reproduce many RGB colors.

Again (due to the fact that process color is full-spectrum), if you restrict yourself to the color space, it seems real. Printed color photos look real. However, we are in worse shape now. CMY cannot reproduce RGB. Neither of them can come close to the real world.

RGB is not CMY is not RBY.

For our purposes, we are discussing three totally separate color spaces. This is true on a practical level, even though reality contains all RBY, and RBY contains all RGB, and all CMY color. This explains why fine art reproduction is such a frustrating exercise, and why it is so difficult to print the newest fashion colors, and why a photograph of the Grand Canyon can never capture the reality.

Four-color process?

So, why is it four-color process? We have been discussing three-color primaries – CMY. Again, reality strikes! The problem is the pigments. CMY inks are really not very close to theoretical CMY. Some of this is due to economics. The CMY pigments available are not economically feasible, or they are not quite the right color, or they are not strong enough, or they are poisonous, or some combination. The compromises we presently use are reasonable and economically viable. They are all a little more expensive than black, but in the acceptable range.

However, they are inaccurate. The three primaries added together do not make black, they make an ugly, muddy brown. This is primarily because the cyan used is weak. In addition, all three pigments have impurities. As a result, a fourth color is used: black. There are several methods of producing the negative used for the black printer. They all involve recording the neutral gray information created by the complementary color graying in the image. Photoshop uses GCR by default, meaning gray component removal.

But there's more: Spot color

Spot color is really not a current printer's term. It is a term made popular by software applications. However, it is useful even though it means many different things to different people. In the context of what we have been talking about, spot colors are specific RBY colors. They can be custom-mixed or bought by the can. They can fit into a system of color or not. The main thing is that they are printed separately, on a separate plate.

Before we go on, we must mention the printing definition of a term used earlier – tint. A tint for our industry is a screen of a color. We have no way to add white other than letting the paper show though. In other words, a tint is a solid color broken up into dots that are described as a percentage of area covered. For example, a 50% screen of square dots looks like a checkerboard. Half the area is one color square, half the other. For printers dealing with negatives, half the area is solid and half is clear.

Process color is created by printing tints of the four process colors on top of each other. A typical color might be described as 100c 50m 0y 10k (standing for the tints involved). K is used for black to avoid confusion with blue, which is written "c" because it is really cyan. In this case, there is solid cyan, overprinted with 50 percent magenta, no yellow, and 10 percent black. This produces a very rich shade of royal blue.

Spot color, however, is mixed pigment – not blended by overprinting tints, but with a paint knife on a mixing table. Brilliant red, warm red, Van Dyke brown, and so on have no specified relationship to CMYK. In fact, many of these colors cannot be produced with process color. These colors are referred to as standard colors. This is sort of funny because they are not standards for anyone. They are really colors manufactured by a specific ink company. They are only standards for that particular company. One company's warm red might be very different from another's warm red. Riso's fourteen standard colors cannot be matched, for example.

Standard colors became a real problem. In the mid-1960s, a company named Pantone gave our industry the first standard color system that was accepted industry-wide. It is called the Pantone Matching System or PMS. PMS color is available at almost every printer in the United States. Although there are some others around the world, PMS is the only universal, spot color system standard that you normally need to be familiar with, in the United States.

The first thing you must understand is this: PMS color is not a full-spectrum system. Even though it covers many colors outside the RGB or CMYK color spaces, it is not based on primary colors. All PMS colors have to be described by RBY or HSV, and 35 percent of PMS colors cannot be reproduced with the tint overprints of process color. Many of them cannot be reproduced with RGB.

PMS (spot) is a completely separate system.

At present, PMS uses fifteen standard colors that are mixed into 1,001 standard mixes. The mixes can be seen in swatch books, which have a swatch of the actual color printed next to a formula. This formula tells the printer which of the standard colors to use and what percentages to mix to create the specified standard mix.

 TIP: In addition, Pantone has metallic and neon swatch books that add another couple hundred standard Pantone spot colors. These are very interesting, and often very beautiful, custom colors. You will pay extra for press washup. It's very difficult to get the metallic particles off the rollers. And there is no digital press equivalent.

With a swatch and a PMS number, anyone can match any PMS color in any facility that puts offset lithographic ink on paper. PMS inks are also available for some other printing methods. However, you must be careful: unless your printing method can use Pantone inks, PMS colors cannot be matched. Pantone sends employees to work in the various ink manufacturing plants to ensure color accuracy. All Pantone approved color has the word Pantone in the name on the label.

High-fidelity (hi-fi) color

Recently, there has been a flurry of activity trying to solve the problem of the different color systems and their color reproductive inadequacies. Pantone has released a six-color system called Hexachrome which seems to be winning, at this point. The goal is to produce a process color system that can reproduce all the colors of the standard color systems plus all the colors of CMYK. The common term, at this point, is hi-fi color. Hexachrome uses CMYK plus green and orange to produce 95 percent of the PMS colors, plus a much more colorful full-spectrum color space.

The ink manufacturers are assuming that some hi-fi system will become the standard. They are also assuming that hi-fi color is perceived to be of high value by the printing industry. The overriding issue, however, is, "Will customers pay the extra costs?" It will obviously cost more money, simply because more color heads are needed.

Hi-fi color will help a lot in such relatively small niches as fine art reproduction, fashion color catalogs, and the like. Companies like Spiegel, for example, can save a great deal of money with more accurate color. The largest reason for returned clothing is that it doesn't "look like it does in the catalog." Hi-fi could cut the return rate substantially. For normal process printing customers, the color accuracy possible with hi-fi color is not yet enough of a difference to justify the increased cost.

The push may come through the six-color inkjets. There are now several large format, hi-fi color inkjets on the market. The people using them are usually involved with top-quality color reproduction. Accurate color still costs a lot of money to print, and will for the foreseeable future. Accurate color on the Web will probably never happen, because surfers don't care. All they want is lots of color. Who cares if it is the same color on their neighbor's set?

Six-color commodity inkjets may increasingly offer hi-fi color. However, there is no way to calibrate them. Even PressReady, which does such a fantastic job of printing accurate color on several of Epson's, Canon's, and HP's inkjets, cannot hand hi-fi or spot color.

Commodity color

This is the bottom line with digital color. Most people don't care. As an industry, printer's have spent over a trillion dollars developing the capability to produce relatively accurate color and no one cares except printers and designers. When is the last time you tossed a brochure in the trash because the color was not accurate? All most consumers demand is what the industry calls acceptable color.

Acceptable color means simply that the reds are red and the greens are green. That skies are blue and skin tones look healthy. This will satisfy 90 percent of printing customers — it is absolute heresy to the printing industry. However, reasonably well-calibrated, process color, digital presses are becoming ubiquitous. The corner copy shop has the capability to toss off a cheap color print that makes the customer ecstatic (even though they still tend to think it is too expensive).

The spectacular growth of color

The traditional portions of our industry are hoping that hi-fi color will keep their traditional presses running. What will probably develop is an additional niche in the printing industry. Our industry is likely to develop along the same lines as many others in the late twentieth century. We will become increasingly diversified. Each niche will have its own preferred printing method. The mass-media color space will be process color, CMYK. With all of its deficiencies, four-color process works well, plus it is increasingly available.

With CMYK laser printers becoming much cheaper than black-and-white LaserWriters were in 1990, we will see phenomenal amounts of color printing. Full bleed, tabloid, duplex color digital presses now cost far less than $30,000. Acceptable production speed only boosts the cost

to around $100,000. This is phenomenal in an industry that as recently as 1990 assumed that a multimillion dollar press was required to print process – plus hundreds of thousands of dollars for prepress equipment. Now process color can be easily printed directly from $2,000 computers to $2,000 color laser printers.

Hi-fi color may never become common enough to appear in copiers and hi-fi color laser printers, although the technology is certainly possible. The governing factor is likely to be economic. As mentioned several times already, modern technology is not primarily concerned with increasing quality. Its main concern is the increase of perceived quality at the same price or cheaper than is currently available. Quantity instead of quality is the normal goal in a economically based, marketing society.

All we have to do is remember that top-quality fine art originals now cost from many thousand dollars to close to a million dollars. The days of printing with hand-ground pigments on handmade 100% rag paper are almost gone forever. Many of the best pigments have gone the way of the hairy mammoth. However, color printing for the masses has gone way up in quality and quantity. Mass-produced process color printing of outstanding quality is now sitting on many people's desktops. It's an exciting time to be alive. Our industry is growing like crazy and will continue to grow for the foreseeable future.

GETTING COLOR ON PAPER

COLOR PRINTING CONCEPTS AND SKILLS

I'm not very enthusiastic about this chapter because process color is a skill that can only be developed by experience. This is one of the places where understanding printing is essential. The majority of desktop designers (and I am certainly glad that my readers are not among that number) do not have a clue about traditional printing techniques. Since the monitor is in color and color can be added at will, many assume that color is no big deal. All you have to do is apply the color, send it to your printer (commercial or quick) and get it printed.

This is not even remotely close to the truth. Before you can even start you need to have a good handle on the color theory we just covered, briefly. This is not something you can pass over. You must understand that monitors are in RGB color and that process color uses different primary colors and a completely different color theory. RGB cannot be printed.

Paint programs

Let's start out with painted or bitmapped graphics. Yes, I know that this is a book on InDesign. And I know you know that all printer output is bitmapped. What we are discussing here is the originating application. Some illustration programs manipulate photographs, scans, and continuous tone art. We've talked about this. As mentioned, we are essentially talking about Photoshop.

The point is that they paint a picture dot by dot, pixel by pixel. The problem here is that you will be drawing in RGB (on the monitor) and printing in CMYK. The dilemma faced with that is that many of the colors on the screen cannot be printed. As a result, you will have to be using printed swatch books to judge final printed color.

 COMMENT: Your results will become more predictable with experience. My warning is this, however, the first printed pieces you design are going to be horrible shocks. The color will be muted, dull, and in many cases a different hue.

The only way around that is a color-calibrated monitor. Until very recently this would cost you $10,000. Currently there are a good selection in $1,500 to $10,000 range. Windows are very much a Johnny-come-lately here. It wasn't until NT 4 and Windows 98 that the PC world even had calibrated monitors. Supposedly Windows 2000 (NT 5) does quite a bit better, but Wintel, in general, requires a lot of caution and much setup time.

Postscript Illustration

PostScript illustration is a completely different animal. These programs can create any kind of shape and apply any color to it. This is what you need for two- and three-color work. These programs make full-color process work a dream. Colors can be added at will to the shapes. But this is the only professional quality illustration software that can draw with spot colors.

For process work you will have the added difficulty that FreeHand and Illustrator render process color on the screen differently than Photoshop or Painter. Even though the Adobe family now has consistent screen color, you will be forced to use printed swatch books to have any idea of the final output. Again the calibrated monitors will help, but remember Spot color cannot be rendered by RGB or CMYK.

WYSIWYG?

Not in color. All I am going to say here is that in digital graphics you will be constantly fighting the three-color schemes used. These color systems are not compatible with or comparable to each other. The only way you can begin to get accurate predictions of printed color is with swatch books.

A particularly difficult situation with fine art is gouache (opaque watercolors). Most gouache pigments fluoresce. This means that they convert ultraviolet to visible light, as a result they glow (like blacklight posters). This fluorescing capability cannot be picked up by a scanner. So, scanned gouache paintings look very different when printed — and there is nothing you can do about it.

RGB color only works on monitors.

Once you have them in the computer and on the screen, it doesn't matter if they are computer generated or scanned. You are in an entirely different color world — RGB. Red, green, blue is a world of light limited by the phosphors available in the tube. RGB is very limited in yellows, yellow greens, and most browns. Take a quick look a the Websafe color palette. There is only one yellow and even it tends strongly toward a harsh greenish yellow.

Printed color (CMY[K]) – called process

When we get to printed materials, we have lost even more color possibilities. Reproduction color is very limited in pigment choice. Here we go back to the original RBY with a real limitation.

This is an entirely new color world, CMY(K). Remember, CMY do not produce black but muddy brown. This is primarily due to the weakness and spectral inaccuracy of the cyan. As a result, K or black has to be added to correct the darker colors. Plus, the blues, greens, and purples are very compromised. CMYK is a very limited version of RBY. Maybe 85 percent of RGB colors can be attempted in CMYK. The reds are very weak and dull leaning strongly toward orange. There are no rich, vibrant purples. The blues are horrible, tending toward lavenders and violets. However, it is a full spectrum color scheme so the mind is fooled. When we look at process color it looks complete. However, do not expect it to match either reality or monitor color. When seen separately it works. However, it is not even theoretically possible to match the original. Use it wisely, with no false expectations.

Process color cannot match reality or monitor color.

All full-color printing is process. Sometimes a fifth color is added to pump up the reds and purples. Hallmark cards has been making money using this trick for years. As far as I know, it is still their tightly held trade secret.

Color handling tips

1. Do not mix spot and process color unless you have a large budget. Process plus two spot colors is a six-color print job. This costs almost 50 percent more to print than process alone. Sometimes you have no choice, but you can usually design around the problem. Remember that every color adds another color plate or head to the press or printer. This means that every printing cost is added again except for the paper.

2. Make sure your spot color naming systems are consistent from program to program. If your illustration program calls Christmas Green PMS 348 and InDesign uses the name Pantone PMS 348C for the same color, you will end up with two separate negatives for the two separate colors.

CONCEPT: Mixing screen tints of spot colors is verboten. It works really well, in theory. I have done a lot of it, but then I have an unlimited supply of student drones who have to do what I ask them. However, mixed spot colors usually cause severe printing problems. Commercial printers will usually not print them unless you sign a release. This is because there is no way to proof mixed spot tints. All proofing materials are either opaque or CMYK.

You will be creating color based on your theoretical understanding of what the resulting mix will be. With experience, you can control these color mixes very well, but all the proofing is in your head. You have to be able to imagine what a turquoise like PMS 326 is going to look like as a 55 percent screen mixed with a 35 percent screen of PMS 200 which is a bright wine red. It will result in a grayed out blue-violet tint of some kind. It will probably be pretty.

The question is, "Can you get the client to trust your taste enough to authorize it?" Based on my experience, this is not likely. Clients and printshops usually want guaranteed color based on either a color proof or a printed swatch. These are simply not available for mixed spot color unless you pay a lot. Even then the proofing methods are often limited in color choice. Most customers get very queasy when you say, "The color is great! Trust me!"

3. Limit your color palette. First of all, this is a sign of good taste and style. You might even try (horror of horrors) a coordinated color scheme. This would be specially true if you were trying to recapture the look of the fifties and early sixties. If you are doing two color, black and a spot color, use the color sparingly and dramatically. The worst thing you can do is simply make all the heads and subheads in color. Remember, that color is always less contrast than black and white. Dingbats and small emphatic graphics work well in spot color as do hand-drawn boxes used for underlines. Color also works extremely well for tinted boxes used as sidebars, mastheads, graphics, etcetera.

4. Approach color with fear and trepidation. Color is ridiculously easy to add on the monitor screen. However, it greatly increases printing costs. It is often not worth the money. Having said that, your clients will certainly demand it. Remember that discretion is a sure sign of refined taste. Be discrete! Do color with style and flair, not sprayed all over like a graffiti vandal.

MORE PROBLEMS

LET'S GET INTO PROCESS PRINTING

Of course, you have guessed by now that the complexities haven't ended. Process color involves four colors printed transparently on top of each other. This creates several problems.

Moiré patterns

Regular patterns have a major problem. If you print two of them on top of each other, you create an incidental interference pattern called a moiré. They are named after the Frenchman who studied them. These moirés can easily create plaid patterns in your carefully produced screened photographs, for linescreens are certainly a regular pattern. Remember, process color requires four screens to be printed on top of each other. So, moirés can be a serious problem.

One of the more common sources of moirés is demonstrated in the figures at the top of the next page. The name is rescreening, and it is caused by screening an already screened piece. In this case, a graduated screen was printed and put back in the scanner. The more

common source is photographs that have already been printed. In projects like photo directories for clubs or classes, you will find that a quarter to a half of all the submitted pictures have been already printed, meaning they are already screened. The dots are usually too small to copydot (unless you have access to very expensive hardware). So they have to be rescreened.

 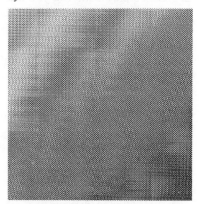

Scanning the printed left square produced the right moiré mess.

The moiré that most of you have probably noticed happens on television when a talk show guest shows up with a pin-striped shirt. Often the stripes are so small that they are not noticeable, but the shirt shimmers with what looks like a glowing, moving oil slick. That's a moiré caused by the stripes on the shirt combining with the horizontal lines of the TV image.

Rescreening is simple in concept, but often horrible in execution. The basic process is to blur the scan to the point where the moiré disappears. Obviously this messes up the photo or scan. However, by carefully using Gaussian Blur to blur "just enough," the effects are usually almost unnoticeable (the printed photos are usually so bad that a little blurring can't hurt too much, anyway). Many scanner plug-ins have rescreening options. As usual, these automatic options only work for the average scan which, as we know well, does not exist in reality. You are better off playing with Gaussian Blur, although it is often slow and tedious at best.

Angled screens

We need to see why angling screens is such a problem digitally. The difficulty is that bitmap, again. Lines are no problem if they remain horizontal or vertical. Even if they are at 45°, they remain straight and even. Any other angle requires contortions.

As you can see, bitmaps chew up lines. In the same way, they really mess up screen angles. What you need to understand is that screens need to be angled for process printing. Angling screens causes many problems with

How lines fit bitmaps

the digital bitmaps. They do not fit well. This causes several problems, of which moirés are the major difficulty.

To avoid moirés, screens need to be at 30- or 45-degree angles to each other. This does not sound like a big deal. After all, we have 360 degrees to play with. But you are not thinking clearly. A screen covers four angles. This is because a screen has two sets of parallel lines at right angles to each other. In other words, a horizontal/vertical screen uses up the 0°, 90°, 180°, and 270° angles. A 45 degree angled screen covers 45°, 135°, 225°, and 315°.

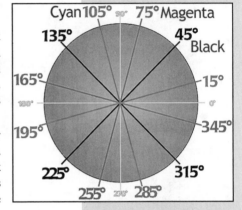

Screen visibility

The next difficulty revolves around the human brain. It would really be a great deal simpler if the brain was not such an incredibly good design. Our minds are indescribably powerful computers. One of the mind's capabilities is pattern recognition. It is especially good at recognizing horizontals and verticals (and even better with horizontal/vertical patterns).

As a result, screens at 0/90° can be seen at 75-line or smaller. However, 45-degree screens are hard to see at 65-line. In practical terms, this means that our halftones are shot at 45° if possible. This helps to fool our brains so that our eyes think they are seeing continuous tone. The 45-degree angle makes the halftones appear to be smoother.

The standard process angles

Now we have to put it all together. The process colors require four screens to be placed on top of each other. This causes horrendous moiré patterns, so a standard procedure was developed, many years ago.

Because the most visible color is black, it was shot at 45°. There are two more angle sets available that are 30° from each other: 75° and 105°. These were given to cyan and magenta. But what to do with yellow? The next smallest moiré is the 15° angle. So, yellow is set between the cyan and magenta, 45° from the black, at 90°. This does create a small moiré. However, it is a yellow moiré. Yellow is almost invisible anyway, so, the small yellow moiré is easily tolerable.

The rosette

There is a small pattern, that is a very complicated moiré, called a rosette. It is the result of properly registered process screens overlapping. The rosette can be seen only with a loupe. With 133-line process, the rosette is around 110-line. In other words, it is certainly an acceptable pattern. It is, however, one of the reasons why 150-line process looks a lot better. The rosette in 133-line tends to make the image look a little grainy.

Yet another problem: Angled cells

The final problem with angled screens has to do with the halftone cell itself. At this point, you may consider this rather straightforward.

The standard process color screen angles with the resulting rosette pattern below.

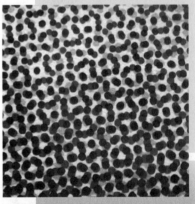

Of course, it is not. The halftone cell is easy to understand, as long as it is 0° or 45°. At any other commonly used angle, it gets ridiculous.

As you recall, the halftone cell takes a group of dots (usually a square) and treats it as a single unit. This cell allows the creation of halftone dots that vary in size. We've mentioned before how messed up the shapes are compared to the old standard of dots that gradually varied in size. The cells are calculated by simple division. The resolution in dpi is divided by the linescreen desired to give you the horizontal dimension of the halftone cell. As just mentioned, this works fine as long as the cell is 0° or 45°.

With all other angles, it gets very complicated because of the limitations of a bitmap. When you rotate a halftone cell, the outside corners of the corner dots have to fit the grid exactly. Bitmaps make no provision for partial dots. A dot is either on or off. This means that the cells have to be squeezed to fit the grid. For traditional printers, these sizes are very strange.

As you can see by this example, the resulting cell has little to do with standard linescreen or standard angles — 101.3099° indeed! In fact, early digital screens did not match the traditional angles at all. As far as printing establishments were

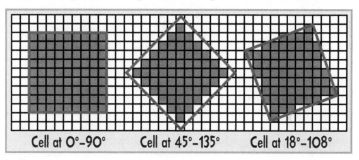

Cell at 0°–90°   Cell at 45°–135°   Cell at 18°–108°

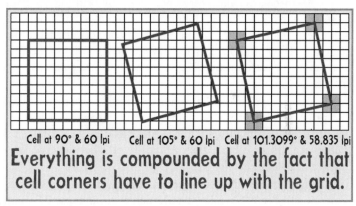

Cell at 90° & 60 lpi   Cell at 105° & 60 lpi   Cell at 101.3099° & 58.835 lpi

Everything is compounded by the fact that cell corners have to line up with the grid.

concerned, digital process color was a horrifying mess of weird angles and moiré patterns. Basically this has become a non-problem. RIPs using PostScript Levels 2 and 3 no longer have that problem.

Stochastic screening

These problems have been part of the push toward stochastic screening. I'm defining stochastic as anything placing dots that do not vary in size in a pattern that appears random. This would include handmade stochastics created with the diffusion dither option of the bitmap mode in Photoshop, and the junk screens of the cheap inkjets. Stochastic screening totally eliminates angling and moiré problems. It is the enabling technology for the newest possibility in process color — hi-fi color.

In addition, traditional process is very dependent on tight registration. Any color out of register by more than half a dot causes color shifts. Stochastic solves that also. This makes stochastic the enabling technology for process on duplicators and digital presses.

High-fidelity color uses a system of six or more process colors. The problems are obvious. With traditional screens, there were no more angles available to eliminate moiré patterns. Stochastic screening solves that.

LET'S PRINT IN COLOR!

It is highly recommended that you learn to work in CMYK on the screen. Now that Apple has released reasonably accurate ColorSync monitors at a decent price, you should have a calibrated monitor. It is the closest approximation to what will be printed. But it is still only approximate. You need to keep a printed swatch book (Pantone makes a good one) next to the keyboard. That is the only way you can keep track of how the images will change when printed. Even then, you will find that experience is the only sufficient teacher.

In the same way, you should always build your colors by the numbers. After a while, you will learn to think in process color, but you need to train your mind.

Duo-, tri-, quadritones, and separations

All these are multilayered halftones. By printing several halftones on top of each other, many things can be done. Separations are the core of process color. They have four halftones on top of each other – cyan, magenta, yellow, and black. They have to be angled, as discussed before, to avoid moiré patterns. Separation procedures are discussed later in this chapter.

These multilayered halftones are used to compensate for the fact that printing ink has a maximum density of around 1.0 on the standard density scale running from 0 to 4.0. This scale is logarithmic, just like the Richter scale is for earthquakes. A density of 2.0 is closer to tens times as dense as 1.0, for example.

Photographs always have a maximum density of at least 2.0 and professional photos can have shadow densities far above 3.0. With printing ink having a dMax of 1.0, something needs to be done to get excellent reproduction quality. Duotones, tritones, and quadritones solve this by printing several layers of ink on top of each other to build up the density to something roughly approximating the original.

Duotones, tritones, and quadritones are halftones that are built in two, three, or four layers. For years, low-quality printers have spread the lie that duotones are a cheap way to add color images to a brochure. This is true in the hands of the monetarily greedy. In fact, they are an expensive way to make your black-and-white photographs richer and more beautiful.

Simply explained, a duotone makes a second halftone from the identical image. This second 'tone contains only shadow dot

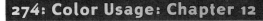

information. When it is printed on top of the first 'tone, the resulting duotone has shadow densities that run from 1.5 to 2.0. A tritone uses a gray for the highlights with the shadows being hit three times to produce densities in the 2 to 3 density range. A quadritone uses two grays and two blacks for the closest approximation to photographic prints with maximum possible densities of nearly 3.0. For best results, as you begin to experiment with these extended density pictures, start with the curves supplied with Photoshop. They will give you a good running start.

Why bother?

For this to be justifiable, you need exceptional photographs. They must be sharp and clear, with detail in both the highlights and the shadows, white whites and black blacks. Because every color adds almost as much cost as the first color (everything except the paper has to be added again), this is a quality choice, not a bottom-line option.

It is true that, if you are already using two colors, duotones are a cheap way to make your halftones look better. However, unless you understand the density range concept, you will be disappointed with the results. The quickprinters pushing this technique rarely understand the density range concept.

Multitone problems

1. Most duotones are made with black and a spot color. There are some good reasons to use a dark brown and a spot color, especially if you need the look of the old sepia tones of the late nineteenth century. The dominant halftone should always be the black one (or the darkest color). There is a tendency to make the colored (or weaker) one stronger, but this tints the highlights as well as the shadows.

2. If your second color is green or blue, tinted highlights tend to make people in the photos look very ill. In the second halftone, all the highlights and upper midtones should be eliminated. Then all the richness is added to the shadows without darkening or coloring the highlights.

3. Spot color proofing is almost nonexistent. This is why we have not discussed multitones done with multiple spot color. Although students do these as experiments, only on very rare occasions can clients be successfully sold on the idea of multitones done with multiple spot colors. They can be extremely beautiful and dramatic. They are very hard to sell unless the client has a lot of printing experience.

4. **Powertones:** There is a software package available that makes amazing multitones with spot color that give incredibly realistic results. The obvious problem is that you will be dependent upon a soft proof on your client's monitor that cannot be duplicated. Approach multispot-colored separations with fear and trepidation.

MAKING CMYK SEPARATIONS

Four-color separations are the primary reason why printing was formerly an arcane craft. It still requires experience and skill, and today's tools provide too much power for the process novice.

However, the procedure is still basically the same as for halftones:

1. Locate the best possible photo
2. Determine the size and resolution (twice the linescreen)
3. Pre-adjust the scan (if you have a decent scanner plug-in)
4. Crop to size (to save as much file size as possible)
5. Clean up the image (especially with store-bought photo prints)
6. Adjust levels using the Curves dialog box in Photoshop
7. Sharpen with Unsharp Mask

The only real additional step (other than the complex adjustments) is the conversion to CMYK mode. Because our goal is to place ink on paper, we need to get to ink colors as soon as we can. You really need to build skill in manipulating ink color (CMYK). Once you have created your masterpiece, all of the image assembly and presswork will be concerned exclusively with CMYK. Therefore, you need to learn to speak their language. You need to learn to think in CMYK.

This book is simply not the place to teach production separation techniques. My new book, *Publishing With Photoshop*, will cover this area thoroughly. What we need to cover here are some tips for dealing with color in InDesign.

COLOR PRINTING PRODUCTION TIPS

1. Do not forget to adjust for dot gain. In process color this is a simple setting in Photoshop. However, you need to remember that tints applied in InDesign will also gain the same amount. If you have a 10 percent dot gain, I would not recommend any screens darker than 80% to 85%; with a 20 percent gain, 70 to 75%; with a 30 percent gain, even 65% can be risky.

2. Remember that the cheaper printing processes have larger dot gain and this means that light tints are also a problem. Commercial printing on high-gloss coated stock might hold a 3% dot in the highlights. Quickprinting with a 30 percent dot gain can easily have trouble holding a 10% highlight dot.

3. Make sure you settle in your mind whether or not you are competent to do professional quality separations. If you are not, carefully choose a service provider to handle the separation conversions. It may well be better to have them scan for you also. If you are providing the scans, do the best you can with RGB scans and let the service provider do the CMYK conversions. In reality, you are often better to let them do the scans also, and merely use 72 dpi FPO scans to show them where to insert the high-res CMYK.

4. Make sure that the costs and difficulty of process color are justified by the content of your project. Often a one- or two-color job on gorgeous paper will look far better than a

process job poorly done — at half the cost or less!

5.   If you are using spot color to cut printing costs, pay special attention to the registration capabilities of your service provider. If their duplicators can only handle a sixteenth inch plus or minus, then all of your colors must overprint and they better not get any closer than a half inch to each other.

6.   Keep careful track of the kind of color you add. If you are quoting a straight four-color process job, adding spot colors (or even RGB colors) are going to add to your quoted printing costs. **YOU CAN'T EXPECT YOUR CLIENT TO PAY FOR YOUR STUPIDITY!**

7.   **Let's repeat this for the brain dead:** Always pick your printer before you begin to design. How can you possibly design within the printing capabilities of your supplier if you do not know who it is going to be?

8.   Always bid in a calibrated color contract proof for your process color jobs. At $50 or more per sig side, this can seem like an extravagance. However, a client's refusal to pay (because he does not like the color) is going to cost someone hundreds or thousands of dollars — or more. That someone will be you if you don't have a signed contract proof — signed by both the client and the supplier. They will, justifiably, point the finger at you.

9.   Avoid nouveaux riche design. One of the surest signs of an amateur is uncontrolled color strewn about the surface of the page. Simply because you can is no excuse! Add color in judicious amounts for specific reasons. Those reasons have to center around improved communication about the client and his or her products or services to the reader. My students have come to call this *"the Windows look."* I don't want to step on toes, but this has been empirically true in the past, mainly because those coming from the PC side have often never been involved with publishing on a professional level. I know that PC users among my readers are not like that any more — but in this business, perception is reality.

10. Use cheap suppliers at your own risk. The main reason they are cheap is that they toss all the color responsibilities on you. Make sure you can handle these tasks, since someone has to do it.

THE NEW REALITY

As I have said many times, the new paradigm for publishing is color: short-run, on-demand, online. All of us are working in color, and more color projects every day. Often our clients think they can handle the simple black and white projects (even though the results are often painful). Color production skills are becoming a necessity for all digital publishers instead of being the lair of the overly elite professionals, like it was in the old paradigm.

However, just because it is now easy, do not make the mistake of thinking it is simple. The complexity of color production can be overwhelming when you first start. The results of your first pieces are going to be a major adjustment as you learn how to compensate in your mind for the RGB to CMYK translation.

1.   What is the basic problem with spot color quadritones?

2.   How and why do you rescreen scans of printed photos?

3.   Why are soft proofs problematic?

4.   Why will and should your first process jobs be scary?

5.   Why are swatch books essential?

WHERE SHOULD YOU BE BY THIS TIME?

By this time you should have earned well over half your grade. You should be working comfortably in InDesign, with your defaults working smoothly. Hopefully you have access to both process printing and spot color printing. Start looking for those skill exams or projects that require the use of color. Especially practice process work with a calibrated proofer.

DISCUSSION

You should be discussing color taste and style with your classmates. You will probably discover that there are some who can make colors you consider ugly into beautiful designs. Discuss the advantages of using a limited palette, and how you can avoid the amateur or *new graduate* look.

Talk among yourselves...

Paper and Media

Knowledge and background needed to pick an appropriate paper for a given project and printer

CONCEPTS

1. **Basis size**
2. **Basis weight**
3. **Calendaring**
4. **Sheet-fed**
5. **Heat-set web**
6. **Sizing**
7. **Filler**

CHAPTER OBJECTIVES

By presenting the basic terms and production procedures, you will learn how to:

1. Compare paper weights
2. When expensive papers are cost-effective
3. How to develop a paper palette
4. Avoid many printing problems resulting from poor paper choices
5. Improve the look of your finished document

LAB WORK FOR CHAPTER

- Continue work on skills and miniskills
- Submit finished theory exams
- Continue work on your approved real project – ideally your second, third, or fourth real project

   There are far too many terms to be covered with a simple list of concepts. These words are also defined in the Glossary in the back of the book.

   Terms: watermark, ink holdout, offset, vellum, smooth, enamel, text, bond, writing, opaque, point, caliper, parent size, vellum bristol, index, tag, newsprint, web sheets

Paper and media

**Hammermill
Laser Plus**® (Featuring Wax Holdout)
Long Grain   500 Sheets
11 x 17-24M-S24/60
For Prepress Proofing and Camera-Ready Masters

↑ Print This
Side Only

White

10452-1

0 10199 00452 9

wausau papers *Royal Felt*®

White Stone

85262

759598 85262 0

23 x 35 – 119M
1000 Sheets-Basis 70

500 sheets: 60# gloss coated: .75"

500 sheets: 60# matte coated: .95"

500 sheets: 60# smooth offset: 1.15"

500 sheets: 60# vellum offset: 1.30"

500 sheets: 60# hi-bulk offset: 1.56"

**The approximate relative thickness
of five common papers used in books.**

Before

we start talking about individual types of projects, there is one final area that must be covered — output media. In our industry, this is normally papers and monitors. Both of these media types are complex, imposing their restrictions upon our designs. Both of these media require planning, for your designs must use these as your base of operation, as it were.

There are thousands of different kinds, styles, colors, and types of paper and printing substrates. Even though monitors seem much more homogeneous, experience quickly shows us that they are even less predictable than paper. However, we have to start somewhere, so let's start with printing substrates which are almost always some type of paper

Your first design decision should be the media.

The first material decision to be made with a publishing project is usually the paper. There are those who simply take what is offered by the copy shop, and that works strongly in your favor. Against that background of cheap white wood pulp, a distinctive paper choice makes a major statement.

Paper manufacturing is huge and capital-intensive

We have not covered, and won't try to cover, the nomenclature, categorizations, limitations, and availability of paper. Paper machines are extremely expensive and often more than a mile long. Entire trees are now chewed up for the fiber and cooked in vats the size of buildings. The output of these massive machines is logs of rolled paper, feet in diameter and yards in width.

The pulp is poured continuously onto a nonending loop of screen hundreds of yards long. The drying rollers are machined to almost unimaginable tolerances in huge arrays that carry the continuous web of paper while it dries. There are thousands of colors, pulp recipes, embossed textures, and so on.

My intention here is to give you a limited introduction to the huge world of paper, to try to give you enough knowledge to ask intelligent questions. What happens with every designer is that she develops a standard selection of papers that meet her needs. There are tens of thousands of different papers manufactured by many dozens of paper mills distributed by hundreds of suppliers. What you will have to do is find the best paper available for the given situation.

Getting samples

Do not hesitate to call your paper supplier. Their expertise goes far beyond a designer's or printer's need. The field is too complex to store in your memory banks unless you sell the material. However, as soon as a paper supplier learns that you are choosing paper choices for your projects, she'll be happy to provide you with swatch book and idea samples.

Some of the best printing in the world is supplied by paper houses with product line idea books. Many of the swatch books contain a page of every color and texture of paper offered in that line with idea-provoking printing to show you some possibilities you may have never seen or thought of. For years Warren Paper produced some of the best books available on varnish usage, photography ideas, and many more in a series that was one of the best sources of ideas for designers. Sadly, it is out of print, but keep your eye open for old copies lying around.

Start by finding papers that you like the look of. Then start asking questions about what papers are kept in stock, get the prices firmed up, and start building your palette of papers. You will find that you come back over and over to certain choices that make the most sense for you, your clients, and your budgets. As you develop your style and reputation, you will find that paper choices are a major portion of that look.

PAPER'S CONFUSING WEIGHTS

As we get into paper, there is much confusion about the weights (not to mention the names): 20#, 65#, 100#, bond, text, enamel, tag, pressure-sensitive — the list seems to go on forever. The good news is that paper weights are very simple to understand.

> **The basis weight of a paper stock is the weight, in pounds, of a ream (500 sheets) of the basis size.**

The basis size (the size the weight calculations are made from) varies arbitrarily with each category of paper. However, there are only three categories that you will need to remember. Unique papers, like newsprint, often have their own basis size. These basis sizes vary for each type of paper. As a result, 24# bond is about the same weight as 60# offset; 140# text is comparable in weight to 55# cover; 90# index is thinner than 65# cover. It seems extremely complicated. The good news is that we only deal with a few categories on a daily basis, determined mainly by the printing technology and the final usage of the printed product.

What you have to memorize is the basis size of the common categories of paper you use every day. Thankfully for most of us, this is only three sizes. Although there are well over a dozen different basis sizes for the various types of paper, there are really only three that you will use regularly.

Papers outside the norm

Before we start, let's just mention the papers that you will come across that you can categorize by name. Newsprint, as mentioned, has a weird basis size and strange weights, but who cares? The newspaper publisher worries about that and you will rarely spec it. Whatever the newspaper uses is fine with you. If you have custom printing done by them, they will show you samples of what they use, give you the price points, and the printing capabilities of the various papers. In general, all you have to know is that it is extremely cheap and very absorbent. You also have to make sure you allow for the fact that everything will print like it's on blotter paper. This is much more important for photos than anything else, so we'll leave that for *Publishing With Photoshop*, my upcoming book about Photoshop and fixing scans.

Paper and media

Mill orders

When you begin looking at paper swatch books and samples, you will quickly discover that some of the most gorgeous papers are not kept in stock. There is not enough demand to keep them in stock. To use those papers you have to make a mill order. This will vary from company to company, but it is usually five to eight cartons. Bear in mind that some trade suppliers, like folder manufacturers and menu specialists, do stock some of these darker, richer, and more unusual papers. They usually advertise in the back of the printing industry trade magazines, (which you might want to subscribe to.)

In addition, at the cheaper printers, you will find three papers sold as cover stock that you need to be careful of: **Vellum Bristol, Index, and Tag**. They are actually the cheapest type of paper — the worst wood pulp. Their only advantage is their price. They look cheap, feel cheap, and cause customers to think your client is cheap. But then if you are making a promo for Billy Bob's Junk Yard, they would work very well. They are very useful, but only if you understand their basic character — **CHEAP**.

Vellum Bristol only comes in 67# and it is the only 67# paper in existence. Index comes in 90# and 110#, and these are the only two papers that use this weight. You will use these fairly often, simply because they are often the heaviest papers that will feed through a laser printer or copier. Tag is so rare that you will always look for it specifically. It's the paper used for those inspection tags with the reinforced holes held to the pipes with twisted wire. Tag is used so little because even most presses cannot feed it — it's too thick.

THE PAPERS YOU'LL USE

The commonly used papers can be broken down into three neat classifications. For most of your daily use, these will be sufficient. All the other categories are either the extremely cheap specialty papers we just mentioned or expensive papers for a particular use: such as label stock for wine or jam bottles; pressure-sensitive or crack'n'peel paper for bumper stickers and labels; plastic stock for posters and banners; latex-impregnated paper for waterproof and durable menus, and so forth. Many of these have different basis sizes. But if you use them at all, you will quickly learn to recognize them by sight.

The three categories of office, printing, and cover stock make up close to 100 percent of the papers sold. Printing papers, by themselves, probably come to three-quarters of the paper manufactured and sold. You may hear figures like "half the paper sold is 60# offset." It matters not. What you need to know is that printing papers contain all the most commonly used sheets and rolls. Of those, 50#, 60#, and 70# offset are by far the most popular, followed by the same weights in coated stock. Almost all paper sold is white. There are hundreds of different whites ranging from almost cream to brilliant, snow white.

Experience is necessary

We will describe these papers in a little more detail, but you need to recognize that this is an unregulated industry. You must learn how specific papers behave on the printers and presses you have to use. Almost all printing companies will have a favorite paper stock that they are convinced works the best for their equipment mix. You will save a lot of money, time, and hassle if you can live with this stock.

Your customers will specify others that you will be forced to use. You will have to be the person who knows what papers cause problems, when and why. Before you specify a paper, call your printer and ask if this paper choice causes any problems that they know of. Some papers feed well, and some don't. Some curl badly and have a pronounced grain direction. You will have to learn what papers are available in your area, what manufacturers and what colors are stocked by the local distributors.

No area has all papers. No one stocks all the colors available for all the papers. Sometimes the paper you really want is only available as a mill order which usually requires five to fifteen carton minimums. Paper is simply too bulky, which means that shipping and storage problems are a major consideration. A carton of paper ranges from around 50 pounds for 10 reams of 8.5x11 precut stock to close to 150 pounds for parent sheet stock (typically 1,000 plus sheets of 23x35 or larger). Buying partial or broken carton quantities normally almost doubles the price. You should ask your supplier about their pricing policies. Often commercial printers buy enough paper to always receive the 16-carton price for any paper carried by their paper distributor of choice.

Obviously, larger cities have better availability. However, some papers are made on the West Coast, some on the East Coast, most in the Upper Midwest, some in the Desert Southwest. Shipping tons of paper thousands of miles raises costs to the point where local papers are much more cost-effective. The building size required for warehousing limits availability. You need to cultivate relationships with your paper sales personnel for help on what is available. It will help more than you can imagine if you find a customer service representative who you can trust for advice.

What you write on: Office papers

First we cover the top category in the graphic to the right. Office papers are distinguished by the fact that they are designed for writing. We do print on them, but they have several characteristics that set them apart. First of all, the basis size is 17"x22", an exact multiple of 8.5"x11". That seems insignificant, but it means

Paper and media

The most commonly used papers

Office papers: Basis size: 17"x22"
SURFACES: cockle, laid, linen, parchment, ripple, wove, rib laid
COMMON NAMES: bond, ditto, ledger, mimeo, onionskin, rag, writing
CHARACTERISTICS: *tough, versatile, often beautiful; has personality only matched by text; is designed for writing; prints better on felt side; can be erased*

Printing papers: Basis size 25"x38"

Uncoated sheets
SURFACES: antique, smooth, vellum, wove
COMMON NAMES: book, offset, opaque
CHARACTERISTICS: *easy folding; wide variety of colors; most common paper; used for books and virtually anything else*

Coated sheets
SURFACES: matte, dull, gloss, cast coat, embossed
COMMON NAMES: coated offset, dull, slick, gloss
CHARACTERISTICS: *good ink holdout; produces ink gloss; smooth surfaces (some mirror-like); usually only comes in white*

Text
SURFACES: antique, embossed, felt, laid, silk, linen, rib laid, vellum • COMMON NAMES: text
CHARACTERISTICS: *premium papers for jobs that require "class"; even cheap grades are distinctive; many are very soft and take embossing superbly; deckle edges; wide range of colors, including deep and "fashion" colors*

Cover stock: Basis size: 20"x26"
SURFACES: any of the above as a matching set
COMMON NAMES: C1S, C2S, cover as a suffix
CHARACTERISTICS: *durable, stiff, strong; opaque for cards, folders, etc.*

that bleeds are rarely cost-effective on office stock unless you design for special sizes or unusual formats.

Because office papers are designed to write on, they are heavily sized. Sizing is a coating that controls absorption. Good examples of unsized paper are blotter paper or paper towels. If bond papers were not sized, ballpoint pens would bleed into and maybe through the paper. However, it is important to note that bonds are sized well on only one side. They are not meant for double-sided use. Paper that is written upon is usually too dented and marked on the back by the pen or pencil to be used for more writing or printing.

In addition to the sizing, writing papers use specially chosen, stronger fibers. This enables erasure of mistakes. It also enables office papers to hold up under the heavy use they receive. They are handled, filed, moved around, copied, and mistreated more than any other kind of paper. The only pieces treated more roughly are things like menus, pocket calendars, and membership cards. Those require either special synthetic stock, plastics, or laminated coatings.

These stronger fibers are not usually diluted with fillers. Fillers are used a lot in printing papers to make the paper opaque, but office stock uses relatively little additional fill. As a result, office papers (bond, writing, ledger, and so forth) have what is called snap. This is especially true for premium bonds containing cotton fiber. Fillers weaken the paper and dull the sound. Much of the experience of top-quality bond paper is in the feel and sound.

Bonds are usually relatively translucent

As mentioned, they are sized on only one side, so they normally are printed on only one side. This means that they do not have to be opaque unlike printing papers. This means that writing papers are the only category that can offer watermarks. Watermarks are made in the paper pulp when it is extremely liquid (80 to 90 percent water). Wire patterns pressed into the liquid pulp rearrange the fibers, making them more translucent. The watermarks are only seen when the paper is held up for reading, and light shows through the back of the paper. There is no dent or surface mark to be seen. You can design custom watermarks. Paper mills will produce custom watermarked bonds for you with relatively small orders. An order of only a couple dozen parent-sheet-size cartons is usually enough. A simple thing like a custom watermark can add a great deal to the perceived image of a firm of CPAs, lawyers, bankers, and other of those types trying to project power, wealth, and influence.

Bonds are usually white or light tints. This is because we write on them and because whiteout is available only in limited colors. This may be necessary no longer now that typewriters are gone. With edited copy, printed on laser printers, the better quality colored sheets can look very classy. At this point, they are still a relatively unusual option that can add a great deal of impact with little additional cost. Make sure you consult with the secretaries who will be using the letterheads before you design, however. Many a beautiful design has sat in desk drawers, unused, because it didn't fit the secretary's normal typing procedures.

Office paper surfaces are often embossed with fabric textures like linen; Chinese paper making bamboo screen textures called laid; unrolled, baked surfaces like cockle; and so on. The better papers are more conservative. A top-quality 100 percent cotton bond has a richness of surface, snap, and feel that is unsurpassed. Remember that this is the same paper used to print our money. You need to read the sidebar on page 290 on counterfeiting.

You should plan on spending $12 to $20 per ream on bond paper. Nothing makes a company seem questionable more than cheap, thin letterhead stock. In many cases, the quality of the paper used for the letterhead, business card, and envelope is the first impression a client, or your client's prospective customer has of quality, ability, and reliability.

WHAT WE PRINT ON: PRINTING PAPERS

As you saw on our category list, printing papers take up far more than three-quarters of papers used. Printing papers are the papers you will be speccing most of the time. They are designed to feed well through a press. They are well-sized, equally on both sides, to control absorption. They use a lot of filler so the sheets are much more opaque. This allows double-sided printing without show-through, on relatively thin papers. Even on paper stock too thin to feed through sheet-fed presses, like 36# to 50# offset , the ink on the other side of the paper is not disturbingly visible.

Most printing papers, except text, are smooth and white. You'll get a feel for this if you try to imagine a novel printed on textured pink paper. These papers are used for all books, magazines, programs, brochures, and the like. The two major types of this smooth white stock are offset (also called uncoated) and enamel (also called coated).

Cheapness

Printing papers, in general, are very cheap. Yes, I am using that term to imply poor quality. Good paper, in general, is found in the office papers. Excellent paper must have a large cotton content. Printing papers are almost exclusively wood pulp. Most of them are the cheapest wood pulp, assaulted by the harshest bleaches to bring it to the brightest white. The only printing papers offering quality are the text grades, and even these are usually cheap wood pulp (even though they come in fancy textures and beautiful colors).

Calendaring

The smoothness of printing papers is accomplished by a stack of steel rollers called calendaring rollers. These highly polished rollers compress and smooth both coated and uncoated printing stock. In fact, calendaring is one of the main distinguishing characteristics of these sheets. All offset and enamel papers are calendared.

There are two reasons for calendaring: smoothness and compression. The second is a definite factor in binding and shipping. The first has to do with requirements most people believe are necessary. Some

Paper and media

Opacity

This is a measurement of how opaque your paper choice will be. Some printers call this *showthrough*. This is the determining factor on whether you can use the thinner (and therefore less expensive) papers. Currently, papers are rated from 0 to 100 on opacity. If you need to print on both sides, the opacity should be in the upper eighties or low nineties. Your paper supplier will know these things. However, they will definitely try to talk you into more expensive sheets (with good reason). Be careful!

of this is due to press operators' claims that smoother papers print better. Some of it is due to paper manufacturers' hype. Most of it is due to the fashion for "slickness" in the 1970s and 1980s, which was largely a reaction to the incredible advances in press and prepress technology.

Smoothness

We've discussed briefly how lithography and xerography work. Both of these technologies do print easier on smoother sheets. Electrostatic printing (xerography) almost requires this smoothness, thus the phrase "suitable for laser printing" on the reams in your office supply center. It is true that electrostatic printing does not work well on strongly textured sheets (the surfaces embossed to look like fabric for example).

In fact, this smoothness requirement is actually a matter of taste. As I read the histories of printing technology, I am struck by the oft-stated fact that one of the main benefits of offset lithography is the ability of the rubber blanket to print well on textured sheets. The blanket is a sheet of rubber mounted to an intermediate cylinder to "offset" the image from the plate to the paper. In my thirty years of printing experience, I have often been pleasantly surprised by how well offset litho works with textured sheets.

Even with electrostatic imaging, the problems of texture are rarely severe. The only real problem is that the hot rollers that melt the toner onto the sheet usually flatten any texture. It takes an extreme texture to cause image breakup. Again, my experience has proven over and over that laser printers print beautifully with slightly textured and non-calendared sheets of paper.

I have often been struck by how well offset litho works with textured sheets.

Another factor to consider is that materials like rubber-based inks commonly used in quickprint and the inks used for digital mimeography only dry by absorption. In these cases, excellence in printing demands that you reject coated sheets and heavily calendared stock.

Excellence in printing simply requires designs within the capabilities of the technology used.

 Discussion point: Increasingly, designers like myself are seeing the overly smooth, slick printing done on super calendared stock as slick, mechanical, unfriendly, and often cheap looking. To use terms of furniture and woodworking, it is the difference between the slick, super-glossy one day coat of polyurethane and the patina that can be produced only by years of hand-rubbed oil and wax application.

Process color prints beautifully on non-calendared, slightly textured, uncoated, or text paper stock. Certainly the dot gain requires adjustments. However, the richness of the paper surface is often much more desirable than the glossy, slap-in-your-face gaudiness of paper where you can see your reflection. Try it, you'll like it.

Compression

The second result of calendaring is genuinely important. The stack of rollers used to smooth the paper also makes it thinner. Pull up that image from your mind about that sandwich of bologna and that pasty white stuff some actually call bread. What happened when you squeezed the bread? Calendaring does a similar thing to the relatively loose mat of fiber that comes off the screen of a papermaking machine.

The importance of this is simple. Let's briefly look at a saddle-stitched booklet. These are booklets, newsletters, or magazines that are folded in half and stitched (printers use wire in rolls that is stitched into place).

There is a real limit on the thickness of such a booklet. If there are too many sheet of paper,

> **7 Sigs: 28 page book**
>
> **36 Sigs: 144 page book**
>
> **The thickness of paper sets the limit for saddle-stitching before large bulges open it.**

the book bulges and separates around the staples. In the printing companies I worked for, we had a rule of thumb that stated that you could not have a saddle-stitched booklet of more than 100 pages. However, this was not really true except for premium grade 60# offset paper. Cheaper sheets, that were calendared less, were restricted to eighty sheets or so. Thinner sheets, like super-calendared 50# coated stock could go up to nearly 200 pages.

As you can see from the illustration on the next page, calendaring has a great effect upon book thickness. Another place calendaring has great effect is with mailing requirements. Post cards, for example, have to be seven thousandths of an inch thick in the States, minimum. A cheap, uncalendared 67# vellum bristol is that thick, but it can take up to an 80# cover stock to reach that thickness with a super-calendared coated sheet.

Offset or uncoated paper

All offset paper is calendared to some degree. The cheaper the paper, the less the calendaring in general. Uncoated sheets and rolls are not entirely white. They do come in pastel (think cheap and ugly looking) colors. Some even come in Day-Glo™ colors (often referred to as neon). Uncoated sheets usually have only two finishes: smooth and vellum (sometimes called antique or wove), depending on the amount of calendaring. Basically this paper is smooth and white.

However, there are major differences in price and quality. The better (#1 premium) sheets are often called opaque instead of offset. They are usually smoother, brighter, and more opaque. They have a quality feel, especially in the heavier weights like 70#, 80#, and 100#.

One thing to remember as you choose paper stock is that different technologies require different paper. We've mentioned this already. The extremely smooth, relatively nonabsorbent opaque sheets will print very poorly on many duplicators and all digital mimeographs.

Paper and media

Brightness

Along with opacity ratings, many papers now have brightness ratings (also from 0 to 100). In many cases, this is one of the most important appearance determinations. A brightness of over 90 will give your project a snap and polish that will go a long way toward causing your readers to react positively to your message. With white paper, the lower the brightness rating the cheaper the printed product looks. Plus, the brighter papers are usually easier to read and easier to print.

The thing you need to remember is that there are many situations where printing on these types of printers is extremely advantageous. With printing prices of around a half cent per sheet per color, including the cost of paper, digital mimeographs are seriously underused. For simple spot color, nonregistration jobs with no continuous tone, the quality is exceptional. In our excitement over the top end of things, we tend to forget that nearly half of all printing fits this description.

500 sheets: 60# gloss coated: .75"

500 sheets: 60# matte coated: .95"

500 sheets: 60# smooth offset: 1.15"

500 sheets: 60# vellum offset: 1.30"

500 sheets: 60# hi-bulk offset: 1.56"

The approximate relative thickness of five common papers used in books.

Enamel or coated paper

Coated paper, commonly called enamel, is designed for offset lithography. Its coating is used to increase ink holdout. Holdout is the term used to describe the amount that ink soaks into the surface of the paper. The more the ink remains on the surface of the paper, the brighter the ink color and saturation. The super-premium cast coated sheets give a brightness, saturation, and clarity that nearly equals a photograph — at 10,000 to 50,000 copies per hour!

Except for very rare cases, enamel stock only comes in white. There is one premium line of highly saturated hues and another that offers a cream coated sheet, but these are very rare. Enamel, or coated stock, differs from offset in only one way — it is coated with clay! It is actually coated with the same clay body as porcelain. The clay (kaolin) is polished on with the calendaring rollers.

All enamel is calendared. The quality levels are usually determined by it. The cheapest are sheets called matte. Here the clay is thin and even the calendaring cannot give an even surface. They are still smoother than offset and have much better holdout, but they look cheap (because they are).

The next quality level is gloss and dull. Here there is quite a variation in quality. I have heard many say that dull is a cheaper grade. This may or not be true. In fact, the dull finish is added by a specially textured calendar roller. The amount of calendaring and the thickness of the clay is the same. Here is where you reach what printers call excellent quality. In truth, it is hard to beat the image quality and the feel of what is called a #2 Dull Enamel 80# or thicker.

The top of the line enamel is called cast coated. The clay is laid on so thick that it can be calendared to a mirror finish. They are also called supercalendered. These sheets are so smooth you can see your reflection in the surface. Printing firms tend to think of these papers as the best papers, but this really is not true. They are very shiny. They print process color very brightly and colorfully. But, they are just wood pulp paper. The ink color is often amazing, which can cause the reader to notice the printing more than the message about the product.

This is because the clay gives the paper great ink holdout. In other words, the ink does not soak into the surface (hardly at all), so the color is very bright and clean. Because it does not soak in, there is relatively little dot gain on the press. The problem is that the shiny stock tends to be garish, cheap-looking, and overly slick. It is hard to sell elegance and top quality on superslick stock.

There is a reason why "Slick Willie" was a nasty nickname. Slickness usually has a mechanical feel that is often associated with coverups, slick presentations, slick salesmen, and so forth. Because most cheap direct mail huckstering is done on slick paper, these associations are increasing. It is becoming increasingly difficult to convey quality, trustworthiness, reliability, and so forth with super glossy papers. (And we haven't even mentioned the readability issues in the midst of all those reflections.)

The truly top-quality papers are 100% rag or pure cotton fiber. These last for centuries without yellowing or getting brittle. They are very strong. Printing papers (except for the extremely rare and very expensive 25% to 50% cotton text) are all pure wood pulp. This means that the papers are relatively limp. They tear easily, plus the surface cracks when folded (especially across the grain), unless it is scored first.

pH: acid and alkaline fillers

Wood pulp papers are extremely susceptible to yellowing and brittleness when traditional fillers are used. These fillers were typically materials such as rosin (the residue from turpentine production). Rosin is very acidic. Most of the great libraries of the world are in serious trouble because the acidic, wood-pulp papers used in books are falling apart before they can be put on microfiche. The most recent solution (beginning in the 1970s) has been to use calcium carbonate (think TUMS®) for filler. This is a high pH material used to make papers that are normally called alkaline.

The paper mills are claiming that alkaline papers will last about 200 years. That is certainly better than the twenty to forty years for traditional wood pulp sheets. (Of course, there is no alkaline paper over forty years old, yet.) Regardless, alkaline paper still does not come close to the quality of 100% rag stock. Wood pulp sheets do print beautifully, however. Plus, most printing is trashed within a month of production.

Text papers

However, we haven't even touched my favorite category of paper — text. The text grades have the most fashionable colors, the best textures, the richest feel and look. It is uncalendared, so it works beautifully for embossing and foil stamping (especially in the companion cover weights). It is quite a bit more expensive, but it is well worth it. Text sheets are the only papers that come in the rich dark blues, hunter greens, maroons, blacks, and so forth. Many of them look as rich as the finest fabric. In most cases, for short runs, a rich text paper costs less and looks better than a second spot color of ink. If you need to imply top quality, excellent service, and reliability, you really need to use text papers.

Paper and media

Counterfeiting

One of the strange things you need to be aware of in current society is that 100% cotton paper is a controlled substance. Paper distributors have to list sales here almost as strictly as pharmacists have to list narcotics. If you purchase a large amount of cotton paper, the Treasury agents will be watching you. With modern printing technology, counterfeiting has become a real problem worldwide. This is the reason for our new *Monopoly* money. It is filled with printing techniques designed to thwart thieves.

... for short runs, a rich text paper costs less and looks better than a second spot color of ink.

In many cases, the best way to win your way into the reader's mind is with the rich look and comfortable feel of a text paper. Two spot colors on a beautiful, elegant, luxurious sheet of paper can have much more impact on the readers than the slap-in-the-face, amazing four-color process color of a cast coated sheet. It also costs less to print and holds up better to the wear and tear of busy schedules.

Heavyweight companions: cover stock

Virtually all the papers mentioned so far come in companion cover weights. This is paper that has the same color, the same texture, the same fiber content, and the same look, but is much thicker and heavier. One way to get an idea of the difference is to make a basis weight comparison; 65# cover, about the lightest cover stock worthy of the name, is roughly equal to 120# printing paper or 48# office stock. It would seem to make sense to use these weights, to help us understand. However, cover stock uses a different basis size (20x26).

This basis size allows for many things needed by cover stock. Because an eighth sheet of 26x40 is 10x13, there is plenty of room for the tabs, spines, and full bleeds often found on covers. It probably wasn't planned that way, however. Little seems to have been planned in the entire paper industry. Most developments simply seemed to happen, followed by codification into rather rigid usage.

SHEET SIZES

All printing papers in the United States are loosely based on the 8.5x11 module used by the American business community. European papers are all metric with sizes like A3, B4, and so forth. The metric sheet sizes have a different proportion. Obviously, care must be taken when comparing the two different sizing systems.

In America, we have an aberration known as legal size. 8.5x14 paper is only available in the lowest-quality papers. In fact, when a client demands that you design something for the 8.5x14 format, the first thing you should do is determine if this is a real need. It is possible that the client is ordering a template to be printed out on the laser printer in their office. Many laser printers cannot print anything larger than legal size.

Even with legitimate use, legal size stock is always a waste of money because 8.5x14 does not cut well out of any parent sheet based on the letter sized module. The standard parent sizes of 23x35, 25x38, and 26x40 only allow you to cut out four legal-sized pieces with a lot of waste. What you are really doing is cutting each legal size sheet out of an 11x17 (tabloid) piece of paper.

The legal size papers commonly available are the specially sheeted dual purpose stock used in copiers. It is given a weight of 20/50# because even the paper companies know that this garbage is neither fish nor fowl. It is only available in the cheapest wood pulp grades and the basic obnoxious pastel colors (with a few poorly done neons tossed into the mix). Is it an office stock with sizing equal on both sides and filler added – or is it printing paper with slightly stronger fibers? The term bastard comes to mind for this unsightly union.

Cover sheet thicknesses

One unusual practice is that cover stock is often sold by the point. There is 8-point cover, 10-point cover, 12-point cover, and so on. Here a point is not a twelfth of a pica. Instead, it is called caliper, stands for a thousandth of an inch, and is measured with a micrometer. This is a place to exercise care. Mailing requirements, for example, state that postcards must be between 7 and 9.5 points thick.

Some papers are much bulkier than others, so weight does not matter much here. Often some of the very cheap cover papers like vellum bristol or index are left uncompressed or use bulky fillers so they reach the caliper needed for postcards.

What counts is the calendaring. The more a paper is calendered the thinner it is, as you saw in the page thickness illustration. An uncalendared sheet like text will be more than twice as thick as gloss coated with the same basis weight. If you do not know how thick a sheet is, look in the paper supplier's catalog. Caliper is usually found in the paper listings right below the name of the paper. If there is any question, or if there seem to be too many choices, call your paper service rep and ask him.

Planning for final thickness is often one of the considerations for the designer. It affects the thickness of the spine on perfect-bound books; the legal stock for postcards; the maximum number of pages for saddle-stitched booklets; and so on. It is usually a simple matter of picking a paper and calling the paper house for a dummy. Most suppliers are happy to supply a folded dummy or the paper to make one (knowing that if it works, they have a sale). Sometimes the paper is sent to the bindery to make the dummy.

PICKING THE PAPER IS IMPORTANT

Paper is often extremely important for small (short-run) jobs. On long runs, paper becomes one of the major expenses. For short runs, paper is often a negligible cost. On huge long-run jobs, setup charges (which include design and artwork) become ignorable. A $5,000 artwork charge means nothing on a $1 million job in which the paper costs might be as high as $750,000. On small jobs (runs of 2,000 or less), setup charges become the dominant factor. For a typical short-run brochure, the artwork could cost $500, the stripping and plates cost $500, the presswork cost $150, and the paper be only $25 or $35.

On these little jobs, going to the most expensive paper on the market would triple the paper cost, but add only 5 percent or so to the overall cost. In the two preceding examples, the short-run case

Digital paper

You need to exercise care when purchasing digital paper, whatever that means. Inkjet papers commonly have plastic sizing that will melt in laser printers. Coated stock must be designed for laser printers or the clay can clog your toner cartridge with just one print. That being said, many of the common offset papers work wonderfully as do many of the text sheets. The only real problem is found with color laser printers. Here the toner is laid on so thick that it may chip off.

adds another $50. In the large job, we would be looking at a $1.5 million increase. For short runs, paper quality is a powerful tool to use for conveying quality.

The difference between a ream of the cheapest bond and the best, 100% cotton bond is around $30. Top-quality text paper is about halfway between. If you are printing only one ream, each additional color of ink will probably cost almost $100 in production costs at a normal commercial printer, and every additional hour of design or image assembly time adds at least $50 plus materials.

 TIP: The smoother text papers print beautifully in many laser printers. With their softness, the shiny areas caused by the hot rollers melting the plastic toner onto the sheet of paper are greatly minimized. The appearance of the project takes a giant leap with these papers. However, care must be taken with color laser printers (see sidebar on opposite page).

*For short run projects,
paper quality is the cheapest option
in quality improvement.*

Even on longer runs, paper choice is critical. Glossy paper is often perceived as cheap because of all the newsstand magazines that use it. Simply going to a dull sheet can greatly increase the perception of quality. Often, for that top-quality image, two-color PMS on a top-grade text works much better than process on cheap coated. In addition, it often costs less.

 INFO: In general, any project needing less than 2,000 sheets of paper is considered short run (unless there are many pages). Projects like these make up half of all jobs printed, according to Frank Romano's *Pocket Guide to Digital Prepress*, Delmar, 1996. That percentage has gone up substantially since then as more and more printing moves into the office. Text papers can help, at relatively no cost, to greatly improve the appearance and quality of your projects.

One of your first, and most important, choices is the paper you will use. It not only sets the tone for the message you are trying to convey to the readers for every piece you design. It also is an important part of your general style of design. Your paper choices provide the environment of your design.

A DIFFERENT WORLD:
THE WORLD WIDE WEB

This is where many designers with a print history will begin having a rough time. On the World Wide Web, we are entering a world of coarse, crude graphics, with little layout control, no color calibration, and no output control. However, like all design problems, this is just another problem to be dealt with. There is hope. Some of the new software, like Dreamweaver and GoLive, promise layout control, but it is still dependent on the abilities and defaults of the individual browser that is reading the site.

The software only changes a little

The best software applications for Web graphic creation are still FreeHand, Illustrator, and Photoshop. FireWorks and ImageReady are more specialized, adding powerful file-size reduction capabilities. Flash offers new and powerful animation abilities, but the download times are still very long. Surely you can recognize that we are still talking about bitmap and PostScript illustration programs. Graphic communication is about using graphics to communicate, and the FreeHand/Illustrator/Photoshop combination is the best no matter what the medium.

This is the primary reason why Web site design and creation are still dominated by desktop publishers. It is basically the same skill set. The drawing and creative skills are almost identical, compromised only by the limitations of the formats used. The layout and design techniques and skills are still largely the same.

The conceptual difference is the interactivity

The main thing to remember is that Web design is conceptually different. James Mohler and Jon Duff in their book, *Designing Interactive Websites*, make a great deal about nonlinear design. Their ideas are very sound, but this is really nothing new when you consider almanacs, encyclopedias, reference books, and so forth.

The basic difference is the interactivity of the Web as a whole. Our rides through cyberspace are all individual searches for content. In fact, due to the present bandwidth restrictions, it may be fairly said that content is at least as important on the Web as in print.

So, exactly like all of the things we have been talking about, the important thing is to determine what the surfer is looking for when they come to your site. Why are they there? You need to meet their needs quickly and efficiently. Unless you are selling games or the like, most of the visitors to your clients' Websites are looking for solid data about the products or services offered by your client – easily, quickly, and efficiently.

InDesign is not a primary Web design tool

The reason that the Web has not been mentioned much in this book is plain. InDesign is not the program to use. For Website design and creation you need Dreamweaver or GoLive. In fact, you can do as I do and meet all of your Web design needs very easily with PageMill. However, a couple of words are in order for this chapter where we are talking about substrates and media used in digital publishing. For the truth is that you will regularly be asked to make a Web version of your InDesign documents.

InDesign's HTML capabilities

The chapter on HTML in InDesign's User Manual looks very

impressive. However, I wouldn't get too excited. As with all page creation on the Web, many rather harsh realities need to be considered. First of all, the completely graphic look of many contemporary designers does not translate well to the Web.

If you truly need to retain the exact look and feel of your InDesign documents, the only true solution is PDF. Taking into account the fact that almost all reading of Web sites is done from printed copies, PDFs are really not a bad solution (except for the file-size load placed on your server). You do need to warn the surfer about the file size and the approximate download times.

If you are designing for an in-house service or intranet, PDFs work exceptionally well. Over an EtherNet connection, PDFs download quickly, print beautifully, and can be just as internally interactive as any Web site.

For traditional Web sites (now there's a silly concept), you will almost always have to rearrange your documents rather radically. On the Web, reading is done in very short bursts. When the needed data is reached, the first reaction is to print the page. All of the other pages need to be clear and concise, offering all the linkage options suggested by the content, so the surfer can arrive at that needed data as quickly and efficiently as possible.

So, what I am saying is this: it is often best to design your documents for print first because of the far higher resolution and typography requirements. You can always dumb down your pages for the Web. However, to make a truly usable Web site, you will need to spend a lot of time designing the site structure, and it will normally be radically different from your print documents.

Even though InDesign can export its documents into HTML pages that look much like their printed version, by the use of cascading styles sheets, you are far better off to think of the conversion as a much more fundamental change. Simply exporting that gorgeous brochure using Cascading Style Sheets (CSS) will usually result in a nonfunctional (albeit beautiful) Web page or site.

LIMITED BY THE ENVIRONMENT

First of all, the Web is severely limited by its output device – the monitor. Although it is true that the Web looks better on high-resolution monitors, less than a third use them at this time. Even if high-res monitors are available, the graphics are still limited to 72 to 96 dpi. Most people use 800x600 pixel monitors, although there are still nearly 20 percent using 640x480. The most recent figures I have seen suggest that even though 800x600 are becoming the norm, the high resolution portion is only growing slowly from a quarter to a third.

Beyond low resolution is the problem of color depth, or the ability of the monitor to display enough colors to satisfy the designer's desires. The figures I saw yesterday show that nearly half of the monitors can only produce 16-bit, with more than 25 percent at 8-bit and around 20 percent with 24-bit. To make sure you've got it, 80 percent of monitors are less than 24-bit. Think about that the next time you drop in that exquisite little 24-bit JPEG.

If your client's customers are mostly graphic designers or digital gamesters, then you can almost count on resolutions of at least 800x600 with 24-bit depth. If those customers are small business owners, you'd better design for 640x480 and 8-bit. Don't be suckered by thinking that rural areas or small towns have lesser equipment. In reality, they often have better and newer hardware. However, the subtlety we take for granted in print is simply not available on the Web.

Platform differences with monitors

On the Web, you have to be cognizant of the vast differences between PC and Mac. It sounds like a simple difference. PC monitors use a gamma of 2.2, and Macs use a gamma of 1.8. To translate the gammas just mentioned. Mac monitors are much brighter, and usually much higher resolution. Images created on a high-res Mac, that look great there, often look very dark and dingy on a PC, not to mention that they look huge. Images created on a PC, that look fine there, are often far too light, with all the highlights blown out; often they are also much too small. This tends to be true, even when you set a Mac's gamma at 2.2 to try and compensate.

This is also true of type. On my high-res monitors, I use 14-point type or larger to make it legible on the screen. The type looks absolutely huge on a PC. This is also why many Web sites created on a PC are completely unreadable on a Mac, because the type is too small to be read, especially if it uses small, light type on a dark or graphic background.

This is probably the place to mention all those who surf with the graphics turned off. In mid-1999, surveys said that there were somewhere between 15 percent and 30 percent of surfers who browse with the graphics turned off. This was largely because of the speed of their connection. We have to remember that the average modem is still 28.8. In fact, virtually all of us who access the Web over a phone line are limited to that speed by the phone line. However, many surf with graphics off because everything they are looking for is in the words anyway.

Pretty depressing, huh? Actually, it's not that bad.

This is an environment where color has no penalty, you can always work in color at no extra cost. Although we are not talking about the impact of process color on cast-coated stock with photos popping off the page, highlit by gloss varnish on a dull varnish background, the color available is good enough to get the reader's attention — 256 colors are definitely better than black and a spot color. All we have to do is design within the medium's capabilities. Careful attention to detail still provides excellence of design. Don't fuss about the limitations. Design within the medium.

Color on the Web

The major thing to remember is all that you have learned about color in print. Color still lessens contrast. A limited color palette is essential to effective communication. The 216 Websafe colors give you more than enough colors to work with.

However, the same things cause problems online. Colored type on a colored background is harder to read *always*. Because of all the color, available so easily, you really need to exercise restraint.

Paper and media

Backgrounds

As we move into a discussion of Web design, one of the major problems is those exquisite background images. In truth, they have become a severe problem with printed materials also. To state it plainly, **BACKGROUND IMAGES ALWAYS MAKE THE COPY HARDER TO READ** — much harder to read. This is true for both print and Web. As reading becomes a rarer skill in our video culture, you should be careful that you don't eliminate your readership by cluttering up the type with that background that may be pretty, but most certainly reduces contrast and makes those important words illegible.

The limiting factor is bandwidth!

This real problem is actually far worse than the limited palette and low resolution. As I mentioned, the average surfer has a 28.8 to 56 kilobit modem. Normal phone connections max out between 3K and 8K per second. Even the 56 kilobit standard is glacially slow when normal color images are dozens of megabytes in size. At 28.8 kilobits (which is well under 4K per second), a 10 MB graphic would take 42½ minutes — minimum (if there is not a break in communication that requires you to start over).

In general, modem connections over phone lines are slow, no matter what hype sold you your particular modem. DSL and cable are not real solutions. All Web traffic ends up on phone lines, at this point. When we reach small satellite transceivers, then we can talk about true bandwidth change.

Download times

Surveys often state that the average surfer cancels out and moves on if the entire page takes more than 30 seconds to appear. I have read articles that suggest anything over 10 seconds is a problem. An informal study of my students indicates that 15 seconds is a practical limit. This means that the entire page must be under 45K (though many agree with me that under 30K is much wiser). Even at the community college where I teach (where we have a T-1 line on an EtherNet network), I consider myself fortunate if I can download at 20K per second. The norm for off-campus sites is still 3K per second or less, even on this very fast network.

Of course, there are always the storied cable modems and even satellite modems. I'm sure you have one — right! I know something of that ilk will probably come in the next decade, but we don't know for sure what it look like or work like *yet*. So the sum of the limitations is that your Web graphics have to be 72 dpi, usually 8-bit, and always under 30K (3K is obviously far superior).

A reality check

Please remember that, outside our community of designers, the average monitor is still 16-bit or less. Many monitors at poorer schools and smaller businesses are still 4-bit. All of those gorgeous, too large, Web graphics crammed into the sixteen colors available is a sorry sight. JPEGs viewed in 8-bit are still severely compromised. Be aware of your viewers!

Those of us in the design community tend to forget how limited the average business PC is. Remember, the Mac is designed by graphic designers for graphic designers and the PC is designed to be cheap. Always check out your designs on both platforms, and as many different browsers as you can.

System color variances: Websafe color

The final platform difference we need to discuss is commonly seen when using GIFs. GIFs use indexed color (8-bit or less). Both PC and Mac have a standard set of 256 system colors (8-bit). Of course they are different sets. Actually, there are 216 common colors in the two different systems. This is the fabled Websafe color palette. Don't get too excited!

Much has been made of using the Websafe palette. In my humble opinion, it is simply more of that anal-retentive nitpicking commonly found in designers who think that the perfect color/design/layout really matters. Basically, *Websafe* is an oxymoronic concept. It is barely possible to have a calibrated PC monitor, so you have no idea what the colors are going to look like anyway. The real solution is not a Web *safe* color palette, but clean, crisp design that looks good no matter how the colors are modified. The concern for dithering is more of the same. Design your graphics so dithering doesn't matter.

Software limitations are simply part of the problems we have to solve as designers. Design is problem solving. Think of what bridges would look like if we had a material that was so strong that a half-inch-thick plate could span a mile while carrying a full load of cars and trucks.

Your task is not to fight reality, but to use available capabilities to create beautiful solutions that communicate clearly to the selected readership.

Some suggested production procedures

First of all, my suggestion for graphic creation on the Web is to work from FreeHand or Illustrator. The key to small, easy-to-read, functional graphics is that they be clear and communicate clearly. One of the major tests of your design is that your pages download in less than 10 seconds on a 28.8 modem over a regular phone line, so it is imperative that you use no graphics without a good reason. When you use a graphic for a good reason, it has to be **SMALL** (in bytes).

The result of this is that many, or most, of your graphics will be words or will contain words. Photoshop is terrible with type, unless it is very large and high-res. Even with Photoshop 5, and its much vaunted type layers, type is clumsy at best. In print, most know that PostScript illustration is the only real solution for powerful type manipulation. If you don't know that yet, at least now you know why you are always outproduced.

In addition, Photoshop is a lousy drawing program. It is not designed for, or meant for, drawing. I know many of you use Photoshop as your primary illustration program. However, it is better used as an image manipulation program that deals with scans and rasterizes original art from PostScript illustration at specific sizes. It cannot do composite paths, complicated blends, or most of the other path combination capabilities we take for granted in FreeHand and Illustrator.

However, it is necessary for adjusting your graphics to the smallest size after they are created. Now that ImageReady is an integral part of Photoshop, all of us have all the tools we need to make superior, and very effective graphics. The new lossy GIFs are a real help. When combined color depth and dithering percentages, wonderful GIFs are easy.

Paper and media

Reversed type

Although it is true that presentation graphics using projected light (like the Web images on your monitor) can be easier to read as light-colored type on a dark background, this is only true at large point sizes with simple and clear fonts. Adding to the problem on the Web is that all of that pretty type shows up very poorly when they print it out to read on paper. The background color often does not print, leaving you with white type on white paper. It's enough to give your client heart failure.

Keeping the high-res needed for print

If you start in PostScript illustration, you'll have a high-resolution graphic available for the conversion. They are actually more powerful, in many ways, than the specialized Web tools which are totally incapable of being used for anything other than the Web. Most designers who do only Web design have simply never paid the money necessary to get the good tools that are a normal part of our graphic design experience. Without the graphic knowledge we have been covering in this book, they cannot come close to the communication effectiveness we have available with the software we use.

Do not even try to mimic your incredible InDesign layout on the Web. It is a different medium. Personally, I usually simply copy and paste the copy out of the print documents into the WYSIWYG Web editor being used. It does save the typing time, but its main advantage is the elimination of formatting. I want to make sure that I have eliminated all formatting that might cloud my view toward clear communication on the Web.

I find that I commonly have to eliminate half of my print copy or more. What we see as terse in print becomes verbose online. When all of the copy is necessary, I am leaning more and more toward PDF delivery. I know they are going to print out that copy to read regardless. The new printing quality Flash content may offer some solution, but then that is pure heresy in a book on Adobe software, isn't it?

A little more reality

At this point, we are still governed by phone lines and hemmed in by AOL. We have to design for our customers. At this point, the only excuse for the fancy stuff would be if our customers are young gamers or seekers of entertainment (as opposed to data). Beyond that, focusing on fancy graphics, wild animations, rollovers, full-page imagemaps, and the rest really misses the point entirely. Most of the Web sites that are done professionally (for money) are greatly inhibited by extraneous graphics and a cluttered interface. You've only got a few seconds to keep them on your site.

The best thing I have ever read about the Web was on one of the Web design sites, and it went something like this:

People do not come to your site to see the killer Web graphics — they come for easily accessible information.

Your customers (or your clients' customers) are not looking for amazing digital dances to amuse and pass the time. They want to know what you are offering, why they need it, and how to get it. The fancy stuff does not help. **IT IRRITATES!** It's the same reason why most of your printed projects are still (and will remain) black and white. In printing, process color is the fancy stuff, and even process color is much easier to justify than that incredible animation with the embedded row of changing interactive buttons where you have to wait seconds for each new image to appear (assuming the screen is not blank while waiting).

At school, as I mentioned, I am running a fast G3, with 128 MB RAM, on a 100BaseT WAN, to a T-1 line, and I still find the fancy stuff merely mildly irritating (entertainment at best). There are many pages, even with this exceptionally fast access, where pages take so long to download that I simply click off in disgust. Even Yahoo's Home Page was like that for a long time. Imagine how a surfer feels on a Quadra or 486, with 16 MB RAM, using a 28.8 modem through AOL. Heck, maybe your customers even live in rural areas where good phone lines are a luxury that hasn't arrived yet.

Always preview your site!

I clearly remember my shock the first time I saw my Web site at school on a computer in one of the PC labs upstairs. It was huge, very dark, and in Times New Roman. That original home page didn't even look like the clean, bright page set in Palatino that I had designed on my screen. I ended up redesigning quite a bit of the page, making the logos and the type smaller, changing the fonts used. This is a much larger problem than you might think.

The first major differences are found in the two opposing operating systems themselves. We have already mentioned that the Microsoft and Mac system palettes are different, with only 213 common colors. A much more important difference is the monitors used. As is true in most things PC, the operative word is cheap. Whenever you have a product and an entire industry that is primarily governed by price concerns, you have a problem. PC purchasers complain if a computer costs more than $2,000, in fact, many now expect them to cost less than $500. This is absurd!

Even with a PC, to get a computer that will do what we need it to do as graphic designers will cost $3,000 or more. You cannot even seriously run a PC before you buy several cards and peripherals that do not come with the machine as standard equipment. However, the real problem here, as far as viewing your marvelously designed site on the Web is concerned, is that any monitor over $500 is considered ridiculously expensive.

Finally, we have the differences in browsers. We assume that there are only two: Explorer or Communicator. But already you can see the problem. About 80 percent have Explorer available. AOL uses a limited Explorer-based browser and they are one of the largest sources of surfers. More than that we have the different version numbers. All of the latest bells and whistles assume that you are using a Version 4.5 browser or better. Only Y2K got the average up to 4.0. Both browsers and all of the different versions of those two browsers show pages differently; check out as many as you can when proofing your Web sites.

In addition, there are many more browser options. I am not just talking about all of the nongraphic interfaces found on many of the bureaucratic systems. There are also several companies eagerly awaiting the alleged Microsoft breakup. I won't even speculate here.

HOW TO COMMUNICATE ONLINE

Web sites are unique bits of graphic communication. On the one hand, they are very cold, uninvolved, impersonal assemblages of digital data. For pixel pushers like us, they are great fun and global on top of that. Some may push the Mac as friendly, but it is not alive and cannot relate to us. The same is true of the Internet, that incomprehensibly vast and intertwined network of most of the computers on Earth. On the other hand, our Web sites reach our customers on a very personal level in a quiet time, where they are isolated within their computer environment, often in the apparent safety of their bedroom, den, living room, or office. Like a Mac, the Web seems friendly, responding easily to our command. More than that, it is a communication medium.

What this means in practical terms is that the Web is a strange type of uniquely personal communication. I've written this book in first person, but none of you really think you are communicating with me. However, if you go to my Web site, find out where I am coming from, and we start an email dialogue, we can develop a pretty tight relationship relatively quickly.

... the Web is a strange type of uniquely personal communication.

In my commercial online school, I have students from all over the world. The farthest one to register, so far, is from the North Island of New Zealand, but I've had many inquiries from most of Asia, all over Europe (especially Italy, for some reason), and the Middle East. Normally, I don't even find out where they are from until we have talked to each other several times. It really does not matter at all. The only differences I have noticed with my student in New Zealand are: their year is very different, being south of the equator; they use metric (but most do that); they hyphenate words differently; and they use plural verbs with companies. Those small differences are merely enough to make things fun.

The other interesting fact is that I know her better than I do most of my students who are in my classroom for a few semesters. The Web seems to promote that. It seems to have something to do with the safety of distance and the relative anonymity of computer-to-computer communication.

The visitors to sites you design really need to touch a human there. They want to know names, email addresses, history, background, and so forth. One of the original successful sites (now morphed into deadlock.com) was for a small hotel in London.

It was phenomenally successful via the simple technique of letting prospective guests wander through the hotel in their imagination. If they wondered about meals, there were pictures, menus, a picture of the cook and her background. The designer (who was then in charge of marketing for this little side-street hotel) said he regularly got bookings from people who made statements like, "I've been wandering around your site for nearly two hours now, having a marvelous time, I guess I'll book a room." The last time I heard, nearly 75 percent of their bookings were coming from the Web site. How did he do that?

The answer is actually very simple. First of all, his writing style is cheerful, friendly, unpretentious, and believable. This is very important. However, more than that, he has a real gift of letting a surfer answer any question he or she might have. Upon visiting the site, you are left with the feeling that the hotel really cares for you, that they genuinely want you to have a wonderful experience staying with them.

The friendliness, openness, and genuine trustworthiness of your site are primary!

This needs to be your focus in Web design. Seems like normal stuff for any type of graphic design, doesn't it? Just as with print, if the surfer reacts consciously to the neat graphics and your incredible design, you've lost him as your client. The best designs are not only invisible, they should also enable the surfer to feel like she can go anywhere she wants and get the answers she needs.

Button bars and communication

By now, you have noticed on the Web site for this book that the communication bars are simple tables with colored backgrounds. Some of you may have even wondered why there weren't amazingly beautiful 3D buttons to guide you on your way through the site. In fact, there are no buttons at all, because tables download like type, *and just as fast.* Not only that, they are clean and easy to understand. I am a little concerned that they are too dark for PCs, but the goal was ease of use.

"Can't I do buttons?" I can hear your whining from here. Certainly you can. But you need to think it out first. If a page is supposed to be 15K to 35K in size (and 15K is far better), then you really need to plan the button sizes accordingly. If you have seven buttons, for example, 3K each will use up almost your entire graphic allotment for the whole page!

It is possible to make one fancy button that can be used repeatedly for all communication links within your site, but that usually defeats the purpose of a button bar by making every link look the same. The argument is, "But, you only have to download them once. After that they are in cache, and show up almost instantly." That is almost true, but that first page is a killer (literally) for anyone accessing on a 14.4 modem with a weak connection. It is certainly not a good first impression for surfers, who are coming for quick, accurate, easily accessible information.

The other problem with the fancy button approach is a little more subjective. Once a person starts with the fancy buttons, it's very hard to stop. The home page at my school (http://www.tvi.cc.nm.us) has this problem. After the first page, the buttons do show up very fast.

Paper and media

TIP! Be careful when using bold styling on your type on Web sites. Bold on the Web often means what it did on the old 9-pin and 24-pin printers. The type is imaged twice, with the second image offset to the right and down a pixel. This is why bolded type on the Web is often hard to read. Simply using the paragraph style for almost everything and changing the point size will greatly improve the look of your sites with no other changes. The only appropriate use of the headline styles is to give the search engine spiders another dose of keywords. Some fonts like Georgia, Trebuchet, and the other freebies from Microsoft's typography site do bold well. You must be careful.

However, the designer couldn't stop there. Every page has large graphics unique to that page. Worse yet, after you get past those new graphics, the typography is very bad, clumsy and difficult to read.

Most of your Web design problems will be solved if you simply remember the reason for the site in the first place. If you are getting paid to design the site, the client needs to make income from it. So, you immediately go back to the same old questions.

- **What's the product?**
- **What's the message?**
- **Who's the client?**
- **Who's the reader?**
- **What does the client want the reader to do?**

With the answers to those questions, you can design a clean site, that downloads fast, is easy to understand, and is easy to negotiate. The client's readers will happily do what is desired because you will have helped them to see that the client's product is something they really need, plus it is easy to purchase, easy to remember, and/or easy to use.

Finally, typos are absolutely forbidden!

PDF multimedia

The last media use for InDesign is the interactive PDF. PDFs make marvelous CD-ROM content with easily added internal relationships including movies, sound, and internal links. In addition, PDFs work very well for presentations. The image quality is better and you can add links to any or every page as needed. In this case you can usually resample down to 72 dpi and still have much stronger graphics than are possible with Powerpoint and the other presentation competitors.

1. What do you know if you are told you will be using a 28# paper?

2. What is the main advantage of text stock for short-run projects?

3. Why is enamel stock often not a quality improvement?

4. Why do you have to be concerned about monitor gamma?

5. Describe the differences between an 80# text and 90# index?

WHERE SHOULD YOU BE BY THIS TIME?

By this time you should have earned nearly all your grade. You should be working comfortably in InDesign. In fact, the software should be ceasing to be an issue as you focus on design problems. More and more InDesign should be an extension of your design process.

DISCUSSION

You should be discussing differences in personal style with your classmates. Discuss the different papers available, which ones you really like, and why. Pick a stock for your personal letterhead that you think represents your stance best.

Talk among yourselves...

Stationery and Corporate Image

CHAPTER CONTENTS

The basic concepts and procedures necessary to produce an effective image package for a client

CHAPTER OBJECTIVES

By presenting the basic terms and production procedures, you will learn how to:

1. Design a useful letterhead
2. Organize data on a business card
3. Recognize an effective logo
4. Consider the actual usage of the image package
5. Produce an effective stationery package

LAB WORK FOR CHAPTER

- Miniskill #6, skill exams #6 and #7
- Submit finished theory exams
- Shift your focus to an effective stationery package for yourself.

Stationery and
Corporate
Image

DU PONT

BIRDS EYE

BAYER
BAYER

SERVING SALMON TO THE GREAT NORTHWEST

Eli's

YUM!

• SINCE 1879 •

Kodak

A company's stance

The earliest forms of graphic design were simple identification marks — often not so simple. The origins of what we today call the logo are found in crests, trademarks, hallmarks, and chops. All of these are identifying marks. Crests identified families. Trademarks identified the products of a particular craftsman, artisan, or designer. Hallmarks provided the seal of approval from guilds, trade unions, and authenticating organizations. Chops were the personal signature carved in stone in China and Japan where a hand-painted signature was worthless (because almost everyone was fluent enough with a brush to copy anyone else's brushmark).

These marks gradually increased in importance as it became more and more necessary to distinguish an original from the copy. Thus, logos are truly the sign and core of graphic design in our marketing economy. The entire focus of our economy is summed up in the logo: My product is better than my competitors' product. My logo reminds you of that. In addition, my corporate image gives subtle reinforcement to the strengths of my product.

Logos as the company signature

Today, the logo is one of the most important tools used to give a company a graphic presence in the world. Even though, contrary to the opinion of many, the logo is not earthshaking; it is the core of a company's style and graphic presence in the marketing community. Because we live in an economy totally governed by marketing, advertising, and promotion, this mark is foundational for a company or corporation.

Marketing has control

Things changed a great deal during the twentieth century. Graphic design to a large extent has become the core of our culture. In a marketing economy, the designer is the person who makes it all happen. We have left behind our roots as a manufacturing, farming economy. Whether that is good or bad is not the issue here. The fact is that we survive and thrive by marketing things that others make.

By the 1950s and 1960s, advertising agencies had grown incredibly powerful and transformed our entire culture. Our culture developed under market pressures. The arbitrators of our lives have increasingly been people whose job survival was based on their success in selling us items of little intrinsic value or differentiation. Everything we use is now marketed.

We have gotten sophisticated enough to reject lies and false claims; marketing must now be based on real benefits to our customers. Why should you use my product or service? Because I can better meet your needs in the following areas: price, ease of use, convenience, emotional gratification, quality, durability, or whatever the truth is for the product.

The logo has been developed into the core of a marketing strategy, the bare bones of the company or corporate image. Often it is the only consistent portion of that image. Here is the core of an image: well-defined and consistent usage. Images only work over a period of time. For this reason, they are normally not fashionable. They make a stylistic statement that the company can live with for a decade or more.

Logos only work over a period of time

We could talk a long time about logo design. In fact, I do that in my second book, *Digital Drawing*. For our purposes, in this chapter, we are going to assume that you have a logo. A logo must have certain characteristics. Does it accurately reflect the true nature of the company? It must give the company a quick, accurate statement of its core image.

Massive (and often simply obsessive) efforts toward corporate image are not our focus here. Logos often a part of million dollar corporate image and product development projects. You will find them to be a real hassle. With that amount of money at stake, the client committee members usually provide sufficient grounds for justifiable homicide.

Our focus here (and a good deal of your future business) is on the new boutique, gift shop, strip mall, construction company, television station, newsletter, photography studio, car dealership, restaurant, bar, hotel, auto parts store, drilling company, candy manufacturer, or whatever comes into your office on a given day. These people genuinely need your help to make themselves known to their clientele. They truly need a distinctive image to set them apart in the live-or-die atmosphere of the modern marketplace. They need a core strategy for their business, and they need to explain this graphically to their customers, suppliers, and financial supporters.

This is not the place or the time for cuteness or your latest graphic ego spasm. You must seriously find out who they are, what they sell, and why their company is better than their competition. Then you can help them go out and do their job by giving them an image they can be proud of, that accurately shows who they are, that answers questions instead of posing problems to their customers, suppliers, and financial supporters.

There are many books on corporate image packaging. However, in this InDesign book, our focus is on document production, in this case the corporate image documents. First the obvious: your logo and stationery package is often a meaningless waste of money unless it is part of a comprehensive plan. When beginning an image project, you must deal with these questions we are hinting at now. Your wonderfully clever ideas are a complete waste of time unless they are tied to an accurate view of the company's true image and character. More than that, the primary thing your layouts must convey is the trustworthiness of the company. Even if you are dealing with a radically fashionable boutique, you must give the customers a sense that they can trust the fashion judgment of the shop's buyers, that the clothing purchased is worth the money, and so forth.

The importance of the font

Here we truly need to look at current usage long and hard. Many designers see an image package as the place to really *strut their stuff*. This commonly assumed attitude does not serve the client well.

The normal standard is that logos, letterheads, business cards, and envelopes must be clean, clear, and businesslike. If it is true that the most important aspect of your design is the trust it engenders in your

Skill #6

PERSONAL STATIONERY

You would be wise (or maybe your instructor has already made this a high priority) to make this one of your major focuses for the next few months. You really need to get a firm grip on who you are and what you have to offer. Don't compare yourself with your wishes. Take a hard look at your competition in the marketplace. You do have a place in this industry, but it must be based on a realistic assessment of your actual gifts, talents, and abilities.

client and his customers, then it would seem obvious that classic typefaces would help. However, there is a strong tendency among designers to use the latest fashionable font for all designs in a given year. Three years later, these fonts look tired, dated, and suspect.

Now, I am not saying that typographic fashion does not have its place. What I am saying is that this place is probably not in a stationery package. Keep the fashion statements to the rest of the graphics in the marketing package. The stationery must have a certain sense of timelessness. An excellent logo should be usable for decades with only minor refinements. The stationery needs to present that logo in a stable, trustworthy package.

The uses of stationery

Judging by designs I have seen over the years, this is the major thing I need to drill into your head. As mentioned, many designers use corporate image packages to build their own agenda, which is impressing the community with their design abilities. Often forgotten in this ego spasm is the simple fact that the letterhead and envelope are used for communication in business relationships. Even business cards are used to cement relationships and to provide a reminder and reference for those relationships. Let's list some stationery uses to help us get a grasp on their design.

Stationery is used for:

1. The presentation of the company to banks, investors, and suppliers
2. The carrier for official announcements, press releases
3. Letters of reference, requests for service, and complaints about bad service
4. Cover letters, proposals, and contracts, and introductions to new clients
5. The base to build invoices, purchase orders, and official financial records

This is all pretty serious stuff. In none of these scenarios do you want a flip, fly-by-night, unreliable image. In all of these instances, you want the public, business associates, or officials to take your client seriously. Obviously, one of your major goals is to make your client believable and trustworthy in a world where many are not.

On the other hand, you definitely do not want your client portrayed as someone who doesn't care about their image. You do not want people to react like your client is still stuck back in the '20s, '40s, '60s, '70s, or even the early 1990s. This is especially true if the client's product or service is on the cutting edge. But it is also true if your client is a dry cleaner who has been in business since 1937. Old images can be transformed into a strong statement about a company's stability and reliability. But it takes careful crafting to place that antiquity into a modern frame of reference.

The need for mottoes

The nice thing about mottoes is that they can be changed with marketing needs. They can add direction to a corporate image plan while you build that stable, trustworthy image. In the case of many companies, you have to build on what has been done, adding to the good parts of its reputation and turning attention away from those aspects that seem to be counterproductive.

A motto, or a new motto, can often add an editorial slant to an existing image that can bring it into current culture. The danger, of course, is that it provides a purely editorial slant. Therefore it must be carefully approved by the client. You do not want to add a focus that doesn't fit well with the client and the sales staff. That being said, a motto can add a good deal of direction to your stationery.

Sizes and proportions

All logos should be roughly square or circular, as we discuss in *Digital Drawing*. You can deal with proportions up to two by three, vertical or horizontal. Anything beyond that is usually a problem. A long, wide logo might work on a ballpoint pen, but it will have a tough time on a keychain, as a dingbat bullet, or as an official seal.

This can be a real problem with companies that have epistles masquerading as names. Sometimes you can make a tight stack of the words in a name to convert it into a usable logo, but legibility is usually the casualty. This is especially true when the logo is reduced to its smaller sizes.

Stationery is used in many color spaces

It should be obvious by now that you are going to need several versions of your stationery. Much of this is determined by the publishing technologies used. In general, you will always need to design a black-and-white (grayscale) version, usually a spot color version, a process color version for digital printing, and increasingly an RGB version for the Web and multimedia.

This makes your color choices critical. Many now suggest that you start with the Websafe color palette to help with consistency across the different color spaces. Of course, picking colors that print the same in spot, RGB, and CMYK does greatly restrict your color choices. This is why you are getting the big bucks. We never said it was easy.

The focus of stationery is the letter. One of the key things lost by many designers is the supposedly obvious fact that a letterhead is merely the framework for the letter. Top on your list of priorities in letterhead and envelope design must be the communication itself. When you open the envelope, the first thing the reader needs to see is the company name and the personal greeting. When the letterhead is folded open, the letter and its content should be unavoidable. Everything on the page should help the reader comfortably digest the content of the letter.

Some design practicalities

The questions to ask before beginning image design are many. Because some of you have not done this yet, it seems appropriate to list some typical questions off the top of my head. This is by no means a complete list:

- What type of person is this meant to attract?
- Are there diverse groups to be attracted by the same logo?
- What am I trying to say about the company or client?
- Is there an existing organization I can tie to with the image style?
- Are any symbols with clear meaning available?

RESUME

This is obviously an extension of skill #8. Even if you plan to start your own business, or if you already have one, you need this exercise in self-examination. Think of it as an introduction, or listing of assets, for client presentations. Remember, if you can't market yourself, how can you market anyone else?

Corporate or company images really involve a great deal of self-examination. As you are searching for the proper graphic expression of your client (especially if that client is yourself), allow yourself to be brutally honest about what really matters, what the focus of the business truly is, and what the nature of the client's customers really are.

Increasingly we need accuracy in our image. The time is long past when you can truly fool the end user of your graphics. It is not at all unusual to find new company direction as the result of a serious examination like that needed for an excellent, functional image package. Conversely, a new image is often required by a new marketing thrust.

When redoing a package for this reason, be careful not to toss the baby with the bath water. Carefully retain the good aspects of the old image. I recently added a "since 1967" near the logo on my stationery. It has become one of my major selling points. That type adjustment can be a major help to your client as she revises her company image and logostyle.

A BASIC PROCEDURE

The normal starting price of an image package is about $600, and this is the very bottom end. This assumes that you can produce it in about a dozen hours or so of work. For yourself, you need to plan on spending several days on any design of this type. The creative process requires thinking time. You need to ask yourself every question you can think of (ask the client too). Then think about it. Like many of us, you might find it very helpful to keep a little sketch pad next to your bed.

As you consider your client's needs and stance, remember that you are looking for a way to stand out from the crowd. They need a uniquely defining look that will separate them from their competition. Visually jot down your ideas as they surface — quick thumbnail sketches (about the size of a thumbnail, done in a minute or two). You'll know you've seriously covered the territory when you have a dozen or so thumbnails. By then, you will be finalizing your concepts into a few solid ideas. Rough them out, either by hand or on the computer. Doing it by hand often allows the human touch to enter your designs.

Finally, scan your roughs and place them in the background as a rough guide to your final image assembly, or do the entire thing in your mind. The methodology is not important. It should only take a few hours to actually render your idea. If it takes much longer than that, you are probably being too precious and too detailed for an image package anyway. Pin them on the wall and live with them for a day or so, THEN show them to the customer.

Do not be surprised or hurt when the client picks the one you like the least. The one you like best probably has associations to a happy, but merely personal, memory. Image design is about pleasing the customer. Your layouts should make him or her proud of the company. It should feel like it fits. They must be comfortable with the image projected.

Standard usage

One of the things you quickly discover as you begin designing image packages is that people have very strong ideas about what is acceptable and what is not. These standards are what I have been calling norms. They are usage parameters that almost everyone assumes.

We have mentioned before that the only way you can keep your designs from being boring is to break at least a couple of rules in every design — and that those departures from the norms must be done intentionally and with good reason. However, this assumes that you know the normal assumptions that everyone is using. What I want to do now is give you a list of some of these norms. You will find that many of them are quite rigid.

Stationery norms

Business cards:

2"x3.5"; .25" margins on all sides; logo about an inch square; logostyle 18 to 30 point; name 8 to 11 point (often bold); title 6 to 8 point (often italic); telephone and email address 9 to 12 point (often bold); address and/or URL 6 to 8 point; motto 8 to 12 point (often italic).

Letterhead:

8.5"x11"; .75" margins or larger (unless it bleeds); logo about 75 percent of the business card; logostyle 18 to 24 point; address, URL, phone, and email address 7 to 11 point; motto 9 to 14 point (often italic); Board of Directors and/or organization membership list 6 to 8 point (often small caps) — it's very important to design the letterhead so it looks empty without a letter.

Envelopes:

#10 business (4.125"x9.5"); logo is letterhead size or smaller; logostyle 12 to 18 point; address 6 to 8 point.; phone numbers on envelopes are considered very gauche; because of printing registration problems, envelopes are often single color; commonly the logo/address block is rotated 90° at the left end of the envelope.

As you format type and lay out the documents, consciously prioritize the copy to organize it. What is the most important copy on the page (from the reader's point of view)? What is the most important copy on the page (from the client's point of view)? Often, for example, important information from the client's viewpoint is different from what the reader will choose to read.

If the executive secretary tells you that the new Web site really needs to be pushed and he wants that emphasized, this does not mean that the reader will care about the URL as they begin to answer the letter. She's reading the letter because she is involved in the content. If a reply is needed, she is looking for the phone number, snail mail address, or e-mail address. The URL may be nice, but it is not primary on a letterhead.

The important thing to keep in mind while you are prioritizing is the need for simplicity and clarity. Too many attention devices function much like the expert roundtables on CNN: that many people talking at the same time is very irritating and causes many of us to switch channels. The same is true of multitudinous subheads and specialized headers all competing for your attention on the same letterhead.

Mini#6

PRITIKAN REDESIGN

Here's a deceptively simple redesign for your normal egomaniacal creative client. When you read the instructions, I'll bet many of you actually think he gave you explicit directions. Don't be fooled!

Business card use

Even if it is true that all of those pieces of data are important, the reader needs help to sort through the chaos. Sometimes you have to arbitrarily assign priorities simply to make the piece readable. In a business card, for example, which items are most important? To understand that, you need to figure out why you keep a business card in the first place.

Is the logo important? Probably, but that is not why you keep a card. You need to be able to instantly recognize that card as belonging to the business you are looking for, but why are you looking for that card? If you are thinking clearly, you'll see that you keep the card for the phone number, e-mail address, URL, and office address, usually in that order. The most important information on the business card is the telephone number (coupled with the name of the person, so you can call them by name when they pick up the phone). The email address is increasingly important, and the Website URL might generate some sales.

The physical address is rarely why you keep a card. Once you have been there (if you ever go there), you can remember where it was. The phone number and e-mail address you need for reference. In fact, isn't the true purpose of a business card to remind you of a relationship?

Letterhead use

As mentioned many times, the letter is the focus. Often you will want a response, therefore the addresses (snail and e-mail) are primary. However, on many letterheads it is also important to show organizational affiliations, certifications, corporate officers and a lot of other visual baggage. The key is to make all this information take a decorative place in the frame around the letter.

Another major focus is taking the secretaries into consideration. If you are using an unusual, asymmetric layout, you will probably need to talk with the secretaries and design a template in their word processor with appropriate margins, so they can actually use your visual masterpiece.

Remember that a stripped down version of your letterhead will be used as the base for fax cover letters, press releases, invoices, and so forth. An outrageous layout is often very intriguing in a letter, but it is then difficult to keep things consistent for the other uses normally needed in business.

Closing thoughts

One of the important things to remember is that the stationery package is really as important as you think it is. It is the foundation upon which the marketing plan is built. It is one of the main tools used to procure financing for the company and often crucial in the early planning stages.

Because of these factors, you will regularly be asked to design the package on spec. In other words, your client will need the package to raise the money to pay you. Rather than simply say, **"DON'T DO THIS!"**, I would rather just caution you.

Remember this simple fact. If he is good enough to con a bank out of money, he may well be good enough to con you out of a free set of stationery. This is definitely a contract you want to get in writing. This is especially true for those who will promise a percent of the profits. You may genuinely believe that you are getting in on the ground floor of a good thing. That may even be true, but get it in writing —signed and notarized. This is especially true if the prospective client is a friend. Dealing with friends often clouds judgment. Do anything you like, but don't get angry if it doesn't pan out. About 90 percent of all startups fail to make it into reality.

However, they make marvelous portfolio pieces to build your reputation!

KNOWLEDGE RETENTION

1. What is the purpose of a letterhead?

2. Why must logos be graphically simple and easily printable?

3. Why are image packages more important in the 21ST century?

4. What needs to be expressed by your personal stationery?

5. Why is a corporate image much more than just a dynamite logo?

WHERE SHOULD YOU BE BY THIS TIME?

You should be actively thinking about and planning for your career in graphic design and/or publishing. If you are going to be seeking employment, what type of company will you be searching for? If you are going to strike out on your own, or with a partner, what creative assets are you focusing on? Are your ideas based on reality or wishful thinking?

DISCUSSION

By now, there is hope that you have made friends and entered into a network of creative resources. If not, get busy!

Talk among yourselves...

15

Brochures and Product Sheets

CHAPTER CONTENTS

Producing the materials to markets specific products and services

CONCEPTS

1. **Rack brochure**

2. **Product sheet**

3. **Catalog**

4. **Response brochure**

CHAPTER OBJECTIVES

By presenting the basic terms and production procedures, you will learn how to:

1. Develop a product sheet
2. Design an effective rack brochure
3. Develop an effective response brochure
4. Discuss what is necessary in a product sheet
5. Explain the different situations where a brochure is used

LAB WORK FOR CHAPTER

- Miniskill #7, and skill exams #8
- Submit finished theory exams
- Produce an effective stationery package for yourself

Outside and first splash hype

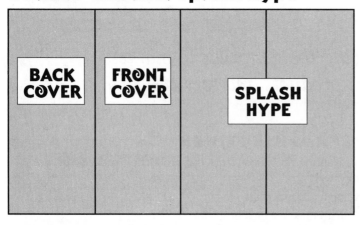

Inside with major pursuasion copy

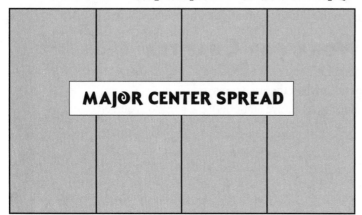

This fold
allows you
to control
how the reader
opens the brochure.

Layout is key to a functioning brochure or product sheet!

Selling the Company's products and services

Although many of you think we have already covered this area by talking about corporate image and logos in Chapter 13, we've never even mentioned marketing products, output, and services of the company. Corporate or company image is more concerned with projecting stability and trustworthiness to entities like banks and investors when looking for financing or selling stock.

When we turn to creating a brochure, your concern becomes much more focused. The question becomes, *"How can I show the reader the genuine benefits of this product or service in a manner that will convince him or her that it is in his or her best interest to purchase and use it?"*

Here we get back the basic statement of design covered in Chapter 10. Every project you create for a client has a message about a product for a client to a reader to get them to do something. These five parts of your design must be covered, and they are your primary concern. Let's review the idea of product.

The product

It is very important to figure out what you are selling – what you are really selling. There are times when your product has no real distinctiveness so you have to sell something intangible. For example, Pontiac has nothing really unique functionally or technologically, so they sell excitement. Automobiles, in general, are virtually identical in technology. As a result they have to sell other attributes. Volvo sold safety for years. Lexus sells the best quality. So, in a very real way, your product is the excitement you experience driving this car, or the admiring glances of the parking valet.

A real benefit

This brings up the first thing we must determine about the product we are selling. Long gone are the days when you could fool the audience. Now that we have had a society controlled by marketing for somewhere between fifty and a hundred years, the readership has gotten remarkably sophisticated. If you lie to the reader, he or she may try your product once. However, once they realize the lie, the resultant negative advertising will have a major, long-lasting effect on your client's profitability.

The first thing you must do to market a product (before you design anything) is list the true benefits. It may be stronger, faster, more convenient, longer lasting, better smelling, more reliable, or a host of other real benefits. Those cute little iMacs really don't sell so well because of the color. They are very fast, reliable, easy to use, convenient, and cheap with all of the production advantages of the MacOS. On top of all that, many people think they look "cool"! There is no one definitive advantage, in this case, it's the entire package.

Negative advertising

One of the major things to remember as you help your client make marketing plans is the impact of word-of-mouth advertising. Here is the standard proverb. "If you please a customer they will tell a couple of friends. If you treat them badly, they will tell forty people – friends, acquaintances, and strangers."

Here's the real point: in an age where everyone is depersonalized and reduced to a number or statistic, good service and the experience of personal relationship will do more than almost anything to increase sales and improve customer relations. This is true even for cut-rate discount stores. It's the key to Walmart's success, for example (think greeters at the door). It's really very simple.

You have to deliver what you promise!

You cannot afford for your client to have one disgruntled customer who is your fault. A dozen angry customers can ruin the entire marketing campaign. A promised benefit that is not delivered can put your client out of business. You must tell the truth about the product!

Effective communication is the basis of your message to the reader.

The true purpose of advertising is to make potential and existing customers aware of the new solution or opportunity your client's product supplies or offers. It is the communication of valued information. There is a good reason why this industry is often called graphic communication. Communication is the basis of your message to the reader.

The good news

By now, you are certainly aware of my opinion that most color usage by graphic designers is mere creative masturbation — designers trying to get themselves off with no thought to anyone else. However, in the brochure, more than anywhere except posters, shining, fancy design is often a real plus. There is still no excuse for splashy graphics that do not communicate. But a brochure is where you need to grab the reader's eye to get him or her to pick it up and read the message you have so carefully crafted.

At this point, we need to have a few words about the effectiveness of color and its use. One of the things about brochures is they usually have a larger budget than most everyday projects. They are usually one of the major products used in a new marketing campaign. As a result, you are almost always doing at least two-color and often process color. In fact, brochures are often one of the few places where the need for hi-fi color can be demonstrated. Brochures are colorful, even if they are black and white. This is where you go out of your way to show off the client and her company in the best possible light.

However, most people have no clue about the use of color. It is seen as a fashion statement, or sheer designer fun. There are many false, even stupid, assumptions about the use of color. The primary one is probably, "Let's punch it up with a little color!" The stupidity continues when the designer is so titillated by the color schemes that all direction is lost. The fact that any color reduces contrast is completely forgotten. The result is often more like fine art than any attempt at communication.

Brochures and product sheets

The need for advertising

One of those strange truths, well hidden in advertising and design books, must be understood. If you are forced to advertise to survive, your product is in severe trouble. For advertising to work, you must be sharing the good news about a product that is of genuine benefit to the reader. If you find yourself struggling to identify some real benefits to the product you are trying to help market, you should be planning on how you are going to replace the income when your client goes out of business.

ANY COLOR REDUCES CONTRAST! Notice that I did not say "reduces impact." However, you need to be clear that any color combination has less contrast than black and white. Extreme care must be used with color to enable communication. Countless color brochures are completely illegible because they lack sufficient color contrast. As a result, leading the reader's eye from the headline benefit statement to sales closer becomes impossible.

Using color to your advantage

To do this we need to look again at what we are trying to do with this brochure. We will get into layout design, tips and tricks in a bit. For now let's be more basic. What is our goal? I would suggest that it is something like this. You want the reader to see your cover design. You want to pique her interest enough so she'll pick it up.

You want her reaction to be, *"This looks interesting. I could really use ..."* You want her to open the brochure, discover a product or service that she can really use, decide to purchase that product or service, and do it. At the very least you need her to contact the company for follow-up information. That's a lot of work for a little piece of paper.

Color can really help. A color accent needs to be placed at every place where you need the reader's eye to stop, in chronological order. How do you determine those locations? For that answer, let's go to Japanese calligraphy.

TIP: For the Japanese (and the Chinese), calligraphy is the highest art form. As a result, they have studied and learned how to generate effective line structures that are beautiful and functional. Even the splashiest, loosest character is readable because of this principle I want you to learn now. The basic rule is simple: accent the beginning, the end, and every important transition point. As you can see below left, the energy of the word Jump comes from the emphasis on these places in the word.

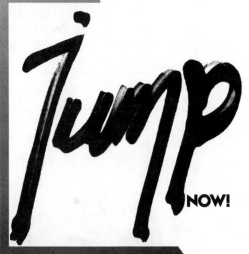

How can you resist ending up at the word "NOW!"? The answer is simple, you cannot.

So how does that apply to color in brochure design? Simply put – hit the cover and the close as hard as you dare. These are the important start and end of a brochure design. Keep color at a minimum throughout the rest of the brochure except to solidly pick out key transition points in the copy as the reader is led through the design by your layout. The reader's eye should be grabbed and dragged inside the copy by the cover. The clear and concise points about the real benefits of the product or service lead irresistibly to the obvious conclusion that this is a product or service that is needed, wanted, and cost effective. The entire visual journey is concluded with an easy and convenient method (or methods) to purchase the product – Web site URL, 800 number, pager number, snail mail address, map, coupon, or whatever devices you are using for this particular brochure promotion. You must give them a way to respond.

Brochures and product sheets

There are many things that can be said about any set of design rules, and there are countless rules. But let's narrow them down to seven key items, at this point:

- **Limit your product**

  You should have a brochure for every product, or at least every product line or group. If you dilute your brochure by having too many products, you end up with a general company brochure or a small catalog that promotes the company. This may be what you need, but recognize what you are doing — and do it on purpose.

- **Make the size appropriate**

  If it is going to sit in a standard rack, the brochure must be 4 inches wide and 9 inches tall with a horizontal headline in the top 2 inches of the front cover (if you live in the States). If they are going to file it in a standard file cabinet, it better be 8.5"x11" unless you are sure that the secretaries who will be filing the brochure have cabinets that will take a 9"x12" folder (if you live in the States). Seriously consider where the reader is going to come across this work of art and make the size fit the area. If it is designed to sit on the cashier's counter in a retail store, you better either design a holder, make it fit a magazine rack, or make it small enough to be tantalizing lying on a corner of the countertop.

- **Make the logo and company name ubiquitous**
  (not dominant though – dominance is reserved for the product)

  Every spread should have the logo and name of the company to reinforce the company image. If the brochure is really a small catalog, follow the experts and have the 800 number or URL at the bottom of every page.

- **Keep it simple**

  If most readers wanted a specification sheet, they would ask for it. If you confuse or overwhelm them, they will stop reading. A benefits list is usually more functional, and better received, than a specification list.

- **Focus on which action or reaction you prefer**

  Do not confuse the reader. Yes, you want to give them options. However, you should focus on the preferred reaction and make all of the others smaller type as a subparagraph or note. If you prefer a snail mailed check, say so (recognizing that you will lose many customers this way). If you prefer online plastic, tell them so (gently asserting the safety and reliability of the service).

- **Be sure to ask**

  Never produce a brochure that forgets to ask the reader to do something appropriate. The most common design mistake is to get the reader excited and then forget to even give a phone and address.

Catalog wisdom

It is easy to prove that the result needed is to have the reader contact the company as a result of the brochure or catalog. The successful catalogs realize that the purpose of a catalog is to gain direct personal contact. Then it is much harder for the customer to leave without a purchase. Even at Web sites, an 800 number works its wonders. A cheerful, helpful, knowledgeable, **REAL** person can really pump up the sales. This reaction will probably increase as we move from the corner store to online shopping.

- **Keep focused**

A brochure is not a book, and rarely a catalog. A brochure needs to offer the reader all the important facts needed for them to make a decision to proceed. Sometimes that decision is to call for more data. There is nothing wrong with that. However, you must remain focused upon the decided purpose and goal of this particular brochure. There are appropriate places for wordiness and chattiness. A brochure is usually not that place.

THE RESPONSE BROCHURE

We have covered much of this all ready. To reword it, a response brochure is a very focused presentation about a specific product, product line, or service. Often it is the fleshing out of a display or classified advertisement. It can be used effectively to reinforce contacts made with magazine ads, 800# conversations, telemarketing responses, trade show booths, or Web site hits — helping the reader respond positively to your message and promotion.

In this case, you assume that the reader has already heard of the company and product, and that they have asked for a brochure. So, you are focused on answering their questions. As a result, one of the first things to do is try to determine what the readers' questions will be. Of course, the basic question is, "Why should I buy this product instead of the competition's versions?"

Almost all products have one or more reasons to buy — cheaper, faster, more efficient, more convenient. This reason should be prominent in the headline on the front cover along with a graphic or photo showing the product (preferably in use). Once you get the reader's attention in this way. You need to lead him or her through to the close where you ask for a specific action: call, write, drop by, buy now.

This is where a great deal of attention has to be paid to the layout. You need to put yourself in the reader's place and try to determine how they will open the brochure, what they will see second, what they will see third, and so forth. To a large extent, this is controlled by your page layout and the arrangement of your folds.

THE PROMOTIONAL BROCHURE

This a commonly called a rack brochure (because it is usually found in a rack — whether that rack is a small wire contraption hanging off a cash register or a large, gorgeous piece of cabinetry in a hotel lobby). For many companies, the rack brochure is their major method of promotion. In my area, for example, tourism is the major industry. Many of the whitewater rafting companies, silversmiths, artists, and Santa Fe style clothing retailers use rack brochures in the multitudinous hotel and motel lobbies as one of their major marketing efforts. In America, this is true almost wherever you live. Rack brochures will probably one of your regular design projects.

Here you have to be very careful to understand what the real product is. If you are advertising bunge-jumping, the draw is not the beautiful canyon and spectacular bridge, the product is the guaranteed, safe, adrenaline rush. For a well-known artist, the product might be the name and reputation. For a newly emerging silversmith, the products are the unique designs and outstanding craftsmanship. For the outlet malls, you'll probably need to focus on price and name brands.

The final concept to remember seems horribly obvious, but it is commonly forgotten in the rush of producing this gorgeous piece of graphic design art. Many things in a rack brochure are determined by their layout needs. Any promotion like this must keep a very strong focus. "What does the reader of this brochure really want?" It may be adrenaline, economy, fun, education, or a host of other attributes. The main thing to remember is simple — you only have the top two inches of the front cover to get their attention and make them look at the rest of the brochure. Think of these brochures as marketing impulse decisions and you will not be far off.

Product sheets

The final marketing piece we will cover here is the product sheet. These are usually flat, two-sided, letter-sized (in the States) sheets that give specifications, abilities, and reasons why this particular product meets the customer's need. These may be separate promotions for every model of an automobile manufacturer, a sheet for each software application sold, a little promo sheet for every size and type of swimming pool available in your client's business, and so forth. Obviously, the list could go on virtually to infinity (we are a marketing economy).

Here the need is very different. You are dealing with a customer who is very close to being sold. They are actually shopping for a product of the type your client sells. The company logo is not primary here (though is should be tastefully visible, as always). The standard parts of a product sheet are: the name and model number of the product; a clear product shot (even if the product is an invisible software utility, shoot the box); a simple concise description; and a clear, easy-to-read benefit list. Often a specification list is needed, but that should go on the back.

Here again, there are several things that need to be remembered. They may pick up the sheet in the showroom, but they will probably be contacting your client from home or the office. Don't forget to include the phone number, address, e-mail, and URL of the Web site. They may be going through a pile of sheets two months later and have no idea where they picked up the one they really want to buy.

 TIP: Always give some indication of price. One of the most irritating things you can do to a potential customer is sell them, only to find out that the price is ten to a hundred times the size of their budget. Another is to afford them no basis for cost comparisons with the inevitable competitors. Always give the manufacturer's suggested price (or the approximate street price, if appropriate). Many sales are lost because companies hem and haw on pricing. How can you trust someone who is afraid to give you a real price? (What are they really trying to hide?) Why do you think the Saturn has been such a popular car? It is certainly not because they are a unique technological achievement.

Brochures and product sheets

 Mini #7

RACK BROCHURE

You are charged with developing a brochure to serve many and varied purposes. Its primary use will be as a handout at trade shows. However, it is also going to be used a great deal in racks and at retail outlets patronized by designers. In addition, it will be attached as a PDF to requests made on the Website and mailed to those requesting more information on coursework available.

Finally, a product sheet is usually not the place for hype, graphic shouting, or amazing graphics — *"just the facts, ma'am."* The potential customer doesn't care at all that your client claims to be the best in the world (competitors are probably making the same claim). Once you have a customer this close to a sale, he or she wants facts to help with decision-making. It may well be true that these "facts" are very subjective, like "the outstanding feel of hand-oiled ebony handles"; "the rush of some of the most dangerous rapids in the Western Hemisphere" or "peace of knowing you are secure." The customer needs an honest evaluation of the capabilities of the product for comparison. This is not the place to be screaming graphically, with "Buy now, while they're hot."

Postal regulations

Because many of these promotional products will be mailed to potential customers, you need to carefully include postal requirements into your plans. In the United States, you can simply call your local post office and they will mail you a sizable booklet with all of the requirements (in exhausting bureaucratic detail). These regulations can be very dangerous. I will never forget that fund-raising brochure we designed for a client (thankfully the blame fell on my art director). We were doing a mass mailing of about 750,000 pieces. The art director thought it would be wonderful to print the enclosed business reply card on bright yellow stock so it could be found easily. It looked great, but the post office refused to mail back a single reply card (they finally told us the paper color was too bright). We had to reprint all 750,000 pieces with the reply card on a white stock. Thankfully, the response was large enough to enable us to keep the client and recoup our losses on future mailings.

There are many areas where the postal regs are extremely important. They specify where the self-mailing area has to be placed and how the folds have to be. They show little things that can be done to save a great deal of money in mailing costs. They specify the setup of bulk rate stamps. For some applications, they even specify layouts, measurements, typestyles, and colors.

LAYOUTS, FOLDS, AND PAPER CUTS

DESIGN AND PRODUCTION TIPS

There are many little tricks to setting up these marketing pieces effectively. I'll cover them in the reverse order from the way they were introduced, simply because the product sheet is the simplest to produce. These are the things that will make or break you as a designer, at least as far as making a profit is concerned.

Product sheets

Because there are usually no folds to worry about, this seems straightforward. However, there are still some elements that need to be considered. The sheet size is the most obvious. But there are a couple of design factors to review first.

Keep in mind that these sheets are probably going to be collected from several vendors and several manufacturers. If the customer is looking at printers, she may come home with two or three model sheets from several different brands. Let's make it personal.

Let's say you are looking for a new color laser printer. You collect product sheets from H/P, Tektronix, Canon, Xerox, and several others. Upon arriving at the office, you start comparing to determine the cost effectiveness, ease of installation, speed, and so forth. What are you looking for – *ways to accurately compare important attributes:* pages per minute, black and white or color; letter, legal, tabloid, or duplex? If you are looking at cost per print, what is the cost at various coverages? What ports and networking are standard and optional? What RIP is used?

The point is this: how do these questions affect your feelings about what type of layout is needed for these sheets? I imagine that your answer is similar to mine – you want everything on one side of a single sheet with clear data so you know you can be comparing oranges with oranges. You do not care at all about flashy graphics. In this case it would be a definite positive if the sheets were actually printed on the printers you are looking at. Very practical stuff for a very practical product is what is needed. Let's look at some of the production practicalities.

Product sheet production tips:

In general, you must take into account how the sheets are going to be used and stored. In most cases, this means that you will be using the normal letter size of your country – 8.5x11 inches in the United States. This is because most business purchase decisions require all of the collected data to be stored in a standard folder in a normal file drawer.

There are certainly cases where this size needs to be different. Consumer products would do well to produce sheets that will fit in a shirt pocket, maybe 3x5 inches or smaller. Maybe it makes more sense to make them a standard rack size for ease of display, 4x9 inches.

Whatever the size you pick, there are several additional factors to consider with your product sheets:

- **Will these sheets be mailed?** Both 8.5"x11" and 4"x9" fit standard envelopes (9"x12" and the #10 at 4.125"x9.5").

- **What is the quantity needed?** If you are looking at thousands of copies, then a full bleed is often an option. If you are printing a few hundred, a bleed is often economically impractical, but process color becomes more feasible.

- **Will the budget allow for process color?** Is process color even a good idea for these products? In certain situations (a charity selling items made by the physically challenged would be one), process color marketing pieces convey the idea that the organization manages its money poorly.

- **How much data needs to be covered?** You may decide that the only way to deal with the mass of data is to make a tabloid sheet folded to letter size so you can accommodate all of the facts with the 11x17-inch area available when you open the cover. However, you need to be very careful here. Keep in mind the

DIRECT MAIL BROCHURE

A major program brochure for Conquering Depression Seminars to be held in the mountains of New Mexico. You are going to design a 16 page brochure that is 5" tall and 7" wide, with the fold on the left side of the cover – containing all of the information about speakers and location.

normal scenario of multiple sheets from several sources spread out on the table so you can easily compare them. You certainly do not want multiple page books or folders (unless you are in an industry where it is common because of the technical specifications required). With a retail purchase, you may be looking at pocket cards.

We are ignoring basic problems that need to be taken care of by the copywriters, though it is often true in the new paradigm that we designers do much of the writing and editing. Areas like answering competitors' claims, listing the benefits desired by the consumer, clearing up common misconceptions, and the like must be handled before you even start the layout.

For the layout and its content, several things are obvious, but regularly forgotten in the rush of production. Keep in mind that product sheets are not usually portfolio pieces used to demonstrate your incredible creative talent and ability.

Product sheet design tips

1. Splashy graphics are of no use and may even be counterproductive *(they may cause loss of sales or consumer trust)*. This is especially true if you are doing sheets for a nonprofit charity or one that is perceived as such like a hospital, insurance company, public utility, and so forth.

2. The name and model must be at the top of the sheet. For some reason, I cannot recall ever seeing a landscape product sheet. They are all portrait – no reason I know of, just the standard.

3. The illustration of the product must be picked for its clarity and how well it shows features and benefits (if possible). You may need a few small illustrations of features that are unique to the market. The reader is looking for easy comparisons, this applies to the illustrations as well. A nontangible sheet like an insurance plan should not have an illustration, even if you think you have a dynamite idea.

4. All features, advantages, specifications, and benefits lists need to be in a clearly defined style with bulleted or number lists. All lists need a headline or subhead that is clear and easy to read.

5. This is one place where sans serif typestyles can be used for everything. However, even here you need to be careful. For example, much of the distinctiveness of Apple's marketing sheets comes from the fact that everything Apple does is in Garamond Light, a very elegant serif type-style. Most of their PC competition uses Helvetica or Ariel.

6. A well-picked font can have a major influence on how the prospective customer views a company's product line. In a design piece that is very controlled and subdued, like a product sheet, font choice is the major graphic factor influencing attributes like believability, trustworthiness, quality, value, and reliability.

7. All of the product lists for a given client need to have an identical layout (as much as this is possible). If there is an identifiable industry layout, you should always use it.

8. The manufacturer's logo and name should be in several locations. In many cases the manufacturer's logo will

need to be subservient to the distributor's logo or the retailer's identification. However, in most cases it needs to be there, at least once. It is often a requirement.

9. Be sure that you have a method to close the sale. Even though this is not perceived as a sales tool, the product sheet is often the only marketing piece physically present when the decision to buy occurs. "This is what you need – buy now" is appropriate.

10. Clear contact information must be present. The purchase decisions will be made at a different place and time from when the product sheet was picked up. You need to clearly include 800 numbers, e-mail addresses, pager numbers, URLs, and so forth. If it is appropriate to give the actual name of a real person, you are a leg up on the competition.

Rack brochure design tips:

The rack brochure has several things that must be considered that are very different from the needs of the product sheet. The following list not only mentions these, but also the practical production setups that will help your project develop smoothly.

1. The cover of the rack brochure has the same problems and the same importance as the magazine sold on the newsstand. All of the marketing hopes for the brochure are based upon the cover attracting appropriate readers who will actually pick this piece out of a host of other similar brochures.

2. Though the entire cover design is crucial, what really matters are the top 2.5 to 3 inches that are seen while the person is standing in front of the rack, scanning its content.

3. Be sure to list the most attractive, most distinctive reason(s) to open the brochure in those top 3 inches. "Fun & thrills! Bungee jumping! Go-cart obstacle course!" makes a much better top area entry than "Merrimak Falls Entertainment, Inc."

4. The rest of the cover needs to be the best hype you can come up with as far as a photo or illustration is concerned. You do not want a shot of those side-by-side cabins. You need a shot of the incredible view through the front window and the porch of one of the cabins.

5. The product shots (like the cabins' interior, the go-carts' obstacles, or the fabulous brand names at the outlet mall) need to be included with a complete description of capabilities, attributes, and benefits on the interior spread.

6. Pricing is not a major factor on a rack brochure. You are selling fun, rest, adventure, discount sales, convenience, or a host of other things. The rack brochure's job is the get the readers to choose to include the site, service, or product in their plans. Don't confuse them with reality – **SELL THE SIZZLE!** Make sure the pricing, location, and so forth are available, but not primary.

Brochures and product sheets

TIP: This weekend my wife and I went for an anniversary "quickie" vacation. The rack brochures that were the most helpful were found on the motel's sign-in desk. They had a rack of beautiful, business-card-sized, two- to six-page brochures that were perfect for decision making after sign-in. The 2"x3.5" size was perfect for scattering many options on the tiny table in the room. *You must carefully think through where the brochure will be used and how large is the rack?*

Rack brochure production tips:

Most of these tips are centered around the unique size of the final product, usually 4 inches wide and 9 inches tall; or the normal method of displaying the final brochure in a rack with many direct competitors. These are not written in stone. One of the local tour bus companies has its own custom rack where it sells advertising slots for mini-brochures that are 1.5 inches wide and 5 inches tall. These look more like bookmarks than brochures. I have seen countless tourists with a pocket full.

The more normal, 4"x9" format does not fit well with normal paper sizes based on the 8.5"x11" standard. A four-page folder can be cut out of an 8.5"x11" sheet. A 9"x16" brochure folded in half and in half fits with not too much waste on an 11"x17" sheet. A 9"x12", letter-fold brochure wastes much of the paper, because it requires the same amount of paper as the 9"x16", four-panel brochure.

A 9x16-inch brochure, if folded properly, gives your client's potential customers a very well programmed information experience (take a close look, below left). It starts with the attention grabber of the front cover, moves directly to a two-page spread that can strongly emphasize the major positive attributes of the client, and then opens to a very large four-panel expanse with plenty of room to close the deal with detail shots, views, options, and so forth. There is still a back cover available for pertinent details like a map, pricing, times, age requirements, and so forth.

TIP: If you have a very tight budget, you can still make a competitive impact with a simple 4"x9" sheet of cover stock set up to work&turn on an 8.5"x11" sheet (see the next page). It can even be done in one color on a nice sheet of paper. Because this layout only requires one plate per color for both the front and the back of the little brochure, you can save you client quite a bit on printing costs while still presenting a very competitive cover design. This type of brochure can be produced in small quantities on your laser printer in your studio *very quickly*.

A letter-fold rack brochure is usually not a very good idea. First of all, it is almost always economically stupid, as mentioned. Secondly, the panel folded inside is clumsy as a visual element. When the reader opens the cover, he or she is confronted with a narrow panel next to a partially revealed interior spread. You usually have to design the left panel of the interior spread so it reads well with both folded flap and the rest of the interior spread. It can certainly be done, but it is never as elegant a solution as the half&half 9x16 or the 8x9 four-page folder (which cuts your paper costs in half).

Outside and first splash hype

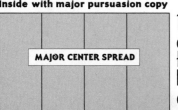

This fold allows you to control how the reader opens the brochure.

Rack brochure layout tips

• Because the cover must be portrait, the layout of any brochure larger than a four-fold has to be landscape. Every attempt with a cover on a different orientation than the rest of the brochure, that I have seen, has been a disaster.

- The key to a good layout in all of these solutions is being careful to maintain even margins around every panel and spread. This requires very careful attention.

- The gutters between columns also have to be carefully located and sized. Because all of these gutters have a fold running down the middle, they are usually made quite a bit larger than you normally find in other multicolumn projects. Because of the fold, your space between columns needs to be at least a half inch (leaving a quarter inch on each side of the fold). Quite often this will be larger than your outside margins on the spread.

- Be sure to drag a guide for each of your folds to help you locate your margins and guides.

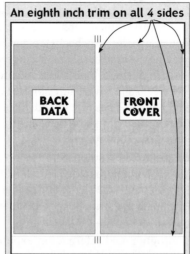

An eighth inch trim on all 4 sides

BACK DATA

FRONT COVER

As you can see, two 4"x9" documents are a tight fit on an 8.5"x11" sheet of paper. They do fit however, and there is more than enough room for gripper at the top or bottom of the sheet. If you can print to the edge of the sheet, even full bleeds can be done, though half dot registration is obviously necessary to line up the front and back accurately.

- Make sure you include an accurate folded dummy of the finished project to your service bureau or printing company. If you are contemplating any unusual folds, make sure that you communicate clearly and get a folding dummy from the actual bindery you are contracted to use on the project.

- Pay special attention to controlling the reader's progress through the brochure. You do not want people opening the brochure from the back forward.

- Never place obstacles in the readers' path by rotating the layout on some of the panels. A map rotated 90° to fit a 4"x9" panel restriction will be a major reading irritant.

- Remember that in this particular type of design project the layout is much more important than the number of colors used.

Marketing brochure production tips:

Marketing brochures have much more layout freedom than rack brochures or product sheets. In addition, they have few size restrictions. We have all seen marketing brochures that are 10 inches by 34 inches roll-folded down to 4 by 10 or so. Many readers take great delight in a brochure that seems to unfold forever.

There is an interesting dichotomy here. Even though it may be argued that a fancy roll-fold brochure that causes delight upon opening

Brochures and product sheets

Work&turn and work&tumble

One of the ways you can save printing costs is to design your piece so that both the front and the back of the document fit on the same side of the paper. This way both sides can be printed with one plate. The paper is just run though once, turned over, and run through the second time with the same plate. With metal plates costing $25 to $100 each, you save this amount for each color. It does require careful layout, but then all printed work takes careful attention. Take a close look at the 4"x9" work&turn layout at the top of this page.

may be very helpful in reinforcing a customer's sense of trust and quality, there is a larger issue. Much later, when the customer thinks or talks about that brochure (this does happen sometimes), my experience suggests they almost never remember the company that produced it (your client).

This places the amazing layouts into the same category as those incredible TV commercials that we would rather watch than the actual programming. In recent years, I have seen TV commercials become a topic of conversation that is almost as common as the discussion of the latest movies. Often a simple question to the person sharing the tale will show you that dangers of this approach. Merely ask, "Who was the commercial advertising?" You will find in many cases that they cannot remember. They may remember the entire script of the commercial, dialog and all, but they often do not remember the product advertised or the company who produced the product and paid for the commercial.

If you recall, in Chapter 10 we made the statement that excellent design should not be noticed. If a potential customer picks the brochure you design and reacts with awe at the design execution and concept, you have utterly failed (unless of course, it is a self-promo piece for your studio). Again your goal is simple – clear communication. You must produce an easily readable message about a specific product that helps the customer trust the client enough to actually purchase the product or service.

With that reminder let's go into some tips and design factors concerning marketing brochures. Here we have a customer who is definitely interested, but it is usually part of a longer decision process.

Response brochure design tips

- Because there are so many options, the environment where the customer will pick up or receive the brochure becomes important. Will they receive it in the mail? Will it be handed to them by your client's sales representative? Will it be lying next to a display of the product (or in a little rack hanging there)? Will the customer store it for future reference or is this a one-time sales pitch that will be disposed of almost immediately?

- If it will be stored for reference, you are almost forced into an 8.5"x11" format (or whatever the standard business storage size is in your country).

- If it is a one-time sales pitch that is likely to be tossed upon reading, you need much more drama and quite possibly an unusual layout. If you do decide on a layout outside the norm, work closely with your printer and binder to make sure you design something that can be produced without a lot of extra expense.

- Always get a folding dummy from the printer/binder, or produce your own. Take a deep breath, put yourself in the reader's place and see how you react to the layout. Does it progress logically? Is there anything out of place, jarring, or vaguely irritating?

- Consciously attempt to program the reader's experience, trying to make it pleasant, easy, obvious, and productive.

- Any panels that are folded inside must be slightly smaller than their enclosing panels to avoid folding problems and damaged paper. For example, the panel that folds inside on a letter-folded 8.5"x11" brochure is normally a sixteenth inch narrower than the outside panels.

 TIP: Because this is a large area of confusion, let me describe the thinking on the 8.5"x11" letter fold. Eleven inches divided by three is $3\frac{5}{8}$" with $\frac{1}{8}$" left over. If you split the eighth in half for the front and back covers, you end up with the following dimensions: front cover $3\frac{11}{16}$"; back cover $3\frac{11}{16}$"; and the panel that folds inside $3\frac{5}{8}$". With the inside panel a sixteenth inch shorter, everything fits perfectly.

Closing comments

Always be conscious of where the brochure or product sheet fits in the company's overall marketing plan (if they have one). For some, the brochure uses their entire budget and must, therefore, be multipurpose. For others, you will be producing several different, tightly focused documents.

The days of printing 50,000 brochures are rapidly going the way of mass-marketed junk mail in general. It is rarely cost-effective any more. This is good news to us. It means a lot more design work is needed. More importantly it removes a lot of the horrendous pressure for results demanded by investing hundreds of thousands of dollars on a single printed product.

KNOWLEDGE RETENTION

1. What are the fundamental conceptual differences between marketing and response brochures?

2. Why should product sheets be clean and simple *graphically*?

3. What determines the size of product sheets?

4. Why is a 4"x9" letter-fold brochure such a waste of money or space, in most cases?

5. Why is so much money lavished on marketing brochures, especially rack brochures?

WHERE SHOULD YOU BE BY THIS TIME?

You should be actively thinking about and planning for your career in graphic design and/or publishing. If you are going to be seeking employment, what type of company will you be searching for? If you are going to strike out on your own, or with a partner, what creative assets are you focusing on? Are your ideas based on reality or wishful thinking?

DISCUSSION

By now, there is hope that you have made friends and entered into a network of creative resources. If not, get busy!

Talk among yourselves...

16

Booklet and Magazine Production

Designing multiple page materials for organizations and events, including: newsletters, programs, magazines, books, and annual reports

CONCEPTS

1. Saddle-stitched

2. Perfect bound

3. Table of contents

4. Front matter

5. Masthead

6. Flag

7. Creep

8. Smythe-sewn

9. Hard cover

10. Spiral-bound

CHAPTER OBJECTIVES

By presenting the basic terms and production procedures, you will learn how to:

1. Develop a consistent look
2. Lay out an effective table of contents
3. Allow planned room for advertising
4. Determine page numbers and booklet size
5. Develop a relationship with the readership

LAB WORK FOR CHAPTER:

- Skill exam #9
- Submit finished theory exams

Booklet and Magazine Production

Dealing with multiple pages

Here we enter several types of projects that require quite a bit of production knowledge. In addition, our format is often determined by production requirements. In reality, of course, this is always the case. However, it seems more important with booklets. This is a product area dominated by bindery concerns and by signature sizes. We will deal with those issues in a little bit.

Of primary importance, as always, is determining the audience. This is a design category where the overall layout, font choices, and graphic style are the main determinants for how well the project is received. These projects are all about building community, a common experience, a group cohesiveness. Newsletters are probably the prime method for doing this. But the same general concerns surround magazines, annual reports, event programs, e-zines, and convention programs.

The questions are the same. *What is the product? Who are the readers? Who is the client (and are they the product)? What is the message? What do you want the readers to do?* **Let's take these in order.**

The product

Usually the product here is less tangible. It is the company, entertainers, the event itself, the city or area producing the event, the political party nominating the candidate, the corporation's financial stability and growth, the organizations or the organization's goals. Often illustrations become much more abstract. Look at the contortions that BASF goes through with its image spots on television. "We don't really do anything, we just make the things that make anything possible." What the heck does that mean? The point being that I am not part of that audience, so it doesn't matter. I'm sure the stockholders recognize the images immediately, maybe even from last year's annual report. In this case, the product is BASF's strength, importance, and diversity,

What about that newsletter for the Humane Society? The product is animal rescue and everything else is subservient to that. What about Albuquerque's Balloon Fiesta program? The product is the ability of the Fiesta to produce gorgeous photo opportunities in a helpful friendly city with amazing weather and wind conditions, plus the camaraderie of the entire ballooning community. As always, once you are sure what you are selling, the message becomes much easier to manage.

The readers

For an event like the Fiesta, the answer seems obvious: the visitors to the Fiesta. They are certainly a large part of it. However, the real importance of the Fiesta program is the communication with the friends of the tourists back home. When the tourists are showing what they did and exclaiming about the fun, beauty, and enjoyment they found in Albuquerque, Santa Fe, and New Mexico in general, an important part of the real readership is found.

A newsletter or magazine is much more targeted. Here you often have an exact readership list with detailed survey data. If you do not, you might be well advised to generate some of that data in an effort to improve the effectiveness of the publication.

A convention program is not only trying to build community; it is usually attempting to prove that the sponsoring organization is a leader in the field and a superior source of needed information. A good convention or annual seminar is built on the needs of the participants. The program (as well as the resulting newsletter or magazine) needs to capitalize on that ability to meet those needs.

The client

Quite often the client is focused on the fundraising aspect of the venture. We certainly need to keep their needs in mind. If they do not raise the necessary funds, we have lost a client. However, we must help them to stay focused on the source of their income — *the service they offer their readers or participants.*

BOOKLET DESIGN TIPS

In general, your first problem is that you will often (normally?) be dealing with relatively amateur editorial staff. Often it is the secretary who has been assigned the newsletter. For some reason, the worst seem to be the Human Resources personnel. I guess that this is because they tend to be so legalistic, but I'm not sure.

Whatever the state of the editor (and any volunteer staff), the real problem is that you will not be dealing with professionals, plus you will almost never have any editorial authority to help. Having said this, these booklets, newsletters, and magazines are an incredible opportunity for you to become indispensable to the company. Many times, I (or people I have known) have started with the newsletter and stationery reprints and taken over all of the design needs of the entire company within a couple of years.

You need to be very gentle here. Often these people you are trying to help have been told amazing falsehoods about the printing process and its capabilities. You'll know you have arrived when you get a timid call asking what can be done with this brochure that came out so horribly.

The normal scenario is simple. You win the bid for the project and they dump a pile of old booklets, a couple of floppies or a ZIP, and an envelope of photos on your desk. "We have to mail this out next week." The determining factor concerning the effort put into the project is whether you have a yearly contract or not.

Quoting the booklet

The major factor that is not understood by many clients is the incredible amount of effort that is required for the first issue. If you are wise, you will have a separate quote for the basic newsletter design, plus a monthly production charge once the design is approved. Often you have to prorate the design charge over the yearly contract.

However you are forced to quote the project, most clients do not expect to pay a great deal for product. The newsletter especially is normally part of their overhead, and is not an income source. This is

Skill #9

PROFESSIONAL UGLY BOOKLET

Here you will design a booklet that requires a good deal of stylistic and illustration knowledge. This one is not for the faint of heart!

not quite so true with magazines, but even here there is tremendous pressure to keep costs down. One of the factors you need to understand is that there are some very real, mass-production benefits in booklet production. I have found that for most booklets, magazines, or books I can be fairly confident that, when all the time spent is totaled up, I will have spent from 10 to 20 minutes per page ($10 to $25 per page) in production time. The 20 minute per page quote is for fairly graphically intensive work. With books and booklets that are almost completely copy, I have quoted as low as $3.00 per page and made a handsome profit.

I can hear several of you whining now, *"My God, how can you expect me to work that fast?"* The fact of it is that hundreds of us can. That's all I get for this book, and that covers everything but the actual writing of the copy — all of the scans, the graphics, the layout, the formatting, the copyediting, and the proofing. When I'm done with my part, the printer gets finished books: PDFs ready to print for each chapter and a CD-ROM ready for mass production. I won't share details of my contract, but it is at the lower end of the figures above, and I am very happy with it.

Master page design

For all booklets you are going to need at least one set of master pages to contain the page numbers. This book has three: the first page with the objectives, the second and third page with the graphics and lead-in formatting, and the main set for all of the rest of the pages in the chapter. For books like this one, it is very important to have page numbers and the chapter name and number on every page. The student needs these reference numbers to help when studying. Any booklet that has a table of contents needs page numbers to help the reader find the articles.

Don't make the mistake of assuming that your reader will read everything.

For newsletters and magazines, you will often need master pages for each regular columnist, for the table of contents pages, for full-page ads, for half page ads with copy, for article first pages, and so forth. Before InDesign, I had two-, three-, four-, and five-column master pages, to keep things visually interesting. Now I set up a grid to use as a guide to PLACE and drag'n'drop the stories into position.

With annual reports you will need master pages for letters, promotional copy for the stockholders, and the financials for the accountants — at least. These printing masterpieces are going through fundamental change now that much of this data can be posted on a secure Web site. You will find that many of them have evolved into fancy multipage brochures with financial summaries pointing toward the full statements on the Web.

Consistency

The prime virtue in all booklets is consistency. To give you an idea of this importance, imagine trying to read a magazine if the layout style varied as often as the advertising does. How would you find the articles to read? Yes, I am fully aware that advertorials have great power, that is why the Feds outlawed them (you now have to put a warning on them). In general, however, your readers should have no trouble at all keeping the thread of the articles as they track through the mass of paid advertisements. In fact, if you recall your behavior, the articles are why you buy magazines.

Even the advertisers need to be reminded that if the readers cannot easily read the articles, their ads won't be seen either, due to dropping readership. Would that we were all so excellent that we could forbid advertisers, like John Wade's great *Before & After* magazine of publishing tips, for example. However, this is not reality for most of us. But ads do have to be put in their place. Readers subscribe to newsletters and magazines because of the contents, not the advertising. Many, like my wife, go through the entire magazine and tear out all the inserts to throw away **BEFORE** she even begins to read the magazine.

Even though it is not politically correct for us to admit it, we all find ads irritating. **EXCEPT FOR THE ADS THAT SELL US SOMETHING WE REALLY WANTED ANYWAY.** The ads need to be the frame that sets off the content of the booklet. You do this through consistent placement and graphic separation.

The masthead

Let's talk a little about some of the pieces. Most misunderstood by the beginner is the masthead. The masthead is not the logo or flag on the front cover. It is the list of personnel and the legalese on the second page or back cover of newsletters (hidden after the table of contents in most magazines). Its normal format is 6- to 8-point type, often centered, listing all of the management personnel in order of power. At the top of the masthead is either a very small version of the flag (sometimes called the newsletter logo) or the logo of the publisher. At the bottom of the newsletter is the mandated legalese with production schedule and circulation data.

The flag

The is the name of the magazine, newsletter, or event. To a certain extent these tips also apply to the corporate name on top of the annual report. There are usually two problems with flags. Either the name is cute and often stupid, or it is an epistle masquerading as a name. The *Middle Rio Grande Conservancy District's Environmental Messenger* is one I remember. Even *Environmental Messenger* would have been bad enough.

What you are hoping for is a punchy name that clearly states the purpose for the booklet. *Publish* magazine is an excellent example, or *Country Living, Good Housekeeping, Fine Woodworking, Sports Illustrated,* and so forth. Current style would not have you add that cutesy logo to the flag. Of course, if you have an asset like Smokey the Bear, you use him.

The normal best is the name in large clearly readable type in an appropriate font, with built-in spaces for the volume and issue numbers, the month, the quarter, the year, or whatever you need to categorize the current issue. Many also add a motto to the flag, but you must be careful to avoid clutter.

The sidebar

There is great graphic advantage in designing in a consistent space for peripheral information, photos, and graphics. I recommend that you make a space like this part of your basic master page design. Even if the editors do not give you information like this, the graphic friendliness and visual interest make sidebars virtually necessary. The important thing to remember is that sidebar contain peripheral information. They need to be part of the frame that sets off the copy.

Table of contents

These lists most clearly show your concern for the comfort and happiness of your readers. Is there anything much more irritating than angrily searching all over the front of a magazine for a simple list to tell you where to find that article you remember but can't locate? Your readership experiences this irritation (at least unconsciously) every time you refuse to help them find the contents. Whoever came up with the idea that hidden tables of contents force the reader to see the ads should be shot. The same is true for catalog design. You will certainly lose more readers than you will gain in sales by making things difficult for the reader.

For a newsletter, the table of contents usually works very well in the built-in sidebar you designed for the cover page. For all other booklets, this table should be on the first available right page. In addition, it needs to be in the same place every month. Your goal is a friendly, comfortable reading experience that provides truly useful or genuinely entertaining content for your readership. This is true even for readers craving excitement and adrenaline rushes.

Margins

These are dependent upon the type of binding, but in general they need to be wider on the inside. Anything less than a half inch, on any side, promotes cheapness *at best*. The more expensive the booklet, the higher quality the content, the wider the margins should be. This is true even if you have full bleed graphics. The absolute minimum is 3/8", 2p3 picas, or 27 points. I have seen incredibly beautiful, graphically intense magazines and books with margins of around 4 inches. A book of photos in a landscape format might have outside margins of 10 inches or more. This book, for example, has outside margins of .75" and inside margins of 2.375". This leaves comfortable room for 1.5" sidebar text blocks.

Front matter

Often there are normal requirements attached to books and booklets. These are commonly called front matter. In newsletters and magazines, these are simply the flag, table of contents, and the masthead. In books, you have the title page, copyright information and ISBN number, preface, dedication, acknowledgements, and so forth. Most categories of booklets have relatively rigid standards. For example, with my last book *Digital Drawing*, I added a summary of the table of contents in response to huge numbers of student requests. They were looking for a simple chapter listing with page numbers to help them quickly locate the assigned chapters for the weekly reading assignments. The publisher flat out bounced the concept because it was too far outside the norm.

The first decision is saddlestitching or perfect binding, with the subsets of perfect binding: comb, 3-ring, spiral, and wire-o binding, with a few more esoteric options.. If you are doing a saddlestitched booklet, the page numbers must be divisible by four. For perfect-bound books, you have much more freedom. In perfect binding, it is relatively easy to slip in a two-page sheet that is four-color, or foil stamped, or whatever you need. This is much trickier in saddle-stitched booklets.

Usually the determining factor are the number of pages and cost. Perfect binding costs more, no matter which iteration you use: case-bound, smythe-sewn, hard cover, spiral-bound, or any of the fancier options. The only thing cheaper than saddlestitching is the three-ring binder, but then there is the cost of the binder.

The limits to saddle-stitching are controlled by the thickness of the paper. The limit is not the ability of the staple to hold the booklet together. Printers actually sew the saddle-stitched booklets together with sewing machines using wire, hence the name. The problem is called "creep". This refers to the simple fact that the insertion of signatures causes the interior pages to move farther and farther away from the fold. When the book is trimmed, the interior pages have margins that get much narrower toward the center of the book.

The problems with creep

AS YOU CAN SEE, NOT ONLY IS THAT EXTRA POINT OF PAPER CUT OFF, BUT THERE IS A LARGE OPEN BULGE AT THE STITCHES.

Imposition software normally adjusts for creep by moving the content progressively toward the center of the book by an amount equal to the actual measurement of the thickness of the paper. Obviously, there are limits to how far you can move the content toward the center. This problem can be lessened with larger interior margins. However, at a certain point, the physical thickness of the paper around the wire stitches causes too much bulge as we saw in the chapter on paper.

The normal limit on page number for saddle-stitched booklets is about 100 pages. Many shops refuse to do more than 72 pages. With text paper, you may be limited to 48 pages. Catalogs printed on a heat-set web press can go as high as 200 pages with super-calendared, light

weight stock. Your printing company will have clearly stated opinions on what they can produce with which papers. Ask them *before* you start designing. You will save yourself a lot of trouble and money.

THE PARADIGM SHIFT

In this particular area of design many things have changed recently. Many newsletters have moved entirely online. I have no idea how many annual reports have been lost to the Web, but it seems silly to pay thousands of dollars or more for incredibly fancy, perfect-bound annual reports when a synopsis will do as well, backed up by a secure Web site. The same is obviously true of that booklet subspecialty, catalogs.

However, do not get the idea that you can work as normal and just convert your documents to HTML. Web documents have very different requirements. A magazine that makes for fascinating reading can be as dull as Thorazine™ online. Here's a list of some of the differences:

1. Reading on a monitor requires a short, pithy writing style with concepts presented in quick visual doses.
2. Web pages are always landscape in orientation. Even when you have a page that requires scrolling, you only see one horizontal area at a time.
3. Point sizes should be a little larger than normal to cover for high-res monitors and the pixelization of the characters.
4. Sidebars become links to other pages. Make sure you provide a method for the reader to return to where they left on the tangent.
5. The table of contents is replaced by the navigation bars or a table cell listing the contents. This table cell must remain consistent on all pages to be effective. Remember that frames usually cause severe problems with bookmarking and download times.
6. A repeating header, and a way back home, is even more important online. In your easy chair it is fairly hard to accidently slip into another magazine or newsletter. It is distressingly easy to do that on the Web.

Cross referencing print and Web

One excellent idea to keep in mind is how print and Web complement each other. Your booklets need to point to a Web site for immediate sales and data capture. Your Web site needs to point to your printed materials with the clear, hand-held instructions, gorgeous graphics, and more structured order. Increasingly, we cannot do one without the other. The Web can't survive without print backup and print is not effective without Web backup.

The important thing to remember is that almost all of us are now doing both. The national average in late 1999 according to TrendWatch™ is that graphic designers spend 45 percent of their time in web design. According to the main cover article of *Publish*, February 2000, by Donnie O'Quinn, *Crossing the Digital Line*, Internet growth has dramatically slowed. The huge digital paradigm shifts slamming publishing since the late 1980s show many signs of maturing stability. We can probably safely assume that we will be working in both for the foreseeable future. The new satellite ISPs will allow us to place more content online. But it appears like it will be a long time before many of us relax on the beach with our latest ebook.

It is likely that it won't even be common to surf the Web from our hammock, even though that is possible now. Even for those of us in the industry who have the technology, a break is necessary. I can't imagine ruining my vacations with online access. But then maybe that is just me.

WHERE SHOULD YOU BE BY THIS TIME?

You should be actively thinking about and planning for your career in graphic design and/or publishing. If you are going to be seeking employment, what type of company will you be searching for? If you are going to strike out on your own, or with a partner, what creative assets are you focusing on? Are your ideas based on reality or wishful thinking?

DISCUSSION

By now, there is hope that you have made friends and entered into a network of creative resources. If not, get busy! Your opportunity is almost over – this puppy is almost complete!

Talk among yourselves...

17

Posters, Flyers, and Billboards

Designing stand-alone advertisements in various sizes, for various purposes

CHAPTER OBJECTIVES

By presenting the basic terms and production procedures, you will learn how to:

1. Conceptualize a poster
2. Take a flyer seriously
3. List the basic design necessities of a billboard

LAB WORK FOR CHAPTER

- Finish it all up – you're out of time!
- **SKILL EXAM #10: DEFAULTS.**
  This skill exam should probably be part of your first few weeks of class. However, it requires a lot of self-directed study, or it must be an in-class lockstep tutorial type of event. For those reasons, it is optional, at the discretion of your instructor or mentor. However, it is highly recommended. All of my students hate it and complain, however, after they complete it, they unanimously tell me that they learned more on this one exam than any other.
  This is why I normally give twice as many points for this exam. It is extremely helpful for page layout beginners.

Grabbing them by the eyes

The final category of print projects we are going to cover in this book are those single-sided sheets mounted to grab your eyes as you walk, ride, or drive by. Posters are the only printed product with fine art pretensions. In fact, posters have so many connections with fine art that if you do not make a major graphic statement of high quality, the effectiveness of your work is severely compromised.

The real shame in recent years is that posters have degenerated into flailing attacks of avant garde, nouveaux riche design. Many of you should keep in mind that ugliness rarely works, no matter how well you couch it in modernism, grunge, or whatever-your-graphic-foible-is. Did you ever stop to think that the reason for the small attendance at modern art, contemporary dance, and so forth is probably due to the nastiness, horror, and ugliness of the work itself? Or maybe the problem is just the avant garde pretensions of the poster designers. By the way, that was free.

Billboards

Let's start with the largest and most clearly defined design categories. The basic rules are simple (if deceptively difficult) — no more than eight words with spectacular graphics. That's it. Simple yes, easy no. You must be able to grasp the entire message in that flash as you whiz by at 50 to 75 mph, no ifs, ands, or buts.

This also means very legible fonts. There is a tendency with billboards to get cute at the expense of effectiveness. I imagine all of us can remember a billboard we thought was very attractive, but we just can't seem to remember who sponsored it.

Billboards are extremely focused advertising. A single, simple message hammered home in the blink of an eye. This is not the place for complicated concepts (unless you are trying for that exceedingly difficult afterglow chuckle that wells up in the reader a couple of miles down the road). It helps to remember those exceedingly effective Burma Shave signs that spread an eight-word joke over several miles. (For those of you who are too young, Burma Shave posted eight-word jokes and slogans, one word at a time, on small signs, a quarter mile apart, throughout the United States in the middle of last century, always finishing with a clean sign containing only their logo.) They were some of the most effective advertising ever done. Usually you didn't remember the joke, just a happy feeling and the words Burma Shave.

Posters

These works of art have two levels. The first is seen from a distance and has the same rules as a billboard. The second level is the selling copy seen a few feet away after the art level has brought you near. The most important is the first art level that grabs your eye at 30 feet, 30 yards, or 30 meters. Like a billboard, you have one shot to grab the reader's attention and hammer home your message.

The second level is almost as important. Again it is important to avoid verbosity. Down and dirty, quick and simple, **GO HERE, BUY TICKETS, ENJOY!** If you are required to put an epistle on the poster, maybe you better think in terms of an attached box containing a brochure that they can take with them. However, never make the mistake of putting all of the copy in the brochure in the box. What happens to the poster when the box is empty?

Flyers

These are miniature posters, cheaply printed. They attempt to do with quantity, what a poster does with quality, what a billboard does with size and money. Never make the mistake of thinking that because they are cheaply printed for throwaway distribution that you can make do with sloppy graphics and type. Flyers need to be as focused as posters or billboards. They are an excellent place to practice your design skills under a tight deadline. The only excuse for a lousy flyer is a crappy designer. Spare us, please!

These are all advertising.

There is a major difference between a fine art print and a poster. That difference is advertising and/or marketing. All three of these products are advertising and marketing tools. Do not ever let that slip your mind. I know all about the temptation to show off your design skills and artistic abilities. My past is filled with self-promotion pieces that are framed all over the country, but no one knows who did them or why. My fine art background killed them as effective marketing tools.

Before beginning to design, you probably need to write down your single, focused marketing goal. The words and message will flow out of that. The quality of the artwork is wonderful, but peripheral. It has to remain peripheral.

WELL, YOU SURVIVED!

Congratulations! I hope it was a fun ride. If you have any questions, feel free to write me: graphics@swcp.com

My Web site is: http://kumo.swcp.com/graphics

If those links have trouble, just search for Bergsland Design. I may go to bergsland.com — the name is very rare, so there should not be much trouble. Please let me know if I can help you in any way.

June 1, 2000

The Teaching Style and Skill Exam Rules

Rules and guidelines to understand what is expected of you in the miniskills and Skill exams

OBJECTIVES

One of the unique aspects of this curriculum is the skill exam concept. This appendix is meant to help you become accustomed to the idea, and to enable you to get to work improving your skills. You will learn:

1. The rules
2. The requirements
3. The benefits
4. The goals

A unique teaching style

In reading industry trade magazines, perusing the many books available, and talking to employers in the new industry, it has become apparent that current textbook and retail book offerings are not meeting the needs of either employers or students. Most publishers are still focused on books that teach software (both textbooks and retail offerings). To quote the chairman of the my industry advisory committee of my Business Graphics & Communication degree, "Software is a moving target." There are no titles that teach page layout from a practical production point of view. This is not graphic design instruction (though that is a part of it). This is not prepress instruction (though this is also a part of it). This is producing functional documents for digital publishing.

The focus is on student needs.

Publishing With InDesign teaches essential skills needed on a daily basis using the best new tool for the task – InDesign. The concepts and skills taught work equally well with PageMaker and QuarkXPress. The basic concepts work equally well on any page layout software including FreeHand. The concepts and skill sets taught in *Publishing With InDesign* are essential to professional production without the titillating illustration techniques that have little practical use once you are hired.

FIVE INSTRUCTIONAL GOALS

- Basic graphic design and publishing knowledge without the egocentric techniques taught traditionally in fine art and design schools that are so overly expensive to produce
- Practical job skills covering the production requirements of offset lithography, screen printing, electrostatic printing, and inkjet printing for commercial printing and quickprint
- Strong thinking and problem-solving skills
- Strategies to determine when to use which types of software
- Basic working knowledge of how to integrate InDesign with rest of the software used by the publishing industry

The problem with tutorials

Publishing With InDesign is easy to read, very practical, and a reference for basic techniques that will be used during your entire career as a professional desktop publisher. These techniques cover concepts that are not going to change. However, this book is not enough. A new method of instruction is necessary also. Current courses around the country are often simply lockstep software tutorials. These tutorial entrances to

digital publishing are generally helpful, but they reach none of the instructional goals listed above. They are usually boring and do not add to skill sets. They merely show software capabilities, not how to use that software.

A new method of instruction is necessary.

Lockstep tutorials are little help to you beyond a bare introduction to the software. They teach the location and capabilities of the various dialog boxes and commands. However, tutorials force you to think in the manner and order of the tutorial creator. The problem is that graphic design projects have thousands of different equally competent and professional solutions. It is impossible for you to solve design problems by trying to think like someone else. Creativity is an extremely subjective process that can be promoted, but never codified. Exams must be open-ended.

There is some need for more directly guided tutorials when you first begin. However, experience has shown that the sooner you can be set free, the faster you learn. We are definitely talking about liberty here, not license. This style of teaching gives freedom within the context of professional production standards. If any solution is unsalable to a real client, you need to redo it, until it is obvious that a real person would pay for it.

THE PROCEDURE AND CONCEPTUAL BASIS OF THE SKILL EXAM APPROACH

Instead of lockstep tutorials, *Publishing With InDesign* includes open-ended projects in the form of skill exams. The miniskills included in the book also give room to express your creativity with slightly more simple projects. The skill exams have been tested for many years to make sure that they actually help you internalize concepts in a production environment. After a tutorial, you can be given a similar project and not be able to do the work. After a skill exam, you can easily transfer those skills to real projects. There are seven miniskills and ten skill exams. They are all located on the Website duplicate on the CD.

You are given relative freedom to pick the exams that will help you the most. This means that some of you will pick the easiest. We always have the lazy ones. If you are one of those lazy ones, you need to look elsewhere for a career. As you can see on the grading policies page on the Website, you are required to do at least three of each type of exam. You can earn the additional points needed (for the grade of your choice) with additional theory, miniskill, or skill exams. Better yet, you can do real-world projects.

Skill exam rules

1.   There is no time limit, unless it is specifically stated in the rules. Regardless, you can practice as much as you like. Remember, these are genuinely skill exams, meaning that you will have to take the time to develop the skills. Please do not assume that you can just toss off the required finished product.

The Teaching Style and Skill Exam Rules

2. You can ask as many questions as you need to ask. Skill exams are designed to teach you a needed skill. We are not interested in your methodology. The required steps of the skill exam are all there for a reason. Read the instructions carefully. You can invent your own shortcuts later, on your own time.

3. If you cannot figure out how to do any part of the skill exam, the instructor or one of the staff will demonstrate it for you. Feel free to ask one of your classmates (but remember they may not know any more than you do).

4. You will finish with a specific product (usually a PDF) that you attach to an email, which you then mail to your instructor for grading and comments.

5. If there is a problem with your final product, the instructor will annotate your PDF and send it back for corrections. There is no penalty for the second try (or third or fourth).

6. If you work in a team with other friends or classmates, you are required to be able to do the skill exam on your own, without help. You need these skills. If the instructor thinks you are trying to get away with avoiding some of the skills, you may be required to demonstrate your skill, at any time.

As mentioned above, there is no way you can cheat on these tests. You have to be able to acquire the skills. At any time, if there is any doubt in the instructor's mind, all he or she has to do is ask you to do the skill while they are watching. Once you have done a skill exam, you should be able to do it again in just a few minutes.

THE APPROACH AND METHOD OF THEORY EXAMS

Current methods normally implement multiple-choice testing for theory concepts. This style is implemented for ease of grading with no thought to its usefulness in analyzing your actual conceptual understanding. *Publishing With InDesign* includes a complete set of theory exams in the short-essay-question style that enables your teacher to accurately assess your comprehension of the materials' conceptual basis. All theory exams are typed into an email for grading and annotation. Experience has clearly demonstrated that the annotation and grading process help more than anything to increase knowledge.

This style of teaching gives you the opportunity to work together with others on the exams. In fact, you are encouraged to work together. Robin Williams (in her popular book, *The Non-Designer's Design Book*, Peachpit Press, 1994) calls it "Open Book, Open Mouth" learning. The questions are open-ended, often requiring higher-level thought processes to answer. Often there is no right or wrong answer, but a search for thoughtful opinion. The goal is to learn to think, not to regurgitate data. The process of writing the answers into the email and reading the annotated email

responses greatly reinforces learning. The very process enables long-term retention of the materials. Trust me. The result of these new procedures will be knowledge and skills which you will not forget when you go to work.

The importance of real-world projects

You should progress (as soon as possible) to real projects for real clients with real deadlines. This enables you to apply what you have learned, making the new knowledge and techniques a permanent part of your skill set. Each school using *Publishing With InDesign* coursework will have the built-in option to supply their own "real" projects.

At my school, students can design and print anything for the school, the local public schools, any government agency or organization, and any state-registered nonprofit corporation. My students unanimously report that projects are their best learning experience in school. Not only do they learn more, but they have much more fun in the learning.

Software versions

Publishing With InDesign is not version-specific, nor are the skill exams. Whenever possible, the exams are written to use any page layout that writes solid PostScript. Most of the screen captures are from InDesign 1.5, but many of the exams have generic captures that can be used with any page layout software. Almost all of the same exams work equally well for PageMaker or QuarkXPress students.

Even though InDesign is the latest and most advanced page layout software, these concepts are standard to all of publishing. However, when you are hired, you will often be forced to use older versions to produce the projects in your job tickets. IN 1998 I had a student with training in PageMaker 6.5, Quark 3.32, FreeHand 7, Illustrator 7, and Photoshop 4 who was hired by a screen printing firm that used CorelDraw 3 exclusively (in Windows 3.1). There was quite a bit of complaining about antiquated software and hardware, but the student adapted fast and became a trusted employee generating hundreds of posters, T-shirts, etc.

Distance learning and online training

Publishing With InDesign includes a complete generic Website on the CD that has been used and tested since 1996. This site is set up for easy inclusion into the distance learning courses taught by any community college, business, or vocational school. The Website includes all the reading assignments, miniskills, and skill exams developed for the coursework using *Publishing With InDesign*.

You have the option to do all or any part of your coursework online (if allowed by the instructor). All theory exams are submitted by email. The miniskills and skill exams are submitted the same way. You simply export the finished projects as a PDF and attach it to an email for grading.

IF YOU ARE WORKING ON YOUR OWN

Many of you will purchase this book from a retail or online bookstore, planning to teach yourself. This will work well. The only problem will be finding someone with the skill and time to help you judge whether you are actually producing professional work.

It is extremely important that you keep your focus on practical and functional design. Readability is a prime virtue. Many would say it is more important than that. Your goal is to communicate clearly and effectively with your reader. Anything less is a waste of your time and your money.

If you can't find a mentor

Even though most of you will be using this book in the context of a class, some of you will not be able to locate an effective mentor. I am offering my services. I teach this course online, open entry, open exit for a small fee. If you think this might be your best option, please check out my Web site: http://kumo.swcp.com/graphics

If that location does not exist, it means that I have done what I have been thinking of for several years. Try bergsland.com

Glossary and Index

Definitions of the terminology used in publishing: traditional and digital, print and Web

 A

Additive color
A color space where the three primary colors add up to white

Application defaults
The defaults for the entire application

Ascender
The strokes of lowercase letters that project above the x-height: bdfhklt

 B

Baseline
The imaginary line that the letters of type sit upon

Basis size
The sheet size used to determine the basis weight

Basis weight
A ream of the basis size: that is, 500 sheets of a 20# bond weighs 20 pounds

Bitmap image
A graphic where every pixel is separately defined

Body copy
The basic reading paragraph of a document

Bond
The most common name of office paper

Bounding box
An invisible frame used to locate the handles of graphics in software that does not use frames

 C

Calendaring
Using a stacked series of large milled steel rollers to polish and compress paper as it comes off the papermaking machine

Caliper
The thickness of cover stock measured in thousandths of an inch

Callout
A paragraph style of enlarged or emphasized body copy used as a graphic device to recapture a reader's wandering attention

Camera ready
Artwork that is black and white, ready to be shot in a copy camera to make a negative or a plate

CMYK
Cyan, Magenta, Yellow, Black: a four-color process used to print full spectrum color

Color depth
The number of digital bits assigned to a pixel; this determines how many colors are available to that pixel

Color reproduction
The ability to reproduce original color in multiple copies — theoretically impossible

Color space

A system of colors defined by a set of three primary colors — which are mixed to produce all of the other colors in the color space

Color temperature

Color defined by its temperature in degrees Kelvin

Commercial printing

Custom manufacturing of printed materials of almost any type

Commodity color

Color that is so common that pricing is based entirely on market value and return on investment — copier color, digital color

Complementary color

Color pairs made up of color wheel opposites

Compression

Replacing patterns in digital code with placeholders, or averaging areas of pixels

Continuous tone

Artwork or graphics that vary in tone or color

Contract proof

A proof used as a contract for the client who promises to pay, and for the printer who promises to duplicate the proof

Creep

The movement of the copy toward the outside of a saddle-stitched booklet, due to the increasing thickness of the paper as the stitched edge

Cross-platform

A workflow accomplished with some of the people on Windows machines and some on Macintoshes or UNIX machines

Customizable shortcuts

The ability to specify personalized keyboard shortcuts for almost all commands

Defaults

What the software and hardware does with no choices made on the part of the designer

Density

A measurement of the lightness or darkness of a scanned or printed area measured from 0 (pure white) to 4.0 (absolute black)

Descender

Those letter portions of lowercase letters that hang below the baseline: gjpqy

Diffusion dithering

Giving the illusion of continuous tone with seemingly random dots; the natural output of low resolution color inkjet printers

Dithering

A coarse arrangement of relatively small dots that gives the illusion of continuous tone, whether grayscale or color — used with low resolution printers

Document defaults

Defaults that only apply to a specific document

Dot

Digitally; the smallest printable unit

Dot gain

The normal phenomenon of dots increasing in size as they are printed. All printers have dot gain except for calibrated electrostatic printers

Dot range

More appropriately should be called the tint range. The range from the lightest highlight to the darkest shadow in tint percentages

Duotone

A technique used to give more shadow density by overprinting two halftones

Electromagnetic spectrum

The visible light spectrum

Electrostatic

A printing method using an electrically charged image. This image then attracts charged toner which is melted onto the paper

Emulsification

The mixing of oil and water

Enamel

Another name for coated offset printing paper

EPS

Encapsulated PostScript — a graphic format

Export

Writing the digital code produced in a format that can be read by other software

Fill

The interior content of a PostScript shape

Flexography

A method of letterpress using relatively soft, flexible plates; dominant in packaging

Filler

A chemical added to paper for bulk and to make it more opaque

Flag

The name of a newsletter or newspaper expressed in a banner style design on the front page

Font

A complete set of characters for a given typestyle

Font family

A group of typestyles of different weights from light or thin to bold, heavy, or black

Format, graphic

Code exported from a digital document in a form that can be read by other documents

Formatting

Arranging copy for readability and comprehension by applying specific paragraph styles

Frames

A containing shape in PostScript

Front matter

Pieces of a book or magazine that come before the real content such as table of contents, forward, preface, and the like

Fugitive color

Color that fades quickly to white

Full-spectrum

A color space that contains colors from all areas of the visible spectrum

Generation

A copy

GIF

Graphic Interchange Format: a graphic format with limited colors and good compression used for low resolution Web graphics

Graphic design

What was formerly called commercial art; the arrangement of copy and graphics for the purpose of clear communication

Gravure

The modern printing technology using intaglio

Gripper

Blank space left at the edge of a sheet of paper to allow the press to grab it and pull it through the duplicator or press

Gutter

The vertical white space left between columns; also used to describe the center margins of a book or booklet

Halftone

Breaking up continuous tone artwork into variable size dots to enable the printing of the illusion of continuous tone

Halftone cell

A group of printer dots producing a halftone dot

Hanging indent

A paragraph style with a left indent, that has a negative first line indent and a tab on top of the left indent to line up the rest of the first line with the indent; used for bulleted or numbered lists

Head

A paragraph style, normally sans serif, used to capture the reader's attention with a real benefit

Heat-set web
A printing press that prints on a roll of paper and has infrared dryers to dry the ink enabling high speed four-color printing

Hi-fi color
A process color system using more than four colors to produce a much larger color space — the most common being Hexacrome™

Highlights
The lightest areas in continuous tone artwork

Hue
The name of a color

Incandescent or Tungsten
An ordinary light bulb uses a tungsten filament and glows with a very yellow light (or low temperature) light

Index
A cheap, low quality, calendared, lightweight cover stock — 90# and 110#

Ink holdout
The ability of a paper to keep the ink on the surface with no absorption of the ink — produces much brighter and more saturated colors and gives much more control of ink densities

Intaglio (now called gravure)
A printing technology that engraves or etches the image below the surface of the plate . The image is filled with ink and the background is cleaned and polished, then the ink is pulled out by squeezing slightly dampened paper into the recessed image. In gravure the background is squeegeed clean with doctor blades

JPEG
A lossy compression method that is only useful for the Web or multimedia shown on a monitor

Kicker
A small introductory subhead that adds more information and more impact to a head, usually all caps and underlined

Leader
Filling the space between the end of the type and the new tab with repeating characters; used for attaching prices to items in menus and so forth

Leading
The old letterpress term for line spacing

Letterhead
The official document used by a company for writing official documents and letters

Letterpress
The modern term for relief printing as developed by Gutenberg; currently used almost exclusively for die cuts, foil stamping, scoring, embossing, and the like

Line
A design element that is primarily distinguished by length and direction

Lineart
Originally, black and white artwork, also called camera ready; currently, the output of PostScript illustration programs

Linescreen
Used to describe the size of the dots used to produce halftones; measured in lines per inch

Link
The digital pointer that causes the PostScript printer or Distiller to use the high resolution original instead of the low res preview that is actually in the document

Linotype
The first mechanical typesetting machine in letterpress — enabled the daily newspaper

Lithography

A printing technology that uses a water receptive background and a grease receptive image — the plate is covered with water and then inked with a roller containing greasy ink

Local formatting

Making changes to paragraph or character specifications without using the Styles palettes

Logo

A graphic identification symbol

Lossless

A compression scheme that loses no data

Lossy

A compression scheme that loses data

Loupe

A magnifying lens used for examining halftone dot structures, color fit, and trapping

Master page

A page containing background images that are automatically placed onto pages of a document

Masthead

The official, legal column listing publication personnel and publishing data required by law

Mill order

Paper not commonly available that must be ordered in multiple carton quantities from the paper mill

Moiré

Interference patterns that appear whenever two or more regular patterns are printed on top of each other; a major problem when rescanning

Morgue

A designer's storage and filing system used to keep samples and references for design ideas

Multimedia

Graphic productions using video, animation, sound, music, and/or interactive linkages

Neutral gray

Colors that show no hue cast

Newsprint

An extremely cheap, low quality, acidic wood pulp paper used for newspaper production

Nouveau riche design

Conspicuous display of the powerful capabilities of publishing and design software "just because you can"

Offset

Lithography presses that print the image first onto a rubber blanket then transfer the image to the paper; allows for right-reading plates

On-demand

Storing documents digitally, then printing only what is needed when it is requested, often with variable data so each printed piece is different

Opaque

A common name of high quality, offset printing papers — #1 Premium sheets

Page layout

The assembly of prepared pieces, graphics, and copy into a finished document

Pantone Matching System (PMS)

The dominant standardized spot color system in the United States

Paragraph rule

A rule attached to a paragraph, either above or below, applied with the Return/Enter key

Parent size

The sheet sizes of paper purchased from a paper distributor, commonly 23"x35" or 26"x40" in United States

PDF

Portable Document Format: a cross-platform format that embeds fonts and graphics with strong compression abilities

Perfect bound

As opposed to saddle-stitched, these books and booklets are trimmed on four sides and have a square binding edge with a cover wrapped around

Permanent color

In printing: color that lasts a year; in fine art, color that lasts a minimum of 200 years

Pixel

Short for picture element; the smallest element of a monitor or scanner

Place (import)

Putting a picture preview in a document with a link to the high resolution version for printing

Point (paper)

Cover stock measured in thousandths of an inch with a micrometer

PostScript

A page description language: the standard for the printing industry and the basis for PDF

PostScript Illustration

Images drawn with PostScript shapes produced by FreeHand and Illustrator (and InDesign)

Primary colors

The three colors from which all other colors in a color space are made through mixtures

Preferences

Settings for some basic application defaults

Process color

A full-spectrum color space using primaries: RGB for Web and multimedia; CMY for color printing (plus K [black] because Cyan is weak)

Pull quote

See Callout: using body copy quotes as a graphic device to recapture readership

Quadritone

A four-color separation using spot colors to give much greater shadow detail and midtone control

Quickprint

Short-run, quick turnaround printing using paper, plastic or digital plates and limited paper choices

RBY

The fine art color space of Red, Blue, Yellow

Registration

The ability of a press to feed paper consistently. The normal standard is a half dot

RGB

The color space of light: Web and monitors

Roughs

Quick proportional sketches used for layouts

Saddle-stitched

Booklets made by folding paper, stapling through the fold, and trimming the three outside edges

Hard cover

Perfect-bound or smythe-sewn books covered with hard cardboard covers

Saturation

The intensity of a color

Scanning resolution

Twice the linescreen

Screen

Another name of a tint using linescreen dots

Screen angles

The angles of the dot grid in the four halftones used for CMYK color: 45°, 75°, 105°, and 90° used to avoid moiré patterns

Screen preview

What you see on the monitor when you place a graphic into a document

Script fonts

Fonts that mimic handwriting: specifically modern handwriting

Secondary colors

Colors made from mixing two primary colors

Self-extracting archive
A compressed archive that will open by a simple double-click of the icon

Separation
Converting a scan of a color image into CMYK

Service bureau
Companies with color expertise, high end color scanners, and top quality imagesetters who prepare designers documents for printing

Shade
A hue plus black

Shadows
The dark areas of a halftone or separation

Shape
A two dimensional piece of a graphic

Sheet-fed
Presses that feed one sheet at a time

Short-run
Printing 2,000 impressions or less of a document or signature

Sidebar
Information placed to the side of a layout that is interesting but not essential

Signature
A sheet of paper with multiple pages arranged upon it, so that after folding and collating, the pages are in the proper order

Sizing
A coating that controls absorption

Smooth
The surface of uncoated, calendared, offset paper

Smythe-sewn
The highest quality of making a book, where the signatures are hand-sewn together and case-bound, usually with a leather cover

Specular highlights
The reflection of a light source on a mirror finish

Spiral-bound
The binding of a book or booklet with spiral wire into prepunched holes

Spot color
Color printed on its own plate or printhead

Standard color
A standard pigment mix of an ink company

Stationery package
Business cards, letterheads, and envelopes

Stochastic
A top quality method of assigning tiny dots in a manner that appears to be random

Stroke
The color and width applied to a PostScript path or the outline of a PostScript shape

Style
A recorded format of a paragraph, character, or graphic available on a palette

Subhead
A lesser headline

Subtractive color
When the primary colors of a full-spectrum color space add up to black

Swatch book
Standard sets of printed colors to enable designers to know what the color will look like when printed

Symbols
A shape with attached meaning

Tag
A very cheap, very thick card stock used for tags

Templates
Saved documents with customized defaults

Text
What software programmers tend to call copy

Text fonts
Fonts mimicking medieval handwriting

Texture
The visual "feel" of shape's surface

Thumbnails
Visual shorthand to record ideas

TIFF
Tagged Information File Format: the most reliable format for printing bitmapped images

Tint (fine art)
A hue plus white

Tint (printed screens)
A partial color expressed in the percentage of area covered by the linescreen dots

Tools
Software routines that change the abilities (and usually the look) of the cursor

Transformation center
A target that appears with a transformation tool

Tritone
Three halftones printed on top of each other for greater shadow detail and density plus better midtone control

Tungsten or incandescent
An ordinary light bulb uses a tungsten filament and glows with a very yellow light (or low temperature) light

Typography
The art of setting and designing professional quality type and fonts

Typesetting
The craft of setting type

Value or brightness
The lightness or darkness of a color

Vector image
An image where shapes are described by outlines of many, very short vector lines

Vellum
A surface description of relatively uncalendared offset paper

Vellum bristol
An extremely cheap wood pulp cover stock

Volume
The illusion of three-dimensional space

Waterless printing
A new high-tech printing technology that uses plates covered with an ink receptive coating covered with an ink repelling coating. A laser is used to burn holes in the repellent coating.

Watermark
A slightly translucent image in office papers

Web printing
Printing onto a roll of paper that is sheeted after printing is completed

Writing
The name of better quality bond or office papers

X-height
The height of the lowercase X

Yak
An extremely smelly and ugly animal with a horrible disposition

Zorro
A hero of Spanish Southern California

Index

knowledge of, 25
Version 5, 46
quickprint, 232-233
See also digital quickprint
quickprinters, 97-98, 242
quotation marks (typesetting), 182-83

R

RBY (red, blue, yellow) color space, 256
Rembrandt van Rijn, 92
RGB (red, green, blue) color space, 256, 262, 268, 310
RIFF (Raster Image File Format), 147
rosette, 272
rotary presses, 93
roughs, 210, 311

S

saddle-stitching, 338-39
sans serif typefaces, 128-29
saturation, 258
screen printing, 97, 231-32
secretarial formatting, 137-38; 140-41
Senefelder, Alois, 93
serif typefaces, 128-29
sidebars, 171
sign printers, 97
Sir Speedy, 32
size(s)
    of document, 177-79
    of files, 250-51
    of paper in printing, 241-42
    and proportions of logos, 310
small caps, 126
snap-to command, 183-84
software, 35-36
spell check, 139
spi (samples per inch), 227
spot color, 264
stationery, 305-13
    logos, 307-8
    uses, 309
stochastic screening, 273-74
stone writing, 93
SuperPaint, 149
symmetry, 194

T

tables of contents, 185
tabs, 121
TARGA (or TGA), 147
templates, defined, 55
text styles, 153-74
thumbnails, 210
TIFF (Tagged Image File Format), 5, 12, 36, 141-47, 149, 248
tools, 62-66
    apply color, 65
    apply gradient, 66
    apply none, 66
    ellipse, 62
    eyedropper, 64
    fill and stroke, 65
    free transform 63

gradient, 64
hand, 64
italics, 130-31
line, 63
pen, 61-62
pencil, 62-63
polygon, 62
rectangle, 62
rotate, 63
scale, 63
shear, 63
selection, 59-60
type, 60-61
zoom 64-65
tritones, 12, 274-75,
TrueType fonts, 251
type size, 119
typesetting, 119-31
    apostrophes, 123
    caps, 123
    double spacing, 120
    em dashes, 122
    en dashes, 122
    fixed spaces, 120-21
    history, 90-91
    hyphens, 122
    index, 185
    kerning and tracking, 124
    quotation marks, 182-83
    returns, 124-25
    small caps, 126
    table of contents, 185
    tables, 185-86
    tabs, 121
    underlining, 122
    widows, 125
typestyles, 127-31
typographic measurements, 119
typography, 115-32
typos (typographical errors), 182, 220\

U

ultrafine screens, 234
underlining, 122

W

waterless printing, 234
Websafe color palette, 297-98, 310
Web site design, 4, 36-37, 301-2, 339-40
weights, 282-83
woodcut, 92
WordPerfect, 5   17
word processing, 136-41
    drag'n'drop editing, 139
    filters, 136-37
    formats, 136
    formatted copy, 137
    rich text format, 137
WYSIWYG, 268, 299

X

x-height, 118-19